T0110359

ALSO BY HAROLD SCHECHTER

NONFICTION:

The A to Z Encyclopedia of Serial Killers (with David Everitt)

Bestial: The Savage Trail of a True American Monster

Deranged: The Shocking True Story of America's Most Fiendish Killer

Depraved: The Shocking True Story of America's First Serial Killer

Deviant: The Shocking True Story of Ed Gein, the Original "Psycho"

The Devil's Gentleman: Privilege, Poison, and the Trial that Ushered in the Twentieth Century

Fatal: The Poisonous Life of a Female Serial Killer

Fiend: The Shocking True Story of America's Youngest Serial Killer

Savage Pastimes: A Cultural History of Violent Entertainment

The Serial Killer Files: The Who, What, Where, How, and Why of the World's Most Terrifying Murderers

FICTION:

Nevermore

Outcry

The Hum Bug

The Mask of Red Death

The Tell-Tale Corpse

THE WHOLE DEATH CATALOG

The WHOLE DEATH CATALOG

A Lively Guide to the Bitter End

Harold Schechter

BALLANTINE BOOKS / NEW YORK

A Ballantine Books Trade Paperback Original

Published in the United States by Ballantine Books,
an imprint of The Random House Publishing Group,
a division of Random House, Inc., New York.

Grateful acknowledgment is made to the following for
permission to reprint previously published material:

Alfred Publishing Co., Inc.: Excerpt from "Fancy Funeral," words and music by
Lucinda Williams, copyright © 2007 by Warner-Tamerlane Publishing Corp.
and Lucy Jones Music. All Rights Administered by Warner-Tamerlane Publishing Corp.
All Rights Reserved. Used by Permission of Alfred Publishing Co., Inc.

Taylor & Francis: Excerpt from "A Revised Death Anxiety Scale" by James A. Thorson and F. C. Powell from
Death Anxiety Handbook: Research, Instrumentation, and Application, edited by Robert A. Neimeyer.
Copyright © 1994 by Taylor & Francis. Used by permission of Taylor & Francis Group LLC.

W. W. Norton & Company: "In Childhood," from *The Artist's Daughter* by Kimiko Hahn,
copyright © 2002 by Kimiko Hahn. Used by permission of W. W. Norton & Company, Inc.

Library of Congress Cataloging-in-Publication Data

Schechter, Harold.
The whole death catalog : a lively guide to the bitter end / Harold Schechter.
p. cm.
Includes index.
ISBN 978-0-345-49964-6 (pbk.)
1. Death. I. Title.
BD444.S383 2009
306.9—dc22 2009013779

www.ballantinebooks.com

Book design by Susan Turner

147468846

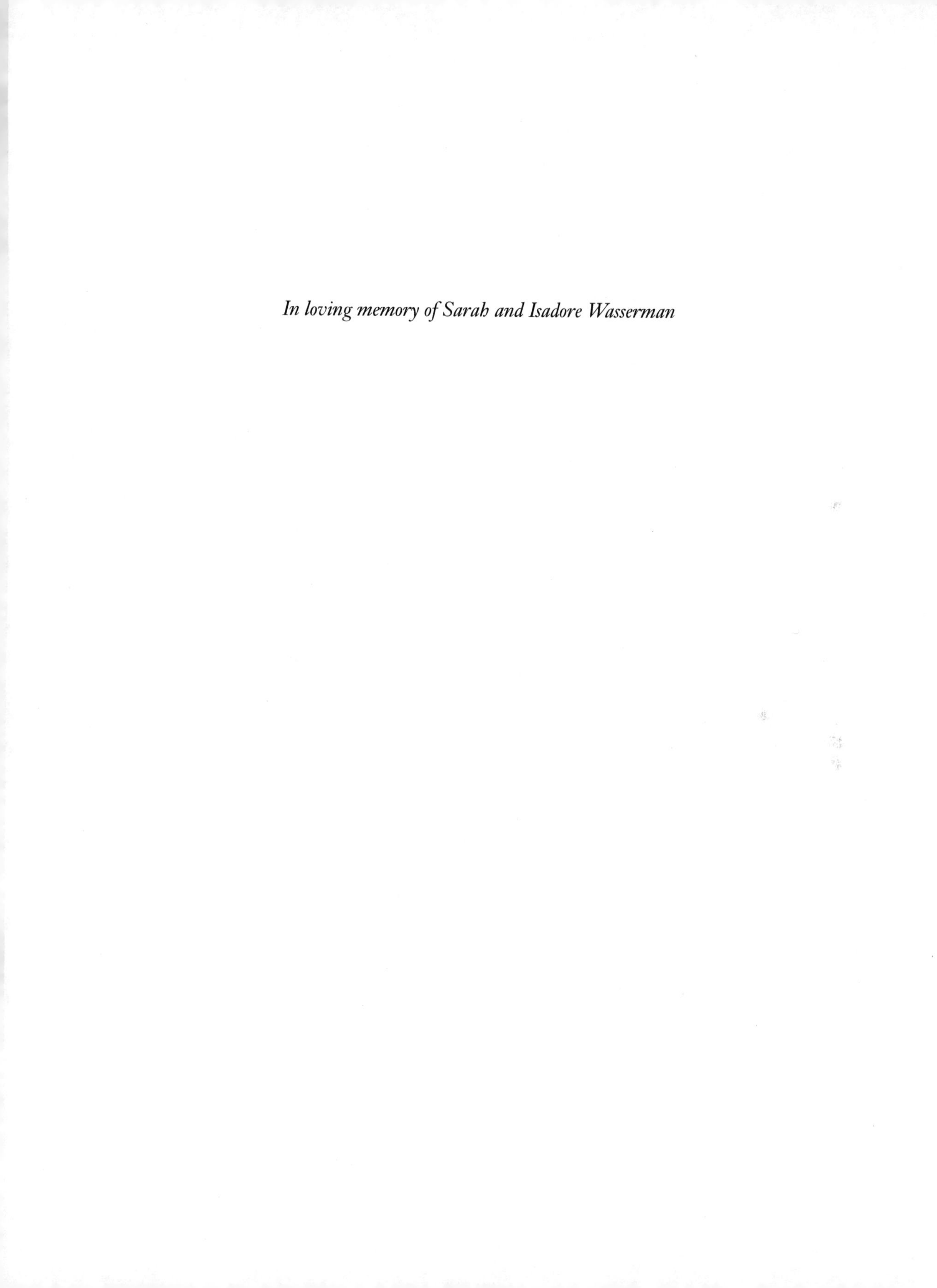

In loving memory of Sarah and Isadore Wasserman

No matter how I struggle and strive,
I'll never get out of this world alive.

—Hank Williams

Contents

THE WHOLE DEATH CATALOG

Introduction

Here's some good news and bad news about personal longevity. Scientists confidently assert that it is entirely possible for a human being to enjoy a robust and active life until at least two hundred years of age. This can be accomplished by, among other things, employing atom-size nanobots to repair cellular damage at the molecular level, exchanging worn-out internal organs for bionic replacements, upgrading the nervous system with a degeneration-proof network of fiber optics, and creating artificial muscle with ultrathin synthetic filaments.

The bad news is that these and other life-prolonging technologies will not be generally available until roughly the year 2108. Which means that everyone now reading this book (as well as, tragically, the person writing it) will be long dead.

Needless to say, this is a bitter pill to swallow, particularly if you happen to belong to the generation that once hoped they'd die before they got old and now fervently pray they'll live long enough to enjoy the full benefits of their AARP memberships. Having grown up in the postwar years—a genuinely golden age in U.S. history (despite a few pesky concerns such as the ever-present threat of nuclear Armageddon)—baby boomers have always taken it for granted that they were blessed with unusually good fortune: born into the best of all possible worlds. To think that the distant future holds a significantly better one—a world in which, thanks to the wonders of biotechnology, death can be put on indefinite hold—really rankles.

Still, if we can't extend our happily self-indulgent lives forever, we can at least go out in style. One thing you can say about us boomers—we're a trendsetting generation. Not to mention a supremely narcissistic one. For a half century, whatever's been happening to us at the moment has clearly been the most important thing in the world. Every phase of life we've passed through—from TVaddicted childhood to Woodstockian youth to thirtysomething yuppiedom to Botox-enhanced middle age—has produced its own cultural craze. Now, with the geriatric years looming, death is sure to be the Next Big Thing.

Certainly the folks in the undertaking biz realize this. In his morticians' handbook, *Funeral Home Customer Service A-Z* (Companion Press, 2004), Alan D. Wolfert, one of the gurus of the death industry, counsels his readers that "boomers are a new and very different breed of customer of funeral services. Understanding their wants and needs and then tailoring services to not only meet but exceed those needs is increasingly essential for funeral homes." And what exactly is it that rapidly aging Aquarians are going to want in a funeral?

The consensus seems to be that we'll be putting the fun back in funerals by eschewing the traditional type of memorial ceremony with all its depressing emphasis on grief, suffering, and bereavement. Instead, we will create our own cool, customized send-offs. A couple of years ago, the parody newspaper *The Onion* ran a piece headlined "Today's Funeral-Goers Want to Be Entertained." "Sure, funerals are still the number-one way to honor and grieve for our dead," the article read. "But if they want to keep their place at the top, there's gonna have to be some big-time changes. Mourners deserve a mind-blowing funeral experience they'll never forget." As Homer Simpson would say, it's funny because it's true.

Take, for instance, the farewell ceremony for that countercultural icon Hunter S. Thompson, whose ashes were launched from a gigantic cannon adorned with a double-thumbed fist clutching a peyote button while Bob Dylan's "Mr. Tambourine Man" filled the air along with a spectacular display of psychedelic fireworks. Not to everyone's taste, perhaps. But that's precisely the point. Nowadays, there's no need to be buried (or cremated) like anyone else. You can keep marching to the beat of a different drum all the way to the grave.

Concerned that you lack the necessary skills to throw a truly memorable funeral, one that expresses the unique, inimitable (albeit now defunct) you? Not to worry. A new branch of the mortuary business has lately sprung up, composed of experts who, taking their cue from professional party planners, will help you arrange the perfect going-away-forever affair, complete with specialty catering, appropriate music, and even give-away "funeral favors." Sort of like a really top-flight wedding or bar mitzvah, only with a cadaver as the guest of honor.

There are also a growing number of companies that cater to the postmortem needs of enthusiasts of every stripe. Is scuba diving your "bag"? Why not have your cremated ashes incorporated into an artificial coral reef off the Florida coast so you can spend eternity submerged in balmy tropical waters? Have you been a fanatical Trekkie ever since the original airing of the show in the fall of 1966? Now, you can proudly assert your undying geekhood by being buried in a fiberglass casket modeled on the popular photon torpedo design as seen in *Star Trek II: The Wrath of Khan*. Is Al Gore's *An Inconvenient Truth* your all-time favorite movie? If so, you might consider having your remains consigned to a biodegradable casket and interred in an all-natural, ecofriendly "green cemetery."

The book you now hold in your hands

contains a wealth of information about these and other alternative forms of body disposal. But (despite its titular tip of the hat to Stewart Brand's bible of hippie-era self-sufficiency), *The Whole Death Catalogue* is not aimed exclusively—or even primarily—at New Agers, back-to-nature types, and do-it-yourselfers. Though our nation's hardworking undertakers have been on the defensive since the publication of Jessica Mitford's 1963 best seller *The American Way of Death*, many (perhaps most) of us still prefer the kinds of services offered by traditional funeral homes, including all-in-one package deals that cover everything from soup to nuts (or, in this case, embalming to interment). Addressing those faced with the painful task of burying a loved one, Thomas Lynch—poet, essayist, undertaker—offers nononsense advice: "If anyone tells you you haven't spent enough, tell them to go piss up a rope. Tell the same thing to anyone who says you spent too much. Tell them to go piss up a rope. It's your money. Do what you want with it." Some people, after all, love to splurge on extravagant all-inclusive resort vacations, while others go in for wilderness backpacking. Choosing one over the other doesn't make you a better person. As another sixties icon so wisely put it, whatever gets you through the night.

As a resource, *The Whole Death Catalogue* is designed to provide practical information on a wide range of mortuary-related matters: how to write a living will, where to find a convenient cemetery, whom to contact when someone dies, what to say in a eulogy, when to start planning for a funeral, et cetera, et cetera. But it's much more than a sourcebook. Covering every conceivable aspect of the subject—historical, cultural, sociological, anatomical, anthropological, and more—it is meant to be an informative and, yes, entertaining read, brimming with amazing facts, amusing anecdotes, revealing insights, and timeless wisdom, as well as loads of cool pictures.

Appropriately enough, a final confession is in order. Death, it turns out, is a more or less inexhaustible topic. No single book could possibly cover the whole subject. Sweeping as this volume is, the title is a slight misnomer. The more accurate one—*The Whole Lotta Death Catalogue*—just didn't sound right.

1

DEATH

Can't Live with It, Can't Live Without It

Is Death Necessary?

Of all the traits that distinguish human beings from other animals—language, toolmaking, the urge to buy other people's unwanted stuff on eBay—perhaps the most fundamental is our awareness of our own inevitable deaths. To be sure, animals possess powerful survival instincts and do their best to avoid getting killed. But (so far as we know) they have no conscious knowledge of how little time they have here on earth. They go through life blissfully unaware that each passing day is bringing them closer and closer to the end.

Humans, on the other hand—particularly as we grow older—are all too keenly aware of how fleeting life is. On the plus side, this can add flavor and poignancy to our existence, making us savor the lovely and precious things in life (as the poet Wallace Stevens says, "Death is the mother of beauty"). But it also burdens us with a heavy load of anxiety and plagues us with the question "Why do we have to die at all?"

From time immemorial, humans have grappled with this mystery. Tribal myths from around the world offer a host of colorful explanations. According to one African tale, when the first humans pleaded with God to stop death, he complied with their wishes, but only on one condition: to prevent the world from becoming too crowded, there would be no more births. Unwilling to endure life without children, the people quickly begged God to return death to them.

In an Indonesian myth, death came into the world when God offered the first man and woman a choice between two gifts: a stone and a banana. Seeing no use for the stone, the pair chose the enticing fruit. At that instant, a voice thundered down from heaven: "Because you have chosen the banana, your life shall be like its life. When the banana tree has offspring, the parent stem dies. So shall you die and your children shall step into your place. Had you chosen the stone, your life would have been like its life, changeless and immortal."

And then there is the Australian Aboriginal myth recorded by the anthropologists Ronald and Catherine Berndt. According to this story, two traveling companions named Moon and Djarbo suddenly fall mortally ill. Moon has a plan to revive them, but Djarbo—believing that Moon's idea is a trick—rebuffs his friend's help and soon dies. Moon dies also, but thanks to his plan he manages to revive himself into a new body every month, whereas Djarbo remains dead. "Thus, Moon triumphed over bodily death while the first peoples of that ancient time followed Djarbo's example, and that is why all humans die."

At first, people never died. As they grew older, they cast off their skins like snakes and crabs and came out with their youth renewed. One day, an elderly woman went to a stream to change her skin. She shed the old skin and threw it in the water, then watched as it floated downstream and caught on a stick. Then she went home, where she had left her little son. As soon as the child saw her, however, he began to cry because he did not recognize her. "You are not my mother. My mother was an old woman." To pacify the child, the woman returned to the stream, found the cast-off skin, and put it back on. From that day on, humans ceased to shed their skin and died.

—Melanesian myth

Of course, these fanciful stories can't be taken seriously. Clearly, they are the products of primitive, childlike minds—nothing more than fairy tales. After all, the real truth, as every biblical fundamentalist will tell you, is that death came into the world when Satan in the form of a talking snake gave a forbidden apple to a naked woman created from the rib of her slumbering mate.

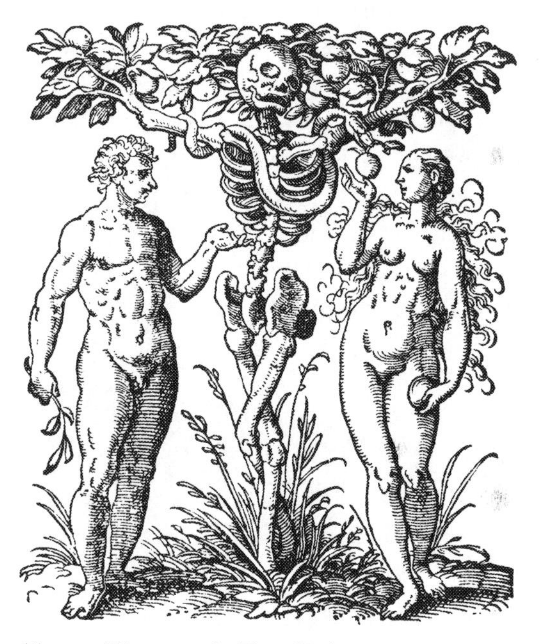

Adam and Eve turn the Tree of Life into the Tree of Death. Sixteenth-century woodcut.

Of course, some scientists reject even this persuasive explanation. As far back as the eighteenth century, the famed botanist Carl Linnaeus, father of modern taxonomy, accounted for death in ecological terms. As Linnaeus saw it, death served to maintain a fundamental balance in nature by ensuring that no single species of plant or animal would overrun the earth through unchecked reproduction. In the following century, Claude Bernard—the founder of modern physiology—viewed obsolescence and death as intrinsic characteristics of living beings, the flip side of embryonic development and birth. "Existence," he wrote, "is nothing other than a perpetual alternation of life and death, composition and decomposition. There is no life without death; there is no death without life."

The Bernardian belief that death is a biological necessity has been endorsed by subsequent thinkers, among them the German physician Wilhelm Fliess (one of Freud's early collaborators), who compared the human body to a "wound up clock that carries within itself the law of its own unwinding." In a similar vein, the Hungarian psychologist Leopold Szondi coined the term *thanatropism* to describe "an unknown force in every living being driving it toward death."

At least one famous nineteenth-century scientist, however, took issue with the view of death as an inescapable aspect of life. The great German biologist August Weismann argued that, contrary to what most people assume, "death is *not* an inevitable phenomenon." Some living beings, he insisted, can exist forever. As proof, he pointed to the case of unicellular organisms, which reproduce themselves by splitting in two and therefore enjoy a kind of immortality.

Clearly, this is an excellent state of affairs if you happen to be an amoeba. Even Weismann, however, acknowledged that higher organisms (including, sadly, human beings) cannot avoid death.

The concepts put forth by Weismann—who is widely regarded as the most impor-

Appointment in Samarra

This famous anecdote [presented here in a version by W. Somerset Maugham] neatly captures an unsettling truth: no matter hard we try—how far and fast we run—we can't escape from death.

"There was a merchant in Baghdad who sent his servant to market to buy provisions, and in a little while the servant came back, white and trembling, and said, 'Master, just now when I was in the market-place I was jostled by a woman in the crowd and when I turned I saw that it was Death that jostled me. She looked at me and made a threatening gesture; now, lend me your horse, and I will ride away from this city and avoid my fate. I will go to Samarra and there Death will not find me.' The merchant lent him his horse, and the servant mounted it, and he dug his spurs in its flanks and as fast the horse could gallop he went. Then the merchant went down to the market-place, and he saw Death in the crowd and he came to her and said, 'Why did you make a threatening gesture to my servant when you saw him this morning?' And Death said: 'That was not a threatening gesture. It was only a start of surprise. I was astonished to see him in Baghdad, for I have an appointment with him tonight in Samarra.' "

tant evolutionary theorist of the nineteenth century after Darwin himself—have contributed significantly to the current scientific understanding of death. Weismann distinguished between what he called the "germ cells"—essentially the sperm and ova that carry our genes—and the "somatic cells" that constitute our bodies. In this view, the body is nothing more than a vehicle for transmitting our genes to future generations. Once this task is accomplished—once reproduction has taken place—the body becomes disposable. There's no biological point in keeping it alive forever. In fact, there are positive advantages to getting rid of it, since the elimination of older individuals frees up important resources for the young and thus ensures the perpetuation of the species, which is all that nature cares about.

Of course, this doesn't entirely explain why humans have the potential to live to a ripe old age and don't simply expire as soon as they fulfill their reproductive mission, in the way of other creatures from praying mantises to salmon. Here, too, evolutionary biology suggests an answer. Thinkers who subscribe to this theory argue that since human offspring require years of parental care, we are genetically programmed to remain alive long past our reproductive prime so that we can protect our children and ensure their survival (scientists call this the "grandmother effect"). Thanks to our kids, we are endowed with "post-reproductive longevity." So the next time you contemplate those college tuition payments, just remember: you may think those bills are killing you, but they're actually helping to keep you alive.

RECOMMENDED READING

André Klarsfeld and Frédéric Revah's *The Biology of Death: Origins of Mortality* (Cornell University Press, 2004) is an excellent survey of scientific theories of death. Another is the first chapter of Jacques Choron's *Modern Man and Mortality* (Macmillan, 1964). George Wald, the eminent Harvard biologist who won the Nobel Prize in 1967, delivered an elegant and wonderfully lucid lecture on the origin of death, which can be found online at www.elijahwald.com/origin.html.

Death Across Cultures

In one sense, people in all times and places have felt pretty much the same about dying. Generally speaking, we'd prefer not to. Apart from this natural desire to avoid death, however, there's no such thing as a single worldwide way of viewing mortality. Cultural attitudes have differed throughout time and across the globe.

Judging from the epic of Gilgamesh—the world's oldest written narrative, which dates back to at least 1300 B.C.—the ancient Babylonians conceived of the afterworld as the "house of darkness," a grim subterranean realm where the dead exist in a state of unrelieved wretchedness. This view led them to adopt an eat-drink-and-be-merry philosophy, articulated in the story by a "wine maiden" named Siduri, who counsels the hero "to make every day a day of rejoicing. Day and night do thou dance and play." In short, it was important for everyone, whether commoner or king, to make the most of his time on earth, since death was an unavoidable catastrophe—the natural, universal (if dreadful) fate of humankind.

Among many aboriginal tribes, on the other hand, there is nothing at all natural about death. In this view, every death—even that of an elderly person—is essentially an act of murder brought about by witchcraft. Slain by a malevolent, unseen enemy, the victim is likely to return as a vengeful spirit.

For the Kaingáng of Brazil, for example, the passing of any individual threatens the welfare of the entire tribe. Transformed into an evil "ghost-soul," the deceased (in the words of funerary scholars Robert Habenstein and William Lamers) "craves a companion from among the living." Surviving spouses are particularly vulnerable and will immediately decamp from the village, armed with a particular variety of large jungle fern—a horticultural charm apparently much feared by ghost-souls. Only after the corpse is safely cremated and buried (in a hole lined with additional ferns to keep the malevolent spirit trapped inside) will the frightened survivor venture to return.

By contrast, Hindus view death not as an evil but as a natural stage in the evolution of the soul, which undergoes successive reincarnations until it attains salvation and is freed from the cycle of dying and rebirth. In the words of one sage: "Our soul never dies; only the physical body dies. We neither fear death nor look forward to it, but revere it as a most exalted experience. Life, death and the afterlife are part of our path to perfect oneness with God."

In Western society, views of death have changed dramatically over the millennia, as French social historian Philippe Ariès was the first to document. Ariès famously identified four distinct stages in European attitudes toward death, from the calm acceptance of the early medieval period to the denial and avoidance characteristic of the modern age.

American death attitudes have undergone major transformations since the days of the early colonists. For the New England Puritans, death was an omnipresent reality. Their median life expectancy was thirty-three, and the mortality rate among children was so high that, according to historian David Stannard, when a young couple in seventeenth-century Massachusetts got married, they "did so with the knowledge and expectation that in all probability two or three of the children they might have would die before the age of ten."

Their familiarity with death, however, did not make the contemplation of their own inevitable end any less anxiety-provoking. As Calvinists, they saw all humans (even newborns) as hopelessly depraved sinners, the vast majority of whom were predestined to spend eternity suffering the torments of hell. They might hope and pray for salvation. But to a very large degree, death remained the "king of terrors."

Nor did they attach any sentimental value to the physical remains of their loved ones. As funeral historian Gary Laderman observes, to the Puritans "the corpse was a horrible sight" that symbolized human sin and corruption. Once the soul had departed, the body was just a vile lump of flesh, undeserving of any special treatment. Thus, the Puritans "did not approve of embalming, elaborate funerals, or extravagant tombs."

The newly dead corpse was "hurried into the ground with little ceremony"—"commended to the cold and silent Grave where it must be entertained with Worms and Rottenness, and turned into putrefaction" (as one Puritan divine so vividly put it).

By the mid-nineteenth century, a far more romanticized attitude toward death had taken hold in the United States. Early Puritan graveyards were bleak, untended places, their stark tombstones carved with winged skulls, scythes, and other grim reminders of life's brevity. Beginning in the mid-1800s, picturesque "garden cemeteries" sprang up across the country: lush, rural burial grounds, as beautifully landscaped as any park and dotted with mawkish memorial statuary—empty cradles and inconsolable pets and little children in peaceful repose.

Death became an occasion for sentimental excess. Ladies' magazines devoted countless features to the latest in mourning fashions; women adorned themselves with "hair jewelry" made from the locks of their deceased loved ones; front parlors were hung with postmortem portraits and memorial lithographs of grieving survivors posed beside tombs and surrounded by weeping willow trees. Shamelessly sappy verse about the tragic deaths of toddlers became a wildly popular poetic genre. Heaven itself came to be seen differently: not as the place where one's soul received its final (and, for the vast majority of humans, dreadful) judgment but (to quote Stannard) as "a domesticated haven, a place where all would be welcomed home"—a kind of celestial version of a comfortable, middle-class Victorian household.

As the Victorian age gave way to the modern era, powerful social factors—urbanization, advances in medical science, the breakdown of tight-knit communities, a growing secular outlook that undermined the traditional faith in an afterlife—caused another major shift in American death attitudes. The dead were segregated from the living, banished from sight. People no longer expired at home surrounded by their loved ones but died in sterile hospital rooms, tended by strangers. The elaborate mourning rituals of earlier times were abandoned, rendered obsolete by the feel-good ethos of contemporary U.S. consumer culture (what sociologists Nathan Leites and Martha Wolfenstein call American "fun mortality"). Funerals became, in the caustic phrase of sociologist Robert Fulton, "low-grief" affairs. With the spread of "perpetual care" cemeteries, visiting the final resting places of departed family members to pay respects and tend their graves became an increasingly quaint and outmoded custom.

Death itself became a taboo topic, something not to be dwelled upon or even spoken of. In her excellent book, *Death's Door: Modern Dying and the Ways We Grieve* (Norton, 2006), Sandra Gilbert relates an anecdote that perfectly captures the extent to which death has become an unmentionable subject in our time. In the mid-1990s, while compiling a book called *Confronting Death*, sociologist David Moller asked the American Cancer Society for permission to include some of its materials. "Its representative," writes Gilbert, "responded with a statement that's distinctively 'modern': 'Absolutely not. In no way do we want to be associated with a book on death. We want to emphasize the positive aspects of cancer only.' "

RECOMMENDED READING

Philippe Ariès's seminal studies of Western death attitudes are, of course, essential reading for anyone interested in this topic. David Stannard's *The Puritan Way of Death* (Oxford, 1977) is an elegant and illuminating book on the topic of early American conceptions of mortality. William Wood and John B. Williamson's contribution to *The Handbook of Death and Dying* (Sage Publications, 2003)—a highly informative essay, "Historical Changes in the Meaning of Death in the Western Tradition"—is also well worth reading.

Philippe Ariès and *Western Attitudes Toward Death*

Philippe Ariès (1914–1984) was, in the strict sense of the term, a true amateur, a word that now connotes a lack of professional skill but originally meant a person who does something for love, not money (it is linguistically related to *amorous*). Certainly he did not earn his keep as a historian. He was a French civil servant who spent his career working for the Institute for Applied Research for Tropical and Subtropical Fruits. But as a part-time scholar (what he himself referred to as a "weekend historian"), he made significant contributions to the study of Western society.

As a historian, Ariès was less interested in momentous events—wars, revolutions, world-changing discoveries—than in the fundamental phenomena of everyday existence. After writing an influential book on the first phase of life, *Centuries of Childhood* (Vintage,

1962), he turned his attention to the final one. The result was his groundbreaking study, *Western Attitudes Toward Death from the Middle Ages to the Present* (Johns Hopkins University Press, 1974).

In this slender volume (which grew out of a series of lectures), Ariès argues that over the course of the second millennium, the European response to death passed through four stages. The earliest—which he labels "tame death"—was distinguished by a resigned acceptance of mortality. "In death," Ariès writes, "man encountered one of the great laws of the species, and he had no thought of escaping it or glorifying it. He merely accepted it with just the proper amount of solemnity due one of the important thresholds which each generation always had to cross."

As the centuries progressed, this attitude underwent a gradual change. By the late Middle Ages, the traditional acceptance of death as the "common destiny of the species" was replaced by a new emphasis on the fate of the individual. This second stage—which was characterized by both a heightened anxiety about the state of one's soul and a growing attachment to the things of this world—Ariès calls "one's own death."

A new attitude appeared at the start of the eighteenth century—an intense, morbid fascination with death that culminated in the excesses of Victorian mourning rituals: extravagant funerals, elaborate widow's garb, lush garden cemeteries, et cetera. The emphasis during this period—which lasted until the early decades of the twentieth century—was on the loss of the loved one: what Ariès defines as a shift from "my death" to "thy death."

Ariès describes our own period as the age of "forbidden death," when the terminally ill are bundled off to hospitals to die alone and out of sight. Death—"so omnipresent in the past that it was familiar"—has become shameful and hidden. If that situation has begun to change—if we are no longer quite so reluctant to confront and talk about death—that salutary shift is at least partly due to the influence of Ariès himself, who elaborated his insights in his last major work, *The Hour of Our Death* (Knopf, 1981).

Geoffrey Gorer and "The Pornography of Death"

It's virtually impossible to find a book about modern attitudes toward death that doesn't pay homage to British scholar Geoffrey Gorer (1905–1985). An anthropologist who spent a decade studying various tribal cultures before turning his attention to modern industrial societies, Gorer published an article called "The Pornography of Death" in the October 1955 issue of the English magazine *Encounter*. Despite its brevity (it ran less than four pages), Gorer's piece proved to be one of the most influential essays of its time.

"The Pornography of Death" appeared when America was in the grip of one of its periodic bouts of hysteria over media violence, particularly the intensely gory crime and horror comic books of the period. Gorer did not believe that these pop entertainments, gruesome as they were, had a harmful effect on young readers. Rather, he viewed them (along with "detective stories, thrillers, war stories, spy stories, science fiction," and other mass-produced fantasies) as a symptom of an unhealthy attitude toward death characteristic of twentieth-century Western societies.

In the previous century, Gorer argued, it was sex that was "unmentionable"—something not to be discussed or even acknowledged in "polite society." Death, on the other hand, was treated openly. People died at home, "the cemetery was the center of every old-fashioned village," and "children were encouraged to think about death, their own deaths and edifying or cautionary deathbeds of others."

Nowadays, the situation is reversed. Sex is everywhere. But the "natural process" of death has become a taboo, forbidden subject. According to Gorer, our refusal to accept the fundamental realities of "corruption and decay" has transformed death into something sick, morbid, "disgusting"—an attitude reflected in the ultraviolent excesses of our popular entertainments.

In short, what sex was to the Victorians, death is for us.

> *At present, death and mourning are treated with much the same prudery as sexual impulses were a century ago.*
>
> —Geoffrey Gorer

The Good and Bad News About Immortality

The ancient Babylonian epic of Gilgamesh, dating back more than three thousand years, is regarded as the oldest written narrative in the world. The story relates the adventures of the hero-king Gilgamesh and his boon companion, Enkidu. When Enkidu falls ill and dies, Gilgamesh—panicked at the thought of his own inevitable demise—sets off in search of eternal life. Eventually, he learns of a plant of immortality growing at the bottom of the ocean. Gilgamesh manages to retrieve this treasure, only to have it snatched away and swallowed by a snake.

That the pursuit of physical immortality forms the central theme of humankind's earliest epic reveals something important:

Death Fun Fact

Though his enduring fame rests on his feats as an aviator, Charles Lindbergh was also involved in the hunt for immortality. In 1930, three years after his solo transatlantic flight made him an international superstar, "Lucky Lindy" teamed up with Nobel Prize–winning scientist Alexis Carrel to create a machine that would extend human life indefinitely. Needless to say, they didn't succeed—though their efforts did produce results that helped pave the way for such lifesaving techniques as open-heart surgery and organ transplants.

You can read the whole story of their strange collaboration in David Friedman's fascinating book, *The Immortalists: Charles Lindbergh, Dr. Alexis Carrel, and Their Daring Quest to Live Forever* (HarperCollins, 2007).

namely, that the possibility of abolishing death is one of our oldest dreams. And indeed, from Gilgamesh's failed effort to Juan Ponce de Léon's equally futile hunt for the Fountain of Youth, the alchemists' quest for the philosopher's stone to our own desperate search for genetic solutions to aging, humans have always sought the magical elixir that will keep them alive forever.

Ironically, according to one eminent scientist, we already *have* achieved immortality—of a sort. In a famous lecture on the origins of death, Harvard professor and Nobel Prize–winning scientist George Wald, drawing on the theories of the German biologist August Weismann, distinguished between our "germ plasm"—the cells that produce the sperm and ova in higher animals and transmit hereditary information—and our bodies or "soma." It is the purpose of the body, said Wald, "to carry the germ plasm, to feed it, to protect it, to warm it in a warm-blooded organism, and finally to mingle it with the germ plasm of the opposite sex." Once this function has been fulfilled, the body "can be discarded." From this point of view, death is merely "the casting aside of the body, of the soma, after it has done its work."

What this all boils down to is the argument that while our bodies are bound to perish, our genetic material—which extends back in an unbroken line through countless millennia and has the potential to exist indefinitely—lives on. "We already have immortality," says Wald. "We have it in the germ plasm."

Of course, as Wald also points out, most of us couldn't care less about our germ plasm and where it's going to be a thousand years from now. What we really cherish is the body—"the thing that looks back at us from the mirror," the repository of our individual identities. And that part is doomed.

In short, this is very good news for your genes. As for you personally, not so much.

America: Paradise Regained?

Ever since Adam and Eve got expelled from the Garden of Eden, humans have been searching for a new terrestrial paradise—a place of perpetual summer where no one ever gets old or dies. From time immemorial, there have been legends about such enchanted realms. The ancient Greeks, for example, told tales of a faraway land called Hyperborea, whose inhabitants lived in perfect health and happiness for a thousand years until, "sated with life and luxury," they leapt into the sea. Indian myths speak of the land of the Uttarakurus, home of the magic jambu tree, whose fruit bestows everlasting youth on all those who taste it. The ancient Persians believed in a timeless utopia ruled by a figure called Yima, while Japanese folklore describes the blessed isle of Horaisan as "a land of eternal spring untouched by sickness, age or death."

America itself has always been regarded as one of these magical kingdoms. When Columbus first reached the New World, he thought he had found the actual Garden of Eden, while the Spanish explorer Juan Ponce de León was convinced that the fountain of youth was located somewhere in Florida.

Two centuries later, newly arrived immigrants still believed that the very atmosphere of the New World could restore a person to youthful vitality. Not long after coming to America, an English settler named Francis Higginson—who had suffered from severe digestive problems all his life—announced that he was cured. "My friends that know me well can tell how very sickly I have been," he wrote in a book about his new life in Massachusetts. "But since I came hither on this voyage, I have had perfect health, freed from pain and vomiting. And therefore I think that a sip of New England's air is better than a whole draft of Old England's ale." Unfortunately, Higginson spoke a little too soon. Shortly after he wrote his glowing testimonial, he suffered a catastrophic illness.

Americans, of course, are still searching for the elixir of eternal youth, though we now call it by other names—Botox, Viagra, Olay Regenerist Deep Hydration Regenerating Cream. Evidence suggests, however, that we are no more likely to achieve long-term rejuvenation than was the overly optimistic Francis Higginson, who by the time his book was published was already dead.

RECOMMENDED READING

For an exhaustive scholarly study of what he calls "prolongevity legends," see Gerald J. Gruman's "A History of Ideas About the Prolongation of Life" (*Transactions of the American Philosophical Society*, n.s., Vol. 56, pp. 1–102).

Time flies: seventeenth-century allegorical emblem depicting winged hourglass with Death's scythe.

"The Wild Honeysuckle"

The transience of existence is one of the perennial themes of poetry. In this 1786 lyric by Philip Freneau, America's first professional poet, the speaker compares the average human life span to the "frail duration of a flower" and offers a consoling thought—"if nothing once, you nothing lose"—that not everyone will find as comforting as the poet evidently intended:

Fair flower, that dost so comely grow,
Hid in this silent, dull retreat,
Untouched thy honied blossoms blow,
Unseen thy little branches greet:
No roving foot shall crush thee here,
No busy hand provoke a tear.

By Nature's self in white arrayed,
She bade thee shun the vulgar eye,
And planted here the guardian shade,
And sent soft waters murmuring by;
Thus quietly thy summer goes,
Thy days declining to repose.

Smit with those charms that must decay,
I grieve to see your future doom;

They died—nor were those flowers more gay,
The flowers that did in Eden bloom;
Unpitying frosts, and Autumn's power
Shall leave no vestige of this flower.

From morning suns and evening dews
At first thy little being came:
If nothing once, you nothing lose,
For when you die you are the same;
The space between is but an hour,
The frail duration of a flower.

The Fellow in the Bright Nightgown

If you were to ask them what death looks like, most people would be able to offer a pretty detailed description: a tall bony guy with hollow eyes and a leering grin, wearing a black hooded robe and wielding a scythe, alias the Grim Reaper. This particular personification, however, is only one of countless guises death has worn throughout the ages.

Courtesy of Joe Coleman.

According to certain accounts, personified depictions of death go all the way back to Stone Age cave paintings that portray it as a giant winged being that battens on corpses. To the ancient Greeks, death was the god Thanatos, son of Nyx (Night) and Erebus (Dark-ness) and brother of Hypnos (Sleep). A winged, bearded, sword-bearing figure, Thanatos would bring the departed to the underworld and turn them over to the boatman Charon, who would ferry them across the river Styx.

In Hindu mythology, the Lord of Death is named Yama. Garbed in red clothes and riding a water buffalo, he carries a loop of rope with which he lassos the souls of the dead. In the Book of Revelations, death is one of the Four Horsemen of the Apocalypse (he's the one on the pale steed), while in Islamic tradition, he is the angel Azrael, a colossal figure with four thousand wings and a body composed of as many eyes and tongues as the earth's population.

During the Middle Ages—when, thanks to the Black Plague, Europe was turned into an immense charnel house—death was most commonly pictured as a rotting cadaver who comes to claim victims of every age and rank. Gwyn Ab Nuud is the name of the death god in early Welsh folklore, a supernatural hunter "who gathers lost souls and escorts them to the land of the dead on a white horse." And in the Haitian Voudon pantheon, death is the dapper Baron Samedi, a skeletal, white-bearded fellow with top hat, tux, and dark shades hiding his empty eye sockets.

Not all death figures are male. Quite the contrary. The mythologies of the world are full of female personifications, from the ancient Roman death goddess Mors (a voracious black-winged figure who would swoop down on her victims

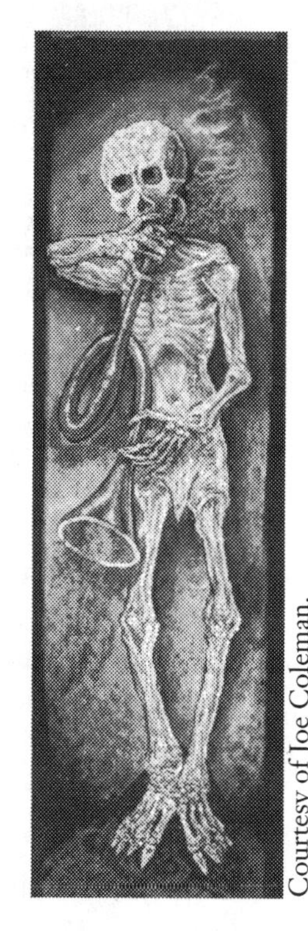

Courtesy of Joe Coleman.

Kitty of Doom

For centuries, death has been represented as a black-hooded, scythe-wielding Grim Reaper who comes knocking on your door when your time is up. It turns out, however, that this image may be wildly off base—at least as far as the residents of one New England nursing home are concerned. At the Steere House Nursing and Rehabilitation Center in Providence, Rhode Island, patients know that they are about to die when an adorable gray-and-white pussycat named Oscar hops onto their bed and cuddles with them.

According to an article by David Dosa that appeared in the July 26, 2007, issue of the *New England Journal of Medicine*, the two-year-old feline has an "uncanny knack" for predicting a patient's imminent demise. Adopted as a kitten and raised in the third-floor dementia unit, Oscar prowls the ward on a daily basis, going from room to room and sniffing the air. In general, he is an aloof creature who shies away from human contact. Occasionally, however, he will leap onto a bed and curl up beside the patient. When that happens, it's a good bet that the person isn't long for this world. To date, more than twenty-five patients who have received these attentions from Oscar have died within four hours of his visit. Indeed, he is considered such an accurate foreteller of death that when nurses see him snuggling with someone, they immediately notify family members that the end is near.

Exactly how Oscar performs his feat remains a mystery. Some observers speculate that he detects telltale scents or picks up subtle signals from the nurses who raised him. Others think that he is simply drawn by the warmth of the electric blankets that are often placed over dying people.

Whatever the case, this furry little harbinger of doom has racked up such an impressive record that he is regarded as a better predictor of death than the doctors who work there. As Dosa writes in his essay, "No one dies on the third floor unless Oscar pays a visit and stays there."

like a great bird of prey) to the Japanese "Snow Queen" Yuki-Onne and Hel, ruler of the Scandinavian underworld. In modern-day Mexican folk culture, death is represented as Santa Muerte (Saint Death), a white-garbed female skeleton carrying the traditional scythe.

Besides these culture-wide representations there are countless other death personifications in high art and pop entertainment. In a famous poem by Emily Dickinson, death is portrayed as a courtly gentleman who offers her a lift in his carriage and conveys her straight to the cemetery. Walt Whitman describes death as a "strong deliveress"—the "dark mother always gliding near with soft feet." W. C. Fields saw death as "the fellow in the bright nightgown," while Ingmar Bergman portrays him as a soft-spoken Swedish chess player in *The Seventh Seal*. In the 1998 box office bomb *Meet Joe Black*, death assumes the form of Brad Pitt, while in a classic episode of TV's *The Twilight Zone* it appears at a frightened old lady's door in the equally hunky guise of the young Robert Redford.

According to thanatologist Robert Kastenbaum, "Personifying death is one of the most ancient and durable methods for coping with death-related anxieties and fears." By giving death a humanlike shape and endowing it with a personality, we deprive it of some of its fearful mystery. In his own studies, Kastenbaum found that people in the United States today tend to visualize death in one of four ways: an elegant, smooth-talking con man; a wise elderly comforter; a cold, robotic being who pursues his lethal work with an unsettling calm; and—most traditionally—a malevolent, macabre creature who revels in destruction: "the sworn enemy of life."

RECOMMENDED READING

Kastenbaum offers an extensive discussion of the psychological research into death personification in his textbook *Death, Society, and Human Experience* (Allyn & Bacon, 2004). An illuminating online survey of the subject is Leilah Wendell's "Selected Cross-Cultural & Historical Personifications of Death," available at www.themystica.com.

ASK DR. DEATH

Dear Dr. Death:
What's the difference between "life expectancy" and "life span"?

Confused

Dear Confused:
Glad you asked, since there is, in fact, an important distinction between these concepts.

The phrase "life expectancy" refers to the number of years that the typical person can expect to live in any given era and place. Back in ancient Rome, for example, the average man could expect to live only into his late twenties (less if he was a gladiator). By 1800, the life expectancy for the average person in the more advanced societies of the West had sky-rocketed all the way up to thirty-five. A hundred years later, it had climbed to nearly fifty in the United States, England, and Sweden. Nowadays, the average American can expect to live into his or her late seventies.

"Life span," on the other hand, refers to the maximum number of years accorded to members of a species—in other words, the extreme limit of longevity, the age beyond which no individual has ever survived. Up until the 1990s, the maximum life span for humans was believed to be 110 years. Then, in 1997, a Frenchwoman named Jeanne Calment died at the age of 122 years and 164 days. (Calment had lived so long that she had clear memories of meeting Vincent Van Gogh, whom she recalled as a "dirty, badly dressed, and disagreeable" fellow.) As a result, human beings now officially have a maximum life span of 122½ years (much better than mice, who are lucky to make it to four, though not nearly as good as Galapagos tortoises, who have the potential to reach two hundred).

The good news in all this is that, thanks to advances in medicine, eating habits, and so on, life expectancy has been steadily increasing for members of advanced societies. The bad news—at least for those of us with dreams of living forever—is that no matter how many crunches you do and trans fats you avoid, human beings (at least as presently constituted) are never going to grow much older than 120 years at the max.

Everybody has got to die, but I always believed that an exception would be made in my case.

—William Saroyan

Death Fear

Though certain extreme circumstances—crushing depression, excruciating pain, having to sit through *Star Wars: Episode I—The Phantom Menace*—can make the prospect of death seem appealing, most people view the inevitable cessation of life with fear and trembling. To be sure, there are seemingly healthy, well-adjusted adults who will tell you that the idea of dying doesn't particularly bother them. Chances are, however, that these Pollyannas are in a serious state of denial.

In various clinical studies, college-age volunteers were hooked up to polygraph machines and asked how they felt about death. Even those who claimed to be completely unconcerned showed heightened psychogalvanic skin response—an indication of deep-seated anxiety at odds with their supposedly carefree attitudes. These tests confirmed the observation made by the eighteenth-century philosopher Jean-Jacques Rousseau: "He who pretends to look on death without fear lies."

According to all available evidence, the dread of death is a universal emotion. "All life fears death," declared the famed British scientist Sir Edward B. Tylor. Cultural anthropologist Ernest Becker goes so far as to argue the terror of death lies at the very root of human behavior—that what drives us is not (as Freud would have it) unconscious sexual desire but a desperate effort to deny our mortality, to control the overwhelming anxiety provoked by the knowledge of our inevitable fate. "The idea of death haunts the human animal like nothing else," writes Becker in his Pulitzer Prize–winning book *The Denial of Death* (Free Press, 1973). "It is a mainspring of human activity—activity designed largely to avoid the fatality of death, to overcome it by denying in some way that it is the final destiny of man."

The fear of death is one of the abiding themes of literature. The ancient Babylonian Epic of Gilgamesh—the world's oldest written narrative, dating back to 1300 B.C.—hinges on the titular hero's terror of dying. After watching his bosom companion, Enkidu, perish of a lingering sickness, Gilgamesh—the greatest warrior in the world, slayer of the monster Humbaba—is reduced to abject fright at the notion that, like his friend, he too will one day "be laid in the earth forever."

Death rules! Seventeenth-century woodcut.

In Shakespeare's *Measure for Measure*, the character Claudio—condemned to death for the crime of fornication—is similarly unmanned when he contemplates the grave. "Death is a fearful thing," he says to his sister, Isabella, hoping to persuade her to save his life by sacrificing her chastity to the play's villain, Angelo. When she suggests that her own honor is more important than her brother's life, Claudio famously replies:

> Ay, but to die, and go we know not where;
> To lie in cold obstruction and to rot;
> This sensible warm motion to become
> A kneaded clod; and the delighted spirit
> To bathe in fiery floods, or to reside
> In thrilling region of thick-ribbed ice;
> To be imprison'd in the viewless winds,
> And blown with restless violence round
> about
> The pendent world; or to be worse than
> worst
> Of those that lawless and incertain thought
> Imagine howling: 'tis too horrible!

For the seventeenth-century English writer William Sherlock, death is "very truly called the king of terrors," while the poet Robert Browning describes it as the ultimate horror—the "Arch Fear."

Of course, plenty of writers have tried to look on the bright side of things and offer various kinds of consolation. The early American poet Philip Freneau, for example, argues that there is no reason to fear death since it is simply a return to the state we inhabited before our conception: "If nothing once, you nothing lose, / For when you die you are the same." The British writer William Hazlitt expresses a similar sentiment:

> To die is only to be as we were before we were born; yet no one feels any remorse, or regret, or repugnance, in contemplating this last idea. It is rather a relief and disburthening of the mind: it seems to have been holiday-time with us then: we were not called to appear upon the stage of life, to wear robes and tatters, to laugh or cry, be hooted or applauded; we had lain *perdus* all this while, snug, out of harm's way; and had slept out our thousands of centuries without wanting to be waked up; at peace and free from care, in a sleep deeper and calmer than that of infancy, wrapped in the finest and softest dust. And the worst that we dread is, after a short, fretful, feverish being, after

> vain hopes, and idle fears, to sink to final repose again, and forget the troubled dream of life!

Of course, it could be said that this argument is itself a symptom of the writer's death anxiety, an attempt to reassure himself that there's nothing to be afraid of. It's an argument, moreover, that not everyone buys. The great English poet Philip Larkin, for example, found it entirely unpersuasive, insisting that there is a big difference between the oblivion that preceded our birth and the oblivion of death, since the former ended with our "being here," while the latter is utter, eternal extinction: "total emptiness forever."

Larkin clearly didn't believe in the afterlife, though people who do are not necessarily better off. Hamlet's "To be or not to be" soliloquy is the most famous expression of one common variety of death fear: the terror of the unknown, of the "undiscovered country from whose bourn / No traveler returns." But even those who think they know exactly what awaits them in the hereafter aren't immune to death anxiety, particularly if their conception includes the very real possibility of suffering the eternal torments of hell.

For other people, it isn't the fate of their souls that worries them but the prospect of undergoing intense pain during their final hours. They do not fear death per se but rather the process of dying—of ending up like Tolstoy's Ivan Ilyich, whose long, torturous passing culminates with three days of continuous screaming, a noise "so terrible that one could not hear it through two closed doors without horror." Of course, there is one great benefit to such prolonged physical agony—at least according to the late social gadfly Erich Geiringer (who was clearly a glass-is-half-full kind of guy). It is, he felt, "a most effective means of banishing concern about death. It is amazing to watch how aversion to death and love of life are blotted out in a very short time by the effects of pain. Those who die in pain die willingly."

This isn't true for everyone, however. For some people, even extreme suffering is better than the ultimate horror of eternal annihilation, of the absolute and irrevocable cessation of our personal being. "I should not really object to dying if it were not followed by death," quips the philosopher Thomas Nagel. Indeed, though sickness and age are supposed to make us more reconciled to death—perhaps even crave it—there are many people who wouldn't trade even the most wretched earthly existence for death. As Shakespeare's Claudio puts it while pleading with his sister:

> The weariest and most loathed worldly life
> That age, ache, penury and imprisonment
> Can lay on nature is a paradise
> To what we fear of death.

Though some experts argue that the fear of death is learned, most agree that it is innate—an inseparable part of our instinct for self-preservation. By programming us to shun potentially life-threatening situations, evolution ensures the survival of the species. As the poet-undertaker Thomas Lynch observes, the fear of death is not only normal—an emotion "that anyone in his right mind has"—but positively healthy, since "it keeps us from playing in traffic."

Of course, there is such a thing as an abnormal fear of death, a morbid obsession known as *thanatophobia.* For people suffering from this condition, the mere thought of death can produce a range of extreme physical reactions, from dizziness and dry mouth to all-out panic attacks. Another common symptom is "unwarranted apprehension of imminent death"—the terrified conviction that every moment is your last, even when you are in the best of health.

Like other phobics, thanatophobes require therapeutic help. But how do ordinary people suffering from run-of-the-mill death anxiety cope? As philosopher Jacques Choron makes clear in his excellent book *Modern Man and Mortality* (Collier, 1964), people resort to various strategies to alleviate their natural dread of death.

There is, for example, the always popular method of ignoring the subject—distracting yourself from unwelcome thoughts of mortality by focusing your attention on something else. In *The Anatomy of Melancholy*, the sixteenth-century English cleric and author Robert Burton advises his readers to "divert their minds" from the contemplation of death by immersing themselves in books. (Nowadays, of course, we are much better off than Burton since we also have iPods, YouTube, and pay-per-view cable TV to keep our minds off any potentially depressing subjects.)

Other people have taken the diametrically opposite approach. Instead of looking away from death, they try to face it head-on—to become so familiar with it that it ceases to be fearful. The legendary actress Sarah Bernhardt, for example, liked to snooze in a coffin, while the great French philosopher Michel de Montaigne "made it a habit to have death not only in his imagination, but constantly to talk about it" (a practice that, however helpful in mitigating death anxiety, is almost guaranteed to play havoc with your social life).

Then there are the various ways people try to minimize death—to convince themselves that it's nothing to be afraid of. The Greek philosopher Epicurus famously argued that "death is nothing, since when we are, death has not come, and when death has come, we are not"—in other words, there's no logical reason to fear death since we won't be around to experience it. (Among many others, however, the poet Philip Larkin views this argument as "specious stuff" since it is precisely the thought of nonexistence—"no sight, no sound, / No touch or taste or smell, nothing to think with, / Nothing to love with or link with"—that is so terrifying.) In the same way, the ostensibly reassuring argument that death is comparable to sleep is also unpersuasive to many people for the obvious reason that when we lay us down to sleep each night, we can be pretty sure (in spite of the bedtime prayer) that we're going to wake up the next morning.

A very different strategy isn't to minimize death but to minimize *life*—that is, to convince yourself that your earthly existence is so empty and meaningless that you won't really lose anything of value when you die. This is the meaning behind the Zen koan "Live each day as though you were already dead." After all, if you're already a "living corpse"—a person who goes through life with no desires, dreams, passions, or attachments to other people or possessions—becoming an *actual* corpse won't be a very difficult transition.

Such utter renunciation of everything that makes life worthwhile may, indeed, be a most effective preparation for death. But as a way of experiencing the few fleeting years vouchsafed to us on earth, it kind of sucks.

RECOMMENDED READING

Besides the books by Ernest Becker and Jacques Choron mentioned previously, there's a fine essay, "The Universal Fear of Death and Cultural Response," by Calvin Conzelus Moore and John B. Williamson, which can be found in volume 1 of *The Handbook of Death and Dying* (Sage, 2003), edited by Clifton D. Bryant. Also recommended: Sandra M. Gilbert's erudite and beautifully written *Death's Door: Modern Dying and the Ways We Grieve* (Norton, 2006).

The Evil Dead

There's a good reason why horror movies are full of cannibal zombies, malevolent ghosts, and rotting skeletons returned from the grave to wreak havoc on the living. These fantasies reflect one of the most deep-seated of all human emotions: the primal fear of the dead.

In his classic 1913 study, *Totem and Taboo*, Sigmund Freud explores the primitive belief that "at the moment of death," even the most "dearly loved relative . . . changes into a demon from whom his survivors can expect nothing but hostility." Your sweet white-haired grandma might have doted on you when she was alive. Once she's dead, however, you can be sure that she'll turn into a malignant spirit, "filled with a lust for murder."

There are different theories about the sources of this ancient belief (Freud, unsurprisingly, attributes it to unconscious ambivalence toward the departed, based—you guessed it!—on the Oedipal complex). But there's no question that, from time immemorial, people have gone to extraordinary lengths to protect themselves from the dead.

Freud himself cites a practice, common among certain aboriginal tribes, of burying the dead on islands or on "the far sides of rivers." Under the apparent theory that demonic spirits are really bad swimmers, these primitive tribespeople "did not feel safe from the dead until there was a sheet of water between them."

In many ancient cultures, corpses were buried with food, drink, and assorted valuables—a way of honoring them but also of making sure that they were happy enough in the afterlife to stay put. Other cultures have taken more extreme measures, burning, binding, or beheading the dead. The common custom of putting pennies or other weights on a cadaver's eyes is also meant as a protective measure: a corpse that can't open its eyes won't be able to find its way home and kill you.

Other vestiges of this archaic belief persist to this day. When Jewish people visit the grave of a loved one, it's traditional to leave pebbles on the headstone. Various explanations for this practice have been put forth—for example, if you want to leave a token of your visit, pebbles make more sense than flowers because they last longer. But some scholars have a different take on the custom, seeing it as rooted in pagan superstition. According to Theodor Reik, the small pebbles left on a gravestone help keep the dead in their place, preventing them from escaping and attacking the living. Grandma may already have a nice headstone over her grave—but some extra rocks to keep her underground never hurt.

Death Anxiety Scale

Not everyone actively dreads the thought of death. There are some people who even see it as a blessing—a "consummation devoutly to be wished," as the melancholy Dane puts it. For most of us, however, Woody Allen's oft-quoted comment—"I'm not afraid of death, I just don't want to be there when it happens"—probably rings truer than Hamlet's suicidal musing. Ask people how they feel about the prospect of dying and the responses, by and large, will fall somewhere between abject terror and stoic acceptance.

If you want to know exactly where *you* fall on this spectrum, there's a simple test you can take. It's called the Death Anxiety Scale and was first devised by a psychologist named Donald Templer. Following is a revised version developed by James A. Thorson and F. C. Powell. For each of the twenty-five questions, give one of these responses: strongly agree, agree, neutral, disagree, strongly disagree.

1. I fear dying a painful death.
2. Not knowing what the next world is like troubles me.
3. The idea of never thinking again after I die frightens me.
4. I am not at all anxious about what happens to the body after burial.
5. Coffins make me anxious.
6. I hate to think about losing control over my affairs after I am gone.
7. Being totally immobile after death bothers me.
8. I dread to think about having an operation.
9. The subject of life after death troubles me greatly.
10. I am not afraid of a long, slow dying.
11. I do not mind the idea of being shut into a coffin when I die.
12. I hate the idea that I will be helpless after I die.
13. I am not at all concerned over whether or not there is an afterlife.
14. Never feeling anything again after I die upsets me.
15. The pain involved in dying frightens me.
16. I am looking forward to a new life after I die.
17. I am not worried about ever being helpless.
18. I am troubled by the thought that my body will decompose in the grave.
19. The feeling that I will be missing out on so much after I die disturbs me.
20. I am worried about what happens to us after we die.
21. I am not at all concerned with being in control of things.
22. The total isolation of death is frightening to me.
23. I am not particularly afraid of getting cancer.
24. I will leave careful instructions about how things should be done after I'm gone.

Death Fun Fact

Did you know that injecting yourself with extract of canine testicles is a surefire way to prolong life? Just kidding! The seemingly self-evident lunacy of this crackpot theory, however, did not prevent the eminent French physiologist Charles Brown-Séquard from advocating it or trying it out on himself. In 1889, at the age of seventy-two, he injected himself with a liquid made from the testicles of a freshly killed dog and claimed it had totally rejuvenated him. Brown-Séquard's highly touted "discovery" did not do much for his life span—he died within a few years. It did, however, inspire countless quacks to peddle a variety of similar elixirs concocted from the sex glands of various male animals, from guinea pigs to goats to monkeys.

25. What happens to my body after I die does not bother me.

Scoring: For the positively phrased statements (numbers 1, 2, 3, 5, 6, 7, 8, 9, 12, 14, 15, 16, 18, 19, 20, 22, and 24), give yourself these scores: strongly agree = 4; agree = 3; neutral = 2; disagree = 1; strongly disagree = 0. For the items that are phrased negatively (numbers 4, 10, 11, 13, 17, 21, 23, and 25), score as follows: strongly agree = 0; agree = 1; neutral = 2; disagree = 3; strongly disagree = 4. Count any items left blank as neutral (score = 2). Then just add up the items to get the total score. The higher the number, the more terrified you are of death.

Source: James A. Thorson and F. C. Powell, "A Revised Death Anxiety Scale," in *Death Anxiety Handbook: Research, Instrumentation, and Application* (Taylor & Francis, 1994.)

All life fears death.

—Edward B. Tylor

Never Say Die

Death is so disturbing that people go to great lengths to avoid the very word. Here, in alphabetical order, are some common euphemisms, along with a few specialized ones.

Asleep in God
Beamed up (restricted to Trekkies)
Bought the farm
Breathed his last
Called home
Cashed in
Checked out
Croaked
Crossed over
Departed
Expired
Found everlasting peace
Gave up the ghost
Gone to a better place

Gone to glory
Gone to his reward
Gone to meet his maker
Handed in his chips
Headed for the last roundup (a cowboy favorite)
Heard the final call
Joined the heavenly choir
Kicked the bucket
Laid to rest
Launched into eternity
Met his Maker
Passed away
Remaindered (popular among publishing types)
Rests in peace
Taking the westbound (hobo slang)
Transitioned
With the angels

"Timor Mortis Conturbat Me"

Aside from the distinction of being the first person to use the *F*-word in print (in a poem titled "Ane Brash of Wowing"), the sixteenth-century Scottish author William Dunbar is best known for his poem "Lament for the Makers," whose famous Latin refrain—"*Timor mortis conturbat me*" ("The fear of death distresses me")—conveys the universal dread of that scythe-wielding "tyrant" whose "awful stroke" no human can avoid.

The hundred-line poem, written in 1508, is too long to quote in its entirety, but here's the first half, modernized for ease of comprehension:

I that in health was and gladness,
Am troubled now with great sickness,
And feeble wit infirmity:
Timor mortis conturbat me.

Our pleasance here is all vainglory
This false world is but transitory,
The flesh is feeble, the Fiend is sly;
Timor mortis conturbat me.

The state of man does change and vary,
Now sound, now sick, now blithe, now sorry,
Now dancing merry, now like to die:
Timor mortis conturbat me.

No state on earth here stands securely,
As with the wind waves the willow,
Waves this world's vanity;
Timor mortis conturbat me.

Unto death go all estates,
Princes, prelates, and potentates,
Both rich and poor of all degree;
Timor mortis conturbat me.

He takes the knights in the field,
Armed under helm and shield;
Victor is he at all melee;
Timor mortis conturbat me.

That strange unmerciful tyrant
Takes, on the mother's breast sucking,
The babe full of benignity;
Timor mortis conturbat me.

He takes the champion in battle,
The captain enclosed in the tower,
The lady in bower, full of beauty;
Timor mortis conturbat me.

He spares no lord for his puissance,
No scholar for his intelligence;
His awful stroke may no man flee;
Timor mortis conturbat me.

I ♥ Death

Not everyone sees death as a fearful prospect. On the contrary, there are people who talk about it as if it were the most beautiful and desirable thing in the world. Such types are technically known as *thanatophiles*: death lovers, the diametric opposite of thanatophobes.

In his consistently fascinating study, *Modern Man and Mortality* (Collier, 1964), Jacques Choron cites numerous literary examples of this sentiment, from the French author Pierre de Ronsard's "Hymn to Death" ("I salute you, blissful and profitable death") to the American poet Mary Emily Bradley's declaration: "O Death, the loveliness that is in thee, / Could the world know, the world would cease to be."

Of course, whether such seemingly heartfelt paeans to death can be taken at face value is an open question. Freudians talk of something called a reaction formation: a defense mechanism that blocks our awareness of deeply disturbing feelings by turning them into their opposite. (The classic case is the aggressively hetero, gay-bashing male whose rabid homophobia masks repressed homosexual desires.)

In short, assertions like Bradley's (or Walt Whitman's insistence that "to die is different from any one supposed, and luckier") may be just another way of coping with the overwhelming terror of extinction.

"I heard a Fly buzz when I died"

What happens at the moment of death? In this famous poem by Emily Dickinson (reprinted from its first 1890 publication), friends and relatives keeping vigil at a deathbed expect something awesome to occur when the speaker breathes her last—perhaps the appearance of God Himself, come to carry the departed soul heavenward. The reality turns out to be considerably more mundane.

I heard a Fly buzz when I died;
The stillness round my form
Was like the stillness in the air
Between the Heaves of storm.

The eyes beside had wrung them dry,
And breaths were gathering sure
For that last onset when the king
Be witnessed in his power.

I willed my keepsakes, signed away
What portion of me I
Could make assignable—and then
There interposed a fly,

With blue, uncertain, stumbling buzz,
Between the light and me;
And then the windows failed, and then
I could not see to see.

Agony to Extinction: The Death Process

In Emily Dickinson's famous poem, "I heard a Fly buzz when I died," death happens in an instant. One moment, the speaker is lying on her deathbed, listening to the titular insect circling her head. A second later, all her senses are extinguished, as though someone has switched off the lights: "And then the windows failed and then / I could not see to see."

That's the way most of us think of death—as a specific moment when a person draws his last breath. In reality, things are more complicated than that. Death isn't a single event—it's a process with definable stages.

The first is what biologists call the *agonal* phase, a term etymologically associated with the word *agony* (both derive from the Greek *agon*, meaning "struggle"). During this period—which generally lasts only a few moments and is often referred to as the "death throes"—the dying person really does seem to be in agony. In truth, however, he or she is too far gone to be aware of any pain and is simply undergoing the violent muscular spasms that accompany the shutdown of the bodily systems. The chest and shoulders may heave convulsively and various ghastly noises—gurgles, rasps, rattles, or even a terrifying bark—might issue from the throat.

The agonal phase is followed by *clinical death*. At this point, the heart stops beating and respiration ceases. There is a brief window of opportunity here for the person to be revived. This highly critical moment has been portrayed in countless movies and TV medical dramas in which frantic emergency room doctors try to jolt a flatlined patient back into life by applying electric defibrillator paddles to the person's chest. (In real life, this technique is only used in cases of heart attacks; to retrieve a person from clinical death requires cardiopulmonary resuscitation or CPR.)

If the attempt to resuscitate a clinically dead patient fails, *brain death* will soon follow. The standard definition of brain death is "the bodily condition of showing no response to external stimuli, no spontaneous movements, no breath, no reflexes, and a flat reading (usually for at least 24 hours) on a machine that measures the brain's electrical activity." The "total and irreversible cessation of brain function" is now the standard criterion for death determination in the United States and most other Western nations.

Even after brain death occurs, there are still two more stages in the utter extinction of a human being: *biological death*, which refers to the permanent, irreversible end of all the

body's life processes; and *postmortem cellular death*, during which the individual cells die and begin to decompose, a process that can last for several hours after biological death.

RECOMMENDED READING

The single best book ever written on the subject of how we die is *How We Die* (Knopf, 1994) by Dr. Sherwin B. Nuland. Much-deserved winner of the National Book Award, this enormously wise, humane, elegantly written work describes, without sentimentality, sensationalism, or sugarcoating, exactly what happens when death occurs by the most common means: heart attack, stroke, cancer, and plain old age. Because the book is so unflinching and honest in its insistence on the messiness, ugliness, and indignities of dying, it has the (somewhat paradoxical) effect of making the whole business seem less terrifying: not an unimaginable horror but a universal and unavoidable event that is the means by which "each of us is returned to the same state of physical, and perhaps spiritual, nonexistence from which we emerged at conception."

THE DEATH CLOCK

Want to know when you'll die? The Death Clock—"the Internet's friendly reminder that life is slipping away" will tell you. Just go to www.deathclock.com, enter your vital statistics (birthday, sex, height, weight, smoking status, etc.), and the Death Clock will tell you how much time you have left, down to the last second!

How Do You Know When You're Dead?

Back in the old days, it was easy to tell if someone was alive or not. If a person had stopped breathing and his heart no longer beat, you could safely assume he was a goner. "I know when one is dead, and when one lives," King Lear cries over the body of his daughter Cordelia. "Lend me a looking glass. If that her breath will mist or stain the stone, why then she lives."

Nowadays, things are much trickier. Holding a mirror up to someone's nose won't cut it anymore. In an age when life support technology has made it possible to keep a human body going more or less indefinitely by artificial means, it's become necessary to draw a more exact distinction between life and death.

In the late 1950s, two French neurologists named P. Mollaret and M. Goulon observed that some patients being kept alive on respirators showed absolutely no electrical activity in their brains. They were in a state of nonbeing that the two physicians called "*coma dépassé*"—beyond coma. These findings ultimately led to the adoption of a new set of standards for determining death: what is technically known as "death by brain criteria," or more commonly "brain death." Essentially, the phrase refers to the complete and irreversible loss of all brain functioning. Based on a landmark report published by the Harvard Medical School in 1968, doctors determine brain death by testing for these vital signs:

1. *Capacity to breathe independently.* Physicians give the comatose patient oxygen,

then shut off the ventilator to see if he can breathe on his own

2. *Gag reflex.* The patient's airway is suctioned. If he fails to cough or gag, his reflexes are no longer functioning.
3. *Pupil reaction.* Doctors shine a light directly at the eye to see if the pupils contract.
4. *Blinking.* Doctors poke the patient's cornea. A live person will blink. A dead one won't.
5. *Eye rolling.* Doctors rotate the patient's head to see if the eyes move around (a phenomenon known as "doll's eyes").
6. *Making a face when ice water is poured into your ear.* Doctors pour ice water into the patient's ear and watch what happens.

Our Bodies, Our Deaths

After all those crunches, push-ups, and bicep curls, you might not want to hear this, but that muscular physique you've worked so hard to achieve isn't going to last forever. Death is not kind to the human body. It is generally agreed that the strongest man in recorded history was Canadian-born weightlifter Louis Cyr, who could press four thousand pounds, push a freight car up a hill, and lift a wooden platform holding eighteen men. He died of nephritis in 1912. Dig him up today and that once formidable upper torso would not be an impressive sight.

Left to its own natural devices, the human corpse passes through several increasingly revolting stages on its way to becoming what pathologists call "dry remains." The first stage is known as "fresh" ("as in fresh fish, not fresh air," Mary Roach helpfully points out in her best seller, *Stiff*). With your heart no longer pumping, your blood begins to sink to the lowest parts of your body—meaning your back and buttocks, assuming that you are supine. Within minutes, the underside of your body will show signs of *livor mortis*—a purple-red discoloration known as "postmortem staining"—while your face, chest, and so on turn a ghastly white.

In the meantime—after growing slack at the instant of death—your muscles start to stiffen. Rigor mortis sets in. It begins two to six hours after death with your eyelids, neck, and jaw, then gradually spreads until your whole body is affected, a process that takes another four to six hours. Your temperature is also dropping during this period, a change known as *algor mortis*. By now, you are a very literal stiff.

Typically, a corpse remains in this rigid condition for approximately one to three days. Then the muscles grow flaccid again. That's when stage two begins and things start to get really ugly.

Stage two is known as "bloat." All living humans harbor bacteria in their intestinal tracts. These bacteria produce foul-smelling gas, which we expel in the usual impolite ways. Our deaths do not stop these bacteria from generating gas inside our guts. Now, however—since our colon, sphincter, and so on have ceased functioning—we can't discharge it anymore. As a result, the gas builds up inside us and (in the words of Richard Selzer, author of *Mortal Lessons*) it "puffs the eyelids, cheeks, and abdomen into bladders of murderous vapor. The slimmest man takes on the bloat of corpulence." The pressure of the gas causes the eyes to bulge, pushes the intestines out through the rectum, and forces foul bloody fluid from the mouth, nose, and other orifices. Beginning in the lower abdomen, the skin turns color—from green to purple and finally, in later stages, to black.

Bloat lasts about a week and is followed by the penultimate stage, "putrefaction and decay." It is during this phase that the body essentially liquefies. Mary Roach compares it to a "slowed-down version" of Margaret Hamilton's death scene in *The Wizard of Oz*, when the Wicked Witch melts into the ground—though the reality is a good deal more repulsive. Giant putrid blisters appear on the discolored skin; the hair, nails, and teeth loosen; the brain oozes through the ears or bubbles from the mouth; the swollen belly bursts; and the internal organs dissolve into an unspeakable soup.

All this, of course, is accompanied by a stench so overpowering that, according to one expert, people who experience it for the first time need weeks to get it out of their nostrils. No deodorizer can mask it. As the pathologist/essayist F. Gonzalez-Crussi observes in his book *The Day of the Dead and Other Mortal Reflections*: "Bathe a decomposing cadaver in sweet perfumes, and it will smell of rotting carrion on a bed of roses."

Gradually (depending on various factors, including the climate), the corpse turns into more or less odorless "dry remains"—"cartilage and bone connected by sinewy ligaments," as one writer describes it.

RECOMMENDED READING

In addition to the three books mentioned previously—Mary Roach's wonderfully witty *Stiff: The Curious Lives of Human Cadavers* (Norton, 2003); Richard Selzer's lyrical *Mortal Lessons: Notes on the Art of Surgery* (Harcourt, 1976); and F. Gonzalez-Crussi's equally elegant *Day of the Dead and Other Mortal Reflections* (Harcourt, 1993)—you'll want to check out Dr. Kenneth Iserson's encyclopedic *Death to Dust: What Happens to Dead Bodies?* (Galen Press, 1994) and Christine Quigley's comprehensive survey, *The Corpse: A History* (McFarland, 1996). Also highly recommended: Jim Crace's bold, beautifully written novel, *Being Dead* (Picador, 2001), which charts both the relationship of two long-married, middle-aged zoologists and the slow decomposition of their bodies after they are murdered on a beach by a passing psycho.

ASK DR. DEATH

Dear Dr. Death:
Let's say I die and no one bothers to bury me. How long will it take for my body to decompose?

Morbid

Dear Morbid:
Like anything else subject to spoilage—uncooked hamburger, iceberg lettuce, sushi—dead bodies decay at different rates depending on environmental conditions.

A body left out in the open in a warm, moderately humid climate will be reduced to skeletal remains in relatively short order—anywhere from one to six months. This is owing in large part to the actions of carrion insects (such as sarcophagous flies) and animal scavengers.

Conditions that keep such creatures from feasting on your flesh will, of course, retard the decomposition process. Since flies can't exist in subfreezing temperatures, bodies left outside in frigid weather will last much longer than those in temperate climates. (The cold also slows the bacterial activity that causes putrefaction.) The effect of a glacial environment on a human corpse was dramatically demonstrated in 1991, when two Alpine hikers came upon the remarkably well-preserved body of what turned out to be a 5,300-year-old man, who quickly became known as "Otzi the Iceman," aka "Frozen Fritz."

If your body is abandoned in a desertlike environment, chances are that it will turn into a natural mummy through the process of dehydration. In her fascinating 2001 book, *The Mummy Congress*, science writer Heather Pringle talks about the Chilean city of Arica, where scores of mummified corpses dating from the Inca period have been uncovered. Bordering on the Atcama Desert—a virtually rainless plateau running from the Andes to the Pacific Ocean—Arica "is blessed with almost perfect conditions for the long-term preservation of the human body," a "relentless and inescapable aridity" that can "dry a human corpse to the texture of shoe leather and keep it that way."

According to an old rule of thumb known as Casper's law, one week of decomposition in the open air is equivalent to two weeks in water. In other words, if your body is dumped in a stagnant lake as opposed to, say, your backyard, you will take twice as long to decompose. You will, however, putrefy in a particularly repulsive way. Here's how journalist Brian Hickey describes it:

> When a corpse is dumped in water, it floats face down. During the first 12 hours, the muscles lock in place, starting with the head and ending with the toes. During the next day or so, that rigor mortis reverses itself; from toes to head, the muscles relax. The skin toughens and pimples. This is called goose-skin, or *anserina cutis*. Then, it becomes swollen and wrinkled, a phenomenon named maceration, or washer-woman's skin. As bacteria start eating away at body tissue, the corpse, now a greenish-red hue, starts emitting a putrid odor. By the third day, gas pockets form internally, causing the stomach to swell. That can split the skin open and form cracks through which greenish-bronze and reddish-brown fluids seep. The water, even if shallow, forces the victim's hands and feet to balloon. Soon, portions of the outer layer of skin will separate from the underlying tissues and slide off. By day 10 post-mortem, the fingernails and more skin start peeling off, body hair starts falling out and silt will have found its way into the airways, lungs and stomach. The body has turned greenish-black. If it's left there for more than a month, the layer of fat beneath the skin will take on a soaplike texture and ooze from the body.

Or—as Dr. Kenneth V. Iserson so succinctly puts it in his definitive 1994 book, *Death to Dust*—a few weeks in water will turn you into "an ugly smelly mess."

DEATH DEFINITION: *Adipocere*

ONE OF THE ICKIER CHANGES THAT THE HUMAN BODY MAY UNDERGO DURING THE PUTREFACTION PROCESS is the conversion of body fat into a substance known as *adipocere* or *grave wax*. Produced by the interaction of fatty tissue, bacterial enzymes, and moisture, adipocere is most frequently found on cadavers that have been immersed in water or buried in wet soil for extended periods. It varies in color from grayish white to yellow or even brown. Depending on various factors, it can have the consistency of grease, semisoft cheese, or coarse soap. It tends to smell like rank cheese.

Bodies that are not exposed to air, insects, or scavengers will start to form adipocere within a month of death, generally on those parts of the body that contain the most fat—the cheeks, breasts, buttocks, and abdomen. Because adipocere formation [aka *saponification*] slows further decomposition, bodies that undergo this process do not turn into skeletons but into bloated, waxy-looking, thoroughly hideous "soap mummies."

For more on this [supremely unappetizing] subject, including images of saponified cadavers, go to www.adipocere.homestead.com, a self-described website "about the soapy, waxy substance many of us will one day become." Also recommended: Christine Quigley's book, *Modern Mummmies: The Preservation of the Human Body in the Twentieth Century* [McFarland, 1996].

If you want to see an actual specimen up close, you can take a trip to the famed Mütter Museum at the College of Physicians in Philadelphia, where a female corpse known as the "Soap Lady" has been on display for more than a century.

Putrefaction: A Handy Guide

How do you know when somebody is putrefying? Here are the twelve major signs as identified by John Glaister and Edgar Rentoul in their standard text, *Medical Jurisprudence and Toxicology* (Livingstone, 1966):

1. A greenish color appears in the lower right abdomen, then gradually spreads.
2. The face darkens and swells.
3. The genitals darken and swell.
4. The abdomen bloats with fetid gases.
5. Putrid blisters form on the skin.
6. The blisters burst and the skin begins to peel off in large, irregular patches.
7. Bloodstained fluid issues from the mouth and nostrils.
8. The eyeballs liquefy.
9. Maggots appear.
10. The nails and hair come off.
11. The abdominal and thoracic cavities burst open.
12. The tissues dissolve into a semiliquid mass.

There is to be a feast. The rich table has been set. The board groans. The guests have already arrived, numberless bacteria that had, in life, dwelt in saprophytic harmony with their host. Their turn now! Charged, they press against the membrane barriers, break through the new softness, sweep across the plain of tissue, devouring, belching gas. . . . Blisters appear upon the skin, enlarge, blast, leaving brownish puddles in the declivities. You are becoming gravy.

—RICHARD SELZER

ASK DR. DEATH

Dear Dr. Death:
I've always heard that a person's hair and nails keep growing after death. How long do they get? I mean, let's say some guy with a crew cut dies and gets buried. If you dug up his corpse a year later, would he have really long hair? And claws? That would be really creepy!

Just Wondering About
Postmortem Hair and Nail Growth

Dear Just Wondering:
You're right, that would be creepy. It would also be impossible. The phenomenon you refer to is just an optical illusion. What really happens is that as a corpse dehydrates, the skin retracts around the hair and nails, making them jut out more prominently. In other words, the hair and nails aren't growing; the flesh is shriveling.

"Ghastly Gropings in the Decay of Graves"

Human decomposition has rarely been portrayed as graphically—not to say sickeningly—as in this short newspaper piece by famed author Lafcadio Hearn who, early in his career, worked as a reporter for *The Cincinnati Enquirer*, where this article appeared on August 26, 1874.

> It may be remembered that a Floater was found Friday and hauled ashore near the Two-mile House. The said Floater was in a horrible condition when stranded; the fishes had devoured the cheeks and left the ghastly grinning teeth exposed; the eyeballs were rolled up so as only to show staring spheres of blood-shot yellow-white; the whole body was enormously puffed up, monstrously swollen, covered with gigantic blisters, revolting and unrecognizable, bearing more resemblance to a vast unshelled turtle than to a human body. Coroner Maley, however, succeeded in identifying it at an Inquest, while the jurymen stood afar off with handkerchiefs to their noses; and the friends of the deceased had the remains subsequently exhumed from Potters' Field and buried in the family lot at Spring Grove.
>
> On Monday evening, however, the widow of the deceased called on the Coroner and begged him to accompany her to the cemetery, as she was intending to have the body exhumed, fearing some mistake had been made, and she wanted Dr. Maley to identify the corpse, if possible, which had by that time been two days underground. The Coroner consented, and performed the gruc-

some duty yesterday afternoon with a degree of nonchalance which would put a ghoul to the blush. On opening the coffin the frightful, acrid, far-reaching stench drove all but the undaunted Coroner from the scene of the action. He, shielding his nose with a pocket handkerchief, and arming his right hand with a glove, set to work without a shudder among the writhing swarms of white vermin which were preying on the decomposing remains. The body had by that time become far more hideous to look upon, the eyes having fallen out, and the protruding tongue crumbling into black rottenness. Nevertheless, the Coroner plunged his gloved hand in the hideous orifice to examine the teeth, and inspected the foul mass of sweltering, shrinking corruption for marks of identification, while the livid worms traveled all over his broadcloth and tried to ring themselves about his fingers. Then, having succeeded in identifying the corpse to the satisfaction of everybody, he trotted home and ate a hearty dinner. Such is the stuff that Coroners' stomachs are made of.

Isn't It Ironic?

Shortly before noon on April 26, 1932, the famous American poet Hart Crane committed suicide by leaping from the deck of a steamship just off the Florida coast and drowning before anyone could throw him a life preserver.

Ironically, Crane's father, Clarence—a successful confectioner from Cincinnati—is famed as the inventor of one of America's most popular candies: the Life Saver!

What a Way to Go

Did you know that the famous American author Sherwood Anderson was killed by an hors d'oeuvre? (He swallowed a cocktail frank at a party without removing the toothpick and died a week later of peritonitis). Or that a California motorist was killed in 1999 when a flying cow—propelled through the air after being hit by another vehicle—crashed through the windshield of his pickup? Or that the fumes from diacetyl, an ingredient in artificial butter flavoring, have caused the deaths of several dozen popcorn factory workers?

These are just a few of the wild and wacky ends described by Michael Largo in his cheerfully macabre volume, *Final Exits: The Illustrated Encyclopedia of How We Die* (Harper, 2006). Arranged alphabetically according to cause of death—from airbags and alligators to yawning and zoöfatalism (a psychological compulsion to get too close to zoo animals)—Largo's book is the definitive guide to the infinite variety of ways that humans have expired. You'll come away convinced that the Grim Reaper is endowed not only with an endlessly fertile imagination but also with a really sick sense of humor. (How else to explain the reputed 1999 death of an Australian circus dwarf named Od who, while performing on a trampoline, accidentally landed in the mouth of a yawning hippopotamus, which swallowed him whole? Or the 1981 fatal immolation of a middle-aged Detroit man whose toupee came off at a disco and who, while trying to stick it back on, accidentally ignited the glue with his cigarette?)

If Largo's book doesn't fully satisfy your appetite for tasty death anecdotes, you can always try *They Went That-a-Way: How the Famous, the Infamous, and the Great Died* (Ballantine, 1989) by the late publishing mogul Malcolm Forbes. Consisting of more than 150 alphabetically arranged capsule biographies, Forbes's collection will fill you in on the final moments of luminaries from Aeschylus ("killed when an eagle mistook his shiny bald head for a rock and dropped a tortoise on it to crack the shell") to John Jacob Astor to Virginia Woolf ("forced a large stone in her coat pocket" and walked into the Ouse River).

A Grim Fairy Tale

They don't call them the Brothers Grimm for nothing. Though most people think of fairy tales as charming little kiddie stories that end happily ever after, many deal with tragedy, sorrow, violence, and death.

In "Death's Messenger," one of the lesser-known tales from the Grimm brothers' world-famous collection, Death is defeated in a wrestling match by a giant. As Death lies panting by the side of the road, a strong and healthy young man wanders by, gives him a refreshing drink of water, and helps him to his feet.

In gratitude, Death promises that—though he can spare no one, including his young helper—he will never sneak up on him. Instead, he will send his messengers to let the man know far in advance when Death is coming. And so the young man goes on his merry way, reassured that he will never die until he receives a warning from Death's messengers.

He enjoys himself and lives a happy, carefree life. "But youth and health did not last long," the story continues. "Soon came sickness and sorrows, which tormented him by day and took away his rest by night. 'Die, I shall not,' said he to himself, 'for Death will send his messengers before that, but I do wish these wretched days of sickness were over.' As soon as he felt himself well again, he began to live merrily.

"Then one day someone tapped him on the shoulder. He looked around and Death stood behind him and said: 'Follow me, the hour of your departure from this world has come.' 'What,' replied the man, 'will you break your word? Did you not promise me that you would send your messengers to me before coming yourself?' 'Silence!' answered Death. 'Have I not sent one messenger to you after another? Did not fever come and smite you, and shake you, and cast you down? Has dizziness not bewildered your head? Did not your ears ring? Did not toothache bite into your cheek? Was it not dark before your eyes? And besides that, has not my own brother Sleep reminded you every night of me? Did you not lie by night as if you were already dead?' The man could make no answer; he yielded to his fate and went away with Death."

2

BE PREPARED

"The Good Death": Achievable Goal or Contradiction in Terms?

Defining a "bad death" is a pretty straightforward affair. In his classic study *Discipline and Punish*, for example, French philosopher Michel Foucault describes at great and grisly length the 1757 execution of one Robert François Damiens for the attempted assassination of King Louis XV. As Foucault tells it, Damiens, after being conveyed to a public square, had the flesh torn from various parts of his body with a red-hot pincer. Then molten lead was poured on the wounds. Then his right hand was scalded with boiling oil. Then his limbs were ripped off by horses. Then his still-living head and trunk were tossed onto a flaming pyre.

Now *that's* a bad death.

Defining a "good death," however, is much trickier. For one thing, different people have different opinions on the subject. If avoiding protracted agony is your criterion for a good death, then being killed instantly in a major traffic accident might fit the bill. Clearly, however, many people would regard such an end as a horrible tragedy.

And then there are cultural variations. Being ripped to pieces by ravenous beasts wouldn't strike most of us as a particularly good death. But in the 1958 movie *The Vikings*, the captive chieftain Ragnar is perfectly happy to get tossed into a pit filled with half-starved wild dogs as long as he can hold on to his sword and go down swinging—a bit of Hollywood hokum, no doubt, but nevertheless an accurate reflection of the manly ethos of the Norsemen, a warrior culture in which dying gloriously in battle was as good as it got.

In our own culture, the concept of a good death can be traced back to the work of renowned psychiatrist Elisabeth Kübler-Ross, whose groundbreaking 1969 best seller, *On*

Death and Dying, became the bible of the contemporary "death awareness" movement. In her studies of the terminally ill, Kübler-Ross famously identified five stages that people presumably pass through as they move toward death: denial, anger, bargaining, depression, and acceptance.

In this scheme, a good death means that you don't get stuck in any of the earlier phases but succeed in reaching the final one, a full and mature acceptance of death as a natural and inevitable part of life. In this way, the individual is able to take charge of his final days—to wrest control from the uncaring grip of a faceless medical establishment and die with dignity and humanity, in a manner and place of his own choosing.

Researchers inspired by Kübler-Ross's work have identified six basic components of a good death, all of which involve the active and fully aware participation of the moribund patient:

1. *Preparation.* To know when death is coming and to understand what you can expect.
2. *Treatment control.* To have a say in medical decisions, including the right to refuse life-prolonging procedures.
3. *Pain and symptom management.* To be assured of adequate relief of suffering at the end.
4. *Surroundings.* To choose the place of death (home, hospice, etc.) and decide who will be present.
5. *Completion.* To take care of "unfinished business," both practical and emotional. This includes putting your affairs in order, settling unresolved conflicts, spending time with friends and loved ones, and saying a proper goodbye.
6. *Affirmation.* Studies suggest that people nearing death are comforted by a sense that their lives have had meaning to themselves and others.

For all the current talk about a good death, however, the fact is that there is no right way to die. Some people leave this world with a smile; others go kicking and screaming.

For the most part, of course, we prefer to see our loved ones die peacefully. But that often has more to do with *us* than with them. As psychiatrist N. H. Cassem points out, "There is a danger that our expectations of others are selfish rather than altruistic. Some want others to grow old quietly, not because there is anything especially good about that, but only so the old won't be a nuisance. So, too, there is a danger we may want others to die quietly, instead of angrily, because it makes us more comfortable. There is no such thing as a best way to die. Dying must have as many styles as living."

In other words—to quote Dylan Thomas—while some people "go gentle into that good night," others (following the poet's own advice) "rage, rage against the dying of the light."

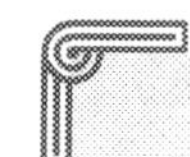

RECOMMENDED READING

Based on six years of extensive research, Marilyn Webb's sweeping *The Good Death: The New American Search to Reshape the End of Life* (Bantam, 1999) concludes that the modern way of dying relies far too heavily on exotic life-prolonging technology while stinting on palliative care. Her conclusions are reinforced by Dr. Ira Byock, whose book *Dying Well: The Prospect for Growth at the End of Life* (Riverhead, 1998) offers practical guidance on how to enjoy life even in the face of death.

In March 2006, the BBC ran a two-part program called *How to Have a Good Death*. The accompanying website offers much useful information, including a practical checklist and a handsome downloadable booklet, *Planning for a Good Death*. The Web address is: www.bbc.co.uk/health/tv_and_radio/how_to_have_a_good_death.

He that begins to live, begins to die.

—Francis Quarles

Mortuary Hall of Fame: Elisabeth Kübler-Ross

Though no one disputes her pioneering contributions to the contemporary "death awareness" movement or her revolutionary impact on the way the terminally ill are treated by the medical profession, Elisabeth Kübler-Ross's once exalted reputation has taken a hit in the years since her own demise in 2004.

Firstborn of a set of triplets, she weighed barely two pounds at her birth in 1926 and was not expected to survive—a circumstance to which she partly attributed her later preoccupation with death. By sixth grade, she had resolved to become a physician. During her teenage years, she hitchhiked through war-ravaged Europe, helping to set up typhoid and first-aid stations. It was during a visit to the Majdanek concentration camp in Poland that she fixed on her life's goal. Profoundly affected by the suffering of the survivors, she decided to become a psychiatrist who helped people deal with death.

After receiving her medical degree in 1957, she practiced briefly in the Swiss countryside before marrying American neuropathologist Emmanuel Ross and moving with him to the United States. She interned at a hospital on Long Island, then accepted a research fellowship at Manhattan State Hospital, where she was appalled by what she perceived as the neglect, even abuse, of dying patients. A two-year stint at the University of Colorado Medical School in Denver, where she taught psychiatry and treated schizophrenic patients, helped her refine interviewing techniques that would prove vital in her later work with the terminally ill.

The turning point in her career—and in the evolution of modern approaches to the palliative care of the dying—occurred during her tenure as professor of psychiatry at the University of Chicago, beginning in 1965. When some theology students approached her for help in studying death, she initiated a series of teaching seminars in which dying patients were invited to come in and speak about their thoughts and feelings to a group of doctors, nurses, and social workers, along with the theology students and their chaplains. This seemingly simple procedure was, in fact, a major breakthrough, shedding unprecedented light on a subject shrouded, even for medical professionals, in fear and denial.

It was from these groundbreaking sessions that Kübler-Ross identified her now-famous "five stages of grief," the supposed sequence of emotional responses that people typically pass through when diagnosed with a terminal illness. As summed up by journalist Holcomb B. Noble, "Denial is the first stage. As his condition worsens and denial is impossible, the patient displays anger, the 'Why me?' stage. That is followed by a bargaining period. 'Yes, I'm going to die, but if I diet and exercise, can I do it later?' When the patient sees the bargaining will not work, depression often sets in. The final stage is acceptance, a period in which the patient is ready to let go."

Kübler-Ross's findings, laid out in her 1969 best seller *On Death and Dying*, made her an international celebrity, a scientist of worldwide repute who helped shatter taboos against the open discussion of death, nurtured the creation of the modern hospice system, and established thanatology as a legitimate medical discipline. In her later years, however, she squandered a good part of her credibility when she grew obsessed with finding proof of an afterlife existence and became involved with a self-proclaimed "spirit medium" who took sexual advantage of his gullible followers.

It is sometimes suggested that what we really mind is the process of dying. *But I should not really object to dying if it were not followed by death.*

—Thomas Nagel

Ars Moriendi

Nowadays, the how-to sections of bookstores are crammed with titles like *The Art of the Deal*, *The Art of Seduction*, *The Art of Happiness*, and *The Art of Staying Young*—works that reflect our contemporary preoccupations with materialism, sex, personal fulfillment, and eternal youthfulness. Back in the late Middle Ages, people read how-to books, too. But in that death-obsessed era, just decades after the bubonic plague devastated Western Europe, the best-known works in the genre fell into the category known as *ars moriendi*: guides that taught readers the art of dying.

The earliest work in this tradition, called *Tractatus artis bene moriendi* (*Treatise on the Art of Dying Well*), appeared in 1415. Composed by an anonymous Dominican friar and aimed at both priests and laymen, it contained six chapters that offered religious consolation as well as specific rites, prayers, and rules of behavior to be followed by both the dying person and those attending him. A widely circulated abridged version—consisting of woodcut illustrations depicting the spiritual struggles of a dying man beset by soul-snaring temptations—was published in 1450.

Over the next two centuries, dozens of similar guidebooks, designed to teach readers how to prepare for a good death, appeared throughout Western Europe. The most famous is *The Rules and Exercises of Holy Dying* (1651) written by the "Shakespeare of divines," Jeremy Taylor, chaplain to King Charles I. Universally regarded as the one true literary masterpiece in the tra-

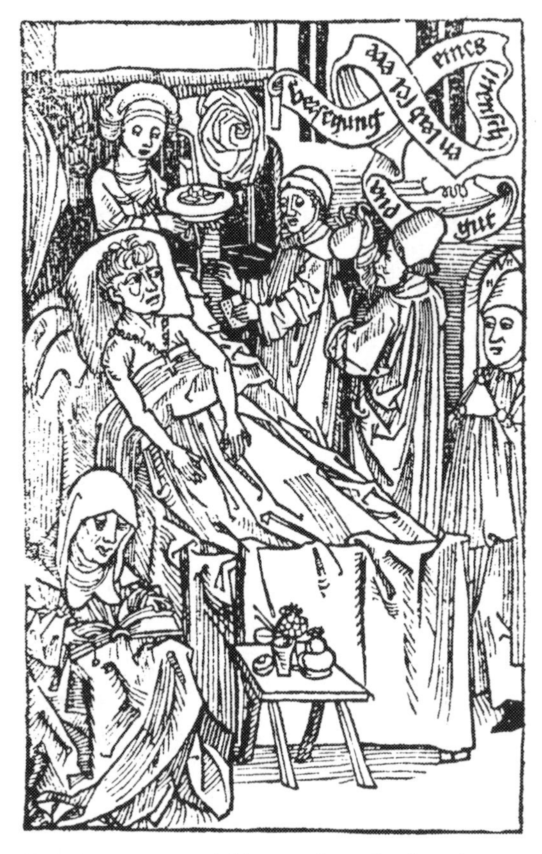

Dying man surrounded by attendants. Attributed to Albrecht Dürer, 1509.

dition, Taylor's book sets forth in rich, poetic prose what he describes as "the first entire body of directions for sick and dying people"—a systematic program that stresses the importance not only of proper deathbed behavior but also of righteous daily living.

Though the *ars moriendi* eventually faded as a vital literary genre, it appears to be making something of a comeback. A recent example is Patricia Weenolsen's *The Art of Dying: How to Leave This World with Dignity and Grace, at Peace with Yourself and Your Loved Ones* (St. Martin's Press, 1996), a practical, straightforward guide that covers everything from how to inform relatives of impending death and preparing for a possible afterlife to the "Twenty-seven Rules for Dying the 'Right' Way."

Death at the Dinner Table: Talking About the Inevitable

In the wise words of Joshua Slocum, executive director of the Funeral Consumers Alliance: "It's time to have death at the dinner table." No, he's not suggesting that you call up the Grim Reaper and invite him over for some of your special Yankee pot roast. He means that we need to become comfortable with death as a topic of ordinary conversation. More particularly, he means that aging parents and their adult children should be able to have free and easy discussions about funeral planning—that the subject should be no more taboo than any other family-related matter.

All too often, people die without conveying their final wishes to their nearest and dearest. The issue is so fraught with anxiety that they don't want to talk—or even think—about it. As a result, their survivors are left in a state of confusion. Should we cremate Mom or bury her? Donate Dad's organs or leave his body intact? Have a formal service conducted by a member of the clergy or a simple graveside ceremony with close friends sharing their memories?

Of course, there are certain people who honestly don't care what happens to them once they're gone. As far as they're concerned, funerals are strictly for the living.

Whatever kind of send-off the kids want to throw is fine by them.

The poet-undertaker Thomas Lynch heartily endorses this attitude. "There is nothing, once you are dead, that can be done *to you* or *for you* or *with you* or *about you* that will do you any harm or good," he writes in his lovely essay collection, *The Undertaking* (Norton, 1997). "Once you're dead, put your feet up, call it a day, and let the husband or the missus or the kids or a sibling decide whether you are to be buried or burned or blown out of a cannon or left to dry out in a ditch somewhere. It's not your day to watch it, because the dead don't care."

Most of us, however, do have preferences, often quite specific ones. And even if you don't, it's pretty inconsiderate to drop the whole messy problem in the lap of your loved ones, particularly at a moment when they're dealing with their own grief. If you really want to make life easier for your survivors—and add to your own ultimate peace of mind—you should make your final wishes clear in either conversation or writing.

Here's a checklist of things to consider, based on recommendations by the Funeral Consumers Alliance:

1. Do you want your organs donated? Which ones? Should they go to any particular medical school?
2. Do you want to be buried? Where?
3. What kind of coffin do you prefer? A cheap pine box? The best casket money can buy?
4. Do you want to be embalmed? Do you want an open-casket viewing of your body?
5. What sort of funeral do you want? Who should officiate? Is there a specific funeral home you wish to handle the arrangements?
6. Do you want a memorial service? Where and what kind—in church, at home, graveside? Are there specific instructions—favorite poems to be read, special music to be played, et cetera?
7. What sort of grave marker do you want, if any? What should the inscription say?
8. Would you prefer cremation? What about your ashes—do you want them preserved? Or should they be scattered? Where?
9. Who should be notified of your death? Who should be invited to the funeral/ memorial service?
10. What information should be included in your obituary?

Given how discomforting it is to contemplate our own deaths, it's no surprise that when it comes to funeral preplanning, most of us are prone to the Scarlett O'Hara syndrome: "I'll think about it tomorrow." But it's important to keep in mind that making these decisions—and communicating them to your family—is good for everyone concerned. It will give you the grown-up satisfaction of taking charge of your own destiny. And it will relieve your loved ones of a terrible burden at a time when they're least capable of coping with it.

Of course, even that argument holds no water with Thomas Lynch. "Why *shouldn't* I be a burden to my children?" he wonders in his book, *Bodies in Motion and at Rest* (Vintage, 2001). "My children have been a burden to me. Lovely burdens, every one of them. . . . And when I die, bearing the burden of burying me or burning me or blasting me into cyberspace should be theirs to do."

Did Lincoln Dream of His Own Death?

People who believe that it's a bad omen to dream about your own death often point to the example of Abraham Lincoln, who reportedly had the following nightmare not long before his assassination.

> About ten days ago, I retired very late. I had been up waiting for important dispatches from the front. I could not have been long in bed when I fell into a slumber, for I was weary. I soon began to dream. There seemed to be a death-like stillness about me. Then I heard subdued sobs, as if a number of people were weeping. I thought I left my bed and wandered downstairs. There the silence was broken by the same pitiful sobbing, but the mourners were invisible. I went from room to room; no living person was in sight, but the same mournful sounds of distress met me as I passed along. I saw light in all the rooms; every object was familiar to me; but where were all the people who were grieving as if their hearts would break? I was puzzled and alarmed. What could be the meaning of all this? Determined to find the cause of a state of things so mysterious and so shocking, I kept on until I arrived at the East Room, which I entered. There I met with a sickening surprise. Before me was a catafalque, on which rested a corpse wrapped in funeral vestments. Around it were stationed soldiers who were acting as guards; and there was a throng of people, gazing mournfully upon the corpse, whose face was covered, others weeping pitifully. "Who is dead in the White House?" I demanded of one of the soldiers, "The President," was his answer; "he was killed by an assassin." Then came a loud burst of grief from the crowd, which woke me from my dream. I slept no more that night; and although it was only a dream, I have been strangely annoyed by it ever since.

This dream certainly seems prophetic. Unfortunately, there is no way of determining its authenticity since it comes from only a single unverifiable source—a book written many years after the assassination by Lincoln's friend and bodyguard, Ward Hill Lamon.

ASK DR. DEATH

Dear Dr. Death:
Someone told me recently that it's impossible to dream about being dead without actually dying. Now I'm afraid to go to sleep at night because I might die in a dream and never wake up. Help!
Believes Everything She Hears

Dear Believes Everything:
Rest easy! Plenty of people experience their own deaths while dreaming and wake up the next morning to tell about it. To be sure, there are cultures that regard such dreams as a bad sign—a premonition of impending disaster. Modern psychiatry, however, dismisses this belief as an old wives' tale and interprets these dreams as a mirror of unconscious feelings: everything from unresolved death anxieties to the hidden wish for a new and different life.

Wills: Last and Living

Most of us accept, in a vague and abstract kind of way, that we probably won't live forever. Deep down inside, however, we find it hard to believe that our time here on earth is depressingly short and that, before we know it, we will be permanently and definitively dead.

One unfortunate consequence of this denial is a tendency to put off all-important end-of-life decisions, sometimes until it's too late. According to one study, roughly 70 percent of American adults don't have a will. This is good news for the legal profession (as one proverb puts it, "The man who dies without a will has lawyers for heirs"). But it's a potentially disastrous situation for everyone else concerned, particularly the spouses, children, siblings, and other relations of those who die intestate (i.e., with no valid will; literally, "without testifying to their wishes").

It's not just your loved ones who are likely to suffer if you die intestate. It's in your own best interest to leave a will. Without one, you won't have a say in how your property, however meager, gets distributed upon your death. The state will make those decisions for you—and rarely in the way you would prefer.

Let's say you're a twenty-year-old college student whose most precious possession is your 2001 black-and-orange Harley-Davidson Sportster 1200 motorcycle. If you should happen to die without a will, the bike will go not to the person most worthy to receive it—say, your best buddy, Wayne—but to your parents, who may give it to someone you hate, like your obnoxious cousin Steve. In their comprehensive book, *Wants, Wishes, and Wills: A Medical and Legal Guide to Protecting Yourself and Your Family in Sickness and in Health* (Financial Times Press, 2007), Wynne A. Whitman and Shawn D. Glisson offer this striking example of what can happen when a person dies without a will:

> In Kentucky, if you die intestate and own real estate, your real estate will first pass to your children or the descendants (your grandchildren or great-grandchildren) of any child of yours who has already died. If you have no children, it passes to your father and mother, or the survivor of them. If neither of your parents is living, it goes to your brothers and sisters or their descendants if they're not then living. And if you don't have siblings, your real estate goes to your spouse. If your spouse isn't living or you're not married, it's left to your grandparents or their descendants (which means your aunts and uncles or your cousins). So let's think about this. If you're married and you own real estate in your name only, and you don't have a will, your spouse will only receive your property if you aren't survived by your children, your parents, your siblings, or your nieces and nephews. This may be what you want—but we bet a lot of you would rather have your spouse receive your real estate before some of your nieces and nephews.

Having a will not only gives you control over the posthumous disposition of your possessions but is a great opportunity to let your family and friends know exactly what you think of them. Bestowing a precious possession on a friend or relative along with a last loving word—"To my dear niece, Suzie, I leave my collection of Victorian bootlace hooks because I know how much she's always coveted them"—can be profoundly meaningful to the recipient. Conversely, what better way to tell your wife how little she meant to you than by bequeathing her your "second-best bed," as Shakespeare famously did? And just think of how satisfying it will be to look down from heaven and see the expression on the face of that greedy, good-for-nothing grandkid who couldn't wait for you to kick off and now discovers, at the reading of your will, that you haven't left him one red cent!

As any financial advisor will tell you, every adult over the age of eighteen—whether single or married, healthy or ill, wealthy or of modest means—should have a will. A will doesn't necessarily have to be complicated ("All to wife" is officially listed as the world's shortest will, according to the *Guinness Book of World's Records*). If you lead a simple life and don't have a whole lot to leave, there are various do-it-yourself options. The simplest is a standard fill-in-the-blanks form, available at any reasonably well-stocked stationery store. Attorney Michael Trachtman has put together something called *My Will Book* (Sterling, 2007), a handsomely bound volume that, when completed according to directions, witnessed, and notarized, is intended to serve as a legal last will and testament in every state. You can also purchase software, such as *Suze Orman's Will and Trust Kit*, that will lead you through the process of creating a will, or make wills online at sites such as LawDepot (www.lawdepot.com), FindLegalForms (www.findlegalforms.com), and LegalZoom (www.legalzoom.com).

Most experts agree, however, that it's best to use an attorney (even if you rely on a do-it-yourself form, you should get a lawyer to review the completed document). A general law practitioner will suffice if your estate is uncomplicated. Otherwise, you'll need a certified estate-planning specialist in the state where you live.

Back in the old days, a last will and testament was the only end-of-life document you had to worry about. Nowadays, thanks to advances in medical technology, experts agree that everyone should also leave a living will. Also known as an advance directive for health care, a living will is a document that specifies the kinds of life-sustaining medical treatments you do *not* wish to receive if you are terminally ill, catastrophically injured, in an irreversible coma, or in a persistent vegetative state with no hope of recovery.

The sidebar on the facing page shows a living will that can be found online. IMPORTANT NOTE: I'm not a lawyer, and I am not suggesting you use this document (it may not even be effective in your jurisdiction); my point is simply to illustrate the kind of thing that's out there. If you are interested in a living will, do the research or seek professional advice in the state where you live.

When indicating the kinds of life-prolonging interventions you do not wish to receive, it's a good idea to be as specific as possible. As Whitman and Glisson put it, "A simple statement of 'no heroic measures' is useless. What's a 'heroic measure'? The definition of heroic is 'exhibiting or marked by courage or daring.' Clearly, that's not a very helpful statement to a heath care provider." Ideally, your living will should name the particular treatments you are not interested in: for example, cardiopulmonary resuscitation (CPR), respiratory support, or artificially administered food and fluids. At the very least, it should state that you do not wish to be "kept alive with artificial support systems."

If you want to be an organ donor, your living will is also the place to say so. You can do

LIVING WILL

I, ________________________________, am of sound mind, and I voluntarily make this declaration.

If I become terminally ill or permanently unconscious as determined by my doctor, and if I am unable to participate in decisions regarding my medical care, I intend this declaration to be honored as the expression of my legal right to authorize or refuse medical treatment.

My desires concerning medical treatment are:

____

____

____

____

My family, the medical facility, and any doctors, nurses, and other medical personnel involved in my care shall have no civil or criminal liability for following my wishes as expressed in this declaration.

I may change my mind at any time by communicating in any manner that this declaration does not reflect my wishes.

Photostatic copies of this document, after it is signed and witnessed, shall have the same legal force as the original document.

I sign this document after careful consideration. I understand its meaning and I accept its consequences.

Dated: ____________ Signed: ____________________________
(Your signature)

____

____

(Address)

STATEMENT OF WITNESSES

We sign below as witnesses. This declaration was signed in our presence. This declarant appears to be of sound mind, and to be making this designation voluntarily, without duress, fraud, or undue influence.

__________________________ ______________________________

(Print Name) (Signature of Witness)

____

____

(Address)

__________________________ ______________________________

(Print Name) (Signature of Witness)

____

____

(Address)

this by simply stating which anatomical parts you'd like to donate and how you'd like them to be used (e.g., "medical purposes only").

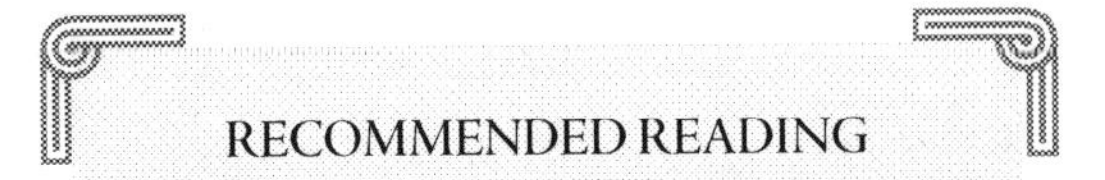

RECOMMENDED READING

Whitman and Glisson's plainspoken and highly informative *Wants, Wishes, and Wills*, which covers every imaginable end-of-life situation you are likely to face, is pretty much the only book you'll need on this subject.

For those dealing with the flip side of the situation—that is, issues that heirs have to cope with—some good books are Dan Rottenberg, *The Inheritor's Handbook* (Fireside, 2000); Ann Perry, *The Wise Inheritor* (Broadway, 2003); and Angie Epting Morris, *The Settlement Game: How to Settle an Estate Peacefully and Fairly* (Voyages Press, 2006).

"Who Gets Grandma's Yellow Pie Plate?"

As any estate lawyer will tell you, soÏme of the ugliest battles fought over a dead person's property have to do not with valuable real estate or large sums of inherited money but with items that would fetch only a paltry sum on eBay. Families are less likely to be torn apart by disputes over Dad's will than by arguments over who gets to keep his old box of fishing tackle or his 1950s Kodak Brownie camera.

Items like these are technically known as "nontitled property"—personal belongings of such negligible monetary value that they're not even mentioned in a will. Often, however, it's precisely these things that possess the greatest sentimental value—which is just another way of saying that they become symbolically charged objects onto which all kinds of potentially explosive feelings and unresolved family issues are projected. For that reason, dividing the personal stuff that belonged to a departed loved one can easily become, in the words of Wynne A. Whitman and Shawn D. Glisson, "a tinderbox of emotion."

To keep your survivors from engaging in nasty fights over who gets what when you're gone, Whitman and Glisson offer the following recommendations:

1. Don't make oral promises. Make a written list of who gets what and be as specific as possible in describing the items (as Whitman and Glisson suggest, "instead of 'my ring,' write 'my ring with two sapphires and one diamond set in platinum' ").
2. Alternatively, you can attach little tags or stickers to your heirlooms, indicating their intended recipients.
3. Think about distributing your special belongings while you're still alive. This will prevent people from fighting over your possessions when you're gone. You will also get to reap the benefits of their gratitude.
4. If there's stuff you think no one wants, get rid of it. That way, your survivors will be spared the dreary task of clearing out your garage, basement, or attic crawl space of all the junk you've accumulated over a lifetime.

A highly recommended resource to help with this task is the *Who Gets Grandma's*

Yellow Pie Plate? Workbook. Produced by the University of Minnesota Extension Service, this ninety-five-page guide supplies all the tools you'll need to pass on your personal belongings in a fair and sensitive way. It's available online at Amazon or can be ordered directly from the extension service by mail, e-mail, or phone:

University of Minnesota Extension
Service Distribution Center
20 Coffey Hall
1420 Eckles Avenue
St. Paul, MN 55108-6068

E-mail orders: order@extension.umn.edu
Phone orders: 800-876-8636

Wacky Wills

In the summer of 2007, Leona Helmsley—widow of New York City real estate mogul Harry Helmsley and a woman so universally detested that she was dubbed the "Queen of Mean"—went to her final reward. When her last will and testament was made public a few weeks later, its provisions appeared to confirm her reputation for egregious behavior. Two of her grandchildren were entirely cut out of her $4 billion fortune, while the single largest bequest—$12 million—was left to her beloved pooch, an eight-year-old Maltese named Trouble.

While the tabloids had a field day with the revelation ("Leona's Dog Gets Her Paws on $12 Mil," blared the *Daily News*), Helmsley was far from the first person to leave a fortune to a pet. Indeed, there have been scores of bizarre bequests throughout the decades. Here are ten of the wackiest:

1. Known for his love of practical jokes, Canadian lawyer Charles Millar (d. 1926) left a will full of prankish provisions. Antigambling crusaders and teetotalers were given shares in racetracks and brew-

DEATH DEFINITION: *Holographic Will*

THOUGH IT SOUNDS KIND OF FUTURISTIC—LIKE SOMETHING FROM A SCI-FI MOVIE WHERE OBJECTS materialize in three-dimensional form, the way Princess Leia does at the start of the original *Star Wars* movie when her image pops out of R2D2, pleading "Help me, Obi-Wan Kenobi; you're my only hope!"—a holographic will is actually (and less spectacularly) a will entirely handwritten, dated, and signed by the testator (i.e., the person making the will).

Since they aren't witnessed and notarized, holographic wills are not recognized in every state and experts advise against leaving them. Sometimes, however, a person has no choice. In 1948, for example, a farmer named Cecil Harris got trapped beneath his tractor and carved his last will and testament into the fender. The fender was eventually accepted as a valid legal document.

eries, three men who detested one another were bequeathed joint lifetime tenancy of a vacation home in Jamaica, and a huge cash bounty was offered to the Montreal woman who produced the most babies in the ten years following Millar's death.

2. In 1871, a hatter named S. Sanborn bequeathed his body to the Harvard Medical School for research purposes with one small proviso: that his skin be flayed and made into a drum that would be used to play "Yankee Doodle" at dawn on Bunker Hill every June 17.
3. Convinced that he would be reincarnated, wealthy Vermont tanner John Bowman left a $50,000 trust fund when he died in 1891 for the maintenance of his twenty-one-room mansion so that he could move right back into his home when he returned. He also instructed his servants to prepare his dinner nightly in case he was hungry when he showed up.
4. When famed ventriloquist Edgar Bergen died in 1978, he left a trust fund of $10,000 for the perpetual care of his dummy, Charlie McCarthy.
5. In accordance with his last wishes, the cremated ashes of "Steady" Ed Headrick—inventor of the Frisbee—were incorporated into limited-edition memorial Frisbees "so that he could fly."
6. In 1862, Henry Budd—a British gentleman with an inordinate loathing of facial hair—left £200,000 in a trust for his two sons on the condition that they never grow moustaches.
7. Following the mysterious disappearance of reclusive copper miner and prospector James Kidd in 1949, a handwritten will was discovered in which he bequeathed nearly a quarter of a million dollars to anyone who could provide "some scientific proof of a soul of the human body which leaves at death," preferably in the form of a photograph.
8. Pennsylvanian Robert Allan Miller was so fed up with the traffic snarl in his hometown of Bethlehem that when he died in 1995, he bequeathed an annual $5,000 reward to the police officer who wrote the most tickets for double parking.
9. Upon her premature death at age thirty-seven in 1977, Beverly Hills socialite Sandra Ilene West—widow of a Texas oil millionaire—was buried, as per her last wishes, in her 1964 powder blue Ferrari, the seat reclined at a comfortable angle.
10. In 1897, an Englishman named Norman Earnest Digweed directed that his estate of £26,000 be placed in trust for eighty years for Jesus Christ should he return within that time.

O death, O death, won't you spare me over till another year?

—Traditional American folk song

Tending to the Terminally Ill

Back in nineteenth-century America, when the average life expectancy was significantly shorter than it is today and people died at home, families knew how to make a loved one's final hours as comfortable as possible. Nowadays, when the terminally ill are generally consigned to hospitals, the average person has little or no idea of how to care for a dying relative—or even how to recognize the active onset of death.

If one of your family members has chosen to pass his or her final days at home, here are the six common signs of imminent death and the recommended measures to make the dying process easier:

Victorian deathbed scene.

SIGN: *Changes in skin color and temperature.* As circulation decreases and less blood reaches the extremities, the hands and feet will turn purple or blue-purple and feel cool to the touch. The fingernail beds will likewise turn bluish. Legs will become blotchy or mottled.
CAREGIVING MEASURE: Use a blanket or some other covering (like a sheet) to keep the person warm.

SIGN: *Decrease in appetite and thirst.* Dying people no longer feel like eating or drinking and find it increasingly hard to swallow.
CAREGIVING MEASURE: Don't try to force your loved one to eat or drink. Keep a glass of water on hand with a straw. Keep your loved one's mouth moist with a sponge, cloth, or spray bottle. Use Chapstick or other balm on the lips.

SIGN: *Changes in breathing.* Respiration becomes highly irregular. There may be shallow breaths followed by deep breaths, several rapid breaths followed by several seconds of no breathing at all, panting, gurgling, or exceptionally noisy breathing caused by the congestion of the lungs.
CAREGIVING MEASURE: Try raising the head of the bed or repositioning your loved one to ease labored breathing. Let fresh air into the room. Medications prescribed by your doctor may also help.

SIGN: *Incontinence.* Loss of bladder and bowel control. Urine may be darkly discolored.
CAREGIVING MEASURE: Keep your loved one clean and dry. Use incontinence pads or a catheter. Change his or her position every few hours.

SIGN: *Restlessness, confusion, agitation.* The person may jerk around in bed, twitch, or pluck at the bedclothes. He or she may not recognize family members and may experience hallucinations and delusions, such as visits from relatives who have already died.
CAREGIVING MEASURE: Speak gently in short, simple phrases. Remind the person of the date and time and the names of the people in the room.

SIGN: *Loss of speech.* The dying person no longer speaks spontaneously and ceases to respond to questions.
CAREGIVING MEASURE: Though a dying person may appear comatose, he or she may still be able to hear you. Always act under the assumption that the patient knows what is going on, however unresponsive he seems. Talk soothingly while holding his hand.

RECOMMENDED RESOURCE

For people taking care of terminally ill relatives at home, the Hospice Foundation of America has published an excellent manual, *The Dying Process: A Guide for Caregivers*. Developed with the participation of various physicians, hospice experts, and grief therapists, this twenty-four-page booklet covers all aspects of the subject, from the physical symptoms of dying to pain management and psychological concerns. It can be downloaded at www.hospicefoundation.org/endOfLifeInfo/documents/general_manual.pdf. Hardcover copies can also be purchased by contacting the Hospice Foundation of America at 1621 Connecticut Avenue, NW, Suite 300, Washington, DC 20009, 800-854-3402.

The goal of all life is death.

—SIGMUND FREUD

"Deathing"

Up until the relatively recent past, giving birth was called "delivery." Then, sometime around the 1970s, another, more touchy-feely word came into vogue: "birthing." Given our society's fondness for such jargon, it was only a matter of time before someone came up with an equivalent term for the process of dying.

That distinction belongs to Anya Foos-Graber, who has devised a technique she calls "deathing" (a word that even her ardent admirers concede is "somewhat strange-sounding"). A blend of Eastern spiritual practices—especially Tibetan Buddhism—and up-to-date NDE (near-death experience) research, "deathing," in Foos-Graber's words, "offers a way to free up dying people so they can utilize the highest potential of the transition called death and experience it as a peak moment." Her method is set forth in her book *Deathing: An Intelligent Alternative for the Final Moment of Life* (Nicolas-Hays, 1989), which includes a step-by-step guide for mastering the technique, along with contrasting case histories illustrating the differences between mere run-of-the mill dying and spiritually enlightened deathing.

Not everybody will relate to Foos-Graber's New Agey approach, which is heavy on concepts such as "spontaneous unfoldment," "harnessing the etheric body," and "entering into the effulgence of the Light with total awareness of the transcendental nature of our being." Still, insofar as her book grows out of the modern death awareness movement that seeks to restore dignity, meaning, and acceptance to the act of dying, it is a worthwhile project. (We just wish she had coined a less clunky word to describe it.)

Quality of Death: The Hospice Experience

Up until the first decade of the twentieth century, fully 85 percent of Americans died in the comfort of their homes and the company of their loved ones. Because medicine was still, comparatively speaking, in the dark ages, a hospital could do little for the desperately ill and only poor people went there to die.

Today, the situation is almost exactly the reverse, with the vast majority of Americans dying in hospitals. "Progress" accounts for this dramatic change. If an acutely ill patient wants the latest in advanced medical treatment, a hospital is the only place to find it. Moreover, because Americans tend not to stay rooted in one place, old people often end up living far away from their relatives and longtime friends and have to rely on paid professionals for end-of-life care.

The net result of these developments is that while the quality of life has been improving for most Americans over the past hundred years, the quality of death has undergone a corresponding decline. We might enjoy luxuries that earlier generations could only dream about—from wall-size TVs to thumbnail-size music players to all-inclusive Caribbean resort vacations—but we also face the dreary (if not terrifying) prospect of dying alone in a faceless medical institution, hooked up to machines and attended by overworked and dispassionate strangers.

In response to this dismal trend, the past few decades have witnessed the growth of a movement whose goal is not to try to ward off death through radical medical intervention, but to provide humane and compassionate care for the incurable—to alleviate the suffering and restore the dignity of the dying. This movement is known as hospice.

The term itself is linguistically related to the words *host* and *hospitality* and originally referred to a lodging place or waystation for travelers in need of assistance. (One of the world's oldest and most famous hospices in the original sense of the term is the Hospice of Great Saint Bernard in the Swiss Alps, which trains dogs to rescue stranded, snowbound hikers.) The current meaning still retains this suggestion of hospitality—only now, the "travelers" in need of care are the ones making the final journey to death.

The modern hospice movement dates back to 1967, when a British physician, Cicely Saunders, founded St. Christopher's Hospice in South London, an institution committed to making the end of life as bearable as possible for both the patient and his family by ministering to the dying person's physical, emotional, social, and even spiritual needs, as well as to those of his loved ones. Inspired by Saunders's work, doctors and other personnel connected to the Yale University School of Medicine helped establish the Connecticut Hospice in 1971, the first such program in the United States. Seven years later, the National Hospice Organization (since renamed the National Hospice and Palliative Care Organization) was founded to "lead and mobilize social change for improved care at the end of life" (in the words of its mission statement). By 1997, more than 2,800 hospices existed throughout the country.

Even with the proliferation of these programs, however, only a minority of Americans—an estimated one in three—avail themselves of hospice care. This is a pity since even though there may be no really good way to die, the hospice option is infinitely preferable to the depersonalized (and often unnecessarily pain-ridden) alternative of death in a modern high-tech hospital.

A dying person can receive hospice care at home, in a special unit within a hospital, or in a separate residential facility. In every case, however, the approach is the same. Central to the hospice philosophy is the conviction that a dying adult has the right to live out his or her final months as comfortably and naturally as possible—not as a frightened and helpless creature reduced to infantile dependence on Olympian medical specialists, but as an autonomous human being who is allowed to make his own decisions and whose wishes and needs (along with those of his family) are of paramount concern.

To achieve this goal, hospice programs deploy an interdisciplinary team of specialists to look after the patient and his family: doctors, nurses, social workers, bereavement coordinators, physical therapists, spiritual advisors, even financial counselors. Very crucially, hospices also reject the traditional medical approach to pain control, which is known as "PRN" (Latin for *pro re nata*, or "as the situation demands")—meaning that pain medication is doled out only when the patient is in urgent need of it. It was Cicely Saunders who came up with what she herself has described as a "very obvious" alternative. Instead of making patients "earn their morphine" by reaching a point of acute suffering, hospices give medication in advance, before the pain begins. The idea is to prevent pain without sedating the patient, so that he or she can experience what remains of life to the fullest extent possible.

Psychologist Beatrice Kastenbaum relates a story about an American nurse who, while visiting St. Christopher's Hospice in London, was surprised to see that—in contrast to the standard American oncology ward—"none of the patients had intravenous fluids hanging by the bedside." When she commented on this fact, Saunders replied: "Isn't it so much nicer to share a cup of tea?" Looking around, the nurse "noted that no patients seemed dehydrated and the staff did indeed share a cup of tea with the patients."

This anecdote epitomizes the essence of hospice care, in which terminally ill patients forgo the dehumanizing indignities of life-prolonging measures for a caring and supportive end-of-life experience.

RECOMMENDED RESOURCES

As *New York Times* health columnist Jane E. Brody wisely suggests, "Patients and families should research hospice options well in advance of needing them." The place to begin is the website of the National Hospice and Palliative Care Organization, www.nhpco.org. Click on "Find a Provider" or call the organization at 703-837-1500.

Shortly before his death, humorist Art Buchwald published a warm and witty account of his time in a Washington, D.C., hospice, *Too Soon to Say Goodbye* (Random House, 2006). If you have any doubts about the benefits of hospice care, this deeply wise and engaging book will dispel them.

For the growing number of people who are thinking about spending their final days at home, Andrea Sankar's *Dying at Home: A Family Guide for Caregiving* (Johns Hopkins University Press, 1999) is absolutely essential. Sensitive, comprehensive, and unflinchingly direct about both the great rewards and equally significant burdens of home dying, this guidebook will tell you, without mincing words, exactly what this experience entails for both patients and their caregivers.

Death Foretold

It's a cliché of countless old movies. Some two-fisted tough guy who has been experiencing unaccustomed bouts of illness finally goes for a checkup. "Give it to me straight, Doc," he says to the grim-faced physician once the examination is over. "How long have I got?" The doctor typically frowns deeply, heaves a long sigh, then delivers the bitter truth: a week, maybe two at the most. The hero takes a moment to absorb the bad news, then squares his shoulders and heads off to take care of unfinished business.

Corny as it is, this type of scene always manages to pack a dramatic punch. But like most of what comes out of Hollywood, it bears little relation to reality. Far from being straightforward with their seriously ill patients—telling them frankly how near they are to death—actual physicians tend to shy away from such grim pronouncements. And "even when doctors *do* prognosticate," writes physician and Harvard sociology professor Nicholas A. Christakis, "they typically overestimate the time a patient has to live, often at least tripling it."

According to Christakis—who sets forth his case in his provocative book, *Death Foretold: Prophecy and Prognosis in Medical Care* (University of Chicago Press, 1999)—the failure of so many physicians to offer accurate, realistic predictions of a dying patient's remaining time stems from various sources. These range from professional hubris—an arrogant belief in their powers to defeat even the most dire diseases—to their own deep-seated, largely unconscious terrors of mortality.

Unfortunately, it's the dying patient and his loved ones who pay the price for this failure to receive a clear prognosis. As an example, Christakis cites the case of a cancer patient's wife:

> The Thursday before my husband died, I thought he was dying and he thought he was dying. But the doctor was talking about aggressive chemotherapy. I asked if this was palliative, and he said that he still hoped for a cure. I was with him at the time of his death three days later, but the room was filled with eight other people hanging bags of blood and monitoring vital signs. It was about as horrifying as anything that could have happened. I don't think the doctors were trying to mislead us. They thought he might be the one case that would have a positive outcome. But if he had been told the truth, his last days could have been spent at home with the children, not filled with painful treatment in the hospital.

"In one study of nearly 5,000 hospitalized adults who had roughly six months to live," writes Christakis, "only fifteen percent were given clear prognoses. In a smaller study of 326 cancer patients in Chicago hospices, all of whom had about a month to live, only thirty-seven percent of the doctors interviewed said they would share an accurate prognosis with their patients, and only if patients or their families pushed them to do so." For the sake of those patients suffering terminal illnesses, Christakis urges doctors to learn how to offer "realistic assessments of how long their patients have to live."

"Sometimes," he concludes, "living life to the fullest requires knowledge of its finitude."

What to Do When Someone Dies

The good news for us twenty-first-century Americans is that—because our friends and relatives enjoy longer, healthier lives—death is something we rarely have to deal with on a personal level. Nowadays, it's entirely possible for someone to reach middle age without ever having attended—much less arranged—a funeral. There is, however, a downside to this happy state of affairs: namely, that when the inevitable *does* happen to an immediate family member, we don't know what to do.

What steps need to be taken in the immediate aftermath of a loved one's death? That depends, to begin with, on where the death occurs. If it happens in a hospital and you are alone at the bedside, immediately notify a nurse, who will summon a doctor to pronounce death. The body may then be moved temporarily to the hospital morgue to await transportation.

When a terminally ill patient dies at home with no medical personnel in attendance, telephone your doctor. If, however, the death is sudden and totally unexpected, call 911. Depending on the circumstances, the coroner may have to be notified. If no further investigation is warranted, the body will then be released for disposal.

Family members will have to be contacted. Call the most important ones right away—children, siblings, parents of the deceased—even if it means waking them up in the middle of the night. (Researchers have found that "those close to the deceased feel left out if they aren't informed about death immediately.") Other friends and relatives will also have to be told the sad news. Don't try to do all this by yourself. Get three to five trusted people and ask each of them to call three to five others.

Assuming that you intend to give your loved one a traditional funeral (as opposed to some trendy alternative form of body disposal such as consigning the cremated ashes to an underwater "memorial reef"), you'll need the services of a funeral home. If you haven't preselected one, get someone you trust—a friend, family member, or a member of the clergy—to help find a suitable establishment and assist in making all the necessary (and difficult) decisions and arrangements. (For help with finding local funeral homes, visit www.funerals.org.)

Once you've settled on a funeral director, he will take charge of the body and dispatch a vehicle to retrieve it from the hospital or other location. (A medical school will also arrange transportation if your loved one has opted for body donation.) The funeral director will also handle or assist with other key tasks, such as placing an obituary notice in the newspaper, securing a death certificate (it's best to get hold of ten to fifteen certified copies, which you may need for various legal purposes), and filing for benefits.

There are a number of practical matters that you'll have to attend to. The Center on Aging at the University of Hawaii's John A. Burns School of Medicine offers the following checklist:

- Contact the Social Security office.
- Contact the life insurance company of the deceased.
- Explore eligibility for civil service and veteran's benefits.

- Notify the lawyer or executor of the estate.
- Alert credit card companies.
- Cancel prescription, newspaper, and other subscriptions.
- Cancel automatic bill payments.

RECOMMENDED RESOURCES

The University of Hawaii's Center on Aging has put together an excellent booklet, *When a Death Occurs: What to Do When a Loved One Dies*, available online at www.hawaii.edu/aging/ECHO4.pdf. Another helpful website is www.funeralplan.com. (One caveat: since the latter is sponsored by the Augusta Casket Company, it automatically assumes that you will be arranging a traditional funeral.)

Two useful books on the subject are *What to Do When a Loved One Dies: A Practical and Compassionate Guide to Dealing with Death on Life's Terms* by Eva Shaw (Dickens Press, 1994) and *Step by Step: Your Guide to Making Practical Decisions When a Loved One Dies* by Ellen Shaw (Quality Life Resources, 2001).

Death Certificates

A death certificate is an official document that has to be filed for various legal and bureaucratic purposes whenever someone dies. The standard format for U.S. death certificates was established in 1978 (you can download a sample at www.cdc.gov/nchs/data/dvs/DEATH11-03final-ACC.pdf).

Typically, the attending physician first fills out those portions pertaining to the cause of the death, then passes the certificate along to the funeral director, who completes the form and submits it to the appropriate municipal or state agency.

If you're a do-it-yourselfer who decides to handle a loved one's final disposition without the use of a funeral director, it will be up to you to fill out and file the death certificate. The form isn't especially complicated, though it has to be completed with care (no Wite-Out permitted) and according to strict guidelines. You can find detailed instructions in Lisa Carlson's *Caring for the Dead: Your Final Act of Love* (Upper Access, 1998).

Since death certificates are public-domain documents in the United States, it's no surprise that—given our prurient interest in celebrity—the Internet offers ready access to the death certificates of assorted superstars, from Elvis to John Lennon to Jimi Hendrix. If you possess the requisite morbid curiosity, just go to Google Image Search and enter the dead celebrity's name plus the phrase "death certificate."

"Not So Fast, Johnson": The Dos and Don'ts of Death Notification

There's an old sick joke that goes like this:

Death Fun Fact

While heart disease and cancer remain the leading causes of death, there are all kinds of colorful ways that people have expired. For example:

- In the summer of 1995, a chef was killed by flying pasta when 150 mph winds hit his restaurant in Mexico City and a bunch of uncooked spaghetti shot through the air and stabbed him in the chest, puncturing his heart.
- In August 1997, a twenty-three-year-old stripper hired to leap out of a cake at a bachelor party in Cosenza, Italy, suffocated inside the giant pastry while waiting for her cue.
- In July 1995, an elderly French golfer, in a fit of frustration after missing three consecutive putts on the final hole, threw his golf bag into a lake, then—after realizing that his car keys were inside the bag—waded into the water and drowned.
- In June 1994, a bubblegum-chewing Aussie died in a traffic accident when he ran his car off the road after blowing a big bubble that burst and stuck to his glasses, blinding him.

These and scores of other zany human tragedies are recounted in Ian Simmons's morbidly amusing collection, *Strange Deaths: More than 375 Freakish Fatalities* (John Brown Publishing, 1998).

An army captain summons his sergeant and says: "I just got a telegram that Private Fitzgerald's mother died last night. You'd better go tell him." So the sergeant lines up his troops and, after taking roll, says: "By the way, Fitzgerald, your mother's dead." When the captain hears about this, he pulls the sergeant aside and says, "Hey, Sarge, that was a pretty harsh way to tell a man that his mother just died. Try to be more tactful next time." A few months later, another death notice arrives by telegram. This time, it concerns the mother of a private named Johnson. So the sergeant calls his morning formation. "Okay, men, fall in and listen up. Everybody whose mother is alive take two steps forward—not so fast, Johnson!"

The butt of this joke is, of course, the fabled callousness of the military establishment, which has often informed families of the most tragic news imaginable—the death of a child—by sending them what amounts to a form letter. But it touches on an issue that also affects countless civilians each year: the proper handling of what thanatologists call the "death notification process."

Most deaths in this country—roughly 78 percent—are "anticipated," which is to say that they are caused by cancer, AIDS, and other terminal illnesses. In these cases, receiving notification of the person's death is rarely traumatic since the news doesn't come as a surprise and may, in fact, afford a measure of relief to survivors, who know that their loved one's suffering is over.

It's the other 22 percent of deaths—the ones caused by vehicular crashes, homicides, suicides, household accidents, heart attacks, strokes, et cetera—that can pose problems for professional "notifiers" such as police officers. There is no really *good* way to tell someone that his or her spouse, sibling, child, or parent has just met a sudden, unexpected, and possibly horrible death. But some ways are worse than others (psychologists Alan E. Stewart and Janice Harris Lord cite the case of a cop who arrived at a couple's home and, finding no one there, left a note on the door informing them that their son had just killed himself).

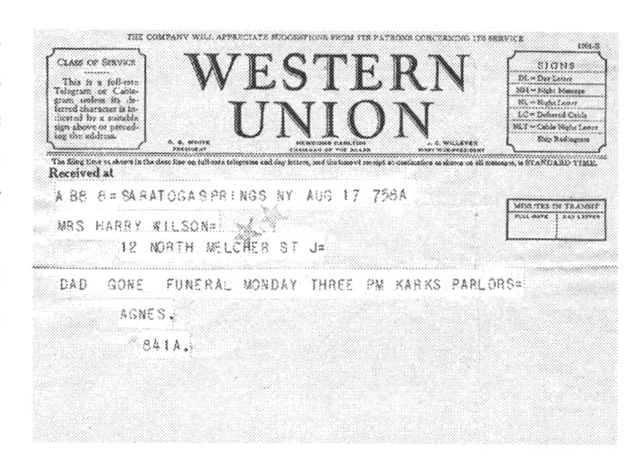
WESTERN UNION
Received at
A 88 8 = SARATOGASPRINGS NY AUG 17 758A
MRS HARRY WILSON=
12 NORTH WELCHER ST J=
DAD GONE FUNERAL MONDAY THREE PM KARKS PARLORS=
AGNES.
841A.

Experts who have studied this subject have identified a number of elements that make for a competent and humane death notification, including:

1. *Proper identification of both the deceased and survivors.* You don't want to show up at a house and tell the woman who answers the door that her husband has just been killed by a hit-and-run driver—only to discover that you're at the wrong address.
2. *Meeting the survivors.* Except in the case of anticipated deaths—when it's okay for a nurse or other hospital official to de-

TIPS FOR TRAVELERS

In March 2007, the Associated Press carried an item headlined "Airline Moves Dead Body to First Class." According to the story, a woman traveling with family members from Delhi to London on British Airways died midflight in her economy-class seat. With the economy section full, the cabin crew—wishing to give the family a measure of privacy—transferred the body to an empty seat in first class. This came as something of a shock to the other first-class passengers, especially the gentleman who awoke to find a corpse beside him.

The airline later issued a statement explaining that about ten of its passengers die in transit each year. Since company policy dictates that "the deceased must not be placed in the galley or blocking aisles or exits," the crew—according to the statement—made the right decision.

Meanwhile, travel experts agree that while it might get you upgraded, death should be avoided when possible.

liver the sad news by phone—notifiers should contact survivors in person and break the news in appropriate surroundings (for example, inside the house, with the family members seated, as opposed to standing on the front steps).

3. *Supplying specific information.* Experts agree that the notifier should provide the crucial details—the when, where, and how of the person's death—in a forthright, deliberate manner, with brief pauses between each piece of information to allow the hearer to absorb the shock.
4. *Avoiding euphemisms.* Without being overly blunt (see the previous joke), the notifier should be open, honest, and plainspoken, using words such as *dead*, *died*, and *killed* instead of *gone*, *passed away*, or *in a better place*. Survivors need to accept the truth.
5. *Dealing supportively with the reactions of survivors.* The shock of receiving sudden tragic news elicits all kinds of reactions, from hysteria to stunned disbelief to violent assaults on the messenger. The notifier must learn to respond constructively to these reactions and avoid saying things that will only make matters worse (such as, "Oh well, you have other children" or "No use crying over spilled milk").

Clearly, the keys to a decent death notification are empathy and tact on the part of the person entrusted with breaking the news. Unfortunately, not every notifier is endowed with these qualities. As a result, the organization MADD (Mothers Against Drunk Driving) has instituted a program of training seminars to educate police officers, sheriffs, and other professionals about the "need for clear, informed, and compassionate death notifications." The goal is to avoid situations like the one described by Stewart and Lord, in which a sheriff's deputy showed up at a woman's house and—speaking through the screen door—informed her that her daughter had just been killed. When the reeling mother cried out that she didn't know how she would survive without her child, the deputy shrugged and said: "Well, ma'am, I guess God is just telling you that it's time to stand on your own two feet."

RECOMMENDED READING

People who work in medicine, law enforcement, or any other field where death notification is part of the job will find practical information in the following: Alan E. Stewart and Janice Harris Lord, "The Death Notification Process: Recommendations for Practice, Training, and Research" in *Handbook of Death and Dying*, volume 2, ed. Clifton D. Bryant (Sage, 2003); R. Moroni Leash, *Death Notification: A Practical Guide to the Process* (Upper Access, 1994); and Janice Harris Lord, *Death Notification: Breaking the Bad News with Compassion for the Survivor and Care of the Professional* (Mothers Against Drunk Driving, 1997).

The Right to Die

In a culture like ours—one that exalts a never-say-die, when-the-going-gets-tough-the-tough-get-going ethos—people who commit suicide have often been perceived as moral weaklings, if not outright cowards. This attitude, however, is not universal. Depending on the circumstances, taking your own life has been regarded as not just acceptable but even honorable in certain times and places. So long as they performed the deed in a suitably manly way—by falling on their sword, say, or cutting their own throats—Roman soldiers facing defeat were admired for killing themselves in order to prevent capture and slavery. The Japanese practice of *seppuku* (more commonly known as *hara-kiri*)—slitting your own belly to avoid or attenuate shame—is an analogous culturally sanctioned form of suicide.

Even some early Christians approved of suicide. Believing that earthly existence only exposed them to suffering and sin and that it was in their best interest to get to heaven as soon as possible, members of early sects such as the Circumcelliones committed suicide en masse by hurling themselves off cliffs. Embracing death through martyrdom was also extolled as a righteous emulation of Christ's sacrifice. It wasn't until the fifth century, when St. Augustine condemned the practice as a violation of the sixth commandment ("Thou shalt not kill"), that the Church pronounced suicide a crime. What was formerly applauded as martyrdom was now reviled as self-murder. In succeeding centuries, the Church did its best to discourage suicide by imposing harsh sanctions on those who committed it. People who took their own lives were denied Christian burial and their remains were subjected to various indignities. In medieval England, for example, such unfortunates were customarily buried during the night at well-traveled crossroads with stakes driven through their hearts. As a further disincentive, their property was also confiscated by the state.

While the Church remained adamantly opposed to suicide, more flexible attitudes began to evolve during the Renaissance, epitomized by John Donne's posthumously published treatise, *Biothanatos*, which argued (in the words of its subtitle) "That Self-Homicide is not so Naturally Sinne that it may never be otherwise"—that is, under certain circumstances, suicide should not be regarded as a crime. In the following century, the philosopher David Hume published his "Essay on Suicide," which systematically refuted the standard religious arguments against suicide and asserted that it was within the rights of the individual to take his own life. By the nineteenth century, a movement was under way in Britain to decriminalize suicide, and by the last decade of the century, people who killed themselves were finally allowed to enjoy such privileges as daytime burial in an actual churchyard without having their property forfeited, their corpses defiled, or stakes driven through their hearts. In certain parts of Europe, suicide even became a fad. The phenomenal popularity of Goethe's 1774 novel, *The Sorrows of Young Werther*—which climaxes with its sensitive artistic hero shooting himself in the head because of unrequited love—inspired a host of real-life imitations throughout Germany (copycat suicides among adolescents, a phenomenon that still occurs with dismaying frequency, has come to be known as the "Werther effect").

Nowadays—apart from the occasional weirdo UFO cult that promotes mass suicide as a ticket to the stars—suicidal behavior is, by and large, viewed as a symptom of severe mental distress that requires emergency therapeutic intervention. The only exception involves the controversial issue variously known as "rational suicide," "self-deliverance," and the "right to die"—that is, the decision of a hopelessly ill, dying person to voluntarily end his or her own life.

There's nothing new about this concept. As far back as ancient Roman times, the Stoic philosopher Seneca articulated what many people still regard as the most cogent rationale for geriatric suicide:

> I will not relinquish old age if it leaves my better part intact. But if it begins to shake my mind, if it destroys its faculties one by one, if it leaves me not life but breath, I will depart from the putrid or tottering edifice. I will not escape by death from disease so long as it may be healed, and leaves my mind unimpaired. I will not raise my hand against myself on account of pain, for so to die is to be conquered. But I know that if I must suffer without hope of relief, I will depart, not through fear of the pain itself, but because it prevents all for which I would live.

Today's proponents of "self-deliverance" offer the same argument. As *New York Times* health columnist Jane E. Brody puts it:

> What is the point of living so long if you can no longer enjoy living? What is the point of living until your mind turns to marshmallow and you are reduced to an existence that is less than human? . . . Why shouldn't an emotionally sound, thoughtful person be able to call it quits when life has dragged on too long? When there is nothing to gain and much to lose from an ongoing existence?

The operative phrase in the above passage is, of course, "emotionally sound." All too often, elderly people resort to suicide because they are in the grip not of intractable physical pain but treatable emotional suffering. As Sherwin B. Nuland puts it in his invaluable book, *How We Die*:

> A very large proportion of the elderly men and women who kill themselves do it because they suffer from quite remediable depression. With proper medication and therapy, most of them would be relieved of the cloud of oppressive despair that colors all reason gray, would then realize that the edifice topples not quite so much as thought, and that hope of relief is less hopeless than it seemed. I have more than once seen a suicidal old person emerge from depression, and rediscovered thereby a vibrant friend.

Even Nuland, however, while insisting that "taking one's own life is almost always the wrong thing to do," concedes that "there are two circumstances in which that may not be so": the "unendurable infirmities of a crippling old age and the final devastations of a terminal disease." He cautions, however, that taking such an extreme measure demands "consultation, counsel, and the leavening influence of a long period of mature thought."

Gerontologist Andrea Sankar, author of *Dying at Home*, concurs with Nuland and offers three specific recommendations for terminally ill patients who are tempted to end their own lives: (1) "If uncontrolled pain is the reason for considering suicide, have the pain evaluated by a hospice physician and nurse. . . . Pain control should be possible to achieve with the help of an appropriately trained professional"; (2) "If the desire is to spare the family the burden of caregiving, allow family members to express themselves about this. They may wish to provide care for the dying in recognition of their love for that person"; and (3) "Seek professional counseling. The dying person may be depressed and afraid. Professional counseling may help the patient deal with these emotions and go on to live out the rest of his or her life."

Since Oregon is the only state in the United States that permits physician-assisted suicide, elderly people who remain intent on ending it all have to figure out a way to do it themselves. Information is published by the Hemlock Society (www.compassionandchoices.org/hemlock), founded by Derek Humphrey, whose 1991 book, *Final Exit: The Practicalities of Self-Deliverance and Assisted Suicide for the Dying*, is the bible of the right-to-die movement.

Famous Last Words

There's a widespread notion that a dying person's final words will hold some special significance—that with his last breath he will offer some blazing insight into the mystery of existence ("Yes, I see it now—life really *is* a bowl of cherries"), a dramatic deathbed confession ("I did it—I kidnapped the Lindbergh baby"), or ultimate affirmation of faith that starkly contrasts with his former skepticism ("Now that I think about it, maybe organized religion isn't so bad after all").

Rarely, however, do farewell utterances meet these high expectations. Considering how many people have died since the invention of writing, the number of memorable last words on record is pathetically small. Check out the many collections of famous last words and you'll find the same old chestnuts repeated again and again: "Goodnight my darlings, I'll see you tomorrow" (Noël Coward); "If this is dying, then I don't think much of it" (Lytton Strachey); "I just had eighteen straight whiskeys. I think that's a record" (Dylan Thomas); "I knew it. I knew it. Born in a hotel room—and God damn it—died in a hotel room" (Eugene O'Neill); and a few dozen more.

Moreover, even many of these statements are of dubious authenticity. Take the last words reputedly spoken in 1920 by the young Notre Dame halfback George Gipp. As he lay in the hospital, dying of pneumonia, he supposedly murmured these immortal words to his coach, Knute Rockne, who later used them to inspire his team in a legendary locker room speech: "Tell them to go out and win one for the Gipper." Since Rockne apparently never visited Gipp during the latter's dying days, however—and since Gipp was never known to his teammates or anyone else as "the Gipper"—it seems unlikely that the famous quote was ever uttered.

Like Gipp's apocryphal exhortation, some famous farewell remarks were clearly fabricated out of whole cloth. Others were emended by friends of the deceased—polished and turned into snappy one-liners. And then there are those frequently anthologized "famous last words" that don't qualify for other reasons. It's a rare collection, for example, that doesn't include Oscar Wilde's supposedly final witticism: "I am in a duel to the death with this wallpaper. One of us must go." As it happens, this bon mot was uttered a month before Wilde's death in November 1900. So unless he remained mute for the last thirty days of his life, it's hard to see how this statement qualifies as his "famous last words."

Among other famous parting statements that invariably make it into the anthologies (and whose validity is open to question) are:

> "How were the circus receipts today at Madison Square Garden?" (P. T. Barnum)
>
> "I am about to—or I am going to—die. Either expression is correct." (French grammarian Dominique Bouhours)
>
> "I've had a hell of a lot of fun, and I've enjoyed every minute of it." (Errol Flynn)
>
> "Turn up the lights. I don't want to go home in the dark." (O. Henry)
>
> "All my possessions for a moment of time." (Queen Elizabeth I)
>
> "I have taken an unconscionable time dying, but I hope you will excuse it." (King Charles II)
>
> "Well, it will be a new experience anyway." (George Bernard Shaw)
>
> "They tell me I am going to get well, but I file a dissenting opinion." (Supreme Court Justice Benjamin Cardozo)
>
> "I've never felt better." (Douglas Fairbanks)
>
> "There's fun in the air!" (Maurice Chevalier)
>
> "I shall hear in heaven!" (Ludwig van Beethoven)
>
> "Die, my dear doctor? That's the last thing I shall do." (British prime minister Henry John Temple)

There are other famous last words that have the ring of authenticity:

> "Why am I hemorrhaging?" (Boris Pasternak)
>
> "God damn." (James Thurber)
>
> "I want my lunch!" (J. Paul Getty)
>
> "Water!" (Ulysses S. Grant)
>
> "It wasn't worth it." (Louis B. Mayer)
>
> "I have a terrific headache." (Franklin Delano Roosevelt)
>
> "Goddamn the whole friggin' world and everyone in it." (W. C. Fields)
>
> "Good night." (Lord George Gordon Byron)

RECOMMENDED READING

You will find all these famous last words and hundreds more in the following collections: Alan Bisbort, *Last Words: Apt Observations, Pleas, Curses, Benedictions, Sour Notes, Bon Mots, and Insights from People on the Brink of Departure* (Pomegranate, 2001); Jonathan Green, *Famous Last Words* (Prion, 2002); Kathleen E. Miller, *Last Laughs: Funny Tombstone Quotes and Famous Last Words* (Sterling, 2006); Ray Robinson, *Famous Last Words: Fond Farewells, Deathbed Diatribes, and Exclamations upon Expiration* (Workman, 2003); Bernard C. Ruffin, *Last Words: A Dictionary of Deathbed Quotations* (MacFarland, 1995); Laura Ward, *Famous Last Words: The Ultimate Collection of Finales and Farewells* (PRC, 2004). You can also find many memorable farewells online at the "Last Word Browser" (www.alsirat.com/last words/index.html).

Famous Last Words: Helpful Tips

If you're determined to go out with a memorable line, here are a few useful things to remember:

1. Generally speaking, when people are on the brink of death, they don't have the presence of mind to come up with pithy observations. Most final utterances are on the order of incomprehensible gurgles or urgent requests for another shot of morphine. For that reason, you'll probably want to compose your dying statement while you still have your wits about you and spend some time rehearsing it so that you sound spontaneous when you finally get around to delivering it.

2. Avoid speaking your last words in a language no one around you understands. (That's what happened to Albert Einstein, who uttered his final words of wisdom in German. Unfortunately, he died in New Jersey, and the only person who heard him was his American nurse, who had no idea what he was saying.)

3. Don't wait too long to speak. You don't want to suffer the embarrassment of expiring halfway through your carefully memorized parting pronouncement.

4. Oh, and one more thing—once you utter your last words, make sure not to say anything else like "Boy, am I thirsty" or "It sure is getting dark in here." Otherwise, you'll have gone to all that trouble for nothing.

3

FUNERAL FACTS

Burial: It's Only Human

The moment is familiar from countless Hollywood westerns. A few badly outnumbered cowpokes are in desperate flight from a bunch of pursuing baddies. One of the good guys gets wounded and dies. Though time is of the essence, his companions refuse to go on until the deceased is given a "proper Christian burial": a hastily dug grave on the prairie, a rough-hewn marker, a few words spoken over the body.

And it's not just in movies that such scenarios are found. Along with love, war, and other epic themes of literature, burial has served as a subject for great works of art. The most wrenching episode in the *Iliad* occurs when the elderly King Priam sneaks into the enemy camp to beg for the return of his slain son, Hector, whose body has been denied a proper disposal by the vengeful Achilles. And the entire tragic action of Sophocles's *Antigone* hinges on the title character's determination to have her dead brother decently interred.

As these examples suggest, the need to provide our friends and relations with a fitting burial is a defining human trait, one of the things that distinguishes us from animals. (Even elephants—who supposedly go to die in "graveyards"—don't bury their dead.) The ancient Greeks and Romans believed that the souls of the unburied were barred from the afterlife. For the Jews of biblical times, an unburied corpse was an abomination, as the prophet Jeremiah makes clear when he calls down a curse upon the enemies of his people: "They shall die of grievous deaths; they shall not be lamented; neither shall they be buried; but they shall be as dung upon the face of the earth; and they shall be consumed by the sword, and by famine; and their carcasses shall be meat for the fowls of heaven, and for the beasts of the earth."

Human burial rites extend back to prehistoric times. Though there are clearly sanitary

Funeral of St. Edward the Confessor, January 1066.

to this custom. Hertz himself believed that the two phases help effect the soul's transition from its former identity as a living member of society to its new status in the afterworld. British archaeologist Timothy Taylor, on the other hand, suggests that the practice of "double burial" stemmed from the archaic belief that the "unquiet soul" of the newly deceased posed a threat to the living and must be prevented from reinhabiting its body, a requirement that lasted "only so long as the flesh lay on the bones." Once "the bones were white, then it was deemed that the person had finally left this life and was no longer a danger to the living. Thus it was that for most of recent human history (roughly the last 35,000 years) funerary rights were twofold: the primary rites zoned off the freshly dead [while] the secondary rites, occurring after weeks or months, firmly and finally incorporated the deceased into the realm of the ancestors."

reasons for sticking a corpse in the ground (as one anthropologist has written, "The smell of decaying flesh might alone be impetus to bury the body"), the elaborate customs surrounding the practice indicate that deeper meanings are involved.

Throughout much of human history, it has been common for people to bury their dead in two distinct stages. The first is what French sociologist Robert Hertz famously called the "wet" phase. During this period, the rotting corpse is divested of its flesh and transformed into a skeleton by any of several means—temporary earth burial, exposure to scavengers, partial cremation, and so on. The denuded bones are then transferred to a communal grave or charnel house. Hertz labeled this the "dry" phase. This practice continues today in parts of the world, particularly in Southeast Asia, where—according to anthropologists Peter Metcalf and Richard Huntington—"the dead are allowed to decompose in large jars, of the type otherwise used to ferment rice wine, and a crowded noisy funeral held when the body is reduced to bone."

Different interpretations have been given

As Taylor explains, archaeological digs in England have revealed a significant shift in burial practices that occurred between the end of the Neolithic period and the start of the Bronze Age. In the earlier era, the bones of the dead—picked clean by birds of prey—were buried "all jumbled together in a long, mounded-up communal tomb or barrow." Sometime over the next thousand years, certain individuals—generally wealthy and powerful men—began to be buried intact under their own small, separate mounds. Surrounded by their possessions—daggers, cloak pins, drinking vessels—they were interred in the fetal position, a fact strongly suggesting "that they believed they would be reborn from their swollen earth mounds into some other world, like babies emerging from the womb."

Other positions have been used throughout the ages: extended, crouched, flexed, sitting, standing, or reclining. In Christian nations, bodies are traditionally buried supine with the head pointing west so that the dead will be able to view Christ's coming at the Eschaton. The only position generally avoided is upside down, though even this is not unheard of. In eighteenth-century England, for example, a small number of people—convinced that the world would be flipped over on Judgment Day—had their corpses placed head down in the grave so that they would be standing upright when the big day arrived. (Jonathan Swift mocks this belief in *Gulliver's Travels*. The Lilliputians, we are told, "bury their dead with their heads directly downward, because they hold an opinion that in eleven thousand moons they are to rise again; in which period the earth, which they conceive to be flat, will turn upside down and by this means they shall, at their resurrection, be found ready, standing on their feet.")

Besides being positioned in particular ways, the dead are generally treated to a ritual washing and dressing before burial. This is both a final act of love and, in many cases, a way of ensuring that the departed will look their best when they reach their final destination. And—refuting the notion that "you can't take it with you"—it has been common through the millennia to bury corpses with various tools, utensils, food, clothing, jewelry, and other "grave goods" that will come in handy in the afterlife.

Though they don't exactly qualify as grave goods, amputated limbs have sometimes been accorded official burials in the belief that they will be reunited with their original owners in the hereafter. "In early America," writes Kenneth V. Iserson, "some grave markers even commemorated buried body parts. A Washington Village, New Hampshire, cemetery contains a marker with the inscription, 'Here lies the leg of Captain Samuel Jones which was amputated July, 1807.' Similarly, the Newport, Rhode Island, cemetery has a marker placed by Mr. Tripp to 'His Wife's Arm, Amputated February 20th, 1786.' " This practice has occasionally proved controversial. In July 1899, for example, the *New York World* reported that a bitter dispute had erupted at the Erste Neu-Sandetzer Lodge on Houston Street after one of its members, Lewis Lowensohn, decided to hold funeral rites for his amputated left leg. "How can he get the society to bury his leg?" protested fellow member Isaac Schmidt. "Suppose he gets well and falls down in front of a trolley car and gets an arm cut off. Will he get his arm buried free, too? He holds only one membership. That entitles him to be buried, but not by piecemeal. He must be buried all at once."

If having a single person buried "piecemeal" in multiple graves represents one end of the inhumation spectrum, then mass burial—a single grave containing multiple occupants—is the opposite. This practice, which extends back to the charnel repositories of ancient times, has existed throughout the ages as the preferred way of disposing of social pariahs, from plague casualties and paupers to the victims of wartime atrocities, who have been dumped into ditches like so much human landfill.

RECOMMENDED READING

For those wishing to dig deeper into the rich field of worldwide sepulchral rites, the following books are must-reads: Robert Hertz, *Death and the Right Hand* (Free Press, 1960); Peter Metcalf and Robert Huntington, *Celebrations of Death: The Anthropology of Mortuary Ritual* (Cambridge University Press, 1991); and Timothy Taylor, *The Buried Soul: How Humans Invented Death* (Beacon Press, 2002).

Ritual Burials: So Easy Even a Caveman Could Do It

No one knows for certain precisely when people first began to dispose of their dead in a ritualistic fashion. For years, conventional scientific wisdom had it that the earliest humans to conduct ceremonial burials were the Cro-Magnons of the Upper Paleolithic period, those prehistoric hunter-gatherers whose anatomical features—high forehead, upright posture, and slender skeletons—were indistinguishable from those of modern human beings.

Indeed, along with their other cultural accomplishments—cave painting, sophisticated toolmaking, the earliest glimmerings of religion—it was their habit of performing elaborate burials that defined the Cro-Magnons as our direct evolutionary forebears, true *Homo sapiens* as opposed to the hulking, thick-skulled Neanderthals they eventually displaced. Archaeologists have un-

DEATH FUN FACT

Did you know that the word *mausoleum*—which has come to mean any grand, stately tomb—derives from the name of a provincial ruler in the ancient Persian empire? When Mausolos died in 353 B.C., to honor his memory, his wife, Artemisia, decided to erect a magnificent shrine at what is now Bodrum, Turkey. (According to legend, she also mixed his cremated ashes with wine and imbibed them—anticipating by a few millennia the behavior of Rolling Stones guitarist Keith Richards, who claimed that he blended his father's cremains with a little cocaine and snorted them.)

Hundreds of craftsmen, including some of the greatest sculptors of the age, labored on the shrine. When it was completed three years later, it was of such unparalleled splendor that it became known as one of the Seven Wonders of the World (along with the Great Pyramid of Giza, the Hanging Gardens of Babylon, the Statue of Jupiter at Olympia, the Temple of Artemis at Ephesus, the Colossus of Rhodes, and the Lighthouse at Alexandria). The great tomb remained intact until the fifteenth century, when it was severely damaged by a series of earthquakes. Nowadays, only the foundation of the mausoleum of Mausolos remains on the original site.

covered Cro-Magnon burial sites containing the fossilized remains of carefully posed corpses ornamented with red ochre, dressed in elaborate tunics, adorned with shell and ivory jewelry, and accompanied by ritualistic grave goods including weapons, tools, and food—clear proof that these early humans followed complex rituals when interring their dead.

In the early 1960s, however, the world of paleoanthropology was shaken up when a pair of archaeologists made a sensational discovery. Excavating a cave in a remote mountain region of Iraq, these scientists uncovered the fossilized corpse of an adult Neanderthal male who appeared to have been interred in a reverential manner, his body strewn with wreaths of multicolored flowers. Since then, other evidence has turned up suggesting that Neanderthals engaged in the deliberate, ceremonial disposal of their dead: bodies arranged in special positions, placed under triangular stones, or accompanied by flint implements.

While some scientists dismiss the significance of these findings (arguing, for example, that the flower pollen found in the Shanidar Cave in Iraq came from burrowing rodents), the growing consensus seems to be that those supposedly knuckle-dragging cavemen, the Neanderthals, were responsible for humankind's first ritualistic burials.

The Wacky World of Funeral Customs

Like all other aspects of human culture—from clothing to cuisine, sexual mores to social etiquette—burial rituals differ dramatically throughout the world.

Among the Ashanti of Ghana, for example, a dying person was traditionally given a final drink of water so that his soul would be refreshed as it ascended the steep hill leading to the afterworld. When death occured, the corpse received a sponge bath, a sip of rum, and a little bag of gold dust tied to his loincloth. A handkerchief was placed between his hands, so that he would be able to wipe away the sweat as he made his final journey. Various provisions—a fowl, eggs, and mashed yams—were placed beside the body. After a raucous wake and the presentation of further gifts to the deceased—a shroud, palm wine, some slaughtered sheep—the corpse was car-

DEATH DEFINITION: *Tumulus*

WHILE THE WORD *TUMULUS* SOUNDS LIKE THE NAME OF A MIDDLE EASTERN APPETIZER THAT GOES WELL with pita bread, it actually refers to a kind of grave. Also known as a barrow, a tumulus (from the Latin word for "bulge" or "swelling") is one of humankind's oldest types of tombs, dating at least as far back as 4000 B.C. Essentially, it is a mound of earth or stones raised over one or more graves.

ried to the graveyard in a procession that periodically paused so that the coffin could be touched to the ground in homage to the earth goddess.

During a Mongolian's final days, he or she is attended by a lama who occasionally plucks out one of the dying person's eyebrow hairs to open an escape route for the soon-to-be-departing soul. Once dead, the body is placed in a squatting position and a blue scarf is tied around its head in such a way that the ends cover the face. Disposal of the body can follow one of three methods. The corpse may be buried in a grave designated by the lama, who selects the appropriate site through a complex ritual involving a white staff, a new rug, and the skin of a black goat. Alternatively, the deceased may be cremated after having his brow anointed with butter and touched seventy-two times with a willow leaf. Or—simplest of all—the body might be abandoned in the wilderness to be stripped of its flesh by scavengers.

The Jivaro tribespeople of the Andes take a different approach. Believing that every death is the work of a malign supernatural force, they break into violent demonstrations—cursing, shaking their fists, and swearing vengeance on the unknown demonic killer—whenever anyone, even a very old person, dies. After dressing the deceased in his best clothes and providing him with all the plantains and manioc beer he'll need for the journey to the afterlife, the mourners begin a nightlong wake, the primary feature of which is a ritual dice-throwing game played with canoe-shaped dice. The following morning, the corpse is buried, often within his own house—a form of body disposal that, as mortuary scholars Robert Habenstein and William Lamers note with nice understatement, "necessitates the abandonment of the place as living quarters." Often, the corpse is armed with a spear "so that he can defend himself against other souls, human or animal, that may come to trouble him in his sleep."

A major concern for the peasants of rural Romania is to ensure that the malevolent spirits of the dead do not return to trouble the survivors. When someone dies, the windows and doors of the house are immediately thrown open to afford the departing soul easy exit. The feet of the corpse are tied together with a kerchief, and a long spiral candle is laid on his chest to light the way to the world beyond. For the next three days, a constant watch is kept over the body "lest it should turn into an evil power which threatens the living." When the body is finally borne to the graveyard, the procession makes a dozen stops along the way so that family members can place small towels on the ground—"symbols of the toll gates through which the soul of the dead must pass in the afterlife." The ceremonies conclude with a funeral feast at which mourners receive ring-shaped loaves of bread.

These customs might seem wildly exotic to us. But then, adorning a cadaver with Nature-Glo mortuary makeup before placing it in a $6,000 Beautyrama Adjustable Soft Foam Bed Casket and displaying it in an air-conditioned "slumber room" with piped-in Muzak can seem equally strange to outsiders. Certainly British-born Jessica Mitford thought so. To her, the average U.S. funeral—with its elaborate corpse preparation, prolonged viewing, and extravagant expenditure—was not just bizarre but grotesque: a high-priced pagan ritual dedicated to the great American gods of commerce and vulgarity.

RECOMMENDED READING

Robert W. Habenstein and William M. Lamers's exhaustive, lavishly illustrated, 850-page *Funeral Customs the World Over* (Buflin Press, 1963) is a standard, if somewhat dryly academic, work on the subject. Less comprehensive, though more fun to read, is Ann Warren Turner's "young adult" book, *Houses for the Dead: Burial Customs Through the Ages* (David McKay, 1976), each chapter of which re-creates, in novelistic fashion, a typical funeral in a particular time and place.

The Mohawks of New York made a large round hole in which the body was placed upright or upon its haunches, after which it was covered with timber, to support the earth which they lay over, and thereby kept the body from being pressed. They then raised the earth in a round hill over it. They always dressed the corpse in all its finery, and put wampum and other things into the grave with it; and the relations suffered not grass nor any weed to grow upon the grave, and frequently visited it and made lamentation.

—*History of the Indian Tribes of the United States* (1853)

God Is in the Details: Religion and Burial

Since the religions of the world share little beyond a mutual hatred of one another's belief systems, it comes as no surprise that they take different approaches to the treatment and disposal of the dead. Here's a brief summary of the burial customs followed by the major religions.

ROMAN CATHOLIC

Prior to death, the moribund person is anointed by a priest who recites a sacramental formula while applying consecrated oil to the forehead and hands of the soon-to-be deceased. (Until relatively recently, this rite was reserved for the final hour of life and was known as "extreme unction." It is now performed at an earlier stage, when someone is dangerously ill but not yet at death's doorway, and is known as the Anointing of the Sick.) This ritual is followed by a final communion, the viaticum.

The funeral rites themselves consist of three parts. The first is the vigil or wake, formerly conducted at the home of the deceased but now typically held at the funeral parlor. During this period, the embalmed body is laid out in an open casket for viewing by relatives and friends. Prayers are conducted and eulogies delivered by loved ones.

Next comes the funeral mass, which generally occurs several days after the death (to allow sufficient time for the wake). It begins with a procession to the church, where the casket is met at the door by a white-robed priest and carried to the head of the aisle. The prescribed funeral mass includes an opening prayer with readings from the Bible, a homily, the liturgy of the Eucharist, communion, and a concluding rite of commendation.

The funeral ends at the cemetery with the brief Rite of Committal, consisting of a blessing of the grave, a reading of scripture, and several prayers. Generally, the family dos not remain at the gravesite for the burial itself but leaves at the end of the ritual.

PROTESTANT

Since—according to one informed estimate—there are over eight thousand denominations within Protestantism, it's impossible to talk about a single Protestant way of death. Indeed, as theologian Merle R. Jordan writes, beyond the "usual practice of a funeral service and a committal service," there are no customs or rites common to all branches of Protestantism.

Generally speaking, a visitation at the funeral home is followed by a relatively brief church service of fifteen to twenty minutes conducted by the minister in accordance with his denomination's book of worship. Typically, the ritual consists of Bible readings, a funeral sermon, a eulogy, and the recitation of poetry and prose, interspersed with organ music and hymns. The casket normally stands at the head of the aisle; if it is open, the mourners file by at the end of the service (some denominations, like Presbyterians, insist on keeping the casket closed "so that attention in the service be directed to God"). A brief committal service is then held at the gravesite.

JEWISH

Among the Orthodox, the corpse is first thoroughly washed by members of a burial society who perform this ritual purification while reciting the required prayers. Since Jewish law forbids the mutilation of the deceased, embalming and autopsy are strictly prohibited unless demanded by local law.

Once cleansed, the corpse is garbed in a simple white shroud made of muslin, cotton, or linen. Males are also wrapped in their fringed prayer shawls, one corner of which is cut off to signify that the deceased is now sundered from his earthly religious obligations. The corpse is then placed in a plain wooden coffin. If soil from Israel is available, it is sprinkled over the body. Shards of pottery, symbolizing the destruction of the Temple, may also be placed on the eyes and mouth of the deceased. The coffin is then sealed, Judaism having no tradition of open-casket viewing.

Burial must take place as soon as possible after death, ideally before sunset on the same day or, at the latest, within twenty-four hours. A brief, simple service—consisting of a selection from the Psalms, a eulogy, and a concluding memorial prayer—is held at a funeral chapel, synagogue, or the gravesite. Once the service is over and the coffin has been lowered into the earth, the mourners come forward to throw shovelfuls of earth into the grave.

ISLAMIC

When a Muslim is on the brink of death, he is attended by loved ones who comfort him and recite supplications to Allah on his behalf. The dying person himself is gently encouraged to offer a final declaration of faith: "There is no god but Allah."

When the end comes, the corpse is washed and then wrapped in a plain white shroud called a *kafan*. As in Judaism, embalming is forbidden and burial is expected to take place as soon after death as feasible. The body is first transported to the site of the funeral service—preferably the outer courtyard of the mosque—where the community gathers to conduct the requisite prayers. The deceased is then carried to the cemetery. Only men are allowed to take part in the actual burial. The body, still wrapped in its shroud, is placed in the grave on its right side, facing Mecca and leaning close to the wall of the grave. (If local law requires a burial container, a simple wood coffin is used.) A stone or wooden slab is arranged over the shrouded corpse to protect it from the dirt. Each of those present tosses three handfuls of earth into the hole, which is then quickly filled up by the men.

HINDU

The Hindu belief in reincarnation forms the basis of its funeral rituals. To expedite the transmigration of the soul to a new body, the old one is consigned to the flames. Thus, while cremation is forbidden by Jewish and Muslim law and optional for Christians, it is standard practice among Hindus.

Since a human corpse is regarded as a source of pollution, survivors do their best to minimize direct contact with the dead. After receiving a ritual cleansing, the body is anointed with sandalwood paste and dressed in new clothes—white for men, red for unmarried girls and wives who predecease their husbands. Next, the deceased is arranged on a bier that is adorned with flowers and sprinkled with rosewater. Mantras are chanted. The bier is then borne to the cremation site beside a river, where a pyre is built. Ghee (clarified butter) is liberally smeared on the body. The chief mourner, typically the eldest son, encircles the pyre three times before igniting it. Once the body has been incinerated, the ashes are collected for disposal in one of India's holy rivers.

BUDDHIST

There is no single way of conducting a Buddhist funeral. "As the religious teachings of Buddha were disseminated throughout Asia," explains thanatologist Robert Kastenbaum, "the beliefs and practices were adapted to indigenous cultural traditions dealing with death." Thus, Buddhists in China, Japan, Thailand, Tibet, Cambodia, Korea, Laos, and Vietnam follow different national and local customs for body disposal.

Still, while Asian funeral practices display tremendous cultural diversity, they tend to follow what Robert W. Habenstein and William Lamers describe as "a general pattern of activity," characterized by "family lamentation, prayers by monks, swathing of the body, offerings to the dead, the preparation of a decorated bier or carrier, a noisy and usually colorful funeral procession, cremation as the preferred mode of disposal, and ancestor worship in some form of cult of the dead."

For Western Buddhists, a funeral is a simple, dignified affair that shuns all lavish expenditure and ostentation. Both cremation and earth burial are permitted—the manner of disposal is purely a personal choice. In either case, a simple casket (which may be open or closed) is arranged at the front of a hall, alongside a shrine holding a Buddha image, flowers, incense, and loving tokens in remembrance of the deceased. Simple rites are conducted that may include readings of poetry, collective chanting of contemplative verses, silent meditation, eulogies, and other tributes. The family then accompanies the body to the graveyard or crematorium, where a brief committal service may be held.

RECOMMENDED READING

For more detailed discussions of burial rites as practiced by the major Western religions, see Earl A. Grollman's anthology, *Concerning Death: A Practical Guide for the Living* (Beacon Press, 1974).

If you're planning a Buddhist funeral, you'll find helpful advice on the website of the Network of Buddhist Organizations, www.nbo.org.uk/funerals/funerals.htm.

DEATH DEFINITION: *State Funerals*

ANYONE OLD ENOUGH TO HAVE MEMORIES OF JOHN F. KENNEDY'S ASSASSINATION KNOWS EXACTLY WHAT A state funeral is since the entire nation sat riveted to the television on the afternoon of November 25, 1963, watching as the slain president was borne to the grave. The images remain indelible: the riderless steed with a pair of backward-facing boots in the stirrups, the long procession of foreign dignitaries marching solemnly along Pennsylvania Avenue behind the grieving family, the military bugler blowing "Taps" at the gravesite, one note cracking like a stifled sob.

Full of pomp and ceremony, American state funerals are granted by law to all U.S. presidents—current, former, and -elect—as well as to other honorees designated by a sitting president. The details vary according to the wishes of the individual, but they all share certain features, including military pallbearers, twenty-one-gun salutes, and flag-draped coffins. After reposing in the East Room of the White House (in the case of sitting presidents), the body is conveyed to the Capitol Rotunda to lie in state for public viewing. Typically, the coffin is borne by a caisson drawn by six horses of the same color (though some individuals, like the unassuming Gerald Ford, have opted for a less formal limousine hearse). A memorial service, attended by international heads of state, is held in Washington, D.C., often at the National Cathedral, after which the body is transported to its final resting place.

Eleven U.S. presidents, including the four who were killed by assassins (Lincoln, McKinley, Garfield, and JFK), have been honored with state funerals.

A Brief History of the American Funeral Industry: Making a Big Production of Death

When a death occurred in the United States before the late 1800s, no one contacted a funeral home and hired a mortician to handle the burial arrangements—mainly because there *were* no funeral homes or morticians. Death (as Gary Laderman documents in his 1996 book, *The Sacred Remains*) was a simple, dignified family affair.

In the rural areas of pre–Civil War America, funerals followed a typical pattern. People generally died at home surrounded by relatives and friends. Immediately afterward, the body was laid out by close relations who washed (and, if necessary, shaved) it, then dressed it in a shroud or "winding sheet" of muslin or wool. The corpse was then placed in a simple pine coffin, frequently built by a family member or neighbor.

Over the next one to three days, the body would remain at home, often in the front parlor, where volunteer "watchers"—relatives, neighbors, and friends—kept a round-the-clock vigil, "sitting up" with the corpse until burial time. Depending on the weather, a tub holding a large block of ice might be placed beneath the coffin, with smaller chunks distributed about the unembalmed body.

On the day of the burial, a service was held, often at the home of the deceased. Hymns were sung, psalms read, a discourse and eulogy delivered. Afterward, the coffin began its journey to its final resting place. Depending on the distance, it would be carried on foot or conveyed in a horse-drawn wagon.

Sometimes the simple home service was followed by a more elaborate one at church. The corpse was borne to the local meetinghouse for a final public viewing and funeral ceremony. Then it was on to the graveyard. A somber procession accompanied the body to the burial site, where the grave had already been dug—occasionally by a sexton, though more often by neighbors or relatives of the deceased.

After the coffin was lowered into the ground, a few last words were spoken by anyone who wished to tender them. The mourners would toss a branch, some straw, or a handful of earth onto the coffin lid—a ritual gesture of farewell. Then the grave was filled while the survivors stood by and watched, or—as frequently happened—they performed the task themselves.

Every stage of this process—from the laying out of the corpse to the sewing of the shroud, the "watching" of the body to the building of the coffin, the carrying of the bier to the digging of the grave—was conducted, for the most part, by family and friends of the deceased. The rural funeral, as Laderman writes, was an "intimate affair" performed "by a close circle of relations."

The situation differed in more urban areas, where upon someone's death an undertaker was immediately summoned to the home to take charge of the body, order a casket, arrange the funeral service, and assume other responsibilities that country dwellers traditionally handled on their own. Even in the towns and cities, however, death was still an "intimate affair" in the early decades of the nineteenth century. People died in their own beds and were laid out in the front parlor, where mourners gathered for home funeral services.

All that began to change in the aftermath of the Civil War. The main reason had to do with innovations in arterial embalming. Widely employed during the war by the pioneering surgeon-chemist Dr. Thomas Holmes, this procedure made it possible to ship dead young soldiers home in a relatively well-preserved state. When Abraham Lincoln's corpse was embalmed for its slow, solemn journey back to Springfield, Illinois, the process gained further legitimacy.

By the closing decades of the nineteenth century, arterial embalming had been widely embraced as the preferred way of preparing the dead for the traditional open-casket viewing. Suddenly, even country dwellers required the services of a person who could

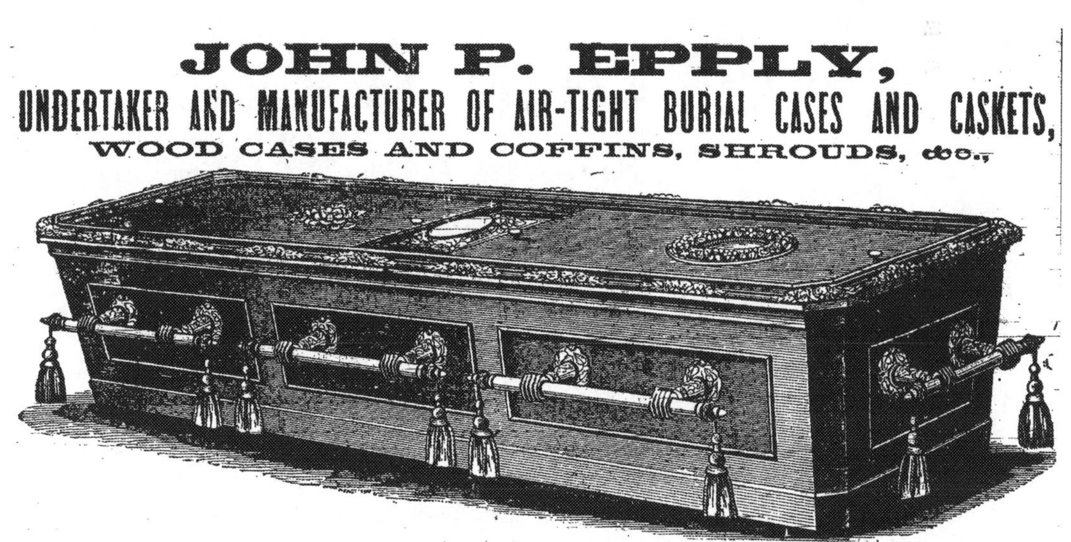

And Wholesale Dealer in Name Plates, Handles, Screws, Escutcheons, Studs, Tacks, Silver Moulding and Lace. Cloth, Velvet, Satin, Merino, Cambric, Ribbon, Silk Fringe, Shroud Trimmings, Crape, Gloves, &c. Embalming Perfectly Done.

THE BEST HEARSES AND CARRIAGES FURNISHED.

OFFICE, CORNER NINTH & PLUM STS., CINCINNATI, O.

Factory and Stables, 182, 184, 186 & 188 West Ninth Street.

handle a trocar and injection pump. To satisfy the public's growing demand for attractive "lifelike" corpses, undertakers had to become skilled in this new, highly specialized technique (which they often learned from traveling embalming-supply salesmen). Before long, they began to conceive of themselves in a different light—as members of a bona fide profession who, by dint of their training and expertise, were entitled to a more elevated social status (and a correspondingly higher pay scale).

By the 1880s, they were publishing trade journals (*The Casket*, *The Shroud*, *Embalmer's Monthly*), establishing mortuary schools with standardized curricula, and joining a professional society whose very name—the Funeral Directors' National Association of the United States (later streamlined to the National Funeral Directors Association, or NFDA)—proclaimed their proud new self-image. No longer did they wish to be identified as mere undertakers, tradesmen who trafficked in funerary paraphernalia and services. Henceforward—through their education, know-how, civic devotion, and ethical conduct—they would win the same respect accorded to doctors, lawyers, and clergymen. Or at least that was the plan.

At first, they continued to make house calls. Notified of a death, they arrived with their chemicals and equipment and set to work in some secluded spot, often the bedroom of the deceased. Not infrequently, a family member stood by and witnessed the procedure. In the early years of the twentieth century, however, a number of factors came into play that changed the nature of the business.

For a variety of reasons—the sharp drop in mortality rates, the rapid rise in the number of hospitals, even the elimination of the front parlor as a standard feature of the middle-class home—death began to disappear from the everyday lives of most Americans. As the new century progressed, people, particularly city dwellers, became increasingly cut off from the earthier realities of existence that had been integral to the lives of their ancestors. A certain squeamishness became the norm.

Back in the old days, if you planned to serve chicken for Sunday dinner, you beheaded, plucked, and butchered the bird yourself. Increasingly, however, people wanted to be sheltered from the disagreeable facts of that process and to purchase their poultry in a ready-to-use and sanitized form. That same attitude extended to mortuary matters. Instead of dying at home surrounded by loved ones, people increasingly expired in hospitals. And the preparation of corpses for viewing (like the processing of farm animals for consumption) became something to be handled far out of the customers' sight, so as not to offend their delicate sensibilities.

THE CINCINNATI COFFIN COMPANY,

CINCINNATI, OHIO. QUINCY, ILLINOIS.

We desire to call your attention to the fact that we manufacture a most complete line of

ROBES AND LININGS.

All goods are precisely as we represent them.

☞ SEND FOR PRICE LIST, ETC.

At the same time, people still wanted the viewing to take place in an intimate, seemingly domestic setting. Not in their actual domiciles, of course—home was no longer a place for anything as depressing as death, and besides, front parlors had gone the way of the horse and buggy. What the modern age demanded was a place designed to suggest the comfort of an old-time parlor but dedicated to the specific purposes of corpse preparation, public mourning, and mortuary display.

Hence, the rise of that peculiarly twentieth-century institution, the funeral home (or parlor). A singular combination of the commercial and the domestic, this modern, all-inclusive establishment not only gathered the full range of funerary services and products under a single roof but also, by serving as the proprietor's actual living quarters, provided the bereaved with a comforting place for their final communion with the dead, an atmosphere suffused with the sacred associations of family and home.

As funeral homes proliferated and the mortuary business blossomed into a full-fledged industry, the disposal of the dead became an increasingly elaborate and costly affair. In the old days, an undertaker might charge sixty dollars for his services: coming to a home, preparing the corpse, providing the coffin, overseeing the funeral, and transporting the remains to the grave. Suddenly, a newly bereaved family would find themselves seated in the hushed receiving room of their neighborhood funeral parlor while the crisply efficient director quietly set forth a range of options that might easily run up expenses into the thousands of dollars.

The age of the modern funeral industry had arrived.

RECOMMENDED READING

The standard history of American funeral directing is *The History of American Funeral Directing* (National Funeral Director's Association, 2001), by Robert W. Habenstein and William M. Lamers. Gary Laderman, a professor of religious history, has produced two highly readable books on the subject, *The Sacred Remains: American Attitudes Toward Death, 1799–1883* (Yale University Press, 1996) and *Rest in Peace: A Cultural History of Death and the Funeral Home in Twentieth-Century America* (Oxford University Press, 2003).

Always go to other people's funerals, otherwise they won't come to yours.

—YOGI BERRA

Funeral Favors

In recent times, handing out increasingly ostentatious party favors has become a standard feature of certain celebratory occasions. The early New England Puritans had a similar tradition—only they didn't practice it at weddings, bar mitzvahs, and kiddie birthday parties. They did it at funerals.

According to Robert W. Habenstein and William M. Lamers, authors of the definitive *History of American Funeral Directing* (National Funeral Directors Association, 2001), the custom of giving "funerary gifts" to mourners originated in England and was transported to the American colonies by early Puritan settlers. Rings, scarves, gloves, books, and various items of needlework were the most common of these handouts.

What began as a heartfelt gesture quickly turned into extravagant showiness. At one early-eighteenth-century ceremony, more than a thousand pairs of gloves were given away; at another, two hundred mourning rings worth a pound apiece—a significant sum in those days. If you were invited to a sufficient number of funerals, you could acquire enough of these items to stock a general store. Habenstein and Lamers cite the case of the Reverend Andrew Eliot of North Church in Boston, who—after tallying "his take for thirty-two years"—discovered that "he had received two thousand nine hundred and forty pairs of funeral gloves." By the mid-eighteenth century, the practice had gotten so out of hand that the General Court of Massachusetts passed a law prohibiting such "prodigious excess" at funerals.

It's a Tough Job but Someone's Got to Do It

For well over a century, members of the "dismal trade" (as undertakers have been known since the 1700s) have come in for more than their fair share of abuse. In novels and movies, they are almost invariably portrayed as money-grubbing vultures, oozing piety as they do their best to squeeze every last penny from their poor, grieving victims. A character identified only as "J.B.," one of Mark Twain's comical creations, is a case in point. Appearing in Twain's memoir-cum-travel book, *Life on the Mississippi*, this shameless rapscallion, who has previously tried his hand with disappointing results at the "insurance-agency business," can't keep from gloating over his new and infinitely more profitable calling. When Twain innocently asks if there is "much profit on a coffin," J.B. crows:

> "Go-Way! How you talk!" Then, with a confidential wink, a dropping of the voice, and an impressive laying of his hand on my arm: "Look here; there's one thing in this world which isn't ever cheap. That's a coffin. There's one thing in this world which a person don't ever try to jew you down on. That's a coffin. There's one thing in the world which a person don't say—'I'll look around a little, and if I can't do better I'll come back and take it.' That's a coffin. There's one thing in this world which a person won't take in pine if he can go walnut; and won't take in walnut if he can go mahogany; and won't take in mahogany if he can go an iron casket with silver door-plate and bronze handles. That's a coffin. And there's one thing in this world which you don't have to worry around after a person to get him to pay for. And that's a coffin. Undertaking?—why it's the dead surest business in Christendom, and the nobbiest."

The mercenary spirit of nineteenth-century hucksters like J.B. continues to pervade the mortuary trade—at least according to Jessica Mitford, who subjects the modern-day funeral industry to merciless ridicule in her 1963 best seller, *The American Way of Death*. Still, while it's easy enough to score satirical points off a business that traffics in products such as Nature-Glo Embalming Makeup and Ko-Zee Burial Footwear, relies on mealy-mouthed euphemisms such as "interment space" instead of "grave," and sponsors seminars on topics such as "Creating Exceptional Funeral Experiences for Today's Educated Consumers," there's little doubt that undertakers perform a vital service for society, one the vast majority of people are only too happy to place into the hands of an experienced pro.

What exactly does that service consist of? The clearest, most complete description of the job—written for the benefit of people who are thinking of entering the profession—appears in the U.S. Department of Labor's *Occupational Outlook Handbook*. According to this source:

- *Funeral directors arrange the details and handle the logistics of funerals.* They interview the family to learn what family members desire with regard to the nature of the funeral, the clergy members or other people who will officiate, and the final disposition of the remains. Together with the family, funeral directors establish the location, dates, and times of wakes, memorial services, and burials. They arrange for a hearse to carry the body to the funeral home or mortuary. They also prepare obituary notices and have them placed in newspapers, arrange for pallbearers and clergy, schedule the opening and closing of a grave with a representative of the cemetery, decorate and prepare the sites of all services, and provide transportation for the remains, mourners, and flowers between sites. They also direct preparation and shipment of remains for out-of-state burials.
- *Most funeral directors are also trained, licensed, and practicing embalmers.* They wash the body with germicidal soap and replace the blood with embalming fluid to preserve the tissues. They may reshape and reconstruct disfigured bodies using materials such as clay, cotton, plaster of Paris, and wax. They may also apply cosmetics to provide a natural appearance, dress the body, and place it in a casket.
- *Funeral directors handle the paperwork involved with the person's death*, such as submitting papers to state authorities so that a formal death certificate may be issued and copies distributed to heirs. They may help family members apply for veterans' burial benefits, and they notify the Social Security Administration of the death. Also, funeral directors may apply for the transfer of any pensions, insurance policies, or annuities on behalf of survivors.
- *Funeral directors also work with those who want to plan their own funerals in advance.* This provides peace of mind by ensuring that the client's wishes will be taken care of in a way that is satisfying to the client and to the client's survivors.
- *Last but not least, funeral directors comfort the family and friends of the deceased*—a task that requires tact, discretion, and compassion.

The Department of Labor stresses the "long, irregular hours" involved in funeral directing. "The occupation can be highly stressful. Many are on call at all hours because they may be needed to remove remains in the middle of the night." The pay is decent, though (despite the accusations of muckrakers like Mitford) money would not seem to be the primary motivation for those considering the profession since the median annual income is somewhere in the neighborhood of $50,000.

To learn more about the profession, go to the Bureau of Labor Statistics website (www.bls.gov) and search under "Funeral Directors."

From Furniture Maker to Undertaker

Check the word *undertaker* in the *Oxford English Dictionary* and you'll find that the modern meaning of the term—"one who makes a business of carrying out arrangements for funerals"—only extends back to around 1700. Before then, no such job existed because there was simply no need for it. Except for the aristocracy—whose corpses were sometimes eviscerated and packed with supposedly preservative spices by authorized barber-surgeons—few people were embalmed or even interred in coffins. Ordinary folk were laid out by relatives, carried on foot to the churchyard, and buried in shrouds.

During the following century, however, the use of coffins became increasingly widespread. As a result, woodworkers started adding them to their inventories. By the beginning of the 1800s, American cabinetmakers typically carried everything from bedroom furniture to burial caskets. Before long, they had branched out into other funerary paraphernalia: palls, shrouds, grave clothes, and assorted mortuary merchandise.

Gradually, these tradesmen began to perform other functions as well: laying out the body in the home, supervising the funeral

From the NFDA "Code of Professional Conduct"

1. Members shall not engage in any unprofessional conduct which is likely to defraud or deceive the public.

2. Members shall not engage in false or misleading advertising.

3. Members shall not pay or offer to pay a commission or anything of value to third parties, such as medical personnel, nursing home and hospice organizations or employees, clergy, government officials or others, to secure deceased human remains for funeral or disposition services.

4. Members shall not use alcohol or drugs to the extent that such use adversely impacts the member's ability to carry out his or her obligation as a funeral professional.

5. Members shall not be convicted of any felony or any crime involving immoral conduct.

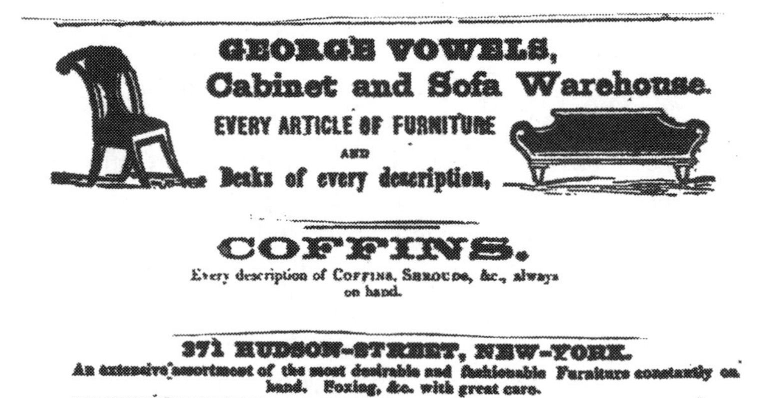

service, providing the hearse, transporting mourners to the cemetery. By the middle of the nineteenth century, funeral undertaking had evolved into a distinct occupation in America—a precursor of the modern profession of licensed mortician or funeral director.

NFDA

The NFDA, or National Funeral Directors Association (not to be confused with other organizations whose acronym is also NFDA, such as the Northeast Florida Dressage Association, the New Frontier Dance Association, and the National Fish Decoy Association), is the world's oldest, largest, and most influential funeral service organization—the NRA for morticians. It traces its origins back to 1880, when two dozen forward-looking Michigan undertakers met to discuss ways of transforming their trade into a bona fide profession. One of the first steps was to dispense with the déclassé designation "undertaker" and adopt the more high-toned title of "funeral director," a decision made after much heated debate at the organization's first national meeting in 1882.

Today, the NFDA devotes itself to various political and public relations activities on behalf of its more than 20,000 members. It lobbies Congress, monitors legislation, disseminates information to the media, and sponsors a yearly national convention. From the first—in its efforts to win the trust and respect of an ever-wary public—it has established constantly evolving standards of ethical behavior, acted to boost the educational requirements for licensed embalmers, and, in general, sought to project an image of its members as "men of means, intelligence, taste, and refinement." Its website, www.nfda.org, features a number of consumer resources, including a toll-free Funeral Service Help Line (800-228-NFDA) and a "Bill of Rights for Funeral Preplanning." In 2004 it adopted, for the first time, a fully enforceable Code of Professional Conduct (www.nfda.org/files/CodeofConduct.pdf). The NFDA also produces a handsome series of free pamphlets, including *Planning a Meaningful Funeral Service*, *Helping Children Through Their Grief*, and *Understanding Cremation*.

Needless to say, foes of the funeral industry take a far more jaundiced view of the NFDA, decrying it as nothing more than a propaganda agency for morticians. Its annual conventions also make a ripe target for critics, who invariably describe these gatherings as ghoulishly festive affairs where the attendees party it up while exhibitors pitch the latest in embalming cosmetics, mortuary fridges, and cadaver deodorizers. For a typically sharp-tongued attack on the NFDA, see Chapter 13 ("The Newest Profession") in Jessica Mitford's *The American Way of Death Revisited* (Vintage, 1998). In a piece called "Merchants of Death," journalist Ashlea Halpern offers a wry, closely observed description of the 2006 National Funeral Directors Association Convention and Expo, held in Philadelphia. Originally published in the *Philadelphia City Paper*, it can be accessed online at www.citypaper.net/articles/2006/10/26/Merchants-of-Death.

The Funeral Home Experience

What exactly happens to you inside a funeral home? Well, that very much depends on whether you are alive or dead—that is, a family member there to make arrangements or the actual corpse.

FUNERAL FLORAL DESIGNS

OF PRESERVED

Everlasting Flowers, Ferns and Grasses.

Never Wilt. Never Fade.

Preserving and Presenting all the Beauties of Nature.

Price List Sent on Application.

☞ Orders by Mail filled promptly on day of arrival, as I carry a large supply, all of my own manufacture.

A. M. NEWBORN,

139 South St. Paul Street, Rochester, N. Y.

If you fall into the former category, you will first be ushered into a hushed and tastefully appointed receiving room by the funeral director, whose demeanor is designed to assure you that, at this supremely difficult moment, you can leave all the details in his capable hands. Without laying it on too thick, he will offer a simple, apparently heartfelt expression of sympathy after you are comfortably seated. With this preliminary out of the way, he will quickly get down to the business at hand.

Gently—but in his perfectly professional manner—he will ask if you have given any thought to the kind of arrangements you wish to make. (Under these emotionally trying circumstances, and particularly if this is your first time dealing with a death in the family, you may feel at a loss. Experts suggest that you bring along a trusted friend—someone less deeply grief-stricken—who can be more objective about the decisions and ask the relevant questions.) Assuming that, like most Americans, you are interested in a traditional burial, the funeral director will then explain your options and present you with an itemized list of his goods and services. Besides the basic fee for his time, trouble, and overhead, these items typically range from cosmetic care of the corpse and use of the chapel and other facilities to the transportation of the mourners and remains to the cemetery.

You may select individual items from the menu or opt for a complete soup-to-nuts package deal. Embalming, though rarely required by law, will almost certainly be part of any package. Since federal regulations prohibit today's funeral director from performing this procedure without express permission, you will be asked if you wish to include it. You have every right to refuse. The funeral director, however, will undoubtedly indicate that unless you wish to bury your loved one right away, with no viewing, embalming is a necessity.

You will be asked for various kinds of information, which the funeral director will jot down on a notepad: personal data for the death certificate, the names of friends and family members who will serve as pallbearers, the type of music you'd like to have played at the memorial service, and so on. It will then be time to choose the burial container.

You may need to steel yourself for this experience. Many people find it profoundly distressing since there is nothing like a roomful of yawning coffins to drive home the terrible finality of death, the awful realization that your mother or father, husband or wife, daughter or son is about to be forever consigned to a narrow box in the ground.

Leading the way downstairs, the funeral director will escort you into the casket selection room, where you will find an array of a dozen or so open coffins, varying in material, quality, and cost. There will be no hard sell from the funeral director, who will simply describe the different options before leaving you alone to wander about the room, examine the merchandise, and decide between, say, the 20-gauge Olivetone at $1,250, the stainless-steel Chateau Slate at $3,295, or the velvet-lined Mahogany at $5,295. Most Americans end up choosing a coffin in the middle price range. With this amount added to the cost of a standard burial package, you can expect to shell out somewhere in the neighborhood of $10,000 for the funeral.

Once the casket has been chosen, it's back to the office, where you will tie up a few loose ends and review the arrangements before taking your leave.

At this point, the funeral director will turn his attentions to your loved one. If he has not already done so, he will immediately have the remains conveyed to his mortuary and wheeled into the white-tiled basement prep room, where—assuming you have opted for a traditional viewing—the body will be embalmed and cosmetically restored (or, as Jessica Mitford gibes, "sprayed, sliced, pierced, pickled, trussed, trimmed, creamed, waxed, painted, rouged, and neatly dressed"). When you next set eyes on your loved one, the spiffed-up body will be handsomely displayed in its shiny new casket—"transformed," as Mitford says, "from a common corpse into a Beautiful Memory Picture."

RECOMMENDED READING

In the opening chapter of his excellent survey of modern-day burial practices, *Grave Matters* (Scribner, 2007), Mark Harris takes the reader inside a typical funeral home as a grieving family makes final arrangements for their eighteen-year-old daughter. A far more scathing look at the funeral home experience can be found in Evelyn Waugh's classic satire *The Loved One* (Little, Brown, 1948). Much useful information is also contained in Constance Jones's *R.I.P.: The Complete Book of Death and Dying* (HarperCollins, 1997).

Funeralspeak

Like the members of other professions (military types, for example, who refer to dead civilians as "collateral damage"), undertakers rely on a great deal of jargon to disguise the disturbing realities of their trade. Here are some of the more common euphemisms employed by the funeral industry, along with their actual meanings:

FUNERALSPEAK	PLAIN ENGLISH
Moved on	Dead
Loved one	Corpse
Cremains	Human ashes
Restorative art	Embalming
Preparation room	Embalming room
Dermasurgeon	Embalmer
College of mortuary science	Embalming school
Display area	Coffin showroom
Celebration of life	Funeral service
Funeral coach	Hearse
Memorial garden	Graveyard
Interment space	Grave
Opening interment space	Gravedigging
Monument	Tombstone
Funeral director	Undertaker

DEATH DEFINITION: *Church Truck*

WHILE THE TERM MIGHT SEEM TO REFER TO A vehicle used to transport elderly and/or handicapped parishioners to and from Sunday services, a church truck is actually a vital piece of mortuary apparatus—namely, a wheeled, adjustable metal cart used to move caskets in funeral homes. We're not exactly sure why it's called a "church truck"—but then again, we have no idea why beer openers are called "church keys."

Mortuary Hall of Fame: Howard Raether

Every now and then, a person comes along who achieves such dominance in a particular field of endeavor that he or she is crowned with an honorific title: the Wizard of Wall Street, the King of Rock and Roll, the Father of Modern Computing. In the twentieth-century death care business, one towering figure earned such a distinction. His name was Howard Raether, and he was known to his admiring peers as "Mr. Funeral Service."

Born and educated in Milwaukee in 1916, where he received his bachelor's and law degrees from Marquette University, Raether began his long funeral-focused career in 1940, when he was retained as general counsel for the Wisconsin Funeral Directors and Embalmers Association. Eight years later, after serving in the U.S. Navy during World War II, he was named executive director of the National Funeral Directors Association, the world's preeminent funeral trade association—a position he occupied for the next thirty-five years.

It was during his tenure that the American funeral industry faced the greatest challenge to its legitimacy since its inception: the firestorm ignited by Jessica Mitford's 1963 bombshell, *The American Way of Death*. Mitford's book took particular aim at the two bedrock practices of the mortuary business, embalming and viewing, which she regarded as crass, morbid rituals perpetuated by the undertaking trade for its own financial welfare. As the public face of the funeral industry, Raether—who genuinely believed that traditional open-casket funerals offered therapeutic benefits for survivors—became Mitford's chief antagonist, defending his profession in scores of radio and television appearances. He also represented the funeral industry during fifty days of public hearings and debate in the early 1980s, when the Federal Trade Commission was about to implement its landmark Funeral Rule.

Revered among his colleagues (who paid him the tribute of bestowing his name on the NFDA's research library, one of the world's largest collections of funeral-related books and historical papers), Raether—in the way such things frequently happen—will forever be linked to his bête noir, Jessica Mitford. In his essay collection, *Bodies in Motion and at Rest* (Vintage, 2001), Thomas Lynch neatly sums up their enduring connection: "Back in the Sixties they would fight it out on radio and TV and in print interviews. She'd talk money. He'd talk meaning. He'd do values. She'd do costs. She said the funeral was a 'barbaric display.' He said the funeral was 'for the living.' They disagreed on almost everything. She died in the summer of 1996. He died in October of 1999. Their old con-

Yellow Pages for Morticians

Are you in the market for a high-performance human crematory? Does your hydraulic embalming table need replacing? Have you been thinking about switching to a different brand of mortuary cosmetics?

No problemo! Just let your fingers do the walking through the *Catalog of Funeral and Cemetery Supplies* issued annually by Nomis Publications of Youngstown, Ohio. From antique funeral equipment to vault sealants, casket accessories to urn beds, embalming supplies to odor control devices, this 250-page directory—the yellow pages of the funeral industry—lists suppliers of every conceivable mortuary product (plus a fair number that most of us would never dream of, such as formaldehyde vapor monitors, and burial garments for stillborns).

Copies of this indispensable volume can be obtained for $30 from Nomis Publications, P.O. Box 5159, Youngstown, OH 44514. For more information, visit the company website at www.yelobk.com.

tentions still shape the meaning and marketing of American funerals."

Step into My Parlor

In the 1979 cult movie classic *Phantasm*, two brothers sneak into the local funeral parlor, which turns out to be a nightmarish mausoleum run by a cadaverous undertaker who transforms human corpses into black-robed dwarf zombies and uses a unique home-security device—a flying metal sphere armed with a skull-piercing corkscrew—to deal with intruders. Needless to say, this is not an accurate depiction of the average American funeral home. It is, however, a fair reflection of the spookhouse fantasies such places inspire.

To dispel the creepy aura that has always clung to their establishments and educate people about what really goes on inside, funeral directors have often opened their doors to the public. As far back as 1929 (according to historian Gary Laderman) one newly opened mortuary in El Paso, Texas, drew a crowd of more than a thousand curiosity-seekers on a single day. Funeral directors across the country continue to offer tours of their facilities. Some, such as the Conley Funeral Home in Elburn, Illinois, even host mortuary visits for schoolchildren—a nice change of pace from those boring field trips to the local art museum.

The interior of a typical funeral home—at least the parts that the public gets to see—is a highly controlled environment, as artificial in its way as a movie set or a Disney ride. Every feature of the surroundings, from the lighting and sound effects to the furnishings and other elements of décor—is designed to produce exactly the right atmosphere of reverent contemplation and solace.

The public areas of a typical funeral home consist of a handsome entrance hall or foyer; a comfortable reception room where the director and the bereaved meet to make arrangements; a spacious and well-lighted casket selection room; one or more visitation (or "slumber") rooms, where the body is laid out for viewing; and a chapel for on-site memorial services.

Besides these spaces, there are also areas off-limits to the public: the private office

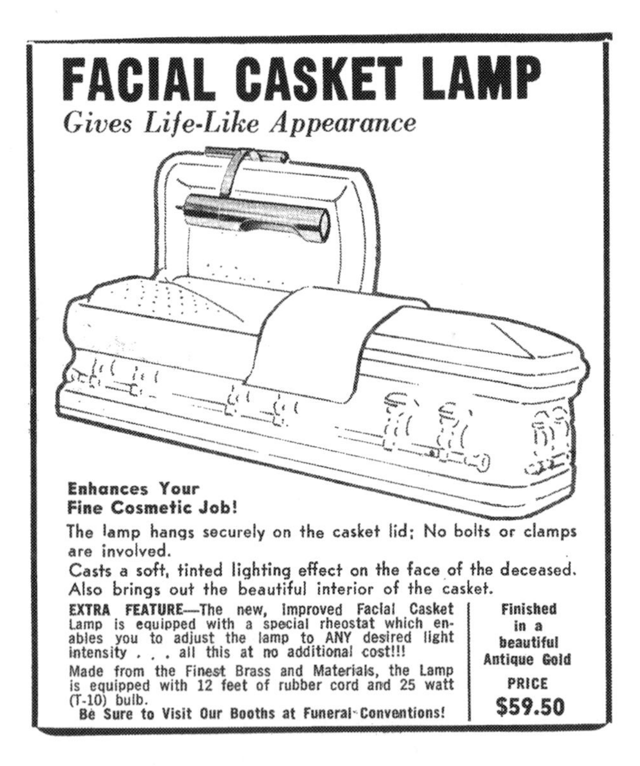

where the funeral director does his paperwork; the living quarters for his family and/or members of the staff; and the tiled, hospital-like preparation room where bodies are embalmed, restored, dressed, and casketed for display.

And then, of course, there's the secret subterranean room where cadavers are turned into black-robed dwarf zombies. (Just kidding!)

RECOMMENDED RESOURCES

A very fine article, "The American Funeral Home: An Archaeology of the Viewing" by Sean Patrick Dockray, is available online at http://spd.e-rat.org/wp-content/uploads/funeralhome.pdf. There is also an excellent chapter on funeral home design in the volume *Successful Funeral Service Practice*, edited by Howard C. Raether (Prentice-Hall, 1971). Times being what they are, you will not be surprised to learn that various funeral homes now offer virtual tours of their facilities. Among them are the Uecker-Witt Funeral Home of Fond du Lac, Wisconsin (www.ueckerwitt.com), and the Eaton Funeral Home of Sullivan, Missouri (www.eatonfuneralhome.com).

Pre-need: Pro or Con?

Whether they work as funeral directors or consumer advocates, people who deal with end-of-life issues will all tell you the same thing: being a responsible grown-up means planning in advance for your eventual demise—talking to your children about your final wishes or, even better, writing everything down so as to make life a little easier for your survivors when you die.

There is no such consensus, however, about another form of long-range death planning: the increasingly popular arrangement generally referred to as "pre-need." This refers to the practice of paying in advance for your own funeral.

In theory, there doesn't appear to be any downside to a pre-need purchase. Everyone seems to benefit. For funeral directors—as Thomas Lynch puts it—"It's money in the bank." For the buyer, the arrangement is supposed to offer peace of mind: the knowledge that, by taking care of business now, you have relieved your loved ones of an enormous burden in the future. It is also touted as a wise financial decision: a hedge against inflation that nails down a major purchase at a guaranteed price.

Unfortunately, there have been widespread abuses in the practice. Indeed, consumer rights organizations that monitor the death care industry routinely warn potential customers that while it always pays to *plan* ahead, it doesn't necessarily pay to *pay* ahead.

Though entering into a pre-need contract would seem to be a foolproof way of ensuring that your loved ones won't be faced with large expenses when you die, some funeral directors have come up with ingenious ways of extorting extra money from survivors. When the sad day of the funeral finally rolls around, family members may suddenly discover that there are hefty additional charges for services not covered in the contract: opening and closing the grave, for example, or placing an obituary in the papers. Or the casket preselected by the purchaser is no longer manufactured and there is a significant "upgrade cost" for the current equivalent model. Funds laid out in advance by pre-need purchasers have also been subjected to various financial shenanigans by unscrupulous funeral industry types.

Though there are distinct advantages to pre-need arrangements, you should carefully examine the pros and cons before you sign up. Read the chapter called "Pay Now—Die Poorer Later" in Jessica Mitford's *The American Way of Death Revisited* (Vintage, 1998), as well as the chapter "The Body Snatchers: Preneed Greed" in Lisa Carlson's *Caring for the Dead* (Upper Access Books, 1998). You should also familiarize yourself with the Funeral Consumers Alliance's "Position Statement Concerning Prepaid Funerals," which can be found at www.funerals.org/Preneed Funerals/Policy.pdf.

GPL

Back in what Jessica Mitford calls the "bad old days"—that is, before the advent of the modern consumer rights movement—people with a loved one to bury had no choice but to pay whatever their local mortician charged for a traditional funeral. Funeral homes rarely explained exactly what they were billing for, other than the casket and the "full range of services." All that changed in April 1984, when—after years of lobbying by groups such as the Funeral Consumers Alliance—the Federal Trade Commission's Funeral Rule went into effect.

The Funeral Rule (which has since undergone several revisions) requires funeral directors to provide their customers with a written, itemized list of goods and services at the start of any arrangement meeting. This document, known as a general price list (GPL), must also contain certain disclosures:

- Consumers have the right to choose only those goods and services they want.
- Embalming is not required by law except in certain special cases.
- A basic nondeclinable service fee will be added to the bill.
- Inexpensive "alternative containers," such as those made of cardboard, are available for direct cremation.
- A price list for caskets is available.
- A price list for "outer burial containers" (or vaults) is available.

The Funeral Rule also stipulates that funeral directors must, if requested, provide prices over the phone (to allow for comparison shopping).

GPLs vary in complexity. Some are as simple as a McDonald's menu, while others offer a dizzying range of options. A relatively straightforward breakdown might look like this:

Basic services of the funeral director and staff	$1,695
Transfer of remains to funeral home	$225
Embalming	$1,015
Cosmetic care, dressing, and casketing	$215
Use of viewing room	$175
Use of chapel for memorial service	$350
Transportation of deceased to cemetery	$175
Transportation of flowers	$85
Transportation of clergy and pallbearers	$85
TOTAL SERVICE COST	$4,020

This charge does not include the cost of the casket, which—if purchased directly from the funeral home—typically adds between $3,000 and $12,000 to the bill.

Besides the itemized lists, GPLs invariably include all-in-one funeral packages, presumably to simplify matters for clients. (A common tactic used by funeral homes is to front-load their GPLs with these discounted bundles, under the theory that grieving family members will simply settle for one of these "bargains" rather than deal with a daunting list of individual items in an effort to trim costs.)

Whether or not the GPL has really made much of a difference in the price of the average American funeral is debatable. As poet-undertaker Thomas Lynch puts it in describing his own business practices: "I used to use the *unit pricing method*. It meant that you had only one number to look at. It was a large number. Now everything is itemized. It's the law. So now there's a long list of items and numbers and italicized disclaimers, something like a menu or the Sears Roebuck Wish Book, and sometimes the federally mandated options begin to look like cruise control or rear-window defrost. At the bottom of the list there is still a large number."

SCI: The 800-Pound Funeral Gorilla

Way back in 1969, a nineteen-year-old longhair named Mo Siegel and his buddy Wyck Hay began gathering wild herbs from the woods around Aspen, Colorado, packaging them in hand-sewn muslin teabags, and selling their concoction to a local health food store. Their enterprise, Celestial Seasonings, swiftly expanded. Before long, their all-natural herbal teas—dubbed with whimsical Sgt. Pepper–style names—could be found in

Find a Funeral Home

Need to locate a reputable funeral home in your area? Try the easy-to-use Funeral Home Directory at www.funeralhomes.com, which allows you to search by city, state, zip code, or (if you have a particular death care provider in mind) business name.

markets throughout the country. This inspiring story of countercultural entrepreneurship culminated in 1984 when the company was acquired for many millions of dollars by Kraft, Inc., which retained the product's playful, Woodstockian packaging under the theory that boomer consumers would prefer to believe that their beloved herbal teas were still being handmade by Mother Earth–loving hippies and not mass-produced by a faceless multinational corporate leviathan.

This same phenomenon—the takeover of small human-scale businesses by a huge corporate entity that keeps its identity concealed behind the original trusted brand name—has, in recent decades, spread to the funeral industry. The most conspicuous practitioner of this strategy is a Houston-based outfit called Service Corporation International or SCI.

Since its founding, SCI—often described as the McDonald's of the mortuary trade—has become the world's largest chain of funeral homes. Its success is based on a state-of-the-art business technique known as "clustering." First, SCI buys up a choice selection of funeral homes, cemeteries, crematoria, and flower shops in select metropolitan areas. Next—as explained in *The American Way of Death Revisited* (Vintage, 1998), the updated version of Jessica Mitford's classic exposé—"the essential elements of the trade are moved to a central depot. 'Clustered' in this hive of activity are the hearses, limousines, utility cars, drivers, dispatchers, embalmers, and a spectrum of office workers, from accountants to data processors, who are kept busy servicing, at vast savings, the needs of a half-dozen or more erstwhile independent funeral homes."

Of course, it is crucial that consumers feel that they are dealing, not with a monolithic corporation—a provider of what Thomas Lynch calls "McFunerals"—but with their friendly neighborhood mortician. To achieve this goal, SCI cultivates anonymity. You won't see the SCI corporate logo adorning any of its more than three thousand funeral homes in North and South America, Europe, and Australia. When the company acquires one of its mom-and-pop operations, it not only keeps the original name of the establishment but often retains the former owner as a salaried manager, thus ensuring that the long-established relationship between the funeral director and his community is maintained.

It's a formula that (with a few setbacks during the late 1990s) has turned SCI into a death industry powerhouse. And the financial prospects only look brighter now that the expression "going back to the land" is about to acquire a whole new meaning for the Woodstock generation.

Coffins and Caskets: What's the Difference?

Since both coffins and caskets are "boxes for the dead" (in the words of poet-undertaker Thomas Lynch), the two terms are sometimes used interchangeably. There are, however, a few significant differences between them.

Most obviously, there is the matter of shape. Coffins, which are generally made of wood, correspond roughly to the form of the human body—that is, they are tapered at the head and foot and wider at the shoulders. They also have lids that lift off completely.

Caskets, on the other hand, are rectangular in shape and usually have hinged lids. Though available in oak, mahogany, walnut, and other species of hardwood, they are also frequently made of metal—copper, bronze, stainless steel, or carbon steel—in a variety of grades, gauges, and finishes.

The deeper distinction, however, is (as Lynch points out) a matter of meaning: the word *casket* "suggests something beyond basic utility, something about the contents of the box. The implication is that it contains something precious: heirlooms, jewels, old love letters, remnants and icons of something dear. So casket is to coffin as tomb is to cave, grave is to hole in the ground, pyre is to bonfire, eulogy is to speech . . . The point is a *casket* presumes something about what goes in it. It presumes the dead body is important to someone."

For more of Lynch's elegant musings on the subject, see his essay "Jessica, the Hound and the Casket Trade" in his collection *The Undertaking: Life Studies from the Dismal Trade* (Norton, 1997).

Coffins for the Big-Boned

As the media never tires of telling us, America has become a junk-food nation with the fattest population on the planet. This is a cause for concern. Obesity can lead to a host of problems, from heart disease and diabetes to an inability to attend the theater because you can't squeeze into a seat. But being seriously overweight can do more than interfere with your life. It can even cause trouble once you're dead.

Most of us realize that it's time to cut back on the cheese fries and quarter-pounders when our clothes don't fit anymore. But some people have gotten so grotesquely out of shape that—once their poor, cholesterol-clogged hearts give out—their bodies won't even fit into a standard-size coffin.

One obvious option for surviving family members of supersized decedents is cremation. But according to the Cremation Association of North America, the average crematorium oven can only accommodate corpses weighing less than five hundred pounds, which (believe it or not) is no longer sufficient for a growing number of morbidly obese Americans. What's a grieving family to do with the six-hundred-pound corpse of a beloved relative who has finally succumbed to an overdose of Oreo sundaes and fudge-iced crème-filled donuts?

Fortunately, a solution is available from the folks at Goliath Casket, Inc., the world's leading manufacturer of burial containers for the terminally overweight. Forrest "Pee Wee" Davis, of Lynn, Indiana, founded Goliath in 1985. A welder in a local casket concern, Davis was a true mortuary industry visionary who foresaw the need for quality jumbo-size coffins years before the American obesity epidemic was in full swing. His first models were made in an old hog barn and came in just two colors and one size. Today, under the stewardship of his son Keith, Goliath produces a wide range of oversize caskets, including a triple-wide colossus that can handle a body up to seven hundred pounds.

FISK'S PATENT METALLIC BURIAL CASES.

Thanks to the ever-expanding waistlines of the American populace, business is booming for Goliath. In the late 1980s, the company sold just one triple-wide model a year. Nowadays, they ship four or five a month, and overall sales have increased about 20 percent annually.

For more information on Goliath coffins, visit the company's website at www.oversizecasket.com.

Unsung Heroes of the Death Industry: Almond Fisk

Americans have always taken pride in their mechanical ingenuity. After all, we're the nation that produced Eli Whitney, Thomas Edison, Alexander Graham Bell, Henry Ford, the Wright brothers, and countless other homespun, do-it-yourself geniuses. Though his brainchild didn't have quite the world-changing impact of the cotton gin, electric lightbulb, telephone, mass-produced automobile, or airplane, one name deserves inclusion in the pantheon of American inventors: Almond D. Fisk, creator of the "Fisk Airtight Coffin of Cast or Raised Metal."

Hailed by funeral historians Robert Habenstein and William Lamers as "the most remarkable coffin ever put into widespread use in America," Fisk's invention, patented in 1848, was a cast-iron container shaped like a human body and equipped with a glass faceplate that, in the words of one contemporary advertising brochure, permitted mourners "to behold again the features of the departed." Resembling a factory-made metal mummy-sarcophagus with a diving helmet on its head, it "retarded the putrefaction process, protected the body against water seepage and vermin, and safeguarded against the spread of disease." The only drawback was that, as originally designed, it was so ineffably creepy-looking that it gave people the chills.

With prices ranging from $7 to $40, the Fisk Metallic Burial Case could be purchased from the inventor himself, who set up a salesroom in New York City, or from one of several companies licensed to manufacture the product. New and improved styles—designed to eliminate "the disagreeable sensation produced by the coffin on many minds" (as one advertisement delicately put it)—were introduced, including models ornamented with molded drapery, finished in imitation rosewood, or trimmed with silk fringe. Even these aesthetic refinements, however, failed to obviate the unnerving effect of Fisk's mummy case. Eventually, the original pattern was abandoned altogether and replaced with rectangular caskets that became hugely popular in the latter part of the nineteenth century.

Fisk didn't live to see the widespread success of his invention. Though the historical records are fuzzy, indications are that by 1862 he was already dead and buried—snugly sealed for eternity in one of his form-fitting metal containers.

Bad Ideas in Coffin Making

Once upon a time, the glass coffin was something found only in fairy tales—the preferred receptacle for preserving poisoned princesses until their saviors showed up to awaken them with a kiss. During the nineteenth century, this fantasy item briefly became a reality when a number of American inventors—in the evident belief that mourners craved a more transparent view of the departed when paying their final respects—took out patents on various airtight glass coffins. Perhaps unsurprisingly, these receptacles—the mortuary equivalent of old-fashioned canning jars—did not catch on big with the public.

The same period of our history produced other seriously bad ideas in coffin manufacture. According to funeral historians Robert Habenstein and William Lamers, the most notable "coffin also-rans" included the cement coffin, the terra-cotta coffin, the papier-mâché coffin, the rubber coffin, the wicker-basket coffin, and—perhaps weirdest of all—the adjustable coffin, suitable for corpses of all shapes and sizes.

DIY Coffins

Just as embalming is rarely required by law anywhere in the United States, there are no federal or local statutes that say you have to be buried in a $5,000 Venetian Bronze casket purchased from your friendly neighborhood funeral home. You can easily get a perfectly nice coffin at a discount rate from one of many online companies such as CasketXpress (www.caskets.net), CasketSite.com, and BestPriceCaskets.com. Even Costco sells them now.

Alternatively, if you wish to return to the dignified simplicity displayed by our pioneer forefathers, there's nothing to keep you from constructing your own plain wooden coffin. Some companies, such as Kent Casket Industries, will ship you a basic pine coffin in flat "knock-down" form. Anyone capable of using a screwdriver can easily assemble it in minutes. (Instructions can be viewed at www.kentcasket.com.) Charles "Outhouse Charlie" Hetrick, a Seattle-area craftsman, offers easy-to-assemble wood coffins that

The Owego Cruciform Casket Co.

PATENT CRUCIFORM AND STRAIGHT LINE CLOTH CASKETS

AS WELL AS THEIR

Fine Finished Wood Coffins and Burial Cases,

PATENT CRUCIFORM CASKET

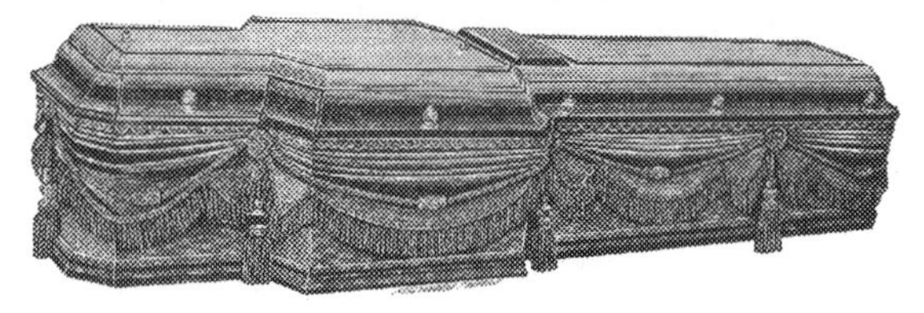

come complete with all the equipment required to build them—a hammer and a packet of nails (check out his website at www.outhousecharlie.com). Putting together one of the handcrafted coffins offered by Ark Wood Caskets of Ashland, Oregon, doesn't require the use of any tools at all. You simply slide the six interlocking boards together, then thread the rope handles through the predrilled holes. (You can see a diagram at www.arkwoodcaskets.com.)

For those with slightly more advanced woodworking skills, do-it-yourself coffin kits requiring a certain degree of manual dexterity are available from various sources. You can order one online at www.mhp-casketkits.com or write to MHP Enterprises, RR#1, S-7, C-34, Crescent Valley, British Columbia, Canada, V0G 1H0. And if you're a serious Mr. (or Ms.) Fix-it type, you can build your own coffin from scratch. Coffin-making instructions are available online from many different sources (Google "casket plans"). You can also find directions in various books. Complete patterns for a simple homemade "burial box" can be found in Ernest Morgan's *Dealing Creatively with Death: A Manual of Death Education and Simple Burial* (Upper Access, 2001) and *Coming to Rest: A Guide to Caring for Our Own Dead* (Dovetail, 1998) by Julie Wiskind and Richard Spiegel. For the serious woodworker, Dale Power's *Do-It-Yourself Coffins: For Pets and People* (Schiffer, 1997) offers step-by-step instructions for six different designs, ranging from a classic pine box to a poplar model that resembles an elegant antique chest and seems far too beautiful to be stuck underground.

Finally, if you are hopelessly inept but would still like to be buried in a simple pine box, you can always buy one from a carpen-

Simple Homemade Casket

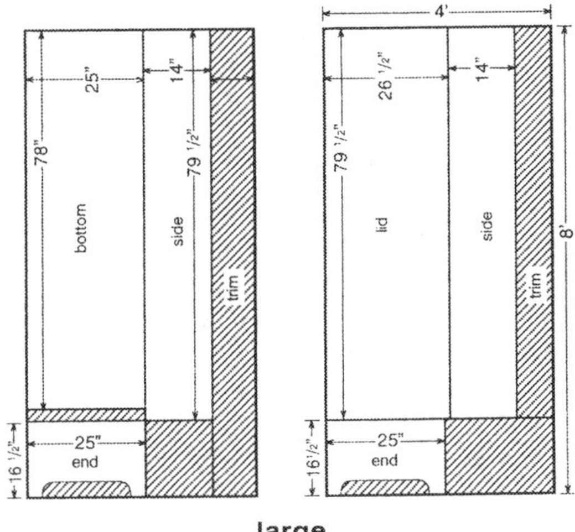

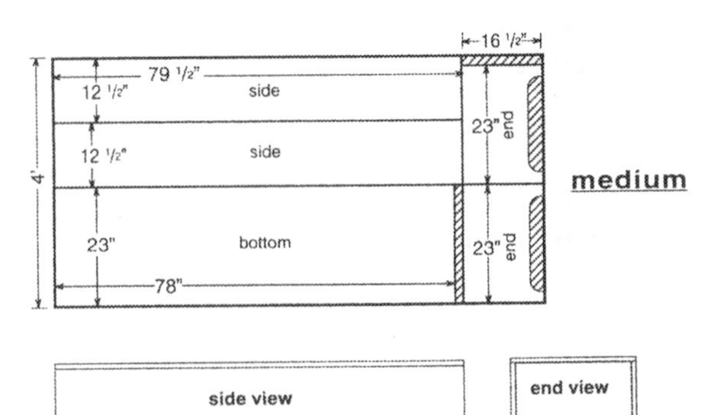

Plans for homemade casket. Courtesy of Julie Wiskind.

ter. In his excellent book *Grave Matters: A Journey Through the Modern Funeral Industry to a Natural Way of Burial* (Scribner, 1997), Mark Harris suggests that you check the yellow pages under "carpenters" and "woodworking" to see if any of your local craftsmen is willing to make a basic coffin for you. You can also find a list of craftsmen who offer handmade wood caskets at www.funerals.org/frequently-asked questions/casket retailers#artisan.

Rent-a-Casket

As every American male knows, there are certain once-in-a-lifetime occasions—your senior prom, your first wedding—when you have to dress up in fancier clothes than you'll ever wear again. The traditional solution, of course, is to rent a tuxedo. Why invest in an expensive getup that you'll need only once?

Well, that same commonsense principle has now been adopted by the death care industry. Increasingly, as a service to their customers, funeral homes have begun to offer rental caskets.

The way it works is this: When you die, your corpse gets to be laid out in a really snazzy upscale casket, so people can ooh and aah over your remains at the wake. Then, right before burial, your body is transferred to a significantly cheaper coffin that nobody but the worms is going to see anyway. The fancy rental casket is typically used for as many as four separate viewings before it is sold at a discount to its final occupant. (Yes, there is now such a thing as a "pre-used" coffin.)

If you're looking for ways to cut down on the high cost of dying, you might want to see if this sensible, money-saving option is available from the friendly folks at your local funeral home.

Kool Koffins

If you're the kind of hip, trendy person who's always taken pride in your stylish appearance, you're not going to want to show up at your own funeral encased in some dull, old-fashioned burial receptacle. While the average American funeral home stocks a wide variety of caskets, most of them are definitely on the stodgy side—the kind of dignified, conservative coffins that haven't changed much in the last fifty years. A Batesville Seville walnut casket with satin finish and champagne velvet interior might represent the finest in mortuary craftsmanship. But fashionwise, it's the funerary equivalent of the boxy, double-breasted Harris tweed suits favored by 1950s bankers. Not exactly the kind of thing that befits a lifelong hipster such as yourself.

Thankfully, there are a number of snazzy options available in today's rapidly evolving mortuary marketplace. If you're a folk art enthusiast, for example, you might consider obtaining one of the amazing caskets crafted by the famous Ga coffin carpenters of Accra, Ghana. These improbably whimsical receptacles are hand-carved and brightly painted wooden sculptures reflecting

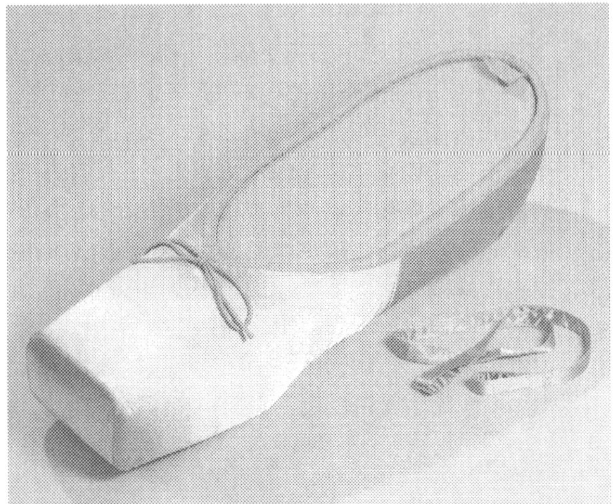

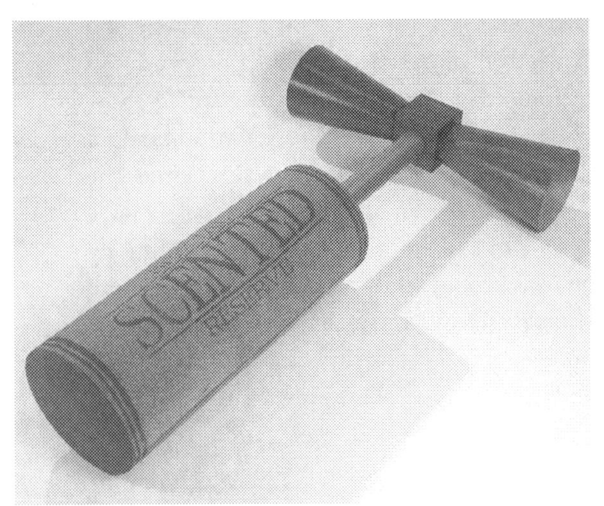

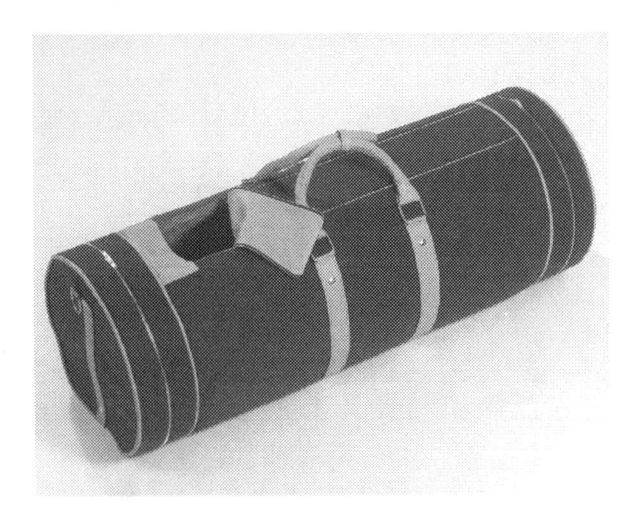

Crazy Coffins: "Guitar," "Corkscrew," "Sports Bag," "Skateboard," "Ballet Shoe." Courtesy of Vic Fearn & Company Ltd. and Museum für Sepulkralkultur, Kassel, Germany.

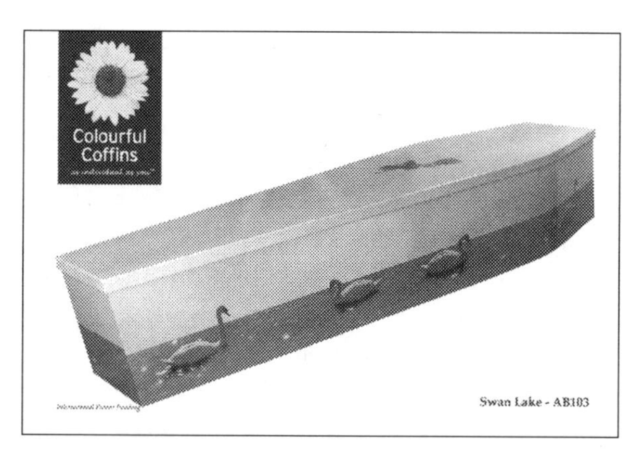

Colourful Coffins: "Swan Lake." Courtesy of Colourful Coffins.

the occupation, status, or character of the deceased. A dead farmer might be buried in an oversize carrot, a fisherman in a giant sardine, a hunter in a great roaring lion, a planter in an enormous cocoa pod. You can read all about these wonderful *objets*—and see dozens of full-color photographs—in Thierry Secretan's *Going into Darkness: Fantastic Coffins from Africa* (Thames and Hudson, 1995). Ghanaian folk-art coffins in a wide variety of styles—from cell phones to airplanes to running shoes—can also be ordered online at www.eshopafrica.com.

Inspired by the Ghanaian tradition, the British coffin-making firm Vic Fearn and Company has begun producing its own spectacular line of "theme coffins" in shapes ranging from electric guitars and corkscrews to skateboards and ballet slippers. So sheerly gorgeous are these caskets that the idea of sticking them permanently underground seems slightly sacrilegious. They would be more at home in a European museum—where, in fact, they have been exhibited (they were the subject of a 2005 show, "Crazy Coffins," at the Museum für Sepulkralkultur in Kassel, Germany).

Colourful Coffins: "Rock 'n' Roll." Courtesy of Colourful Coffins.

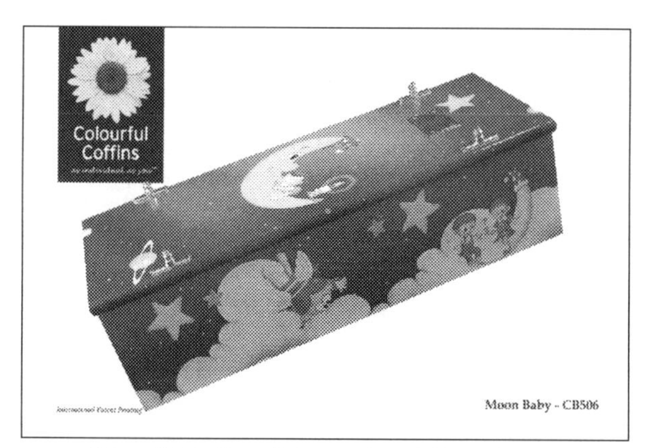

Colourful Coffins: "Moon Baby" child's coffin. Courtesy of Colourful Coffins.

If the Ghanaian caskets are folk art and the Vic Fearn versions high art, another British company, Colourful Coffins of Oxford, produces burial receptacles that fall under the category of commercial art. Adorned with bright, blandly pretty images—leaping doplins, rural sunsets, English countrysides, autumnal forests—these coffins are ideal for anyone who has ever wanted to be interred in a giant Hallmark greeting card. You can see them for yourself at www.colourfulcoffins.com.

A Brief History of Embalming

Though the artificial mummification of corpses dates back to the days of the pharaohs, embalming (literally, preserving a dead body by anointing it with balm, i.e., a concoction of resin and aromatic spices) has a relatively recent history in Western civilization. With rare exceptions, the ancient Greeks and Romans didn't practice it (on the contrary, the former often buried their dead in limestone *sarkophagi* designed to speed up decomposition). Nor did the Jews, who frowned upon embalming (along with cremation) as a desecration of the body.

Following these traditions, early Christians likewise shunned embalming. In the third century, St. Anthony denounced it as a pagan custom and declared that he had gone into the desert to ensure that his own body would not be artificially preserved upon death:

> And if your minds are set upon me, and ye remember me as a father, permit no man to take my body and carry it into Egypt, lest, according to the custom which they have, they embalm me and lay me up in their houses, for it was to avoid this that I came into this desert. And ye know that I have continually made exhortation concerning this thing and begged that it should not be done, and ye well know how much I have blamed those who observed this custom. Dig a grave, then, and bury me therein, and hide my body under the earth, and let these my words be observed carefully by you.

Up through the late Middle Ages, embalming was rarely performed in Europe—and then only on personages of great eminence and wealth. Upon his death in 814, Charlemagne was embalmed, garbed in imperial robes, and placed in a seated position in his tomb at Aachen Palace. Both William the Conqueror (d. 1087) and Edward I (d. 1307) were also embalmed. The method employed in each of these cases was a rough approximation of Egyptian mummification. After the internal organs were removed and the blood drained from the major arteries, the eviscerated cavity was washed with alcohol and vinegar, then packed with aromatic spices and cotton. The incisions were sewn up, the veins cauterized, and the rectum and other orifices plugged with oakum. Then the entire cadaver was anointed with a mixture of turpentine, rosewater, and chamomile before being tightly wrapped in layers of wax-impregnated cloth.

Other preservative methods were occasionally used. Funeral historians Robert Habenstein and William Lamers describe the case of one medieval nobleman whose long-entombed cadaver—"sheeted in lead and boxed in an elm coffin"—was exhumed in the late eighteenth century. "When the lead was opened," they write, "the body was revealed to be lying wholly perfect in a liquor resembling mushroom catchup. Someone tasted the preservative and found that it tasted like 'catchup, and of the pickle of Spanish olives.' "

It was not until the Renaissance that embalming became more widely practiced in Europe. The main impetus behind the search for new and improved methods of corpse preservation sprang from the renewed interest in human anatomy, not only among physicians and surgeons but among artists as well—most famously Leonardo da Vinci, who dissected several dozen cadavers and (with his usual preternatural inventiveness) conceived a system of intravenous injection that anticipated by several centuries the embalming methods of the modern era.

In Elizabethan England, funeral embalming—along with bloodletting, tooth extraction, and haircutting—was the exclusive province of the barber-surgeons. For more than a century, members of this powerful guild jealously guarded their legal prerogative to perform the procedure. Because of its expense, only the rich and powerful could afford it. In the early 1700s, however, a growing number of English tradesmen-undertakers—whose business had previously been confined to selling coffins and assorted mortuary paraphernalia (as well as cabinets, upholstered chairs, and other household furnishings)—began to practice cut-rate embalming: basically a crude form of human taxidermy that consisted of scooping out the viscera and filling the hollow torso with sawdust and tar.

In the meantime, various European scientists had been experimenting with the more sophisticated technique of arterial injection. Various fluids were employed in these early attempts, including arsenic-and-alcohol solutions and "camphorated spirits of wine." The results were decidedly mixed. One seventeenth-century Italian physician, Girolamo Segato, managed to turn a corpse into stone by infusing its tissues with a solution of silicate of potash.

Far more effective was the method pioneered by the celebrated eighteenth-century anatomist William Hunter, who preserved anatomical specimens with a combination of old-fashioned cavity packing and an arterial injection process that utilized oil of turpentine mixed with other ingredients. In 1775, Hunter used this procedure to embalm the wife of Martin Van Butchell, a colorful London quack, whose marriage contract supposedly stipulated that he could maintain control of his spouse's fortune only "as long as she remained above ground." Working with a colleague, Hunter injected the late Mrs. Van Butchell with his special embalming recipe (enhanced with vermillion dye to give a rosy hue to her flesh). She was then outfitted with glass eyes, garbed in a fine linen gown, and placed in a glass-lidded case for display in her husband's drawing room, where she became such a popular attraction that Van Butchell was compelled to place a notice in the London newspapers limiting visiting hours to "any day between Nine and One, Sundays excepted." Eventually, Van Butchell remarried. For some reason, his new wife wasn't thrilled about having her predecessor's corpse in the parlor, and Van Butchell was forced to donate it to the Royal College of Surgeons, where it remained until 1941, when—along with other rarities—it was destroyed during the London blitz.

Because he was the first to describe the method in print, Hunter is generally credited as "the originator of the injection technique of preserving human remains." (The great Dutch anatomist Frederik Ruysch had successfully embalmed human specimens via arterial injection a century earlier but never disclosed the details of his process or the ingredients of his fluid.) Even so, another hundred years would pass before this procedure became standard among undertakers.

In the meantime, people continued to rely on other methods of corpse preservation, including steeping dead bodies in alcoholic beverages. When Lord Nelson was killed at Trafalgar, for example, his officers—unwilling to dispose of his body at sea—stuffed him in a cask of rum so that his corpse could be returned to England. (According to legend, when the cask was eventually opened it was found to be nearly drained of liquor. Supposedly, the British sailors—unable to manage without their daily dole of rum—had surreptitiously siphoned off the liquid contents of the cask. Thereafter, the phrase "tapping the admiral" became slang for sneaking unauthorized swigs of liquor.)

In America, corpse preservation remained in a rudimentary state until the mid-nineteenth century. Simple refrigeration was the most common approach. To keep it fresh for a few days until burial, a body might be laid on a "cooling board"—a plank of wood drilled with holes and placed upon some blocks of ice. In 1846, two Baltimore undertakers patented the world's first "corpse cooler": basically a metal ice chest designed to sit atop a recumbent torso and delay the decomposition of the internal organs. More elaborate models—including "cold air caskets" equipped with easily refillable ice compartments—soon followed.

The Civil War marked the beginning of the end of the "ice age" of American corpse preservation. By the late nineteenth century, the crudely refrigerated contraptions of the antebellum era had been rendered all but obsolete by various developments in the field of embalming: the widespread manufacture and marketing of preservative fluids and the discovery of formaldehyde; the refinement of new techniques and the invention of specialized implements such as the trocar (a long, hollow needle used in cavity embalming); the founding of the first schools of embalming and the publication of the earliest textbooks on the subject; the growing professionalization of the undertaking trade; and the appearance of journals such as *Embalmer's Monthly*. By the dawn of the twentieth century, embalming was well on its way to becoming a major mortuary enterprise in the

Undertaker humor: ad for Oriental Embalming Fluid, circa 1890.

United States—the bedrock of the burgeoning death care industry.

RECOMMENDED READING

Besides providing exhaustive instruction on corpse preservation procedures, Robert G. Mayer's standard textbook, *Embalming: History, Theory, and Practice* (McGraw-Hill, 2000), contains a concise, highly readable historical survey of the subject. For an excellent work that places the development of modern embalming methods in the larger context of the Civil War and its transformative effect on the American relationship to death, check out Drew Gilpin Faust's *This Republic of Suffering* (Knopf, 2008).

DEATH FUN FACT

While certain cultures (such as the ancient Egyptians) have gone to great lengths to preserve dead bodies, others have taken the opposite tack. Ancient Greeks, for example, buried their dead in coffins carved from a special limestone that was supposed to speed decomposition. As a result, these coffins were called *sarkophagi*, or "flesh-eaters" (from the Greek *sarx*, meaning "flesh," and *phagos*, meaning "to eat"). The word *sarcophagus* subsequently came to mean any stone coffin.

Thomas Holmes

Calling someone the "father" of his particular field is the highest professional accolade that can be bestowed on a man. There's the father of medicine (Hippocrates), the father of history (Herotodus), and the father of geometry (Euclid). In the field of mortuary science, that honorific belongs to the legendary Thomas Holmes—the father of modern embalming.

Biographical facts about Holmes's early life are sketchy. A native New Yorker, he was born in 1817 into a well-to-do mercantile family and appears to have developed an early interest in medicine. He attended the College of Physicians and Surgeons of Columbia University in the early 1840s, though whether or not he received a degree is a matter of debate among his biographers. According to some sources, he was expelled before graduation because of his habit of removing cadavers from the dissection room for his own personal investigations.

In any event—with or without a degree—he managed to wangle a position as examining physician in the city's coroner's office, a job that afforded him an ample supply of cadavers for study. He remained there for several years until, at the age of thirty, he married, moved to Brooklyn, and established a thriving family practice in his Williamsburg neighborhood. By then, he had also begun experimenting with innovative embalming techniques.

Until the mid-nineteenth century, the most common methods for preserving dead bodies in the United States were either ice refrigeration or treating the body with compounds such as arsenic, mercury, and zinc,

Early embalmers occasionally displayed their handiwork in public, as portrayed in these panels from Rick Geary's graphic novel, Lower Broadway. Courtesy of Rick Geary.

whose toxic fumes made them hazardous to handle. Holmes not only concocted a more efficacious (and much safer) embalming fluid—guaranteed, or so he claimed, to preserve bodies "forever, or at least as long as stone"—but also patented a pump for injecting it into the cadaver's arteries.

He began to publicize his new technique in 1850, when he put one of his embalmed subjects on display in a lower Manhattan "undertaker's store." Thanks to extensive press coverage, the exhibit became a citywide sensation, drawing thousands of spectators.

It was the Civil War, however, that really made his reputation. In 1861, Holmes was in Washington, D.C., when Colonel Elmer E. Ellsworth, a close friend of Abraham Lincoln's, became the first prominent casualty of the conflict. Invited to handle the embalming, Holmes did such an impressive job that when the body was laid out in the East Room of the White House, the dignitary escorting Mary Lincoln declared that Ellsworth looked absolutely "natural, as though he were sleeping a brief and peaceful sleep."

Holmes's success earned him a commission as an official "embalmer-surgeon" for the military. There was an urgent need for a man of his skills. Thousands of young soldiers were dying far from their homes. The arterial injection embalming method pioneered by Holmes made it possible to keep their bodies in a decent state of preservation during the long voyage back to their families.

Of course, there were only so many casualties he and his assistants could handle. He soon had plenty of competitors who employed his techniques while aggressively (not to say shamelessly) promoting their own services. Some posted handbills along the roadsides, where passing troops would be sure to see them. Others sent employees to the front lines to distribute circulars complete with prices ($50 for an officer, $25 for an enlisted man, coffins included). Still others ran newspaper ads with attention-grabbing slogans:

Bodies Embalmed by Us
NEVER TURN BLACK
But retain their natural color and appearance!

Little wonder that one Union general put a stop to these "ghastly advertisements" since they were having such a "demoralizing influence" on his men.

Before the war ended, Holmes himself had resigned his commission and opened a private business in Washington, charging twice as much as his less-renowned rivals to embalm, box, and ship a body home. In later years, he estimated that between 1861 and 1865, he had personally embalmed "4,028 soldiers and officers, field and staff."

Back in Brooklyn after the war, Holmes—who was then operating a neighborhood drugstore—continued to experiment with his embalming fluid. Dissatisfied with his original formula—which had a tendency to distort the features of his subjects—he eventually concocted a new and improved brand that he called Innominata and sold for $3 a gallon. The show window of his pharmacy was an attention grabber, featuring prominent signs for both his embalming fluid and a homemade root beer he had perfected in his lab. There was also a preserved human arm on a marble slab.

After his death in 1900, workmen found a number of bodies buried in his cellar. At first, Holmes was suspected of having been a homicidal maniac, but the police quickly determined that the corpses—most of them young children and infants—had been legally obtained from the city morgue and used as subjects for his experiments. In accordance with his last wishes, Holmes himself—who believed to the last that no one besides himself could do a decent job of preserving the dead—was buried unembalmed.

RECOMMENDED READING

If you can get hold of it (which is easier than it used to be, now that the entire run of the magazine is available on CD), there's a fine, lively bio of Holmes—"That Was New York: The First Embalmer" by Trentwell Mason White and Ivan Sandrof—in the November 7, 1942, issue of the *New Yorker*.

Equal-Opportunity Embalming

During the early years of the American embalming business, the vast majority of practitioners were white guys. Even back then, however, there were a few notable exceptions—pioneering death workers who brought a bit of diversity to the trade.

During the Civil War, when the process of arterial injection embalming first became popularized through the efforts of Thomas Holmes and other military embalmer-surgeons, an African American slave named Prince Greer arrived at the Nashville home of a Tennessee undertaker named W. P. Cornelius. Inside Greer's buckboard was the body of his master, one Colonel Greer, a member of a Texas cavalry regiment who had been slain in battle. Fulfilling his master's dying wish, Greer asked Cornelius to embalm the body so that it could be shipped back home to Texas.

Once the job was done, Prince Greer asked if he could remain at Cornelius's premises and indicated that he would be willing to perform whatever chores were required to earn his room and board. Cornelius—who had just lost the services of his assistant, a young army doctor named E. C. Lewis who had been trained by Holmes himself—offered to teach Greer how to embalm. The results were later described by Cornelius in his memoirs:

> Prince Greer appeared to enjoy embalming so much that he himself became an expert, kept on at work embalming during the balance of the war and was very successful at it. It was but a short time before he could raise an artery as quickly as anyone and was always careful, always of course coming to me in a difficult case. He remained with me until I quit the business in 1871.

What became of Prince Greer in later years is unknown, but his work with Cornelius makes him the first documented African American embalmer in U.S. history.

Women took a bit longer to break into the business. Perhaps the most important early female embalmer was Mme. Lina D. Odou (1853—1919). The daughter of a French diplomat, Odou had a cosmopolitan upbringing, traveling with her family around the capitals of Europe. While living in London in 1868, she met and befriended Florence Nightingale, who became a mentor to the fifteen-year-old girl. After training as a nurse, Odou served with the Red Cross in France, then spent several years working privately for various aristocratic families throughout Europe.

It was during this period that she became aware of a pressing need for women embalmers. Victorian prudery was at its height. To many people, the thought of a male embalmer handling the unclothed body of a beloved female relative was unacceptable. "Over and over again," Odou later explained, "I heard mothers ask undertakers if they could not furnish women embalmers for their dead daughters, and many others to whom the dead are sacred asked the same question." Odou resolved to master the skill herself.

After studying in Switzerland, she moved to the United States, where she continued her training under some of the leading figures in the burgeoning field of mortuary education, including Auguste Renouard and A. Johnson Dodge, founders of two of the earliest schools of embalming in the United States. By 1901, Odou had formed a partnership with the famed New York City undertaker Frank E. Campbell and, in early 1901, opened the Lina D. Odou Embalming Institute at Campbell's funeral establishment on West Twenty-third Street in Manhattan.

In the following years, Odou and her assistants handled all the female corpses at Campbell's. At the same time, she became a forceful advocate for the education of female undertakers, publishing editorials on the subject in trade journals and founding the Women's Licensed Embalmer Association. Her example inspired other pioneers in the field, including Mrs. E. G. Bernard of Newark, New Jersey, and Lena R. Simons of Syracuse, New York, both of whom founded embalming schools of their own.

Unsung Heroes of the Death Industry: Roy F. McCampbell

Back in the early years of the twentieth century, when electricity was transforming the world, countless Thomas Edison wannabes were cranking out all kinds of electrical contraptions. Marketed under impressive-sounding, pseudo-scientific names—the Dynamizer, the Spectro-Chrome, the Electro-Magneto Resonator—these crackpot devices were touted as miracle cures for everything from baldness and backaches to blindness and cancer.

Quack healers weren't the only ones devising bizarre, futuristic gizmos. In the 1920s, one enterprising Chicago undertaker got in on the act. His name was Roy F. McCampbell, and he occupies a special place in the annals of embalming as the first (and, so far as is known, only) person ever to try preserving a human body by means of electrical current.

According to an article in the May 1923 issue of the trade magazine *Undertaker's Journal*, McCampbell, after years of "laborious toil," had succeeded in manufacturing a machine that could mummify a cadaver at the flip of a switch. After experimenting on a bunch of cats and dogs, he tried out his device on a human subject, the male "victim of a fatal gunshot wound." The powerful electrical currents not only caused the complete dehydration of the corpse—reducing its weight by fully one-fifth—but (according to McCampbell) "positively killed" all the bacteria conducive to putrefaction. The results were impressive: a beautifully preserved (if somewhat shrunken) body with a face that "retained its naturalness."

Measuring seven feet in height, eight feet in length, and more than three feet in width, the one-and-a-half-ton apparatus was, as the article put it, "not of a portable nature." An accompanying photograph depicts something that resembles an MRI machine in the shape of a Medici tomb: an enormous white sarcophagus with a sliding body-tray and an instrument panel full of dials, gauges, and switches.

Besides the convenience of the process, McCampbell proudly proclaimed its great economy, estimating that—"when figured in terms of kilowatt hours"—the approximate cost for embalming a full-grown adult body was "eighteen to twenty-five cents." Sadly, this groundbreaking invention never caught on, and McCampbell's prototype seems to have vanished forever.

Embalming: Don't Try This at Home

Undertakers will tell you that embalming is both an art and a science (though their concept of "art" tends to be a tad different from yours and mine; as one standard textbook puts it, "The *art* of embalming is the raising of the vessel, but the *science* of embalming is knowing which vessel to raise"). In any case, it's a complex procedure that can be performed only by a board-licensed practitioner who has graduated from an accredited mortuary school and put in one to two years of apprenticeship at a funeral home.

Though no two cases are alike—a body afflicted with crippling arthritis presents different problems from, say, the autopsied corpse of a shotgun victim—the basic steps of embalming are as follows:

1. Don the appropriate protective gear: waterproof bodysuit, surgical cap, latex gloves, shoe covers, gauze mask, and plastic goggles.
2. Place the body on a stainless steel or porcelain embalming table. (Make sure the person is actually dead. Having a body leap up with a howl when the first needle is inserted can be very disconcerting for everyone involved.)
3. Remove all clothing and valuables from the body, including jewelry, religious articles, and expensive Swiss watches. Resist any temptation to pocket the last. (Remember your embalmer's code of ethics!)
4. Disinfect the body by spraying or sponging it with a strong disinfectant solution, then scrub it with germicidal soap. Shampoo the hair, clean under the fingernails, swab out the mouth and nasal passages. Shave the face clean of hair (even on women and children), unless the corpse sports a particular style of facial adornment—whiskers, goatee, walrus moustache, et cetera—in which case you should trim it neatly.
5. Arrange the body into the position you wish it to assume in the coffin. Since rigor mortis will have already set in, this entails massaging the muscles and flexing the limbs to make them more pliable for manipulation. The head should be elevated on a rubber block (which will ultimately be replaced by a casket pillow) and tilted slightly to the right, so that when the mourners approach the open casket at the time of the viewing they will see the full face of the deceased, not simply the profile.
6. Close and secure the eyes so that the person seems to be sleeping peacefully. This is done by inserting a plastic, lens-shaped "eyecap" under each lid. Little spurs on the cap hold the lids in place. For extra insurance, you may also superglue the upper and lower lids together, taking care not to mess up the eyelashes.
7. Close and secure the mouth by the method of your choice. The most common involves a spring-activated "needle injector"—a kind of surgical staple gun that shoots wired barbs deep into the upper and lower gums, allowing the jaws to be drawn shut. The mouth can then be worked into a natural position using cotton, creams, and mortuary putty.
8. This completes the preparation stage of the procedure. You may now proceed with the actual embalming. There are two stages to the process. The first is known as *arterial embalming*: replacing the blood with formaldehyde-based preservative. After filling the tank of your embalming machine with your favorite brand of fluid, select a suitable spot on the body—for example, the left side of the neck near the collarbone—and make an incision with a sharp scalpel. Then, using a wire hook, probe the gash until you have located the carotid artery and gently pull this vessel to the surface. (This will be your injection site.) Now do the same with the neighboring jugular vein. (This will serve as the drainage vessel.)
9. Insert the injection tube of the embalming machine into the exposed artery and a

drainage hose into the vein. Hit the on switch to start the machine pumping. As the embalming solution circulates through the arteries, the blood will be forced out through the veins, exit via the drainage hose into the gutter of the embalming table, and disappear down a porcelain basin (or "slop sink") hooked directly to the municipal sewer system.

10. Once the blood has been completely exchanged for embalming fluid, the arterial tube and drainage hose are removed, the blood vessels tied off, and the incision at the base of the neck sutured. It is now time for stage two: suctioning out the goop from the body's internal organs and replacing it with preservative—a process known as *cavity embalming*.
11. Take your trocar (a long, hollow metal tube that terminates in an arrowlike point and is connected at the other end to an electric pump known as an aspirator) and thrust it into the corpse's abdomen. Poke it around so that it punctures each of the internal organs in turn—heart, lungs, stomach, colon, intestines, liver, and bladder—and suck out the contents.
12. Once you have vacuumed out the viscera, remove the trocar, disconnect it from the aspirator, and attach the hose to a bottle of formaldehyde. Shove the trocar back into the abdomen and flood the cavity with the fluid. Remove the trocar and close the unsightly external puncture holes either by suturing them or by plugging them with threaded plastic doodads known as "trocar buttons." Pack the anus and (where appropriate) vagina with phenol-soaked cotton. Rewash and dry the body.
13. The embalming is now complete and the cadaver is ready to receive the undertaker's final and most artful ministrations: the cosmetic "restoration" intended to transform even the most gruesomely deformed cadaver into a handsome semblance of its formerly living self—a "beautiful memory picture," in the lingo of the trade.

RECOMMENDED READING

If you're looking for a professional textbook that will teach you everything you need to know about embalming, you can't do better than the third edition of Robert G. Mayer's *Embalming: History, Theory, and Practice* (McGraw-Hill, 2000). For a vivid, powerfully written account of a typical embalming—one that will really make you feel what it's like to perform the procedure—check out "The Embalming of Jenny Johnson," the opening chapter of Mark Harris's *Grave Matters: A Journey Through the Modern Funeral Industry to a Natural Way of Burial* (Scribner, 2007). Jessica Mitford also offers a vivid and typically acerbic description in *The American Way of Death* (Simon & Schuster, 1963).

If embalming is taken out of the funeral, then viewing the body will also be lost. If viewing is lost, then the body itself will not be central to the funeral. If the body is taken out of the funeral, then what does the funeral director have to sell?

—John Kroshus (as quoted by Jessica Mitford)

How to Beat the High Cost of Embalming (Hint: Skip It)

Many people assume that a dead body must be embalmed before burial. This is a belief that undertakers are only too happy to encourage since it allows them to add a few thousand extra dollars to their (already hefty) bills. The only problem is, it's simply not true.

Up until the mid-nineteenth century, bodies were rarely embalmed in America since the modern arterial injection technique wasn't invented until the Civil War. Once perfected, it quickly became the cornerstone of the burgeoning funeral industry—the specialized, quasi-scientific procedure only a certified mortician could perform. By the mid-twentieth century, corpses were embalmed so routinely that most people assumed it was obligatory. It wasn't until the 1963 publication of Jessica Mitford's landmark exposé, *The American Way of Death*, that the public learned the truth: that embalming is a very recent and peculiarly American practice based on a number of dubious rationales.

Some traditions forbid it altogether. Orthodox Judaism, for example, decrees that a person must be buried within twenty-four hours of death and allowed to decompose naturally in the earth. But even if you're not Jewish (or Muslim, another faith that regards embalming as a form of desecration), there are few compelling reasons to be embalmed.

Just a handful of states require it by law—and only in highly specific circumstances. (In Kansas, Idaho, and Minnesota, embalming is mandatory if a body is to be shipped by plane or other common carrier; in Alaska and New Jersey, it's required if the body is to be transported out of state and won't reach its destination within twenty-four hours of death; and in Alabama, it must be done for any out-of-state transport by any means.) It is not required in *any* state if burial takes place within twenty-four hours.

Despite the claims of morticians who insist that embalming helps safeguard society from contagious disease, medical authorities have determined that unembalmed corpses pose no threat to the public health. And though grieving survivors like to think that embalming will keep their loved ones in a state of eternal preservation, the sad fact is that even a corpse treated with heavy-duty chemicals will eventually rot.

So why embalm? The usual reason is to prepare the body for the traditional viewing at a funeral home. Even in this case, however, embalming isn't necessary if the mortuary is equipped with refrigeration facilities.

And, of course, there are alternatives to a prolonged public display of the deceased. Family members can view the body privately right after death, then keep the casket closed at the funeral home. A visitation—at which friends and family members gather to offer condolence and comfort to the bereaved—can also be held at home without the body present at all.

In short, "beyond the fact that embalming is good business for the undertaker" (as Mitford writes), there aren't a whole lot of persuasive reasons to do it.

Death Fun Fact

The word *hearse* can be traced back to the Latin word *hirpex*, meaning "rake" or "harrow" (a piece of farming equipment that, in the old days, consisted of a wood frame fitted with iron teeth, used to break up clods in plowed land). Since hearses bear no resemblance at all to either of these agricultural implements, this seems to be a puzzling etymology.

Originally, however, the term *hearse* was not applied to a vehicle used to transport corpses to the cemetery—for the simple reason that such vehicles didn't exist before the early 1600s. Back then, people were buried so close to home that their bodies were simply carried to the local churchyard on the shoulders of family members or friends. During the funeral service, however, the coffin was often enclosed within an ornamental framework of wood or wrought-iron. These structures had spikes sticking from the top to hold candles or other decorations (such as banners, in the case of the aristocracy). "With its rows of upended spikes," writes funeral vehicle historian Walter M. P. McCall, "the ornamental framework indeed resembled an inverted rake or farm harrow."

Eventually, these ceremonial structures—known as *herses*—became so elaborate that some of them looked like miniature Gothic cathedrals. As they grew more cumbersome, and as cemeteries were laid out at greater and greater distances from densely populated towns, they could no longer be carried to the gravesite by hand. They were placed on wheels and drawn to the cemetery by horses. By the mid-seventeenth century, the term *hearse* had assumed its modern meaning.

American Hearses: Going in Style

We tend to assume that our modern-day inventions are always better than the once-trendy objects they replaced. And this is often the case. A pocket-size cell phone that can take pictures, download video games, and play "Highway to Hell" when it rings is considerably cooler than a princess telephone with an illuminated dial.

Still, there are exceptions. Take automobiles. While today's boxy, nondescript cars may outdo their predecessors in terms of gas mileage, safety features, and comfort, there's no way that a Honda Civic can match, say, a 1959 Chevy Impala for sheer automotive pizzazz.

The same holds true in another vehicular category: hearses. A brand-new Cadillac Medalist "funeral coach" may offer the latest in graveyard transport technology: galvanized steel inner structure, patented loading door, sixteen-roller bier for easier casket handling. But sleek as it may be, it's still a pretty stodgy

Fourteenth-century wrought-iron hearse.

piece of machinery compared to some of the amazingly designed hearses of the past.

Though the average early American hearse was little more than a black-painted farm wagon pulled by a single horse, fancy funeral equipages had become standard by the mid-nineteenth century. The well-appointed hearse of the post–Civil War era typically had tasseled velvet drapes behind French plate-glass windows, a roof ornamented with decorative wooden urns, a cloth-covered driver's seat flanked by tall carriage lamps, and a matched set of black horses. Styles became even more lavish as the century progressed. By the 1890s, the finest American "funeral cars" featured intricately carved wooden panels in the shape of heavy draperies, ornate side columns, silver-plated roof rails, and other embellishments.

Apart from ceremonial occasions such as state funerals, horse-drawn hearses essentially disappeared from the American scene by the start of World War I. As early as 1905 (according to funeral transport historian Walter M. P. McCall), at least one enterprising undertaker had mounted a hearse body onto an automobile chassis. Four years later, the Crane and Breed Company of Cincinnati introduced the world's first factory-built "auto-hearse." Equipped with a four-cylinder, thirty-horsepower engine, the inaugural model was a black-painted trucklike affair with a single, somewhat bizarre decoration sitting on its roof: a facsimile of the famed tomb of Scipio, an ancient Roman sarcophagus housed in the Vatican museum. Within a few months, a new and more lavishly appointed model was on the market. In addition to the rooftop replica of Scipio's tomb, this one featured the traditional design elements found on Victorian hearses: richly carved wood draperies framed by elaborate columns. By 1919, the tall, boxlike, heavily adorned automotive hearse—essentially the body of a horse-drawn "funeral car" attached to a motorized chassis—had become the industry standard.

Like virtually everything else in American culture, from women's clothing to pop music to sexual mores, hearse fashion underwent a radical change during the Roaring Twenties. Apart from a few manufacturers who clung to old-fashioned styles, U.S. makers of funeral vehicles switched to a jazzy modern design in keeping with the spirit of the age. The new look, which came into vogue in the first years of the decade, was the long low limousine. While a few models were decked out with the usual gloomy adornments, most were so uncluttered that—apart

Evolution of the American hearse, 1883–1968.
Courtesy of Walter P. McCall Collection.

from the cast metal "funeral coach" nameplates displayed in the windshields—it was virtually impossible to distinguish them from luxury passenger cars.

By the time of the Great Depression, however, the once-snazzy limousine hearse, with its low rectangular body, had come to seem staid and outmoded. The preferred new look during the 1930s featured a curvy, aerodynamic coach. At the same time, ornate side panels of carved wood made to resemble draperies—a design element dating back to the horse-drawn era—made a major comeback. The resulting combination of streamlined bodies bedecked with Victorian embellishments resulted in some truly spectacular vehicles, such as the lavishly draped eight-columned Sayers and Scovill Olympian model of 1934 and the 1939 Eureka, whose interior—with Gothic inlaid wood ornamentation, sconce lights, and statuary angels—resembled a miniature cathedral.

As the 1940s dawned, various hearse makers continued to decorate their vehicles with carved wood panels (some in the shape of arched church windows instead of drapes). The outbreak of World War II, however, put an abrupt halt to funeral car production. Like the rest of the U.S. auto industry, hearse makers devoted their resources to the war effort, turning out a variety of specialized military vehicles. When hearse production resumed in the mid-forties, fashions had changed again. The old carved-panel look was gone for good. In its place was the stately "landau" hearse, featuring a faux-leather rear roof with bow-shaped chrome bars on either side.

The 1950s witnessed the last gasp of

really eye-catching hearses, with some of the spiffier models sporting such typically space-age features as rocket-ship fins and twin-bullet taillights. Since then, all trace of ostentation has vanished from American funeral coaches, which now conform to a single style, the impeccably tasteful landau hearse: stately, dignified, and so devoid of personality that only a corpse could love it.

RECOMMENDED READING

Thomas McPherson's out-of-print *American Funeral Cars and Ambulances Since 1900* (Crestline, 1973) is the bible of serious hearse historians. A more up-to-date survey is Walter M. P. McCall's lavishly illustrated *American Funeral Vehicles 1883–2003*, one of the many highly specialized books for "transportation enthusiasts" published by the Iconografix company of Hudson, Wisconsin.

Hearses for the Harley Crowd

Few people are as image-conscious as bikers. If you're roaring down the highway on a customized chopper, you've got to look the part: bald head, handlebar 'stache, massive arms covered with the perfect mix of patriotic and satanic tattoos, a black T-shirt printed with a bad-ass slogan on back: "If you can read this, the bitch fell off." That sort of thing.

Given how important it is to maintain

HEARSE OF THE RISING SUN

American hearse makers have produced some spectacular vehicles over the years (such as the limited-edition 1929 Sayers and Scovill "Signed Sculpture" model, with bronze relief side panels depicting a grieving angel clutching a memorial wreath). For sheer exotic splendor, however, nothing made in the United States matches a Japanese *reikyusha*.

Used to transport a body from the funeral home to the crematorium, the *reikyusha* is an eye-popping hybrid of modern automotive technology and traditional Asian design. Its body consists of a standard luxury car, such as a Cadillac or a Toyota Crown, which is subjected to a radical modification. The roof behind the driver's seat is cut away and the entire rear section of the car is converted into a kind of flatbed onto which is mounted an elaborately carved wooden shrine, covered in gold and adorned with dragons, lions, and other traditional devices. The result resembles a miniature Buddhist temple grafted onto a limo.

The earliest prototypes of the *reikyusha* first appeared around 1910, though it was not until the post–World War II era that a Tokyo hearse maker named Yonezu Saburo began producing these vehicles on a large scale. Today, the Yonezu Corporation manufactures about 70 percent of all Japanese hearses.

this outlaw image from cradle to grave, no self-respecting biker, after living fast and dying young, is going to want to be conveyed to the cemetery in anything as stodgy as an ordinary limousine hearse. Fortunately, a few visionary entrepreneurs have come up with the perfect solution: the motorcycle hearse.

This ingenious product comes in two styles. Most popular is the sidecar model. Though its history is a little vague, it appears to have been pioneered in the United Kingdom following World War II, when motorcycle enthusiasts began removing their sidecars so that coffins could be carried on the chassis. The practice grew in popularity throughout the 1990s, particularly among British bikers. In 2002, the Reverend Paul Sinclair, a Pentecostal minister based in Derbyshire, England, launched a company called Motorcycle Funerals Ltd. (www.motorcyclefunerals.com), Britain's first (and only) provider of professional sidecar hearse funeral services.

Motorcycle hearse. Courtesy of Al Skinner Enterprises, LLC.

Here at home, a number of individuals have entered the same business. For a modest fee of $300 plus $1 per mile round trip from his headquarters in Wrightsville, Pennsylvania, Al Skinner of Biker Burials (www.bikerburials.com) will transport his motorcycle hearse—a Harley-Davidson Road King with custom-built sidecar assembly—to your home and carry your dear departed to the grave in *Easy Rider* style. The Starwalt Motorcycle Hearse Company of Springfield, Illinois (www.motorcycle-hearse.com), offers a similar service with a high-tech hydraulic rig for convenient casket handling. Starwalt also offers its sidecar hearses for sale, so for a mere $14,200 (or $5,500 for a basic nonelevating model) you can start your very own motorcycle funeral business—or just ride around with a coffin attached to your chopper, an accessory guaranteed to enhance your hell-on-wheels rep.

Bikers nostalgic for the vanished glories of the American past—when the bullet-ridden bodies of sociopathic Western outlaws were conveyed to Boot Hill in high style—might prefer the second, more elaborate type of motorcycle hearse. This consists of a full-scale old-fashioned glass-sided hearse hitched to a three-wheeled "trike" motorcycle. You can hire or purchase one of these impressive rigs from the Tombstone Hearse Company of Alum Bank, Pennsylvania (www.tombstonehearse.com). Another outfit, Justin Carriage Works of Nashville, Michigan, also sells handsome pseudo-

Victorian trailer-style motorcycle hearses, along with a wide range of other handcrafted vintage vehicles (www.buggy.com).

All Aboard for the Cemetery!

One of the more curious contraptions ever built was the self-contained, all-in-one "funeral bus," which enjoyed a deservedly brief life in the years just before and after World War I. Designed to eliminate the need for multivehicle processions, this colossal conveyance, the size of a trolley car, was big enough to accommodate an entire funeral party—undertaker, pallbearers, and two dozen mourners—along with the casket. Though used briefly in a few big cities, the funeral bus never caught on and quickly lapsed into extinction (you can see one of the few surviving examples, a 1916 Packard model, at Houston's National Museum of Funeral History).

Hearse Clubs: For Connoisseurs of Fine Vintage Funeral Coaches

Some people grow sad when they pass a funeral cortege on the road. Others feel a twinge of superstitious dread. And then there are those who look at the lead vehicle and think, "Wow, that's one sweet ride!"

If you fall into the latter category, you might consider joining one of the many "hearse clubs" that have sprung up across the country. The members of these organizations share a deep appreciation of vintage funeral vehicles (many of which are indeed masterpieces of automotive craftsmanship). They buy and lovingly restore old hearses (as well as funeral limousines and flower cars), drive them around on weekends, have festive get-togethers, and exchange photos, anecdotes, and customizing tips in newsletters and on websites. In short, they are no different from any other automotive aficionados—except the objects of their affection aren't old Studebakers or Corvette convertibles but '62 Cadillac Royale side-loading funeral coaches and '41 Meteor hearses with carved Gothic side panels. Plus, they tend to have more facial piercings than the average member of the Antique Automobile Club of America.

Indeed, in recent years, a schism has developed between those collectors (often members of the funeral industry) who take their hobby very seriously and believe that hearse owners should comport themselves with a befitting dignity and the growing ranks of (often heavily tattooed and leather-clad) individuals who like to tool around in funeral vehicles for the sheer transgressive fun of it. The latter are likely to outfit their rides with ghoulish vanity plates (DST 2 DST, YOU NEXT, etc.), keep a coffin in the rear compartment, and, on special occasions, drive around with a life-size skeleton in the passenger seat.

One of the better-known hearse clubs is Grim Rides. Founded by Amy "the Hearse Queen" Shanafelt of Sunnyvale, California, Grim Rides is a group of self-described "funeral car fiends" who "get together once in a blue moon to hang out and talk hearses."

The club also maintains an impressive website that features classified ads, a nationwide directory of hearse clubs, a catalogue of funeral-related toys and model kits, a bookstore, and a truly mind-boggling filmography of every movie in which a hearse appears, however fleetingly (including *The Muppet Movie*, *The Brave Little Toaster*, and *That Darn Cat!*). You can also view the photo gallery of hot babes posed beside (or atop) vintage hearses and visit the online store to order Grim Rides T-shirts. Check it all out at: http://members.aol.com/hearseq/grimrides.htm. Other hearse club websites worth visiting are:

www.hearsedriver.com

www.angelfire.com/zine/TheHearseEnthusiast

www.gravesights.org

www.hearseclub.com

www.phantomcoaches.org (which, upon being opened, will regale you with a performance of Chopin's famous funeral march)

www.societyoffuneralcoaches.com (not a hearse club but an online gathering place where devotees of mortuary transport can share their passion)

Mortuary Masterpiece: The 1921 Rock Falls Hearse

If you've been dying to get a good look at a classic American hearse but can't make it to the National Museum of Funeral History, you're in luck. Just go to the museum's website at www.nmfh.org and follow the menu to the 1921 Rock Falls Hearse. There, you will be able to take a guided tour of one of the most opulent "funeral coaches" ever built in this country.

Constructed by the Rock Falls Manufacturing Company of Sterling, Illinois, this eye-popping vehicle measures eight feet in height and more than nineteen feet in length. Individual links on the virtual tour allow you to examine every amazing detail, from its six-cylinder Continental "Red Seal" engine to its lavish interior (complete with a stained-glass window on the divider between the cab and rear compartment) and its intricately hand-carved wooden body (which took craftsmen more than a year to complete).

Of course, nothing beats a firsthand view of this beauty, so if you're ever in Houston, head out to 415 Barren Springs Drive, where you'll be able to marvel at this and other amazing specimens of the hearse maker's art.

Funerals: The Consumer's Last Rights

As cultural historian Gary Laderman points out in his excellent study *Rest in Peace* (Oxford University Press, 2003), efforts to reform American funeral practices date at least as far back as the 1920s, when a book by one Quincy L. Dowd denounced the undertaking trade for encouraging "foolish consumer impulses" in the public. In the following years, other, similar books appeared, deploring both the public's appetite for "vulgar display" and the funeral industry's readiness to feed it with extravagantly wasteful burial ceremonies.

It wasn't until the publication of Jessica Mitford's *The American Way of Death* in 1963, however, that funeral industry fraud became a cause célèbre in this country. Mitford's scathing exposé—made even more devastating by her caustic wit—set off a media firestorm, raising public awareness of the greed, gouging, and outright deception rife in the undertaking business.

Even so, another decade passed before the federal government—under pressure from consumer rights crusaders—finally took action. After several years of hearings, the FTC instituted a trade rule designed to protect the public from the predatory practices of unscrupulous funeral providers.

According to the Funeral Rule, undertakers must:

- provide printed itemized price lists for their goods and services
- offer price information over the telephone

- disclose that, except in certain special cases, embalming is not required by law
- allow the consumer to purchase a coffin elsewhere (from a discount online dealer, for example) and not charge a fee for its use
- make "alternative containers" of unfinished wood, cardboard, or other inexpensive material available for direct cremations

Today, there is no shortage of consumer advice available to the public. Even the National Funeral Directors Association, the main lobbying group for the death care industry, offers consumer resources on its website (www.nfda.org). Far more detailed is the guide posted by the Federal Trade Commission, which you'll find at www.ftc.gov/bcp/conline/edcams/funerals/coninfo.htm.

As all funeral industry watchdogs will tell you, saving money on funerals boils down to a few very basic principles, the same ones that apply to any significant purchase:

1. *Shop around.* Compare prices from at least two funeral homes. You can visit them in person or inquire over the phone. Also, check out casket prices at various online suppliers for the best deals. If you can do this in advance—before the need arises—so much the better.
2. *Get a written price list.* All funeral homes are required to provide a printed general price list, specifying their fees.
3. *Avoid "emotional overspending."* Funeral directors often play on the heartstrings of vulnerable family members in an effort to get them to spring for the costliest funeral. Remember: you don't need to go into debt to honor the memory of your loved one.
4. *Know your rights.* Laws regarding burial vary from state to state. It's important to know which goods and services are mandatory and which optional. The bible for this information is Lisa Carlson's *Caring for the Dead: Your Final Act of Love* (Upper Access, 1998).
5. *Simplify, simplify.* By following Henry David Thoreau's famous injunction, you can cut costs on funeral expenses. Experts suggest, for example, that you limit the viewing to one day (or even one hour) before the funeral, dress your loved one's body in a favorite outfit instead of exorbitantly expensive burial clothing, purchase a simple coffin in lieu of the $5,0000 mahogany model, hold an intimate personal memorial in some place that was meaningful to the deceased and forgo an elaborate service in a rented chapel, et cetera.

RECOMMENDED RESOURCES

The torch first ignited by Jessica Mitford is currently being carried by the folks at the Funeral Consumers Alliance, the nonprofit educational organization that keeps close tabs on the death care trade and publishes a very helpful series of pamphlets, including *Ten Tips for Saving on Funerals*, *Common Funeral Myths*, and *How to File a Funeral Complaint* (see page 128).

Another important source of funeral-related facts is the AARP, which offers several good publications on the topic, including one called *Funeral Goods and Services*. You can get it free of charge by writing to AARP Fulfillment, 601 E Street, NW, Washington, DC 20049, or going to the website, www.aarp.org.

Online, you'll find loads of consumer information, including links to dozens of articles, at a site called FuneralHelp.com. An indispensable book is the aforementioned *Caring for the Dead* by consumer firebrand Lisa Carlson, executive director of the FCA. This thick volume is both a muckraking exposé in the Mitford tradition and an exhaustive how-to guide that will keep you from getting ripped off. Included is a complete state-by-state guide to funeral regulations.

"Fancy Funeral"

Though it seems doubtful that the highborn British muckraker Jessica Mitford spent much time listening to country music, she would undoubtedly have endorsed the sentiment behind Lucinda Williams's song "Fancy Funeral" from her 2007 CD, West. Here's how it goes:

Some think a fancy funeral
Would be worth every cent
But for every dime and nickel
There's money better spent

Better spent on groceries
And covering the bills
Instead of little luxuries
And unnecessary frills

Lovely yellow daffodils
And lacy filigree
Pretty little angels
For everyone to see

Lily of the valley
And long black limousines
It's three or four months' salary
Just to pay for all those things

So don't buy a fancy funeral
It's not worth it in the end
Goodbyes can still be beautiful
Without the money that you'll spend

'Cause no amount of riches
Can bring back what you've lost
To satisfy your wishes
You'll never justify the cost

FCA, USA

Funeral Consumers Alliance is a nationwide federation of nonprofit "information societies" dedicated to "protecting a consumer's right to a dignified, meaningful affordable funeral." It is headquartered in Burlington, Vermont, with affiliates in virtually every state of the Union.

Among other vital services performed by this worthy organization, FCA acts as a mortuary watchdog, closely monitoring the funeral industry and exposing its abuses. It also offers a series of how-to pamphlets, containing practical and levelheaded advice on topics ranging from funeral preplanning to grief management to money-saving burial tips.

A particularly useful publication available from FCA is *Before I Go, You Should Know: My Funeral and Final Plans*. Adorned with deliciously macabre drawings by Edward Gorey, this sixteen-page booklet allows you "to stay in charge of your affairs right up to the end of your life and even a bit beyond" by recording your last wishes: whether or not you want to be buried, cremated, embalmed, viewed, memorialized, et cetera. You can check off the kind of coffin (or urn) you prefer, write down what you do and do *not* want at your funeral service, and include facts useful for an obituary and death certificate. It also lets your survivors know where to find important papers (e.g., your life insurance policies, bank accounts, etc.) that will facilitate the orderly handling of your estate.

As a safe but readily accessible place to store it, the folks at FCA recommend the inside of your refrigerator or freezer. To that end, the booklet comes packaged in a heavy plastic envelope with a Gorey-designed refrigerator magnet labeled "Matters of Life and Death Inside."

To learn more about this organization, become a member; order *Before I Go* kits, how-to pamphlets, and other publications; then write to Funeral Consumers Alliance, 33 Patchen Road, South Burlington, VT 05403 or go to www.funerals.org.

Scams and What to Do About Them

There's no doubt that only a tiny percentage of funeral directors are outright crooks. Even Jessica Mitford acknowledged that the "vast majority" of undertakers subscribe to a code of ethics. The problem, as she saw it, is that the code itself is inherently self-serving: designed for the benefit of the businessmen, not the consumers. While undertakers like to think of themselves as high-minded professionals, most of them (according to Mitford) are really "merchants of a rather grubby order, preying on the grief, remorse, and guilt of survivors."

Through decades of trial and error, the American death care industry has perfected ingenious ways of pressuring people into spending outrageous sums on extravagant funerals. Professional service manuals, for example, teach something called the "keystone approach" to coffin sales—a method of arranging casket showrooms that, through subtle psychological manipulation, discourages consumers from buying the cheapest models. There's nothing really deceptive about such a technique. It's just good old-fashioned (albeit slightly sleazy) salesmanship. If you want to learn more about this and other tactics used by undertakers to squeeze every last penny from grieving survivors, you can't do better than Mitford's classic *The American Way of Death*, Lisa Carlson's *Caring for the Dead*, or *Profits of Death* by former funeral industry insider Darryl J. Roberts.

Beyond everyday ploys such as the "keystone approach," there are a number of flat-out frauds that consumers occasionally encounter. Here are a few to watch out for:

1. *The old bait-and-switch*. Unscrupulous undertakers have been known to charge a premium for a deluxe casket or urn, then deliver a much cheaper item, claiming that the original model is no longer

available but that the substitute is of equivalent value.

2. *Sham "discounts."* To entice people into buying a coffin directly from their funeral home (instead of purchasing one at a lower cost from an outside source), some shady undertakers will offer a supposed "package deal" with a reduced-price coffin. Instead of the list price of, say, $4,000, the consumer will only have to pay $2,500 for the very same model. It seems like a bargain. What the consumer doesn't know, however, is that the undertaker has tacked an additional $1,500 service fee onto the bill to make up the difference.
3. *Misrepresentation.* In violation of the Federal Trade Commission's Funeral Rule, some undertakers will mislead consumers into making unnecessary purchases—by telling them, for example, that embalming is required, or that they must buy an expensive coffin for a cremation, or that a high-priced reinforced-concrete grave liner is mandatory at a particular cemetery, or that a deluxe "protective" casket will preserve a body indefinitely.
4. *Pre-need shenanigans.* People who enter into pre-need arrangements—paying in advance for their own funerals—naturally assume that they are covering all expenses so that their families won't have to worry when the time comes. It's a shock, then, when—as sometimes happens—survivors are told that there is an extra charge for certain basic services (such as opening and closing the grave) or that the coffin that comes with the contract is a cut-rate "nonprotective" model and if they want one with a "protective" sealer, they'll have to upgrade at a cost of an additional $600.

If you encounter these or any other rip-offs, the Funeral Consumers Alliance recommends that you take certain steps. First, try to resolve matters directly with the funeral home. If that doesn't work, you might have to file an official complaint. According to the FCA pamphlet *How to File a Funeral or Cemetery Complaint* (available upon request from Funeral Consumers Alliance, 33 Patchen Road, South Burlington, VT 05403, 800-765-0107):

> All states, except Colorado and Hawaii, have a funeral board or agency that regulates funeral directors. About half the states have some sort of cemetery regulation. Your complaint should be addressed to the regulatory board when there is one. In addition, if there's a possibility of criminal action, it would be a good idea to file a complaint with the state's Attorney General's Department of Consumer Affairs. These addresses can be found on the state government's website. Or call the FCA office if you don't have Internet access.

Note: The most despicable of all predators who batten on the bereaved aren't undertakers but those con men who target elderly survivors, generally widows. These vultures will study the local obituaries, then swoop down on a victim, claiming that they are owed money for some expense incurred by the deceased: a debt, an insurance premium, or a high-priced sales item (like a deluxe Bible) that has been ordered but unpaid for. Do not fall for these scams!

Funerals for the YouTube Age

Back in the preautomotive days, when vehicles ran on literal horsepower, people might need several days to make it to a funeral, particularly if they lived in rural areas. (Embalming became a big business in the late 1800s partly because it allowed corpses to stay relatively fresh while faraway family members made their long-distance journeys.) The advent of modern means of locomotion—first trains, then cars and airplanes—obviously reduced travel time significantly. Even today, however, there are occasions when it's impossible to reach a funeral on time, if at all.

Thanks to the Internet revolution, a solution is now at hand. An outfit called Online Funeral offers a way for mourners to pay their last respects without ever budging from their desktop PCs. Touted on the company's website as "the most advanced and comprehensive system for funeral homes," this service offers such features as real-time live Internet viewing of the visitation, an online video of the funeral service (which can be transferred to a CD and sold to survivors, thus providing a "valuable new revenue stream" for the funeral director), an online condolence message center, and more. Funeral home operators can even have additional hidden cameras installed in other parts of their establishment to monitor the staff and make sure that no hanky-panky is going on.

For more information on this product—which, according to the company's PR material, is guaranteed to give grieving families "the confidence that the funeral home they have selected is state-of-the-art"—go to www.online-funeral.com.

Bereavement Fares

Since airlines charge a premium for last-minute reservations, smart travelers try to book their seats way in advance. At times, however, such foresight just isn't possible—for example, when you get a long-distance call that a family member has died suddenly, and you have to fly to the funeral on short notice.

To prove that they are not soulless entities that care only about the bottom line, airlines have traditionally offered special "bereavement fares" to people who find themselves in this trying situation. In theory, this is a decent and humane gesture. In practice, however (since airline companies pretty much *are* soulless entities that care only about the bottom line), it usually turns out to be less generous than it seems.

The problem with most bereavement (aka "compassion") discounts is that they apply only to the airline's highest-priced, non-advance-purchase, unrestricted fare. So while you might save as much as 50 percent on a one-way ticket, you can still end up spending a bundle—much more, in fact, than you'd spend by booking a regular flight.

One traveler, cited in an article that appeared in *USA Today*, needed to get from Kansas City, Missouri, to Phoenix for his father-in-law's funeral. The half-price bereavement ticket he was offered by United came to $380. When he checked online, however, he found a regular flight on a different carrier for only $250. (Indeed, some airlines can beat their *own* bereavement discounts with cheaper flights.)

Getting a bereavement fare also requires that you provide the airline with certain documentation, including the name and phone number of the funeral home and, sometimes, a copy of the death certificate.

Increasingly, as the airline industry revamps its pricing strategies, major carriers are doing away with their bereavement fares. Delta, for example, eliminated them a few years ago after introducing a simplified pricing scheme called "Simplifares" that offers low-priced last-minute tickets.

Other major carriers, however—American, United, Northwest, Continental—continue to offer bereavement discounts. The major benefit of these fares is that they usually have more flexible travel rules than other last-minute tickets (most are refundable, for example, and allow date changes and open-ended returns). In terms of price alone, however, you might well find a cheaper flight online or through a travel agent.

A Meal to Die For

Having a big feast right after planting a loved one in the ground might seem at first blush a bit peculiar, if not actively disrespectful of the dead. Throughout the ages, however, and in cultures all over the world, such postfuneral meals have been an important part of the healing process—an occasion for friends and family to gather around the bereaved and offer comfort.

Some scholars theorize that funeral feasts were originally held for the benefit of the newly deceased. Back in ancient Roman times, for example, people evidently believed "that the dead required nourishment in some way, and that the tedium of their existence in the tomb could be relieved by participating in a feast held by their relatives and friends at their place of burial." Following a funeral, therefore, the mourners would throw a party at the gravesite—thus allowing the dead person to take part one last time in that most popular of all ancient Roman pastimes, the drunken orgiastic revel.

For the most part, however, cultural anthropologists agree that the funeral meal evolved as a way to help the living. From Bali to Belgium, Iceland to India, Mexico to the Mississippi Delta, it's traditional for mourners to share a postmortem meal. Customs vary, of course. Some are simple, some lavish. Though most are held after the burial, some take place beforehand. And the mood can vary from festive to somber. But the impulse behind these occasions is the same: to provide a communal support system, to show the bereaved that they are not alone, and to help assuage their sudden sense of abandonment and isolation.

And the funeral meal serves another function, too. Indulging in a hearty dinner after returning from the cemetery proves that we're still very much alive. In that sense, as Lisa Rogak suggests in her mortuary cookbook, *Death Warmed Over* (Ten Speed Press, 2004), the postfuneral meal is a way of affirming life in the presence of death—of thumbing your nose at the Grim Reaper.

Menus for funeral meals vary widely, of course, depending on cultural tradition. Rogak's book offers a range of international recipes, from Hungarian Funeral Goulash to Irish Wake Cake to Mexican *Pan de Muerto* (bread of the dead). And in their delightful book *Being Dead Is No Excuse: The Official Southern Ladies Guide to Hosting the Perfect Funeral* (Hyperion, 2005), Gayden Metcalfe and Charlotte Hays provide instructions for such standards as Can't-Die-Without-It Caramel Cake and Liketa Died Potatoes, along with Gouda Cheese Grits and the mandatory Tomato Aspic with Homemade Mayonnaise ("Can you be buried without tomato aspic? Not in the Mississippi Delta you can't").

Not only down South but throughout America, traditional funeral fare seems designed to ensure that the mourners won't outlive the dearly departed by very long. Among the alarmingly artery-clogging offerings typically served at American funeral meals are Wisconsin cold bacon-cheese dip, Mormon funeral potatoes (consisting of hash browns, cream of potato soup, sour cream, grated Parmesan, and butter), and pig tails cooked in sauerkraut, a dish popular in the Baltimore African American community.

But like all other culinary practices in what one writer has dubbed the "United States of Arugula," even these traditions are evolving. Interviewed about the changes he's noticed in his nearly forty years of partaking in the Jewish postfuneral ritual known as the "Meal of Restoration," Rabbi Sholom Lipskar of Bal Harbour, Florida, observed: "You're getting a lot more vegetable trays and less of the fried, fatty foods. Nowadays people are more health conscious."

RECOMMENDED READING

Besides the two books mentioned previously, you'll find recipes—along with practical advice on everything from writing condolence notes to composing your own obituary—in Jessica Bemis Ward's *Food to Die For: A Book of Funeral Food, Tips, and Tales* (Southern Memorial Association, 2004).

There's nothing like a morning funeral for sharpening an appetite for lunch.

—Arthur Marshall

Eat, Drink, and Be Buried

In the popular mind, the New England Puritans were a bunch of finger-wagging killjoys who frowned on all earthly pleasures. Even the Puritans, however, occasionally allowed themselves to eat, drink, and be merry. Especially at funerals.

Colonial New England funeral feasts were surprisingly lavish affairs. According to historians Robert Habenstein and William Lamers, the menu at one of these occasions "featured beef, ham, bacon and fowls, supplemented by fish, oysters, 150 eggs, peas, onions and potatoes, followed by cheese, fruit, and sweetmeats"—all washed down with "rum, wine, beer, gin and brandy." The bill for this blowout came to nearly $850—the equivalent

Pennsylvania Ducth Funeral Pie

This traditional postfuneral treat is both easy to fix and lip-smacking good. At 400 calories a slice, it's a bit of an indulgence if you're watching your weight. But what the heck—you only live once!

1 tablespoon cornstarch
1/2 cup sugar
1 3/4 cups water
2 1/2 cups seedless raisins
2 teaspoons grated lemon zest (yellow part only)
2 tablespoons lemon juice
2 tablespoons butter
Prepared pastry for two-crust 9-inch pie, unbaked

Preheat oven to 400°F. Mix cornstarch with sugar, then gradually stir in the water. Add raisins and cook over low heat, stirring constantly, until mixture thickens. Remove from heat and add the grated lemon zest, lemon juice, and butter. Pour filling into prepared pie shell. Place top crust over pie, crimp and trim edges, and cut slits to allow for escaping steam. Bake 30 minutes or until done.

Makes 8 servings.

of "between five and ten thousand dollars in modern purchasing power."

The Puritans may have persecuted heretics, hanged their neighbors as suspected witches, and put people in the stocks for laughing out loud on the Sabbath, but on the plus side, no New England mourner ever left a funeral hungry!

Eulogies

Being asked by bereaved family members to say a few words at a funeral is clearly a sign of their high regard for you, as well as a mark of the special place you occupied in the life of their loved one. But it can also seem like an intimidating responsibility, especially if you're not particularly comfortable with public speaking.

If you are invited to deliver a eulogy, there are a number of tips to keep in mind. To begin with, you'll need to spend time preparing your remarks and writing them down. This is no time for improvisation. Even people possessed of extraordinary rhetorical gifts have to rely on the written word. Mark Antony's rousing "Friends, Romans, countrymen, lend me your ears" eulogy in *The Tragedy of Julius Caesar* seems to be delivered off the cuff. But in reality, it was composed by Shakespeare.

Not that anyone expects you to be Shakespeare. What is required is a simple, straightforward tribute to the deceased, delivered in a natural, conversational voice. People who have analyzed the ingredients of successful eulogies agree on a number of points:

1. *Make it brief.* Anywhere from three to ten minutes is the normal length, though it's a good idea to consult beforehand with the family or officiating clergyman. If a number of speakers are lined up, you might be told to keep it shorter. (Remember: a single typewritten, double-spaced page takes roughly a minute to read aloud.)
2. *Keep it personal.* A eulogy is not the same as an obituary—that is, it's not meant to be a biography of the departed or a summary of his or her achievements. It's a personal, sincerely felt tribute that captures something true about the subject, something that made him or her so special to you.
3. *Be specific.* Don't just generalize about what a wonderful, witty, loving person the departed was; recall a particular anecdote that captures his or her personality. In a eulogy delivered for his malapropism-prone grandfather, for example, writer Garry Schaeffer recalled the time that—while dining together at a Spanish restaurant—the old man ordered the "Gestapo soup."
4. *Don't be overly glum.* As Schaeffer's example indicates, it's perfectly appropriate to inject some humor into a eulogy. Indeed, in a fine *Esquire* magazine piece, "How to Give a Eulogy," writer Tom Chiarella flatly declares, "You *must* make them laugh. Laughs are a pivot point in a funeral. They are your responsibility. The best laughs come by forcing people not to idealize the dead." At the same time, it's important to remember that you are not there to perform a stand-up routine or deliver a roast.
5. *Be honest—up to a point.* Telling the truth about the person is important, but you want to emphasize the positive. A funeral service is no place for brutal honesty. It's one thing to elicit warm chuckles from the audience by describing the departed's lovable quirks. But feelings are raw at these times, and you'll want to avoid anything that smacks of criticism. Likewise, a eulogy is not an occasion for you to offer a tearful confession or belated apology for some wrong you committed against the deceased. Remember: this is not about you.
6. *Let your feelings show.* It's okay to choke up or shed a few tears while recalling the deceased. But you don't want to get carried away in a tide of emotion. That's why it's important to rehearse your eulogy before you deliver it.

Added to these are a few rules of thumb recommended by Tom Chiarella: "Don't read poetry unless you knew it going in. Don't use Bartlett's. Don't do imitations. Don't sing unless they ask you. Even then, consider not singing."

RECOMMENDED RESOURCES

Tom Chiarella's essay can be found at the *Esquire* website, www.esquire.com. Two slender but helpful guides are Garry Schaeffer's *A Labor of Love: How to Write a*

Eulogy (GMS Publishing, 1998) and Leo Seguin's *How to Write and Deliver a Loving Eulogy* (Seguin Books, 1998). If you're interested in reading some world-class eulogies, Ted Tobias reprints several dozen in his book, *In Tribute: Eulogies of Famous People* (Bushky Press, 1999).

For those who feel absolutely incapable of composing an original eulogy, there are online companies that offer fill-in-the-blank eulogy forms or, for a slightly higher fee, custom eulogies prepared by a professional writer. You'll find these services at www.lovingeulogies.com and www.instanteulogies.com.

Wake Me When It's Over

The word *wake* is linguistically connected to *watch*, as in surveillance. Strictly speaking, a funeral wake is the custom of keeping vigil over a corpse from death until burial by family, friends, and neighbors (or, in some places, paid watchers). The practice is ancient and widespread and appears to spring from a variety of motives—from the practical need to keep rats and other vermin away from the body to various archaic fears, such as the superstitious belief that unless a close watch is kept over the dead, evil spirits might come and whisk it away to the netherworld.

While many traditional wakes were simple, somber affairs—a pair of old friends conversing quietly all night at the kitchen table while the deceased lay upstairs in the bedroom—others involved a good deal of boisterous merrymaking. Irish wakes in particular are known for their carousing, though other cultures, too, practice festive food-and-drink-fueled wakes. Such postmortem partying is generally seen as a life-affirming act of defiance—a kind of rowdy thumbing of one's nose at death. Some anthropologists also believe that these raucous prefuneral gatherings are meant to ensure that the deceased really *is* gone for good and can therefore be safely interred. After all, if all that drunken revelry doesn't wake Grandma up, nothing will.

Nowadays, particularly in America, the word *wake* is often used interchangeably with *visitation*—not a lively at-home get-together in the presence of the deceased, but a subdued viewing of the embalmed corpse at a funeral parlor.

RECOMMENDED READING

A lovely depiction of an old-fashioned American wake can be found in the story "Miss Tempy's Watchers" by the New England writer Sarah Orne Jewett. Originally published in 1888, this simple but quite moving tale concerns two women in a small New Hampshire farming community who have volunteered to keep vigil over the body of their neighbor, Miss Tempy Dent, over the course of a long night. It is frequently included in anthologies of classic American literature and can be found in its entirety online at http://faculty.uml.edu/mpennell/amlit2/Tempy.htm.

Two worthwhile studies of traditional Irish funeral customs are Sean O'Suilleabhain, *Irish Wake Amusements* (Mercier Press, 1967) and E. Estyn Evans, *Irish Folkways* (Routledge, 1957).

Oh, and Never *Ever* Wear New Shoes to a Funeral

Given the number of actual real-world perils we're constantly being warned about—from identity theft to trans fats to untended airport baggage—you'd think there'd be enough things in life to watch out for. But superstitious people know that you can never be too careful. So here are fourteen death-related folk beliefs to add to your list of worries.

- If a bird flies into your house through a window, someone in your family will die.
- If your left eye twitches, there will be a death in your family.
- If you dream of muddy water, there will be a death in your family.
- If someone in your household dies and you don't cover your mirrors, the first person to see his reflection will be the next to die.
- If three people are photographed together, the one in the middle will die first.
- If thirteen people sit down at a table to eat, one of them will die before the year is out.
- If you rest a broom against a bed, the person who sleeps there will die.
- If, during the twelve nights preceding Christmas, you dream of a loved one lying in a coffin, that person will die within the year.
- If you walk or ride past a cemetery without tucking your thumbs into your fists, one of your parents will die.
- If you see an ant in winter, all the members of your household will die.
- If you don't hold your breath while walking or driving past a cemetery, you will die.
- If you see an owl in the daytime, you will die.
- If you point at a passing funeral procession, you will die.
- If you count the cars in a funeral cortege, you will die.

Please note: Even if you scrupulously heed these warnings and never point at a passing funeral procession, count the cars in a cortege, or walk by a cemetery without holding your breath, you will still die. But hopefully not so soon.

Hand of Glory

Beyond providing medical students with the raw material for their dissection classes, human corpses don't, by and large, have much practical use. If you believe in witchcraft, however—and have access to the dead body of a person hanged for murder—you can whip up a nifty little item that will have all kinds of useful (if highly illicit) applications.

Known as the "Hand of Glory," this black-magic charm not only purportedly has the power to unlock the door to any house but, when used at night, will prevent the sleeping inhabitants from awakening. The value of this amazing implement for any professional burglar can hardly be overstated.

The trick, of course, is procuring one. First, you'll have to sever the hand of a hanged killer while the corpse is still dangling from the gallows. If you can manage this during a lunar eclipse, so much the better. (There is some disagreement about which hand works best, though the consensus seems to be either the left hand or the one that wielded the murder weapon.)

Next, wrap the hand in a shroud and squeeze out as much blood as possible. Then place the exsanguinated hand inside an earthenware jar, add salt, saltpeter, and black pepper, mix well, and let stand.

While the hand is curing, make a candle. Most experts recommend that you use fat rendered from the dead man's flesh, along with virgin wax and sesame oil. Ideally, the wick should be made from a strand of corpse hair, though freshly spun flax will do in a pinch.

After two weeks, remove the hand from the jar, brush off any clinging powder, and place it in an oven fired with fir branches. (You can also dry it in the sun, though only during the dog days of summer.) After one hour, the hand should be ready. Remove from the heat and curl it into a fist, leaving just enough space between the middle and ring fingers to accommodate the candle.

Place the candle in the appropriate space, squeeze the fingers tight, and there you have it—your very own Hand of Glory, ready to light your way into the homes of unsuspecting victims. E-Z? U bet!

Living Funerals

Obviously, the worst thing about your own funeral is that, being dead, you are unable to hear all the wonderful things people are saying about you or to see how broken up everyone is by your untimely demise. Lots of people (especially adolescents in their most self-pitying moods) fantasize about their funerals, but outside of the occasional literary classic such as Twain's *Tom Sawyer*, hardly anyone gets to attend his own memorial service while still alive.

All that has begun to change, however, thanks in large part to Mitch Albom's inspirational megaseller, *Tuesdays with Morrie* (Doubleday, 1997). Near the start of that book, the title character—Albom's terminally ill mentor, Morris Schwartz—decides to throw himself a "living funeral":

> He made some calls. He chose a date. And on a cold Sunday afternoon, he was joined

> in his home by a small group of friends and family. . . . Each of them spoke and paid tribute to my old professor. Some cried. Some laughed. . . . Morrie cried and laughed with them. And all the heartfelt things we never get to say to those we love, Morrie said that day. His "living funeral" was a rousing success.

Of course, living funerals aren't everyone's cup of tea. Some people regard them as overly egocentric. Others worry that the occasion might turn into a roast.

Still, in the opinion of some specialists in dying and grief, a living funeral can serve an important therapeutic function. If nothing else, as Robin O. Winter and Bruce A. Birnberg point out, it can help the dying person "avoid the social isolation so common to those with a fatal illness." By arranging for his own living funeral, for example, Morrie let "his close friends and family know that he was willing to talk about his illness and death and that they did not have to be afraid to visit him."

(*Please Note:* It is important not to confuse a living *funeral*, which can be a deeply meaningful and gratifying experience, with a living *burial*, which is to be avoided at all costs.)

The Dead Beat

Unlike, say, the Nobel Prize—or, for that matter, any other award you receive while alive—getting your obituary in the *New York Times* isn't exactly the kind of honor you can bask in. Still, it's a distinction that many people aspire to. Unfortunately, unless you're internationally famous, there's no guarantee that you'll end up in the *Times*. According to obituaries editor Bill McDonald, the individuals who make it are those who have contributed something significant "to the wider society or some corner of it"—a fairly broad category that in recent years has included everyone from Dr. Albert Ellis, founder of an influential school of psychotherapy, to Harold von Braunhut, the guy who came up with the brainstorm of selling dehydrated brine shrimp as frolicking pet "Sea Monkeys."

Like other major newspapers, the *Times* has full-time staffers who compose obituaries. Though becoming an obituary writer ("working the dead beat" in the lingo of the trade) wouldn't seem to be the first-choice dream job for any hotshot young journalist hoping to score a Pulitzer, a number of outstanding writers have turned out obits for the *Times*. Indeed, some have achieved a fair degree of renown, at least among the kind of people likely to attend the Annual Great Obituary Writers' International Conference in Las Vegas.

Alden Whitman, the paper's chief obituary writer from 1965 to 1976, is regarded as a great literary innovator in the field, the person who pioneered the technique of interviewing major figures while they were still alive to garner information for their future obituaries. The late Robert McG. Thomas Jr. is revered among aficionados for his skill at summing up a subject's importance, as in this classic opening from the October 9, 1995, issue: "Edward Lowe, whose accidental discovery of a product he called Kitty Litter made cats more welcome household company and created a half-billion-dollar industry, died at a hospital in Sarasota, Fla."

More recently, Margalit Fox has become a fan favorite for her snappy obits on everyone from Anna Nicole Smith and Sidney Sheldon to such obscure but intriguing individuals as Conrad Spizz, "a tough-talking, cigar-chewing artisan of smoked fish whose work was enshrined behind glass at some of New York's best-known food shops" and Richard S. Prather, "a hugely popular mystery writer of the 1950s and '60s whose novels were known for their swift violence, loopy humor and astonishing number of characters with no clothes on." It is thanks to writers like these—along with colleagues at other major dailies (like Alana Baranick of the *Cleveland Plain Dealer*, winner of the 2005 American Society of Newspaper Editors Best News Writing Award in the obits category)—that we are living, as journalist Marilyn Johnson puts it, in the "Golden Age of the Obituary."

As Johnson makes clear in her improbably delightful book, *The Dead Beat: Lost Souls, Lucky Stiffs, and the Perverse Pleasures of Obituaries* (HarperCollins, 2006), a *New York Times* obituary adheres to a format as fixed as an Elizabethan sonnet. The opening sentence identifies the deceased, provides a crisp explanation of what he or she did to deserve a *Times* obit, and ends with the date and place of death. ("Serena Wilson, a noted dancer, teacher and choreographer who was widely credited with helping to popularize belly dancing in the United States, died last Sunday in Manhattan.") A simple declaration of the subject's age and place of residence at the time of death completes paragraph one. ("She was 73 and lived in Manhattan.")

The second paragraph cites the source of the news—generally a family member, spokesperson, or some other reliable figure—and, when possible, gives the cause of death. ("The cause was a pulmonary embolism, her son, Scott, said.") Providing this upfront information became standard practice at the *Times* after an embarrassing incident in December 2003 when—based on an unconfirmed story in another newspaper—the obits page mistakenly reported the death of Broadway dancer Katherine Sergava. "From that day forward," explains Bill McDonald, "it has been ironclad policy at the *Times* to devote the second paragraph of every obit to answering a simple question about a death that every reader is entitled to ask: How do you know—who told you? We now insist on attribution. We will not publish an obituary until we can confirm the death."

The announcement of the subject's death is typically followed by what Marilyn Johnson calls the "song and dance"—"an expansive section of one or more paragraphs, an anecdote or even a full-blown scene that illustrates the turning point in the story of the subject's life." ("One day in the early 1950s, [her husband's] band was booked for an engagement that required a belly dancer. Never mind that it was a Dixieland band; Mr. Wilson quickly got hold of arrangements of Middle Eastern standards like 'Miserlou.' His wife, drawing on her training, gamely volunteered to dance. That was the start of a fascination with belly dance on the part of both Ms. Wilson and her husband, who learned Middle Eastern drumming and often performed with his wife.")

Next, the writer backpedals a bit to provide a straightforward chronology of the subject's life. ("Serene Blake was born in the Bronx on Aug. 8, 1933; she changed the spelling of her first name as a young adult. As a child, she performed with her parents' vaudeville act, Blake & Blake, which did musical and comedy numbers. She also studied with the celebrated dancer Ruth St. Denis, who was known for her sinuous, Eastern-inspired choreography.")

Adding spice to the obit are quotes from experts, friends, and relatives that are sprinkled throughout the piece. ("Reviewing a performance by the troupe at Lincoln Center Out of Doors in 2001, the *Village Voice* wrote: 'Her dancers, working those rhumba, chiftetelli, and kashlimar rhythms, showed classic Serena training—elegant carriage, willowy arms and hips that make tiny flicks like a clock's second hand.") The stock ending is a list of survivors. ("Ms. Wilson's husband and son, both of Manhattan, are her only immediate survivors.")

The vast majority of *Times* obits are written from scratch by the three full-time staffers. These tend to be relatively short—anywhere from two hundred to a thousand words—and are produced on extremely short notice, often within a day of the subject's death.

In addition to these "dailies," the paper keeps a file of twelve hundred or so "advances"—prewritten or "draft" obituaries of major figures from the worlds of politics, art, science, sports, and so on. These run anywhere from one thousand to ten thousand words and, depending on the eminence of the person, might begin on page one. Though some are produced by the regular obits writers, most, as McDonald explains, are supplied by the wider newsroom staff or by outside authorities and freelancers. Since these "advances" are prepared years, if not decades, before the death of the subjects, they are regularly updated.

Though you have to be someone significant to land an obituary in a major metropolitan newspaper, anyone can get a mention on the obits page if his loved ones are willing to spring for a death notice—a small classified ad paid for and placed by family or friends. Death notices, which are telephoned into the paper, fall into several categories. The first is the short formal announcement, intended to notify friends, acquaintances, and business associates of the person's death and the details of the funeral service ("SMITH—John. On July 25. Devoted husband of Mary, father of Suzie and Tom, grandfather of Ellen, Jane, and Anna. Reposing at Gleason Funeral Home, 26 Main Street, Friday 2–5 and 7–9 P.M. Interment, St. Charles Cemetery, Saturday at 11 A.M.").

Another common type is the so-called condolence notice, typically placed by friends and associates of the deceased. ("JOHNSON—Ellen. The partners and staff at the firm of Abel, Bartley, and Crowe express profound sorrow at the death on December 2 of Ellen Johnson, beloved wife of our friend and partner Richard P. Johnson. We express our deepest sympathies to Richard and to all other members of the family.")

More elaborate death notices sometimes include such extended tributes to the deceased that they amount to miniature, family-written obituaries. ("BRONSON—Harry, on May 18. With his father Edward, he began his career building affordable homes for returning World War II veterans in the suburb of Midgeville. By 1957, the Bronson Company had constructed more than 1,200 attractive and solidly built homes. When not devoting himself to work, Harry loved to spend his time outdoors, hiking through the woods or fishing for trout. Though honored for his many contributions to his community, his proudest achievement was being named 'Sportsman of the Year' by the Smithville Wilderness Club in 2006," etc., etc.)

RECOMMENDED RESOURCES

Marilyn Johnson's charming, chatty book about the art and "perverse pleasures" of obituaries is a must-read for anyone interested in the subject. If you'd like to read obits by some of the journalistic titans to whom she pays tribute, check out Alden Whitman's *Come to Judgment: Diverse Notables Who Found Fame and Earned Obits in the* New York Times (Viking, 1980), Robert McG. Thomas Jr.'s *52 McGs: The Best Obituaries from Legendary* New York Times *Reporter Robert McG. Thomas Jr.* (Scribner, 2001), and Marvin Siegel's compilation *The Last Word: The* New York Times *Book of Obituaries and Farewells* (William Morrow and Company, 1997).

Aspiring obit writers should acquaint themselves with *Life on the Death Beat: A Handbook for Obituary Writers* (Marion Street Press, 2005) by Alana Baranick, Jim Sheeler, and Stephen Miller, a highly informative how-to guide that includes such indispensable advice as "Rule No. 1: Make Sure They're Dead." A very readable scholarly work that examines shifting societal values as reflected in thousands of historical obituaries from 1818 to 1930 is Janice Hume's *Obituaries in American Culture* (University Press of Mississippi, 2000).

The Internet, of course, is full of information. Obituary Central (www.obitcentral.com), which bills itself as "the headquarters for finding obituaries," provides links to many useful websites. The Pattee Library of Penn State University also features an excellent website on the topic (www.libraries.psu.edu/newsandmicroforms/obits.htm).

As part of its online "Talk to the Newsroom" column, in which various editors answer questions submitted by readers, the *New York Times* ran a very informative discussion of the obits department by Bill McDonald in September 2006. It's available at www.nytimes.com/asktheeditors.

Greetings from the Grave

"Hi, I'm Art Buchwald and I just died."

That's the way the late great humorist Art Buchwald introduced himself on a video posted on the *New York Times* website the day after his death in January 2007. Released along with a traditional printed obituary, Buchwald's "video obit" was the first in a planned series called "The Last Word," featuring prerecorded interviews of various luminaries to be broadcast online after their deaths.

The project was the brainchild of reporter Tim Weiner, who came up with the concept of videotaping high-definition "oral histories" of "people whose deaths are likely to be Page One news." At the time of Buchwald's demise, ten other subjects—including one former U.S. president and a world-famous scientist (rumored to be Stephen Hawking)—had been taped for their eventual video obits.

Though you won't receive international

media coverage, you don't have to be a Pulitzer Prize–winning author to have your very own video obituary. Thanks to the folks at My Last E-mail, that privilege is now available to anyone. For a range of fees—depending on how elaborate a tribute you wish to create for yourself—you can post anything from a simple text message to a full-fledged online memorial, complete with a ten-minute video clip. For further information, go to www.mylastemail.com.

A less extravagant way to send e-mails from beyond the grave is offered by a French-based website called Après La Mort (After Death), which allows you to create messages that will be sent to the recipients of your choice once you have died. According to the home page, the idea first came to the webmaster when he was tooling around in his car one day and started thinking about a secret he'd never been able to share with a particular friend. *Et voilà*—the idea was born: "the possibility of being able to leave the kind of message you would not have dared to say to someone whilst alive." Despite this titillating premise—that your postmortem e-mail will contain some deep, dark revelation, far too embarrassing to be uttered in life—you can actually leave any kind of message you want, no matter how boring. And the service is free! Just go to www.apreslamort.net.

DEATH FUN FACT

Ever wonder what people will say about you when you die? Well, if you'd been President Gerald Ford, Pope John Paul II, or Bob Hope, you would have had a chance to find out. These individuals were among a bunch of world luminaries whose draft obituaries, written in preparation for their eventual deaths, were accidentally posted online by CNN.com in April 2003 before any of them had actually passed to the Great Beyond.

According to legend, Mark Twain was also the subject of a premature newspaper obituary that supposedly led to his famous quip, "Reports of my death are greatly exaggerated." The truth of the matter is that while Twain was visiting London in 1897, his cousin James Ross Clemens fell seriously ill. A reporter got wind of the story but mistakenly thought that it was Twain himself who was near death. This bogus news found its way to the *New York Journal*, which promptly reported Twain's imminent demise. No formal obituary, however, was ever published. When Twain learned of the story, he issued a statement that read: "The report of my death was an exaggeration." Much later, in recounting the episode, he revised this not especially memorable remark to the wittier saying.

Obit for an Obituarist

Along with comfort and joy, Christmas Day 2007 brought tidings of sadness for obituary lovers throughout the world: news of the passing of one of the titans of the genre, Hugh Massingberd, dead at age sixty of cancer. A classic English eccentric who once posed for an official photograph decked out as a Roman emperor with a garland of sausages, Massingberd gained renown as the "father of the modern British obituary" during his tenure as obituaries editor of the London *Daily Telegraph* from 1986 to 1994. Prior to his arrival at the newspaper, the standard obituary was (no pun intended) a deadly affair, consisting of a ponderous recitation of the subject's honors and achievements. Massingberd revolutionized the form by offering witty and irreverent (not to say gleefully scandalous) observations about the departed, such as his characterization of one aristocratic expat as a man whose "chief occupations were bongo drummer, confidence trickster, brothel-keeper, drug-smuggler, and police informer." In another obituary much cherished by cognoscenti, he described a once-renowned scholar of the Dead Sea Scrolls whose crackpot theories had transformed him into a laughingstock as "the Liberace of biblical scholarship."

To fully appreciate a Massingberd obituary, it is necessary to be conversant with his highly specialized vocabulary—with what Margalit Fox calls his "carefully coded euphemisms." In her *New York Times* tribute to her colleague, Fox helpfully provides "an abridged Massingberd-English dictionary" for the benefit of American readers:

"Convivial": habitually drunk
"Did not suffer fools gladly": monstrously foul-tempered
"Gave colorful accounts of his exploits": a liar
"A man of simple tastes": a complete vulgarian
"A powerful negotiator": a bully
"Relished the cadences of the English language": an incorrigible windbag
"Relished physical contact": a sadist
"An uncompromisingly direct ladies' man": a flasher

Though Massingberd is gone, his work lives on in *The* Daily Telegraph *Book of Obituaries: A Celebration of Eccentric Lives* (Macmillan, 1995) and five other collections, each of which—as he himself was quick to point out—makes "splendid bedtime reading."

4

GRAVE MATTERS

From Mass Grave to Memorial Park: The Rise of the Modern Cemetery

Though the word itself derives from the ancient Greek *koimeterion* (meaning "sleeping place"), the cemetery as we know it today—a parklike tract of land with neatly marked individual plots—is a modern invention.

Early Christians living in Rome interred their dead in catacombs—underground burial chambers hewn out of the soft volcanic rock surrounding the city. An estimated six million Christians were entombed in these elaborate subterranean networks, which were also used as places of refuge during times of religious persecution. As writer Penny Colman describes them in her excellent book *Corpses, Coffins, and Crypts: A History of Burial* (Henry Holt, 1997):

> The actual graves were cut into the walls, and the walls were frequently painted with religious scenes and portraits of religious leaders. In order to reduce odors, the bodies were usually covered in plaster and sealed in the tombs, and perfumes were constantly burned. When the first level of the catacomb was filled, the second level was built under it. Some catacombs went down six levels.

In succeeding centuries, churches became the sepulchral site of choice for the devout. At first, only martyrs were interred within the sanctuary itself. Gradually, bishops and other members of the ecclesiastical elite were granted the same right, their decaying corpses installed beneath the altars, behind the walls, or under the stone floors. It wasn't long before kings and aristocrats were demanding the same privilege. People of less exalted rank were consigned to the hallowed ground of the churchyards.

Eventually, the overstuffed vaults within the churches produced an insufferable atmosphere—an "abominable smell," as one

Early Christian catacombs.

observer described it, "impossible to conceal however much the sacred edifices were fumigated with incense, myrrh, and other aromatic odors." At the same time, the churchyards grew so packed with uncoffined remains that it became impossible to dig a new grave without turning up bones, skulls, and other human carrion.

The most notorious of these early European burial spots was Paris's Cimitière des Innocents—the Cemetery of the Holy Innocents—a sprawling mass graveyard in the heart of the city where, for eight hundred years, countless corpses from eighteen parishes were brought for disposal. The shockingly crude burial procedure employed at des Innocents—where communal burial trenches were left open for months while they filled with decaying corpses—was graphically described by one eighteenth-century visitor to the city:

> The dead bodies are laid, side by side, without any earth being put over them until the ground tier is full; then, and not till then, a small layer of earth covers them, and another layer of dead comes on, till by layer upon layer, and dead upon dead, the hole is filled with a mass of human corruption.

By the 1700s, des Innocents had become so gorged with decomposing remains that, as travel writer Tom Weil puts it, the earth "fairly seethed and bubbled" with putrefaction. So noxious was the fetor emanating from this massive charnel pit that, in 1785, it was closed by parliamentary decree, its reeking contents were exhumed, and millions of bones were transferred to an underground gypsum quarry that became known as the Catacombs and still remains a popular Parisian tourist attraction. From that point on, cemeteries were banned from the precincts of the city.

In early December 1804—the same week that Napoleon was crowned emperor—a landmark event in mortuary history took place outside of Paris. On a hillside in an eastern suburb, the Cimitière du Père-Lachaise was officially opened. Named after a Jesuit friar—François d'Aix de la Chaise, confessor to Louis XIV—Père-Lachaise represented nothing less than "a turning point in one thousand years of Western history" (according to culture scholar Richard A. Etlin). Designed as both a pastoral resting place for the dead and a rural retreat for city dwellers, it became the world's first modern—which is

Père-Lachaise Cemetery. Nineteenth-century engraving.

to say, carefully laid-out and landscaped—cemetery.

Because of its distance from the city, Père-Lachaise initially attracted few paying customers. But after a number of notable remains were transferred to the site—including Molière's, La Fontaine's, and the purported bones of Abelard and Héloïse—it became wildly popular among wealthy Parisians, who began to erect hundreds of elaborate sarcophagi, often in the form of miniature chapels. Its charming parklike atmosphere did not survive for very long. By the mid-nineteenth century, it was already well on its way to becoming a sprawling, overcrammed necropolis, "full of tombs, not trees" (in the words of cemetery historian Harold Mythum). By then, however, its main innovations—"provisions that bodies lie only side by side, not atop one another; that cemeteries should be made park-like places, garnished with greenery; that families could buy plots in perpetuity; and that survivors could erect monuments for specific decedents"—had already set the standard for other cemeteries on both sides of the Atlantic.

In the United States, the first modern "garden cemetery" modeled after Père-Lachaise was Boston's Mount Auburn, established in 1831 just outside Cambridge. Prior to that time—as David Charles Sloane explains in his illuminating book, *The Last Great Necessity: Cemeteries in American History* (Johns Hopkins University Press, 1991)—the burial places of white Americans fell into several categories.

The earliest pioneers were laid to rest in whatever remote part of the landscape they happened to die in, whether forest, plain, or prairie. Their isolated graves might be marked with slabs of stone or wood, "crudely scrawled with the deceased's initials." Often, however, they were left completely anonymous.

Such lonely burial spots were "soon replaced by clusters of graves as the pioneers' homesteads grew into small settlements," writes Sloane. By the early 1800s, the family graveyard had become a common feature of the American frontier. Often "set among the trees on the outskirts of a farmer's field," these domestic burying grounds were usually surrounded by a simple wood fence or stone wall. "Markers were placed irregularly within the small enclosure, with an occasional child's grave disturbing the line of the row because of the smaller size of the grave. The farmer periodically cut away the overgrown grass, and his wife tended any flowers planted inside the wall."

One notable exception to this practice was found among the early New England Puritans, who buried their dead around their meetinghouses. Early Puritan graveyards tended to be barren, untended plots, their stark slate markers carved with grim reminders of mortality in the form of winged skulls, hourglasses, bones, and coffins.

As the nation grew and cities expanded, members of other denominations—following contemporary European custom—interred their dead either in cellar vaults beneath their houses of worship or, more commonly, in the soil of the adjoining churchyards. Sloane cites New York City's Trinity Church as a prime example of this practice:

> Trinity's church vaults and churchyard were the primary burial places for the city's English elite and also much of the rest of the Protestant English population. Contemporaries estimated that by 1800, after one hundred years of use, Trinity churchyard held the remains of over one hundred thousand New Yorkers. Vaults were spread throughout the church and tunneled out from the church into the ground surrounding the building. The burial ground encompassed only a few acres, and no corpses were removed, so space was reused many times. Burials raised the level of the churchyard by several yards during the century; by the nineteenth century, it sat well above the surrounding streets.

As in Europe, the overcrowded conditions in these metropolitan burial places brought increasingly loud protests from health officials. Reformers demanded the closing of all church graveyards within large cities, decrying them as "stinking quagmires"—"receptacles of putrefying matter and hot-beds of miasmata." Their fears appeared to be confirmed in 1822, when sixteen thousand New Yorkers were carried off in a yellow fever epidemic that was particularly virulent in the vicinity of the Trinity Church burying ground.

Keenly aware that his own city was vulnerable to the same hazard from its decrepit neighborhood graveyards, a Boston physician, botanist, and Harvard professor named Joseph Bigelow launched a crusade to establish a large rural cemetery, modeled partly on Père-Lachaise, outside the municipal limits. Joining forces with the Massachusetts Horticultural Society, Bigelow and his associates acquired a picturesque seventy-two-acre tract of land along the Charles River where, in 1831, they opened Mount Auburn.

Entering through an Egyptian-style gateway, visitors found themselves in an oasis of rolling hills, thick woods, charming dells, and pristine lakes—grounds so lovely and serene that, as Emily Dickinson observed, it seemed "as if Nature had formed the spot with a distinct idea of being a resting place for her children." With its pastoral charm and sophisticated memorial architecture and statuary, Mount Auburn became an immediate draw, not only for Bostonians who flocked to it on weekends but (as Sloane writes) for travelers "from other American cities who came there to admire its magical setting and to plan how to emulate it in their own towns and cities."

By 1861, more than sixty of these sylvan burial spots had sprung up across the country: Brooklyn's Green-Wood, Philadelphia's Laurel Hill, Cincinnati's Spring Grove, Cleveland's Lake View, and many more. Visitors came by the thousands to wander the graveled footpaths, ride along shaded carriage avenues, admire the splendid plantings, and derive consolation from the sheer natural loveliness of the settings.

It wasn't until the early decades of the twentieth century that an entirely new type of cemetery appeared on the American scene—a burial place "that captured the attention of the nation unlike any cemetery since Mount Auburn," writes Sloane. This was the so-called memorial park, of which the first and most famous (or, depending on your point of view, notorious) example was Los Angeles's Forest Lawn.

Founded in 1906 on a piece of land that had proved worthless for any other use, Forest Lawn limped along as a dreary, underutilized graveyard until the arrival, in 1913, of a new manager named Hubert Eaton. A visionary midwestern businessman, Eaton fervently believed that cemeteries should, insofar as possible, avoid anything that might depress a visitor by actually reminding him of death. Viewing the Victorian garden cemeteries as excessively grim—"unsightly stoneyards" whose elaborate tombs did nothing but "chill the heart" with reminders of mortality—he resolved to create a "gladsome" new kind of burial ground, "as unlike other cemeteries as sunshine is unlike darkness." Forest Lawn, he declared, would be a place

> devoid of mis-shapen monuments and other customary signs of earthly Death, but filled with towering trees, sweeping lawns, splashing fountains, singing birds, beautiful statuary, cheerful flowers; noble memorial architecture, with interiors of light and color, and redolent of the world's best history and romances . . . a place where lovers new and old shall love to stroll and watch the sunset's glow, planning for the future or reminiscing of the past; a place where artists study and sketch; where school teachers bring happy children to see things they read of in books; where little churches invite, triumphant in the knowledge that from their pulpits only words of Love can be spoken.

To achieve his lofty aim, Eaton—or "the Builder," as he preferred to be called—introduced a number of radical innovations. To purge any trace of gloom from his "Garden of Memory," he banned traditional upright tombstones. Only inconspicuous bronze markers, flush with the ground, were permitted. The rolling landscape was kept as neatly manicured as a suburban front lawn, its gentle contours sporadically broken by neatly trimmed shrubs and small stands of evergreens (no deciduous trees were allowed "because the loss of leaves reminded visitors of death"). Burial sections were identified by sugary names: Eventide, Babyland, Sweet Memories, Vesperland, Kindly Light, Sunrise Slope, and Dawn of Tomorrow.

Though certain activities, such as picnicking and bike riding, were forbidden, the public was actively encouraged to treat the park as a recreation area. Indeed, under Eaton's leadership, Forest Lawn was turned into a kind of amusement park—a "Disneyland of death," as it was later dubbed—complete with museums, replicas of famous artworks, thematic courts organized around inspirational and patriotic exhibits, guided tours, and gift shops. Eaton also revolutionized the way cemeteries did business, opening a magnificent mortuary on the premises and turning his "garden of graves" into a one-stop, full-service shopping place that handled its customers' every postmortem need.

Forest Lawn was an immediate and stunning success, attracting thousands of paying customers (who were wooed through aggressive marketing techniques unprecedented in the burial business), luring millions of weekend visitors, and even becoming a favorite site for weddings. The original location in Glendale was eventually supplemented by five other branches in the Los Angeles area. At the same time, memorial parks modeled on Eaton's creation sprang up across the United States—more than six hundred by the mid-1930s. For sheer excess, however, nothing matches the original, which for more than fifty years has served as a ripe target for satirists—a symbol of middlebrow vulgarity, unabashed commercialism, and childish refusal to face the harsh facts of mortality that characterize the "American way of death."

RECOMMENDED READING

Besides the works mentioned previously, significant books about the development of the American cemetery include James J. Farrell, *Inventing the American Way of Death, 1830–1920* (Temple University Press, 1980); Kenneth Jackson and Camilo José Vergara, *Silent Cities: The Evolution of the American Cemetery* (Princeton Architectural Press, 1989); Blanche Linden-Ward, *Silent City on a Hill: Landscapes of Memory and Boston's Mount Auburn Cemetery* (Ohio State University Press, 1989); Barbara Rubin, Robert Carlton, and Arnold Rubin, *Forest Lawn: L.A. in Installments* (Hennessey and Ingalls, 1979); and Adela Rogers St. Johns, *First Step Up Toward Heaven: Hubert Eaton and Forest Lawn* (Prentice-Hall, 1959).

My God! Can it be possible I have
To die so suddenly? so young to go
Under the obscure, cold, rotting, wormy ground!
To be nailed down into a narrow place;
To see no more sweet sunshine; hear no more
Blithe voice of living thing; muse not again
Upon familiar thoughts, sad, yet thus lost!
How fearful! to be nothing!

—Percy Bysshe Shelley

ASK DR. DEATH

Dear Dr. Death:

Our high school English teacher, Mrs. Grundy, is making us read Shakespeare's Romeo and Juliet *and my local bookstore is out of the Cliffs-Notes, so I'm stuck reading the whole play, which is, like, really hard. There's one part where Juliet says she'd rather hide "nightly in a charnel house / O'er covered quite with dead men's rattling bones" than marry some other guy besides Romeo. Here's my question: what's a charnel house? It sounds kind of gross.*

Kimberly from Mrs. Grundy's second-period English

Dear Kimberly:

A charnel house is a place—often a small chapel-like building—where dead bodies and old human bones are stored. They have existed throughout the ages and can still be found in some parts of the world.

In medieval Europe, charnel houses could be found in many small villages, sometimes connected to the church. When the cemetery became full, the old graves were dug up to make room for new occupants and the exhumed bones were stacked inside the charnel house. Shakespeare himself was apparently terrified that his corpse would meet this fate and left a famous warning on his tombstone, supposedly composed by himself:

> Good friend, for Jesus sake forbear
> To dig the dust enclosed here:
> Blest be the man that spares these
> stones,
> And curst be he that moves my bones.

The world *charnel* itself is a variant of *carnal*, meaning "flesh," though there was little flesh to be found on the skeletal contents of a typical charnel house. When Juliet thinks about hiding there, she pictures herself lying among "reeky shanks and yellow chapless skulls"—stinking old leg bones and decaying skulls missing their lower jaws.

As you so aptly put it, Kimberly—*gross!*

Take Me Out to the Graveyard

Just because a graveyard is a hallowed site where grieving people go to memorialize their dead family members doesn't mean that it can't serve as the perfect place for a delightful weekend outing featuring live entertainment and brunch. That, at any rate, is the thinking behind a growing trend among historical American cemeteries.

Over the past few years, a number of venerable burial grounds have found themselves in dire financial straits. Home to many beautiful old tombs and monuments that require expensive upkeep, they are unable to generate income in the usual way—that is, by selling interment sites—since they have run out of room for new bodies. As a result, they have begun to experiment with a novel approach, raising funds for badly needed maintenance and repairs by luring visitors with a variety of fun-filled events and activities—or, as an article in the May 25, 2007, *New York Times* puts it, by "rebranding themselves as a destination for weekend tourists."

Take Laurel Hill Cemetery in Bala Cynwyd, Pennsylvania, a 170-year-old graveyard containing all kinds of funerary treasures, from mausoleums adorned with Tiffany windows to splendid examples of Victorian mortuary sculpture. Its traditional revenue stream having dried up (less than 1 percent of its space is available for new burials), conservators have cooked up a variety of ingenious fund-raising schemes, including a day devoted to "bird-watching among the buried," a guided visit to the graves of notorious inhabitants (the "Sinners, Scandals, and Suicides" tour), and—in commemoration of the six *Titanic* victims buried on the premises—a "nine-course re-creation of the last supper aboard the ill-fated ocean liner," complete with liveried waiters and an orchestra playing the "Blue Danube Waltz."

SEARS, ROEBUCK & CO., CHICAGO, ILL. 17

OUR SPECIAL $20.70 HANDSOMELY ORNAMENTED TOMBSTONE.

Delivered on the Cars at Our Quarry and Marble Works in Vermont.

AT REST

GIVE US FOUR TO SIX WEEKS IN WHICH TO FINISH, LETTER AND SHIP.

1902 Sears, Roebuck catalogue tombstone ad.
Courtesy of The Winterthur Library: Printed Book and Periodical Collection.

To raise money for the Congressional Cemetery in Washington, D.C.—the city's oldest graveyard, containing monuments designed by Benjamin Henry LaTrobe, architect of the Capitol Building—officials have sponsored a John Philip Sousa concert performed by a seventy-piece marching band and a dog parade featuring costumed canines decked out as historical figures. Other cemeteries in need have resorted to everything from jazz performances in the memorial chapel to elaborate brunches prepared by star chefs and served in the crematorium.

Not all of these special events are thrown for preservation purposes. Some are designed to attract potential customers. That explains the Renaissance fair with strolling troubadours and jousting knights held at the Oakwood Cemetery in Troy, New York, an 1848 graveyard that still has enough burial space for the next two hundred years. "We want visitors to think, 'Wow, I'd like to spend eternity here,' " one cemetery trustee explained to the *Times*. "It's our way of saying, 'We'd love you to stay with us permanently.' "

Ten Cemeteries to See Before You Die

1. PÈRE-LACHAISE, *Paris*

One of the wonders of the necropolitan world, this wildly picturesque, world-famous graveyard is a must-see tourist destination for any art lover, cultural connoisseur, aficionado of mortuary architecture, or fan of the Gothic sublime. A true city of the dead, consisting of 118 suffocatingly overcrowded acres, Père-Lachaise can be navigated only with the aid of a guidebook, a map, or one of the knowledgeable locals who hang around the entrance and are always available for tours. Among the countless luminaries interred on the grounds are Frédéric Chopin, Isadora Duncan, Eugène Delacroix, Yves Montand, Marcel Proust, Gertrude Stein, Oscar Wilde, and (of course) that icon of sixties rock decadence, Jim Morrison.

Whether you're paying homage to your favorite artist, marveling at the astonishing works of funerary sculpture, or simply strolling nervously past the ineffably creepy tumbledown mausoleums whose unhinged doors and shattered stone floors suggest that their occupants have recently escaped from the grave, you're guaranteed to have a memorable time at this legendary necropolis.

> Address: 16 rue du Repos, 20th arrondisement, 75020 Paris (entrances on rue des Rondeaux, bd. de Ménilmontant, and rue de la Réunion)
> Metro: Gambetta, Philippe-Auguste, or Père-Lachaise
> Hours: Mon.–Fri. 8 A.M.–6 P.M., Sat. 8:30 A.M.–6 P.M., Sun. 9 A.M.–6 P.M. (5:30 P.M. in winter)
> Tel.: (33) 1 55 25 82 10

Virtual Père-Lachaise

Thanks to the miracle of the Internet, you can now visit the world-famous Père-Lachaise Cemetery without having to subject yourself to the hideous ordeal of a Paris vacation. A beautifully designed website allows you to stroll through the sylvan avenues of the necropolis and marvel at the spectacular gravesites of dozens of its most illustrious residents, from Balzac and Chopin to Edith Piaf and Marcel Proust. (American interloper Jim Morrison is there, too.) Just go to http://dying.about.com/od/Fascinationwithdeath/Fascination_with_Death.htm and follow the link to the virtual tour.

2. THE CATACOMBS, *Paris*

Though not, strictly speaking, a cemetery, the Catacombs of Paris should definitely be part of any sightseeing tour of great international funerary sites—unless you happen to be even slightly claustrophobic or squeamish about spending time in the company of several million exhumed human bones. Located deep beneath the city streets, this former gypsum quarry was consecrated as a burial place in 1786, at which time the bones from the notorious Cimetière des Innocents were dug up and transferred to its underground grottoes. "Other overcrowded churchyards soon followed suit," Judi Culbertson and Tom Randall inform us in *Permanent Parisians*. "At dusk the bones were loaded into carts, which were followed by priests chanting the burial service. No attempt was made to individualize the remains."

To reach the Catacombs, you are required to undergo a subterranean journey not unlike the one experienced by poor Fortunato in Poe's "The Cask of Amontillado." After descending a seemingly endless flight of narrow stone stairs and proceeding along a dank, dark, oppressively cramped passageway, you will finally arrive at the ossuary entrance, whose lintel is carved with the heartwarming greeting "*Arrête! C'est ici l'empire de la mort*" ("Stop! This is the kingdom of the dead"). If you choose to ignore this warning by crossing the threshold, you will find yourself wandering past a series of large recesses in the stone walls. Each is fronted by a retaining wall of skulls and tibias (some quite artfully arranged) behind which looms an enormous pile of indiscriminately commingled bones. The remains of many illustrious Parisians are here, though you won't be able to pick them out of the jumble. When you finally reemerge into the world of the living, you will never have felt so grateful to see the sky.

Note: If it crosses your mind to abscond with a macabre souvenir, you should strongly resist the temptation, not only because of the inherent sacrilege of the act—which is tantamount to grave robbing—but because you will be searched as you depart.

Address: 1 place Denfert-Rochereau, 14th arrondissement, 75014 Paris
Metro: Denfert-Rochereau
Hours: Tue.–Fri. 2–4 p.m.; Sat.–Sun. 9–11 a.m., 2–4 p.m.
Tel.: (33) 1 43 22 47 63

3. HIGHGATE, *London*

One of the best-known garden cemeteries of the Victorian era, Highgate is renowned for its elaborate funerary architecture and impressive landscaping. Its original section—now known as the West Cemetery—was designed by architect Stephen Geary, who supplied it with a handsomely terraced layout, gently winding paths, and imposing features. Most notable are the famed Egyptian Avenue—entered through a massive archway flanked by lotus-decorated columns—and the Circle of Lebanon, a somber structure of twenty sunken tombs surrounding a vast cedar tree. During its early years, when the cemetery was filled with plantings from an on-site greenhouse that employed more than two dozen full-time gardeners, Highgate became the burial place of choice for fashionable Londoners. By 1854, fifteen years after its opening, its success led to the creation of a second section across the road, the so-called East Cemetery, whose most famous permanent occupant is Karl Marx. Eventually, the original West Cemetery suffered a severe decline. The tombs and mausoleums fell into disrepair (when they weren't actively vandalized) and the once carefully tended grounds became choked with trees and undergrowth. In 1975, West Highgate was closed to the public. It has since enjoyed an extensive and ongoing restoration and its beautiful stone monuments and notable graves are once again available for viewing, albeit on a restricted, guided-tour-only basis.

Address: Swain's Lane, Highgate, London N6 6PJ
Hours: The cemetery is open every day except December 25 and 26. The cemetery is closed temporarily when there is a funeral in progress. *East Cemetery:* Open from 10 a.m. weekdays, 11 a.m. weekends. Closing time: Apr. 1–Oct. 31: 5 p.m. (last admission 4:30 p.m.), Nov. 1–Mar. 31: 4 p.m. (last admission 3:30 p.m.). *West Cemetery:* Admission to the West Cemetery is by

guided tour only. Weekday tours: There is one tour at 2 P.M. (guaranteed for 12–15 people). It is advisable to book in advance by telephone, and visitors are requested to arrive at 1:45 P.M. There are no weekday tours in December, January, and February. Weekend tours (for which there is no booking) take place each hour at 11 A.M., 12 noon, 1 P.M., 2 P.M., 3 P.M., and 4 P.M. (last tour at 3 P.M. from November 1 to March 31), again guaranteed only for 12–15 people each. It is advisable, especially in holiday seasons, to come at least half an hour before the scheduled time.

TEL.: (44) 020 8340 1834

4. PROTESTANT CEMETERY, *Rome*

The name by which this tiny plot of land is commonly known—the Protestant Cemetery—is somewhat of a misnomer since Jews and other non-Christians are also buried on the site. Its Italian name, *Cimitero acattolico* (non-Catholic cemetery) is a more accurate designation. By whatever name it's called, however, this urban oasis—with its towering cypress trees and proximity to the ancient Pyramid of Cestius (an Egyptian-style tomb built around 12 B.C.)—is widely regarded as one of the world's most glorious graveyards. Henry James deemed it "the most beautiful thing in Italy," while poet Percy Bysshe Shelley couldn't think of a better spot to spend eternity. "It might make one in love with death," he declared, "to think that one should be buried in so sweet a place."

Shelley, who drowned in a boating accident not long after making this comment, would get his wish. His cremains (minus the heart, which was snatched from the flames by his friend Edward John Trelawney) are interred on the grounds, beneath a stone with an inscription from Shakespeare's *The Tempest*: "Nothing of Him that Doth Fade / But Doth Suffer a Sea Change / Into Something Rich and Strange." Not far away lie the remains of Shelley's fellow immortal, John Keats, whose tombstone features a famous (if overly pessimistic) inscription by his friends Joseph Severn and Charles Brown: "This grave contains all that was mortal, of a YOUNG ENGLISH POET, Who on his Death Bed, in the Bitterness of his Heart, at the Malicious Power of his Enemies, Desired these Words to be engraven on his Tomb Stone: Here lies One Whose Name was writ in water."

Indeed, given the smallness of the cemetery—which was founded in 1734 and is said to be the oldest burial ground in continuous use in Europe—it may well contain, as writer Elizabeth Rosenthal claims, "the highest density of famous and important bones anywhere in the world." Other renowned occupants include Goethe's only son, August; nineteenth-century American novelist Richard Henry Dana, author of *Two Years Before the Mast*; Italian philosopher Antonio Gramsci, a founding father of European Communism; English poet and critic John Addington Symonds; Josef Myslivecek, the eighteenth-century Czech composer credited with inventing the string quartet; and the American Beat poet Gregory Corso. Among the graveyard's many beautiful works of funerary art is the sculpture *Angel of Grief*, an enormous weeping angel that adorns the tomb of its creator, American artist W. W. Story, and his wife, Emelyn, for whom it was designed.

Unfortunately, despite its historic significance, the Protestant Cemetery has never received landmark status from the Italian government and the public financing that goes along with it. As a result, it has fallen into such extreme disrepair that it has been placed on the World Monument Fund's watch list of the one hundred most endangered sites on earth. At present, it is managed by a committee of volunteer conservators whose hope (as Rosenthal writes) is that the World Monument Fund listing "will bring in financing, so that they will be able to restore the cemetery to its former glory and preserve the important monuments within."

ADDRESS: Via Caio Cestio 6, Rome
DIRECTIONS: Take the metro to the Porta San Paolo stop (Piramide), cross the square to the Via Caio Cesto, and follow the wall to the entrance.
HOURS: 8–11:30 A.M., 2:30–4:30 P.M.; closed on Wednesdays
TEL.: 06 5741900

Mount Auburn Cemetery. Nineteenth-century engraving.

5. MOUNT AUBURN, *Cambridge, Massachusetts*

America's first garden cemetery, Mount Auburn consists of 174 picturesque acres (most of which, despite its official Cambridge address, actually lie in adjacent Watertown). Nestled in a bend of the Charles River, its lush, wooded landscape—featuring over fifty-three thousand trees—has served as a quasi-rural retreat for nature-hungry city dwellers since the cemetery opened in 1831. Mount Auburn still draws more than two hundred thousand visitors a year and is regarded as a mecca for birders, who flock there to catch glimpses of dozens of species, including white-throated sparrows in the fall, yellow-rumped warblers in the spring, and northern waterthrushes and great crested flycatchers in the summer.

To the true taphophile, of course, the real attraction is the cemetery's magnificent collection of historic tombs and memorials. Among the luminaries buried there are Louis Agassiz, Robert Creeley, Mary Baker Eddy, Felix Frankfurter, Buckminster Fuller, Oliver Wendell Holmes, Winslow Homer, Henry Wadsworth Longfellow, James Russell Lowell, Bernard Malamud, and B. F. Skinner.

ADDRESS: 580 Mount Auburn Street
Cambridge, MA 02138
HOURS: Oct.–Apr., 8 A.M.–5 P.M.;
May–Aug., 8 A.M.–7 P.M.
TEL.: 617-547-7105

6. GREEN-WOOD, *Brooklyn, New York*

Four times the size of Père-Lachaise, this sprawling 474-acre rural cemetery was founded in 1838 and quickly became one of the nation's leading tourist attractions, drawing upward of a half million visitors a year in its heyday. With its rolling hills, winding paths, charming ponds, and magnificent mortuary sculptures, it was precisely the sort of lush arboretum-cum–memorial garden that appealed so intensely to Victorian sensibilities.

Though the crowds are considerably

smaller today, Green-Wood (designated a National Historic Landmark in 2006) remains a delightful spot for a Sunday outing and a taphophile's paradise. As the preferred interment spot for eminent nineteenth-century New Yorkers, it boasts a veritable who's who of famous Victorian occupants, including Henry Ward Beecher, Horace Greeley, Nathaniel Currier and James Merritt Ives, Samuel B. Morse, and Louis Comfort Tiffany. There are also plenty of later notables, ranging from world-famous artists such as Leonard Bernstein and Jean-Michel Basquiat to legendary gangsters such as Albert Anastasia and Johnny Torrio. Altogether, roughly six hundred thousand individuals are interred on the grounds and it continues to average nine burials and/or cremations per day. Its many sculptural highlights include a life-size statue of the goddess Minerva saluting the Statue of Liberty; the exquisite Griffith monument, featuring a bas-relief of a nineteenth-century housewife waving farewell to her husband as he hurries to catch a trolley car for work; and the imposing tomb of tobacconist John Anderson in the shape of a Greek Revival temple.

Address: 500 25th Street
Brooklyn, NY 11232-1755
Subway: Take the R train to 25th Street in Brooklyn, then walk up the hill one block to the main entrance at 5th Avenue and 25th Street.
Hours: 7:45 a.m.–5 p.m. daily
Tel.: 718-768-7300

7. WOODLAWN, *Bronx, New York*

Founded in 1863 when the Bronx was still farmland, Woodlawn Cemetery became the favored burial place for the fantastically wealthy robber barons of the Gilded Age—a necropolis with such a rich concentration of elaborate tombs that it has been likened to the Valley of the Kings in ancient Thebes. In a beautiful parklike setting filled with magnificent trees—white oak and weeping beech, umbrella pine and cork, goldenrain and silver bell—visitors can view some of the most spectacular mausoleums ever erected on American soil, many designed by the most famous U.S. architects of the day, including John Russell Pope, Raymond Hood, James Renwick, James Gamble Rogers, and Stanford White (the architects, respectively, of the Jefferson Memorial, Rockefeller Center, St. Patrick's Cathedral, Yale University, and the Washington Square Arch). The long-dead nabobs who occupy these ornate tombs—which resemble everything from Greek and Egyptian temples to the chapels of Renaissance chateaux—include R. H. Macy, F. W. Woolworth, J. C. Penney, Jay Gould, H. O. Armour, and Henry Westinghouse.

Besides its dense population of plutocrats, Woodlawn also boasts a long list of resident celebrities, many of whose graves are adorned with beautifully designed monuments. Among its most renowned occupants are Irving Berlin, Miles Davis, Duke Ellington, Oscar Hammerstein, W. C. Handy, Fiorello LaGuardia, Bat Masterson, Herman Melville, Joseph Pulitzer, Damon Runyon, and Elizabeth Cady Stanton.

Address: Webster Avenue and East 233rd Street, Bronx, NY 10470
Subway: Take the #4 train (Lexington Avenue express) to the end of the line (Woodlawn Station). At the base of the station walk about a half block. The Jerome Avenue entrance is on the right.

Alternatively, take the #2 or #5 train to 233rd Street Station. Walk three blocks along 233rd downhill. Cross over Webster Avenue. The cemetery entrance is on the left.
HOURS: 8:30 A.M.–5 P.M. daily
TEL.: 718-920-0500

8. FOREST LAWN, *Glendale, California*

Clearly every taphophile worthy of the name will want to visit all six branches of Forest Lawn. But if, for whatever reason, you must limit yourself to a single site, the original memorial garden in Glendale is the one to see. Even the Hollywood Hills cemetery—with its magnificent Plaza of Mesoamerican Heritage, Birth of Liberty Mosaic, and replica of Boston's Old North Church—can't match the wonders to be seen at Glendale. Among its artistic and architectural highlights: an exact facsimile (with added fig leaf) of Michelangelo's *David*, standing sixteen feet nine inches high and carved of white Carrara marble; a mosaic reproduction of John Trumbull's famous patriotic painting *The Signing of the Declaration of Independence*, consisting of seven hundred thousand pieces of Venetian glass tile and measuring three times the size of the original; an immense stained-glass re-creation of Leonardo da Vinci's *Last Supper*, based on the artist's original sketches; the world's largest wrought-iron entrance gates, surpassing in size the ones at Buckingham Palace; Polish artist Jan Styka's panoramic depiction of the Crucifixion, said to be the largest framed painting in the world at 195 feet long by 45 feet high; and the Wee Kirk o' the Heather, a "faithful reconstruction" of the little church in Glencairn, Scotland, where "bonnie Annie Laurie" of Scottish folk tradition worshipped.

There are even graves to be seen at the cemetery, though they are not, of course, blighted by anything as dreary as tombstones. Among the many celebrities interred at Glendale are Humphrey Bogart, Nat "King" Cole, Sammy Davis Jr., Walt Disney, Buddy Ebsen, W. C. Fields, Errol Flynn, Clark Gable, Jean Harlow, Chico Marx, Mary Pickford, James Stewart, and Spencer Tracy.

ADDRESS: 1712 S. Glendale Avenue
Glendale, CA 91205
HOURS: 8 A.M.–5 P.M. daily
TEL.: 323-478-2339

9. HOLLYWOOD FOREVER, *Hollywood, California*

Founded in 1899—a dozen years before the pioneers of the nascent film industry began setting up shop in southern California—Hollywood Memorial Park (as it was originally called) became the preferred final resting place for the early stars and moguls of the silent screen. With the advent of Forest Lawn, however, the older cemetery lost much of its cachet and eventually declined into one of those sad relics of former Tinseltown glamour, like the Brown Derby restaurant or the character played by Gloria Swanson in *Sunset Boulevard*. It hit its nadir in the mid-1990s when it fell into bankruptcy and lost its license to sell its remaining plots. Some families—alarmed at the sorry state of the increasingly decrepit graveyard—went so far as to disinter their loved ones and bury them elsewhere. Fortunately for film lovers and taphophiles alike, this historic cemetery was saved by a pair of farsighted funeral home entrepreneurs, the Cassity brothers of Forever Enterprises, who bought it for a song in 1998 and set about restoring it to its former glory.

Among the many Hollywood legends who repose on its grounds are Rudolph Valentino, Douglas Fairbanks, Cecil B. DeMille, and Jesse Lasky, founder of Paramount Pictures. Other permanent residents include such minor (but intriguing) figures as Virginia Rappe (the victim at the center of the notorious Fatty Arbuckle murder trial, one of the most sensational criminal cases of the Roaring Twenties); the beloved cowlick-sporting Little Rascal, Carl "Alfalfa" Switzer, shot dead in a sordid altercation over $50; and William Randolph Hearst's mistress, Marion Davies.

In contrast to Forest Lawn—whose "Builder" regarded headstones as a blight on the landscape—Hollywood Forever is also graced with some exceptional mortuary markers, including a monument shaped like a rocket ship and the tombstone of the inimitable Mel Blanc, who provided the voices of Bugs Bunny, Daffy Duck, Porky Pig, and countless other classic cartoon characters and whose epitaph reads: "That's All Folks."

Address: 6000 Santa Monica Boulevard
Hollywood, CA 90038
Hours: 8 a.m.–5 p.m. daily
Tel.: 323-469-1181

10. HOPE, Barre, *Vermont*

This 85-acre cemetery was established in 1895 when it became clear that the town's original graveyard, Elmwood, was about to reach its limit. The burial place of choice for the town's large population of immigrant Italian stonecutters, Hope features hundreds of stunning monuments carved from its world-famous granite. Among its sculptural

Hope Cemetery Memorials: chair, car, soccer ball, and marriage bed. Courtesy of Jim Eaton.

highlights are a half-size replica of a racing car, a biplane on its way to the heavens, an enormous soccer ball, an upholstered armchair, and a set of twin beds with the pajama-clad husband-and-wife occupants sitting up and holding hands. (For a good online guide to the various monuments, go to www.central-vt.com/visit/cemetery/.

ADDRESS: 201 Maple Avenue, Barre, VT 05641 (entrance on Merchant Street)
HOURS: Daily, dawn to dusk
TEL.: 802-476-6245

RECOMMENDED READING

To learn more about these and many other outstanding burial sites, check out the excellent series of illustrated guidebooks by Judi Culbertson and Tom Randall, *Permanent Parisians* (Cheslea Green, 1986), *Permanent New Yorkers* (Chelsea Green, 1987), *Permanent Californians* (Chelsea Green, 1989), *Permanent Londoners* (Chelsea Green, 1991), and *Permanent Italians* (Walker and Co., 1996).

Legends of Père-Lachaise

A place as creepily atmospheric as Père-Lachaise is bound to spawn all kinds of bizarre urban legends. In *This Must Be the Place* (Collier, 1989), his engaging memoir of Paris in the 1920s, Jimmie Charters—bartender at the famed Montparnasse watering hole The Dingo—recalls a regular named Leaming, a mysterious American who "loved to tell weird stories which he always insisted were true."

One of the weirdest involved a beautiful Russian princess who had escaped the revolution with a fortune in jewels and settled in Paris in 1919. When she died just two years later at the age of twenty-five, she left "a most curious bequest."

"It provided," claimed Leaming, "that a large vault should be built in Père-Lachaise cemetery. She herself was to be placed, totally nude, in a coffin made entirely of glass. The coffin was to be sealed hermetically in such a way that her body would be preserved in perfect condition for many years" and arranged in an upright position so that the body would appear "to be that of a lovely woman standing in a natural way." The remainder of the vault was to be "furnished with a fine bed, table, bookshelves and books, and even a bath with running hot and cold water."

The strangest part of the story, however, was yet to come. As Leaming explained to his rapt barroom audience:

> Her fortune of well over a million francs is left to a man who shall pass one entire year within the vault, along with the lovely ivory-skinned lady. He will not be alone, for her eyes are wide open and they seem to follow one to every part of the room. During that year, the lucky man is to have whatever he chooses in the way of books and phonograph records; he may work on sculpture, painting or writing, anything he chooses. He may have what materials he likes. There is no window in the vault, but ample air and light is provided by a skylight. In the door is a small sliding passage by which his food will be brought to him three times a day. He may

> order of his heart's desire of meat or drink. The lucky man will even be allowed to take half an hour's exercise in a garden nearby which is closed to everyone except himself and his guard. He may not speak to the guard, for the latter is deaf and dumb.

There was one other crucial feature of the vault, said Leaming: an electric buzzer near the door. "The man who lives there has but to push the button and at once the guard will come, open the door, and give him his liberty. But of course, if he leaves before the end of one year, he forfeits his claim to the inheritance."

According to Leaming—who insisted that he might take up the challenge himself—only two men had made the attempt, "a Dutchman who stayed two months and later went insane" and a Russian who lasted only one night before fleeing.

"Both said that the terrible part was the night, in the dark," reported Leaming, "when the body of the nude girl seemed to take on a luminous quality."

ASK DR. DEATH

Dear Dr. Death:

In reading the discussion of Hollywood Forever Cemetery, I was shocked to learn that Carl Switzer—the beloved, cowlicked Alfalfa of Our Gang *fame—was "shot dead in a sordid altercation over $50." Can you elaborate?*

Devastated Alfalfa Fan

Dear Devastated:

Certainly. Once his *Our Gang* days were over in 1940, Switzer had a spotty career, landing bit parts in various movies, including *Lassie*, *It's a Wonderful Life*, and *The Defiant Ones*. He also popped up occasionally on TV, appearing a few times on *The Roy Rogers Show*, where he reprised the comical off-key singing that had endeared the character Alfalfa to millions. For the most part, however, he had become one of those Hollywood has-beens who are forced to scramble for ways to keep body and soul together. In Switzer's case, he worked at various unglamorous jobs, including bartending. He also bred hunting dogs and hired himself out as a professional hunting guide.

In January 1959, Switzer borrowed a dog from a friend, Moses "Bud" Stiltz. When the dog ran away, Switzer posted a $50 reward for its return. A few days later, someone found the dog and claimed the reward, which Switzer promptly forked over. It wasn't long, however, before Switzer—a notoriously prickly personality who became even nastier when he drank—decided that Stiltz should reimburse him the $50. On the evening of January 21, a drunken Switzer showed up at Stiltz's Mission Hills home and demanded the money. A violent quarrel ensued. It climaxed when Switzer drew a knife and charged Stiltz, who shot him in the belly with a handgun. Switzer died of blood loss on the way to the hospital at the age of thirty-two. Stiltz was ultimately acquitted, the incident being ruled a justifiable homicide.

For more information about the depressing demise of Alfalfa and scores of other celebrities, see James Robert Parish's *The Hollywood Book of Death: The Bizarre, Often Sordid, Passings of More than 125 American Movie and TV Idols* (McGraw-Hill, 2001).

The Only Travel Book You'll Ever Need (Assuming You Spend All Your Vacation Time Visiting Cemeteries)

Making a pilgrimage to Graceland to stand in awe of Elvis's collection of gold records, marvel at the magnificence of the Jungle Room, and stand reverentially at the King's grave is, of course, part of the patriotic duty of every right-thinking American. But where do you go if you want to pay your respects to one of the lesser deities of rock and roll—Buddy Holly, say, or Roy Orbison?

DEATH DEFINITION: *Taphophile*

ARE YOU THE KIND OF PERSON WHO LOVES TO SPEND YOUR FREE TIME TOURING CEMETERIES? ARE TOMBstone rubbings your favorite genre of visual art? While other people devote themselves to ending hunger in Third World countries and promoting global peace, do you regard the preservation of old graveyards as the single worthiest cause a human being can embrace?

If the answer to any or all of these questions is yes, then you are almost certainly a taphophile.

A combination of the Greek words for "tomb" and "lover," a taphophile is a person who has the same kind of passionate interest in graveyards that bibliophiles have in books, cinephiles in movies, and oenophiles in fine wines. Taphophiles love to study, read about, and visit cemeteries, often in the company of like-minded enthusiasts.

If you'd like to get to know other taphophiles and maybe even join a club and organize group trips to various picturesque graveyards (an activity known in taphophile circles as "cemetery crawls"), there are any number of websites you can check out, including www.taph.com and www.alsirat.com/taphophile. Particularly good is www.thecemeteryclub.com, whose founders also publish a magazine for taphophiles, *Epitaphs: The Magazine for Cemetery Lovers by Cemetery Lovers*.

the park, bear right, take the next right and the next left. Stop on the drive about 100 feet before it makes an abrupt left. On the curb to the right are markers for the Western Jewish Institute. Jerome's stone can be found five rows back.") Want to pay your respects to *Twilight Zone* creator Rod Serling? You'll find him at Lakeview Cemetery in Interlaken, New York, north from town on Route 96, then east on County Road 150. "Enter the cemetery and bear right at the first two forks. Go past the concrete holding house on the left, turn right at the four corners, and stop at the twin cedar trees on the left. A hundred feet further left is the flat stone that marks Rod's grave."

Not to worry. Thanks to Tod Benoit, tireless tracker-down of the "final resting places of the famous, infamous, and noteworthy," you can easily locate the burial sites not only of America's greatest musicians but also of major figures in nearly every field of human endeavor.

Organized into a dozen useful categories—including "Sports Heroes," "Television and Movie Personalities," "Baby Boomer Icons," and "Greats of Literature, Philosophy, and the Arts"—Benoit's comprehensive guide, *Where Are They Buried? How Did They Die?* (Black Dog & Leventhal, 2003), provides a capsule biography of each of its more than 450 subjects, along with details of his or her death and—best of all—precise directions for finding the gravesite.

Let's say that, like so many other people, you've always dreamed of visiting the grave of the beloved Stooge Jerome "Curly" Howard. Benoit will tell you how. (Proceed to Los Angeles's Home of Peace Memorial Park at 4334 Whittier Blvd., just west of the intersection of I-5 and I-710. Then "enter

Though Benoit's book is a must-have for every serious dead-celebrity sightseer, another indispensable resource is the Find a Grave website (www.findagrave.com). Although its biographical entries are briefer and its burial plot directions not as obsessively precise, Find a Grave will tell you where to find the graves of more than fifty thousand deceased notables, divided into more than thirty categories—everything from actors to architects, magicians to Medal of Honor recipients, Supreme Court justices to organized crime figures. (Benoit will tell you exactly where to find the graves of Al Capone and Benjamin "Bugsy" Siegel, but if you have a hankering to see the final resting place of "Machine Gun" Jack McGurn—one of the perpetrators of the St. Valentine's Massacre—you'll have to consult Find a Grave.)

OTHER RECOMMENDED READING

Besides Benoit's book, other fine, somewhat more specialized guides are available to the dedicated necrotourist. These include *James Dean Died Here: The Locations of America's Pop Culture Landmarks* (Santa Monica, 2003) by Chris Epting; *Hollywood Remains to Be Seen: A Guide to the Movie Stars' Final Homes* (Cumberland House, 2001) by Mark J. Masek; *Stairway to Heaven: The Final Resting Places of Rock's Legends* (Wener, 2005) by J. D. Reed and Maddy Miller; and *The Tombstone Tourist: Musicians* (Pocket, 2003) by Scott Stanton.

Cemetery Shopping Tips

If you plan to be buried in the traditional way—as opposed to opting for some newfangled alternative such as cryonic preservation or getting turned into a synthetic diamond—it's a good idea to purchase a cemetery plot well in advance of your demise. By doing so, you will spare your grieving survivors a lot of last-minute stress when they're least capable of coping. You will also save your family a significant amount of money. According to experts, a plot purchased "pre-need" can be half the price of what the same piece of real estate will cost when it's urgently required—that is, when

A Taphophilic Treat for *Titanic* Tourists

If you're a serious *Titanic* buff—or a hard-core fan of James Cameron's 1997 blockbuster—you'll certainly want to make a pilgrimage to Fairview Lawn Cemetery in Halifax, Nova Scotia, the final resting place of more than one hundred people who died aboard the doomed luxury liner.

As viewers of the movie know, drowning was not the only cause of death when the *Titanic* went down. Some passengers and crew members—kept afloat by life preservers—died of exposure in the frigid water. In the days immediately following the disaster, several ships were dispatched from the nearest port city, Halifax, to retrieve whatever bodies could be found. Altogether, 328 corpses—men, women, and 2 children—were recovered. Of those, 119 were buried at sea. The rest were brought back to Halifax, where they were embalmed by volunteer undertakers from around the Maritime Provinces.

Fifty-nine of these *Titanic* victims were shipped back home for burial. The remaining 150 were interred in three Halifax graveyards: 10 bodies in the Jewish cemetery, Baron de Hirsch; 19 in the Catholic cemetery, Mount Olivet; and 121 in the nondenominational cemetery, Fairview Lawn. The plots and simple gravestones were paid for by the doomed ship's owner, the White Star Line.

the purchasers are in no position to shop around for a better bargain.

In choosing a cemetery, there are a number of questions to ask yourself. To begin with, in what manner of graveyard do you wish to spend your decomposing years? The two main types are the traditional cemetery with upright gravestones and the memorial park as pioneered by Forest Lawn—the kind whose expansive lawns are free of unsightly tombstones and that rely instead on ground-level bronze markers to signify the presence of departed loved ones.

Next, as with all real estate purchases, you must consider the issue of location. A cemetery adjoining a suburban industrial park in Frostbite Falls, Minnesota, is likely to charge less for a grave than one located on a beautiful hilltop with a sweeping view of San Francisco Bay.

Similarly, plots *within* a given cemetery often vary significantly according to location. A grave near a piece of sculpture, a fountain, or some other special feature of the cemetery will almost certainly be more expensive than one in a "nonfeature section" (to use the lingo of the trade). The question to consider is: Do you really want to shell out all that extra money for the privilege of spending eternity in the vicinity of a half-size replica of Michelangelo's *David*—particularly when you will be spending it as a decayed mass of organic matter encased within a tightly sealed container several feet underground?

If the cemetery features an aboveground mausoleum, you might want to consider it as an alternative to earth burial, particularly if you, like so many people, have an aversion to the thought of ending up as subterranean worm fodder. Being entombed in a nice, clean, dry mausoleum crypt is generally no more expensive than traditional burial since it eliminates the various fees involved with the opening and closing of a grave, as well as the cost of a tombstone or other memorial marker.

As with all other major purchases, it's incumbent on you to be an educated consumer. Find out who owns and manages the cemetery, if there is an endowment care fund for the perpetual maintenance of the premises, and what the various ancillary costs of burial amount to. Grave-shopping mavens agree that it's wise to pay a personal visit to any prospective cemeteries so you can tour the property and check out its condition for yourself. If you find, for example, that a particular cemetery is distinguished by its blighted trees, badly overgrown plots, and vandalized tombstones defaced with swastikas, you'll probably want to pass on it.

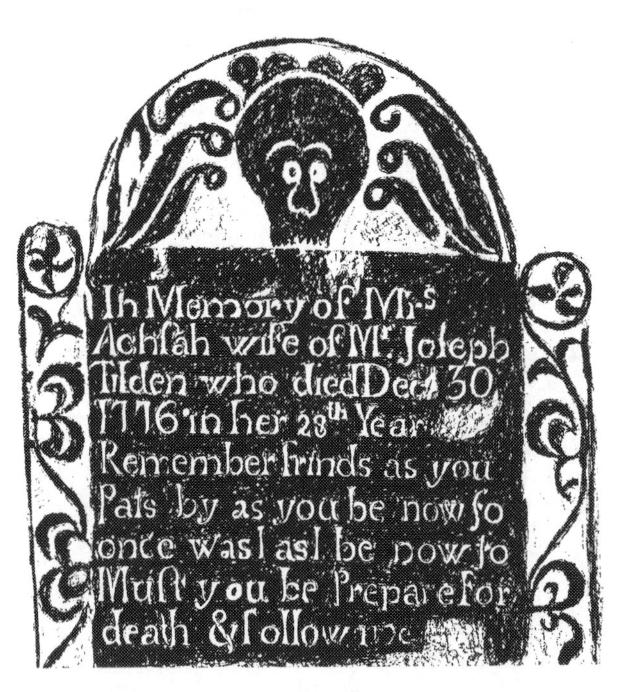

RECOMMENDED RESOURCES

For solid information on cemetery shopping, check out the Consumer Resource Guide compiled by the International Cemetery and Funeral Association at www.icfa.org/cemeteries.htm. The Alton Memorial Sales Company of Alton, Illinois, also maintains a very informative site at www.altonmemorialsales.com/faq.htm. A brisk, seven-step guide, "How to Purchase a Cemetery Plot," can be found online at www.ehow.com/how_3461_buy-cemetery-plot.html.

The Ultimate Cemetery Locator

If you're conducting genealogical research, looking for a convenient place to bury a loved one, or just curious to know how many graveyards exist in, say, North Dakota, the book you'll want to consult is *Cemeteries of the U.S.: A Guide to Contact Information for U.S. Cemeteries and Their Records* (Gale Research, 1994), edited by Deborah M. Burek. This massive tome provides information on more than 22,600 currently operating and inactive cemeteries in all fifty states, plus overseas military cemeteries where large numbers of American servicemen are buried.

Each entry provides basic data—the cemetery name, address, telephone number, religious affiliation, visiting hours, and so on—plus a bunch of other useful information, including the years of operation, any former names the cemetery went by, the availability of records, the name of the person to contact with questions, and interesting historical and architectural tidbits.

Originally published at $155, the book is currently out of print, and a used copy (if you can find one) will set you back even more. Given the cost, it's the kind of volume that only a professional genealogist or hard-core taphophile will want for his or her personal collection. Mere dilettantes of death will have to settle for visiting their nearest research library to pore over a copy.

Though man has lost his claim to uniqueness as a toolmaker, war planner, and even serial murderer, there is a case, made at length by paleontologists, that humans are still unique in having burial rituals for their fellows. Man is no longer the toolmaker, but the gravedigger.

—Adam Gopnik

Gravedigging: A Dying Art

As anyone who's read *Hamlet* knows, gravedigging used to be an extremely specialized occupation that required a strong back, a high tolerance for dirt, and the ability to engage in clever repartee with tragically indecisive Danish princes. Nowadays, things are different. There's still a lot of dirt involved, but opportunities to trade witticisms with doomed Shakespearean heroes are much less common. Nor—thanks to the technological advances that have occurred during the last four centuries—is the job quite as physically demanding as it once was.

Even as recently as the mid-twentieth century, gravediggers were forced to rely entirely on hand tools and their own muscles. They hauled their implements to the burial site in a wheelbarrow, used wood planks to measure off the dimensions of the plot, excavated the hole and squared off its edges with a shovel, then—once the coffin was in place—filled up the grave again by hand. It was a backbreaking job, but one that many of its practitioners performed with a keen sense of professionalism, taking pride in the perfection of each handmade grave.

Today's gravediggers have it easier. They can use backhoes for the digging, hydraulic equipment to shore up the sides of the grave, mechanized devices to lower the casket into the ground, and dump trucks to replace the dirt. To be sure, a fair amount of manual labor is still necessary. And it's still possible to find the occasional gravedigger who does things the traditional way.

If you want to read a beautiful description of this latter type of old-fashioned craftsman, you can't do better than the concluding pages of Philip Roth's powerfully depressing 2006 masterwork, *Everyman*, in which the nameless protagonist, during a visit to his parents' graves, encounters the cemetery caretaker, who patiently explains the painstaking daylong process: locating the plot with a seven-foot metal probe, cutting the sod to precisely measured dimensions, shoveling out a neatly edged six-foot-deep hole. Even this individual, however—who spurns backhoes because they can damage the soil—uses a small tractor to cart away the excess dirt.

The website www.careerplanner.com offers this job description for aspiring cemetery workers:

> Prepares graves and maintains cemetery grounds: Locates grave site according to section, lot, and plot numbers and marks area to be excavated. Removes sod from gravesite, using shovel. Digs grave to specified depth, using spade and shovel or backhoe. Places concrete slabs on bottom and around grave to line it. Mixes and pours concrete to construct foundation for grave marker, using premixed concrete, wheelbarrow, and handtools. Positions casket-lowering device on grave, covers dirt pile and sod with artificial grass carpet, erects canopy, and arranges folding chairs to prepare site for burial service. Sets grave marker in concrete on gravesite, using

shovel and trowel. Mows grass, using hand or power mower. Prunes shrubs, trims trees, and plants flowers and shrubs on grave. Removes leaves and other debris from graves, using leaf blowers and weed eaters. May drive vehicles, such as backhoe, truck, and tractors.

Though incomes vary, the standard salary for today's cemetery worker is about $9 an hour. So if you're looking for an outdoor job involving manual labor, rudimentary gardening skill, an extremely quiet work environment, and meager pay, gravedigging may be right for you!

Written in Stone

One great disadvantage of opting for an alternative form of corpse disposal—such as having your ashes scattered at sea or getting your body planted in an all-natural "green cemetery" that forbids grave markers—is that you miss out on the fun of having a tombstone inscribed with an elaborate epitaph.

The practice of placing memorial messages on grave markers dates back to antiquity (the word itself is compounded of the Greek prefix *epi-*, meaning "upon," and the word *taphos*, meaning "tomb"). In his seminal 1962 study, *Themes in Greek and Latin Epitaphs* (University of Chicago Press, 1962), poet and scholar Richard Lattimore analyzes hundreds of sepulchral inscriptions from the ancient world and divides them into various themes, from the simple farewell ("Happy voyage!") to the curse leveled against potential violators of the grave ("I, Idameneus, built this tomb to my own glory. May Zeus utterly destroy anyone who disturbs it").

The dire-threat-to-grave-defilers type of epitaph fell out of fashion in subsequent centuries. (One notable exception is Shakespeare's supposedly self-composed epitaph, "Good friend for Jesus sake forbeare / To dig the dust enclosed here. / Blest be the man that spares these stones / And curst be he that moves my bones.") At least since the 1600s, the fundamental purpose of the epitaph has been to keep alive the memory of the deceased by transmitting basic biographical information. Many old tombstones both here and abroad offer nothing more than the simplest facts: "John Chapman, shipwright, died 10th August, 1789." Others add loving tributes to the deceased. These can range from a simple appreciation—"Devoted wife of Hiram"—to an extended encomium, as in this specimen collected by the Reverend Timothy Alden, who published a two-volume compilation of early American epitaphs in 1814:

SACRED TO THE MEMORY OF MRS. SARAH LITTLE, RELICT OF THE LATE REV. DANIEL LITTLE, WHO DEPARTED THIS LIFE, 19 DECEMBER 1804, AGED 78. POSSESSED OF A FEELING MIND ENCLOSED IN A DELICATE FRAME, WITH A HEART TRANSFUSED WITH THE MILD SPIRIT OF CHRISTIANITY; WITH THE WORLD UNDER HER FEET, AND THE EYE OF FAITH STEADFASTLY FIXED ON HEAVENLY JOYS; FOR A SERIES OF YEARS, SHE ENDURED EXCRUCIATING PAIN AND MUCH BODILY INDISPOSITION; AND, AT LAST, CALMLY RESIGNED HER BODY TO THE TOMB IN THE WELL ASSURED HOPE OF A RESURRECTION TO A BLESSED IMMORTALITY.

Another common type of epitaph, examples of which can be found as far back as ancient Rome, is the message from the dead to the living. The most famous of these is:

Remember friend as you pass by
As you are now so once was I.
As I am now you will surely be
Prepare thyself to follow me

As a stroll through any old cemetery will attest, the vast majority of tombstone writings offer little in the way of originality. Still, British and American graveyards have yielded enough weird and wacky epitaphs to fill a shelf's worth of volumes with titles such as *Curious Epitaphs*, *Select and Remarkable Epitaphs* and *Epitaphs: Quaint, Curious, and Elegant*. Epitaphs of this variety tend to fall into various categories. There is, for example, the type of inscription that details the cause of death—anything from childbirth to fatal disease to a tragic accident:

Eighteen years a maiden,
One year a wife,
One day a mother,
Then I lost my life

Nearby these gray rocks
Enclos'd in a box
Lies Hatter Cox
Who died of smallpox

In memory of Ellen Shannon
Aged 26 Years
Who was fatally burned
March 21st 1870
By the explosion of a lamp
Filled with "R. E. Danforth's
Non Explosive
Burning
Fluid"

There are epitaphs to departed spouses that convey a wide range of emotions, from inconsolable grief to unabashed glee:

Sacred to the memory of Mary
The lovely and beloved wife of Frederic
Madden. She who was to me the light,
the breath of life is gone!
And memory now is as the faded flower
Whose lingering fragrance
just recalls how sweet,
How beautiful it has been!

Stranger call this not a place
Of fear and gloom,
To me it is a pleasant spot
It is my husband's tomb!

There's the ever-popular punning epitaph that plays on the departed's name:

Here lies Matthew Mudd
Death did him no hurt
When he was alive he was Mudd
But now he's only dirt

Owen Moore
Gone Away
Owin' More
Than he could pay

Here lies
Johnny Yeast
Pardon me
For not rising

In bracing contrast to the saccharine tombstone inscriptions so beloved by the Victorians, there is the occasional "good riddance"–style epitaph for unlamented decedents:

EBENEZER DOCKWOOD
AGED FORTY-SEVEN
A MISER AND A HYPOCRITE
AND NEVER WENT TO HEAVEN

HERE LIES EZEKIEL AIKLE
AGE 102
THE GOOD
DIE YOUNG

There is the occasional epigraph that doubles as a classified ad:

SACRED TO THE MEMORY OF MR.
JARD BATES WHO DIED AUG. THE 6TH
1800. HIS WIDOW AGED 24 WHO MOURNS
AS ONE CAN BE COMFORTED LIVES
AT 7 ELM STREET THIS VILLAGE
AND POSSESSES EVERY QUALIFICATION
FOR A GOOD WIFE

HERE LIES JANE SMITH, WIFE OF THOMAS SMITH, MARBLE CUTTER. THIS MONUMENT WAS ERECTED BY HER HUSBAND AS A TRIBUTE TO HER MEMORY AND A SPECIMEN OF HIS WORK. MONUMENTS OF THE SAME STYLE 350 DOLLARS.

Some epigraphs are short and sweet:

BEEN HERE
AND GONE
HAD A GOOD TIME

THIS IS WHAT I EXPECTED BUT NOT SO SOON

ONCE I WASN'T
THEN I WAS
NOW I AIN'T AGAIN

There are witty self-composed epitaphs, such as the following three by, respectively, the English comedian Spike Milligan, humorist Dorothy Parker, and actress Joan Hackett:

I TOLD YOU I WAS ILL

EXCUSE MY DUST

GO AWAY—I'M ASLEEP

Finally, there are the unclassifiably bizarre epitaphs, like this one found on a Colonial-era tombstone in Great Barrington, Massachusetts:

OH WOULD THAT I COULD LIFT THE LID AND PEER
WITHIN THE GRAVE AND WATCH
THE GREEDY WORMS
THAT EAT AWAY THE DEAD!

RECOMMENDED READING

These epitaphs and hundreds more can be found in Charles L. Wallis, *Stories on Stone: A Book of American Epitaphs* (Oxford University Press, 1954); E. R. Shushan, *Grave Matters: A Collection of 500 Actual Epitaphs* (Ballantine, 1990); David M. Wilson, *Awful Ends: The British Museum Book of Epitaphs* (British Museum Press, 1992); and Kathleen E. Miller, *Last Laughs: Funny Tombstone Quotes and Famous Last Words* (Sterling, 2006). You can also find an extensive collection of memorable epitaphs online at the Epitaph Browser (www.alsirat.com/epitaphs).

Stone Love

A necessity for any nature hobbyist—whether you're a bird watcher, butterfly chaser, wildflower lover, or seashell collector—is the compact, lavishly illustrated field guide that allows easy identification of the objects of your obsession. If you happen to be the type of outdoorsperson who loves to spend a beautiful summer day traipsing through old graveyards instead of pursuing silver-bordered fritillaries or trying to catch a glimpse of a yellow-belled sapsucker, you'll definitely want to get your hands on Douglas Keister's *Stories in Stone: A Field Guide to Cemetery Symbolism and Iconography* (Gibbs Smith, 2004).

Designed for the devoted amateur taphophile, this slender, exceptionally handsome volume contains hundreds of stunning photographs of intricately carved tombstone insignias, from plants and flowers to birds and bees, mythical beasts to human body parts. The hidden meaning of each symbol is explained in a concise accompanying text. The result is a kind of glossy, full-color code book deciphering the pictorial language of tombstones.

Let's say, for example, that—as so often happens—you find yourself in an old Italian cemetery, puzzling over a gravestone carving of an odd-looking creature with the head and wings of an eagle and the body of a lion. Armed with Keister's manual, you will quickly discover that this figure is actually a griffin and that from the fourteenth century onward it was commonly used "to portray the dual nature of Christ—human and divine—because of its mastery of the earth and the heavens." Keister (an award-winning photographer of historical architecture) also devotes a chapter to various organizational symbols, making it easy to tell if the occupant of a particular grave was a Freemason, Shriner, or proud member of the Loyal Order of Moose.

The Virtual Tombstone

You don't have to be a taphophile to love the Tombstone Generator, one of the coolest and cleverest sites on the Web. The main page consists of a large color photograph of a handsome marble tombstone standing in a manicured graveyard. Below the picture is a five-line form on which you can enter whatever name and epigraph you wish. You click on the "Create Tombstone" button and—voilà!—the image reappears, engraved with your custom tombstone message.

You can have all kinds of fun with the Tombstone Generator. Compose your own epigraph and see how it will look when it's carved in stone. Engrave the memorial with the kind of X-rated message not normally found in cemeteries. Or inscribe it with the name of someone you hate and pretend they're dead. The possibilities are endless! You'll find this ingenious site at www.jjchandler.com/tombstone.

Dead Men tell no tales
but their tombstones do.
—Tom Weil

Finally! A Magazine Addressed to the Needs of Taphophiles

Check out the magazine racks and you'll find publications for enthusiasts of every stripe: wine lovers, dog lovers, cigar lovers, book lovers, you name it. Up until now, however, cemetery lovers have been left out in the cold. (Of course, cemetery lovers are used to being out in the cold—when they're traipsing around a New England graveyard in late fall, for example, making rubbings of Puritan tombstones.)

Well, this grave (so to speak) injustice has finally been rectified. Along with her husband, Bill, Minda Powers-Douglas, author of the book *Cemetery Walk* and founder of the indispensable taphophilic website www.thecemeteryclub.com, has recently launched *Epitaphs: The Magazine for Cemetery Lovers by Cemetery Lovers*. A slick, handsomely produced quarterly, *Epitaphs* features the kind of must-read articles you simply won't find in the *New Yorker* or *Family Circle*: items such as "Finding Graves with a Dowsing Rod," "Cemetery Road Trips," and "Antique Funeral Collectibles: A Hobby with a Life of Its Own."

The magazine can be purchased for $8 an issue or at a yearly subscription rate of just $30. For more information, go to the Cemetery Club website or write to:

Epitaphs Magazine
P.O. Box 1163
Moline, IL 61266-1163

(Die-hard taphophiles will also find tons of useful and entertaining information at—you guessed it—www.taph.com.)

Epitaphs *magazine.*
Courtesy of Minda Powers-Douglas.

The Tombstone of Tomorrow—Today

Clearly, in the age of laptops, BlackBerries, and touch-screen cell phones, tombstones are a dreary relic of a time when humans were forced to convey information by the primitive technique of inscribing it by hand. Certainly, no baby boomer worthy of the name is going to want to be memorialized by a boring slab of stone featuring little more than his vital statistics and a hackneyed epitaph.

Happily, help has arrived, courtesy of the visionary entrepreneurs at Vidstone LLC, a company with offices in Florida and Colorado. For a mere $2,000, farsighted consumers can purchase a high-tech device dubbed a "Serenity Panel." Equipped with a small memory chip and a seven-inch LCD screen, this weatherproof, solar-powered, digital "scrapbook" mounts to the front of a gravestone and can play a ten-minute prerecorded video tribute to the deceased.

To be sure, there are a few kinks in the system. Since it operates on sunlight, it won't work if the gravestone is under a tree or facing west. It also has an estimated life span of fifteen years—considerably shorter than the average carved-in-stone tombstone inscription, which tends to last for, oh, several centuries. Also, it's catnip for vandals.

Still, it has one major selling point that no true boomer can resist: it's really cool!

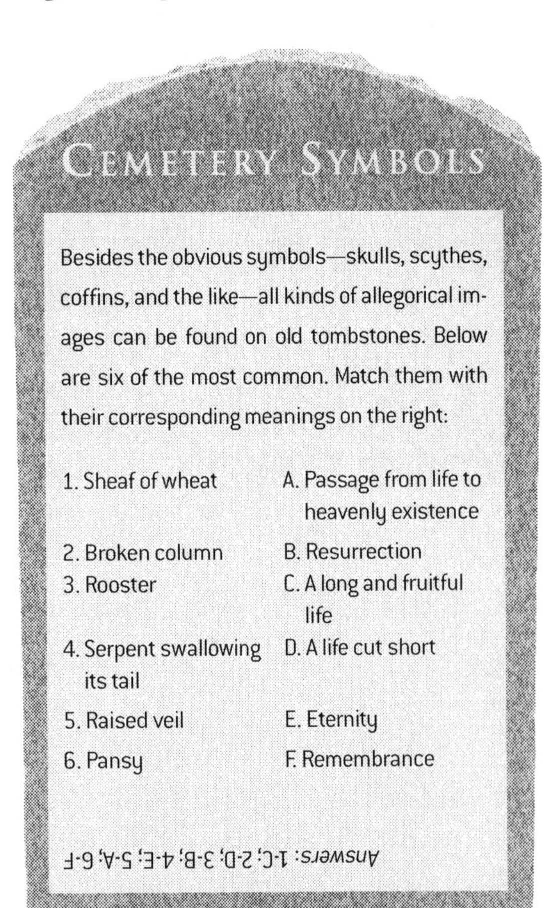

CEMETERY SYMBOLS

Besides the obvious symbols—skulls, scythes, coffins, and the like—all kinds of allegorical images can be found on old tombstones. Below are six of the most common. Match them with their corresponding meanings on the right:

1. Sheaf of wheat	A. Passage from life to heavenly existence
2. Broken column	B. Resurrection
3. Rooster	C. A long and fruitful life
4. Serpent swallowing its tail	D. A life cut short
5. Raised veil	E. Eternity
6. Pansy	F. Remembrance

Answers: 1-C; 2-D; 3-B; 4-E; 5-A; 6-F

Buried Alive

One of the nice things about being alive today as opposed to, say, anytime prior to the mid-1800s is that doctors have become much better at determining whether someone is actually dead or not. As a result, there are far fewer cases of premature burial than there were in the past.

Though accounts of overly hasty body disposal date back to antiquity (Pliny the Elder records two instances of supposedly dead Romans who awoke on their flaming funeral pyres), it wasn't until the mid-eighteenth century that a full-fledged premature-burial panic seized Western Europe. It was precipitated by the publication, in 1746, of a book titled *Dissertation sur l'incertitude des signes de la mort* (*The Uncertainty of the Signs of Death*) by a French physician, Jean-Jacques Bruhier. At a time when a common test for death was placing a feather on someone's lips to see if it moved, Bruhier believed that doctors needed a more reliable way to tell when their dying patients had truly expired. Since the only surefire sign of death was putrefaction, bodies (so Bruhier argued) should not be consigned to the grave until they started to rot, in order to avoid the horror of living interment.

Other medical authorities saw some problems with this approach (primarily the sanitary drawback of keeping a corpse around the house until decomposition set in) and offered recommendations of their own, ranging from tickling the patient's nose with a quill or introducing a crawling insect into his ear to shoving a red-hot poker up his anus—a procedure guaranteed to awaken anyone in even the deepest cataleptic trance. All agreed, however, that—owing to the primitive state of then-current death verification techniques—premature burials had become a common, if not rampant, occurrence.

Self-declared experts cited the most alarming statistics—one claimed that "at least one-tenth of all human beings were buried before they were dead"—while newspapers both here and abroad trumpeted horror stories like this one from a Pennsylvania weekly:

> Farmer George Hefdecker, who lived at Erie, Pa., died very suddenly two weeks ago, of what is supposed to have been heart failure. The body was buried temporarily four days later in a neighbor's lot in the Erie cemetery pending the purchase of one by his family. The transfer was made in a few days, and when the casket was opened at the request of his family, a horrifying spectacle was presented. The body had turned round, and the face and interior of the casket bore the traces of a terrible struggle with death in its most awful shape. The distorted and blood-covered features bore evidence of the agony endured. The clothing about the head and neck had been torn to shreds, as was likewise the lining of the coffin. Bloody marks of fingernails on the face, throat, and neck told of the awful despair of the doomed man, who tore his own flesh in his terrible anguish. Several fingers had been entirely bitten off and the hands torn with the teeth until they scarcely resembled those of a human being.

Accounts like these—along with fear-mongering books such as Joseph Taylor's *The Danger of Premature Interment* and William Tebb's *Premature Burial and How It May Be Prevented*—set off a wave of hysteria that swept through Western Europe and quickly spread to America. Edgar Allan Poe's 1845 story "The Premature Burial" might strike the modern reader as the purely fanciful product of his bizarre imagination—something only Poe could dream up. In truth, however, it is an accurate reflection of a widespread fear of the time (albeit rendered in the author's typically overheated style):

> It may be asserted, without hesitation, that *no* event is so terribly well adapted to inspire the supremeness of bodily and of mental distress, as is burial before death. The unendurable oppression of the lungs—the stifling fumes of the damp earth—the clinging to the death garments—the rigid embrace of the narrow house—the blackness of the absolute Night—the silence like a sea that overwhelms—the unseen but palpable presence of the Conqueror Worm—these things, with the thoughts of the air and grass above, with memory of dear friends who would fly to save us if but informed of our fate, and with consciousness that of this fate they can *never* be informed—that our hopeless portion is that of the really dead—these considerations, I say, carry into the heart, which still palpitates, a degree of appalling

> and intolerable horror from which the most daring imagination must recoil. We know of nothing so agonizing upon Earth—we can dream of nothing half so hideous in the realms of the nethermost Hell.

To avoid this "appalling and intolerable horror," Poe's contemporaries often resorted to extraordinary measures, directing their family physicians to remove their heads, slit their throats, drive needles under their toenails, or puncture their hearts with long metal pins after death. Undertakers did a booming business in "security coffins," the most popular model of which was the Bateson Life Revival Device—essentially a casket equipped with a miniature belfry that poked out of the ground, so that—should the occupant wake up and discover himself buried alive—he could ring the bell and alert the outside world to his predicament.

For all the hysteria surrounding the subject, however, modern historians generally agree that Victorian fears of living interment were seriously overblown. To be sure, there undoubtedly *were* instances of premature burial, particularly during certain epidemics, when victims were often hurried into the grave to minimize the risk of contagion. But much of the evidence cited by nineteenth-century alarmists as proof of premature burial can be attributed to other causes. As the British physician and writer Jan Bondeson explains,

> writers made much of a cadaver found, for example, lying on its side; this position could just as well be consistent with the tilting of a coffin while it was being put into the grave. If the corpse's face was contorted or the arms and legs drawn up, an imaginative journalist might describe the horrid scuffle in the coffin, but neither of these changes is inconsistent with the natural decomposition of the body after death. A shattered coffin in a vault might, similarly, be due to the swelling of the corpse during putrefaction. Even the gruesome phenomenon of a dead pregnant woman bearing a child could be caused by the highly increased intra-abdominal pressure during decomposition. In several nineteenth-century reports, the prematurely dead individuals are said to have eaten their fingers or even their entire arms; modern textbooks in forensic medicine have demonstrated that such bodies were probably attacked by rodents.

In short, like today's media-induced panics over supposedly pervasive (but actually quite negligible) threats like bird flu, serial killers, and poisoned Halloween candy, the Victorian fear of premature burial—though not wholly unfounded—was largely generated by a sensationalizing press.

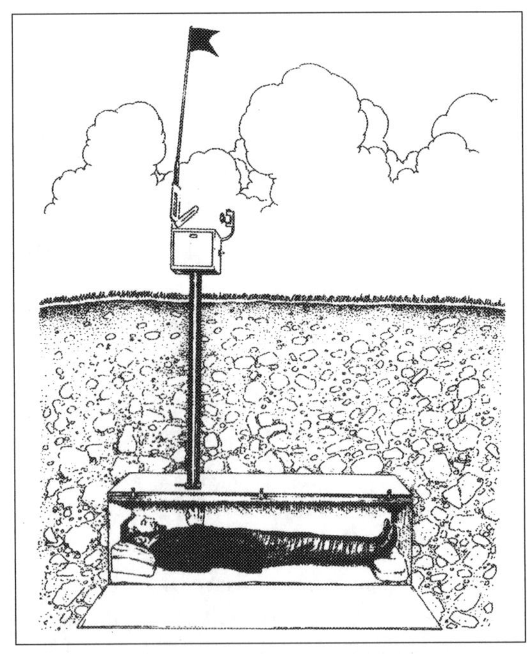

Victorian security coffin equipped with breathing tube and signal flag.

RECOMMENDED READING

The single best work on this subject—indeed, the only one you'll really have to read—is Jan Bondeson's *Buried Alive: The Terrifying History of Our Most Primal Fear* (Norton, 2001), a book-length elaboration of a chapter in his equally fine collection, *A Cabinet of Medical Curiosities* (Norton, 1999).

There was a young man at Nunhead
Who awoke in his coffin of lead.
"It was cozy enough,"
He remarked in a huff,
"But I wasn't aware I was dead."

—Victorian limerick

The *Lebenswecker*: If *This* Doesn't Wake You Up, Nothing Will

One of the more unusual medical implements available to nineteenth-century physicians was the *Lebenswecker* (life-awakener). Invented by a German quack named Carl Baunscheidt and marketed in English under the name "Resuscitator," this ingenious device was essentially a hollow, spring-loaded wand equipped at one end with a cluster of thirty razor-sharp needles. Among its other uses, it was recommended by its inventor as a surefire way to prevent premature burial.

Here's how it worked. To make sure that someone was really dead, the doctor placed the business end of the *Lebenswecker* against the person's chest and activated the spring—

DEATH FUN FACT

Common sense—as well as euphemisms such as "at rest"—suggests that when you're dead and buried, you basically don't budge from your supine position. Amazingly enough, however, corpses not only can move but have been known to shift around in the coffin. As a cadaver decomposes, the muscles shrivel and contract, pulling the arms and legs into a contorted position, which can create "the false impression that the corpse has awakened and tried to push up the coffin lid." The putrefactive gas that builds up in the abdominal cavity can also burst out with enough force to move the whole body around. According to Jan Bondeson in his 2001 book, *Buried Alive*, these "perfectly natural phenomena" go a long way toward explaining the widespread nineteenth-century fear of premature burial, which "derived from accounts of corpses and skeletons found in unnatural positions upon exhumation of coffins."

whereupon the needles popped out and punctured the flesh. If the patient remained unresponsive after several attempts, the doctor might apply it elsewhere—to what the instructions delicately described as the "sensitive" parts of the body. (Exactly what that meant was made clear by an accompanying illustration depicting a nude Aphrodite and Adonis with a single fig leaf covering their privates). If *that* didn't do the trick, you could be pretty sure that the patient was indeed deceased and suitable for burial.

"One Summer Night"

During the nineteenth century, when "resurrectionists" earned their keep by digging up freshly interred corpses and peddling them to anatomy schools, the fear of grave robbing was rife both here and abroad. So was the fear of premature burial. It took a particularly diabolical mind, however, to combine those two anxieties into a single nightmarish fantasy. Such a mind belonged to Ambrose Bierce, Gilded Age America's master of the macabre. In this creepy little yarn from his 1893 collection *Can Such Things Be?* the famously mordant Bierce concocts a hair-raising (if wildly improbable) scenario that climaxes with a grisly punch line.

> The fact that Henry Armstrong was buried did not seem to him to prove that he was dead: he had always been a hard man to convince. That he really was buried, the testimony of his senses compelled him to admit. His posture—flat upon his back, with his hands crossed upon his stomach and tied with something he easily broke without profitably altering the situation—the strict confinement of his entire person, the black darkness and profound silence, made a body of evidence impossible to controvert and he accepted it without cavil.

But dead—no; he was only very, very ill. He had, withal, the invalid's apathy and did not greatly concern himself about the uncommon fate that had been allotted to him. No philosopher was he—just a plain, commonplace person gifted, for the time being, with a pathological indifference: the organ that he feared consequences with was torpid. So. With no particular apprehension for his immediate future, he fell asleep and all was peace with Henry Armstrong.

But something was going on overhead. It was a dark summer night, shot through with infrequent shimmers of lightning silently firing a cloud lying low in the west and portending a storm. These brief, stammering illuminations brought out with ghastly distinctness the monuments and headstones of the cemetery and seemed to set them dancing. It was not a night in which any credible witness was likely to be straying about a cemetery, so the three men who were there, digging into the grave of Henry Armstrong, felt reasonably secure.

Two of them were young students from a medical college a few miles away; the third was a gigantic Negro known as Jess. For many years Jess had been employed about the cemetery as a man-of-all-work and it was a favorite pleasantry that he knew "every soul in the place." From the nature of what he was now doing it was inferable that the place was not so populous as its register might have shown it to be.

Outside the wall, at the part of the

grounds farthest from the public road, were a horse and light wagon, waiting.

The work of excavation was not difficult: the earth with which the grave had been loosely filled a few hours before offered little resistance and was soon thrown out. Removal of the casket from its box was less easy, but it was taken out, for it was a perquisite of Jess, who carefully unscrewed the cover and laid it aside, exposing the body in black trousers and white shirt. At that instant the air sprang to flame, a cracking shock of thunder shook the stunned world and Henry Armstrong tranquilly sat up. With inarticulate cries the men fled in terror, each in a different direction. For nothing on earth could two of them have been persuaded to return. But Jess was of another breed.

In the gray morning the two students, pallid and haggard from anxiety and with the terror of their adventure still beating tumultuously in their blood, met at the medical college.

"You saw it?" cried one.

"God! Yes—what are we to do?"

They went around to the rear of the building, where they saw a horse, attached to a light wagon, hitched to a gatepost near the door of the dissecting-room. Mechanically they entered the room. On a bench in the obscurity sat the Negro Jess. He rose, grinning, all eyes and teeth.

"I'm waiting for my pay," he said.

DEATH DEFINITION: *Thanatomimesis*

A COMBINATION OF *THANATO-* (MEANING "DEATH," FROM THE GREEK GOD THANATOS) AND *MIMESIS* (MEANing "Imitation," as in *mimic*), the word *thanatomimesis* means—you guessed it—the imitation of death. It is used in two basic ways.

First, it describes the deliberate or instinctive feigning of death, usually as a survival strategy. This behavior is commonly known as "playing possum" since members of that particular species will protect themselves from attack by falling to the ground, growing limp, and assuming a vacant, slack-mouthed appearance. When the enemy loses interest and leaves (why kill something that's already dead?), the possum will spring up and scamper away. The same ploy has come in handy for humans, especially cowardly ones such as Shakespeare's Falstaff, who—in accordance with his credo "Discretion is the better part of valor"—plays dead on the battlefield of Shrewsbury and so lives to fight (or rather to avoid fighting) another day.

The term *thanatomimesis* can also refer to physical symptoms resembling death, such as those associated with comas, hypothermia, and catalepsy. The last—a trancelike state accompanied by extreme rigidity of the limbs—afflicts an inordinate number of characters in the fiction of Edgar Allan Poe: they are invariably pronounced dead by their attending physicians, whisked off to the graveyard, and buried alive.

Stretched naked on a long table lay the body of Henry Armstrong, the head defiled with blood and clay from a blow with a spade.

The Undead: Fact or Fiction?

Apart from the occasional sexual psychopath who takes perverted pleasure from drinking the blood of his victims, vampires don't really exist. And yet stories about resuscitated corpses who return from the grave to batten on the living are found all over the world. Where do such widespread folk beliefs come from?

Explanations vary. According to Freudian analysts, vampires—like all other supernatural creatures—are really fantasy projections of unconscious dreads and desires: monsters from the id. Others have put forth a less psychoanalytic theory. Most notable among these is the scholar Paul Barber in his persuasive and highly readable book *Vampires, Burial, and Death* (Yale University Press, 1988).

According to Barber, the belief in vampires arose among the peasantry of preliterate cultures who gave superstitious explanations for perfectly natural postmortem phenomena. Following the death of a Serbian peasant named Peter Plogojowitz in 1725, for example, a number of his fellow villagers fell ill and died. Immediately, stories began to spread that Plogojowitz had turned into a vampire and returned from the grave each night to attack his former neighbors in their beds. When Plogojowitz's corpse was exhumed, witnesses were horrified to discover that his body looked plumper than before; his hair and nails had grown; his skin had sloughed off and been replaced "with a new one"; and his mouth was full of fresh blood. When a stake was driven through his heart, he let out an audible groan.

To Plogojowitz's benighted neighbors, all this was incontrovertible proof that he had, indeed, become one of the undead. Modern science teaches us, however, that there is nothing at all unusual about these seemingly supernatural phenomena. When bodies decompose, they bloat; the skin contracts (thereby creating the illusion that the hair and nails have grown) and eventually peels off; and bloody fluid issues from the mouth. As for the groaning, when a death-swollen corpse is punctured, the escaping gases can produce a noise that, to credulous ears, can sound like a cry of pain. The supposedly telltale signs of vampirism in other exhumed corpses—ranging from open eyes to erections to apparent movement in the coffin—can also be explained as the normal (if seriously unpleasant) events that happen when our bodies rot in the grave.

Pet Cemeteries

In the view of some people, elaborate pet funerals are just one more vulgar example of American conspicuous consumerism, like diamond-studded cat collars and designer dog apparel. In truth, however, there is nothing either new or uniquely American about the practice.

Various creatures sacred to the ancient

Egyptians—from cats and crocodiles to baboons and ibises—were interred with the same care and ceremony lavished on human beings. Among the Chiribaya people of pre-Columbian Peru, dogs were not only laid to rest in their own cemeteries but also provided with warm blankets and food for the afterlife. And horses have received special posthumous treatment throughout the millennia, from Roman times (when champion chariot teams were accorded stately funerals) to the era of Buffalo Bill (one of whose favorite steeds, Old Charlie, was buried at sea with full honors).

Pet cemeteries themselves have existed since at least the 1800s. One of the oldest, founded in 1899, is the famed Cimetière des Chiens, located on the Île des Ravageurs, a small island in a northwestern suburb of Paris. Despite its name—which means "Cemetery of the Dogs"—this renowned "zoological necropolis" contains the graves of a large assortment of creatures: cats, birds, rabbits, horses, hamsters, turtles, and fish, as well as a scattering of more exotic beasts, including a lion, a gazelle, a desert fox, and a monkey.

Among its most famous occupants is the original Rin Tin Tin, canine star of several dozen wildly popular Hollywood adventure movies in the 1920s. ("Rinty," as he was nicknamed, was born in France and, in the waning months of World War I, adopted as a pup by an American doughboy who brought him back to Los Angeles. Upon his death in 1931, the celebrity pooch was returned to his native soil.) The cemetery also features an impressive monument to an authentic canine hero—a St. Bernard rescue dog named Barry, who saved forty snow-stranded hikers in the Alps before being killed by the forty-first, who mistook the big shaggy dog for a bear.

Across the Channel stands another famed animal burial ground dating back to the Victorian era—the Hyde Park Pet Cemetery. Between 1880 (when a dog belonging to the Duke of Cambridge was interred in the garden behind the gatekeeper's lodge) and 1915 (when the plot was full and further burials prohibited), three hundred dogs—

PET CEMETERY ALERT!

Warning! If you are a cat owner living in a small New England town and your beloved feline has just died, you might want to check out Stephen King's 1983 novel, *Pet Sematary* (or the very faithful 1989 movie version), before deciding on how to dispose of the remains. A reworking of W. W. Jacobs's classic story "The Monkey's Paw," *Pet Sematary* not only stands as one of the spookiest books ever to issue from the pen of America's favorite horrormeister but also offers a very useful rule of thumb for every animal lover: namely, never bury your departed pet in a neighborhood cemetery located next to an ancient Indian burial ground, particularly if the latter is somehow endowed with the power to bring corpses to life.

along with the occasional cat—were laid to rest there. In keeping with the aristocratic pedigree of its original occupant, only upper-crust pets were permitted. Their neatly laid-out graves are marked with miniature tombstones inscribed with simple, heartfelt epitaphs, including (inevitably) an occasional quote from Shakespeare: "In memory of Ginger Blyth of Westbourne Terrace. His 'little life was rounded with a sleep.' "

The oldest pet cemetery in our own country is the Hartsdale Pet Cemetery in Westchester County, New York. It began life as an apple orchard, part of the country retreat of Dr. Samuel Johnson, a prominent Manhattan veterinarian. In 1896, Dr. Johnson permitted a bereaved friend to bury her pet dog on his property. When newspapers got wind of the story, he was besieged with requests from other New Yorkers, looking for a tranquil spot to inter their departed pets. Johnson set aside a three-acre section of his hillside orchard as a burial plot and it was soon dotted with tiny tombstones and other commemorative markers. Today, the Hartsdale Pet Cemetery is the permanent resting place of more than seventy thousand animals, including the pets of many one-time celebrities, from tough-guy movie star George Raft to former New York City mayor Jimmy Walker and the legendary jazz drummer Gene Krupa.

In the hundred-plus years since Dr. Johnson first allowed a friend's dog to be buried on his property, pet cemeteries have proliferated across the country. According to the International Association of Pet Cemeteries and Crematories, there are currently more than six hundred active pet cemeteries in the United States. Some are connected to other pet-related businesses (kennels, veterinary hospitals, animal shelters, etc.) and some are full-time operations dedicated specifically to animal disposal, while others are specially designated sections of human burying grounds.

A large number of ancillary businesses have also sprung up to serve the needs of bereaved pet owners: everything from memorial stones (www.rainbowbridgepetmemorials.com) and condolence gifts (www.doglovergiftbaskets.com) to online counseling services for grieving pet owners (www.grievingyourpet.com).

RECOMMENDED READING

Tom Weil's engaging guide, *The Cemetery Book: Graveyards, Catacombs, and Other Travel Haunts Around the World* (Barnes & Noble, 1993), contains a long and informative chapter on international pet cemeteries. For those who like to adorn their coffee tables with lavishly illustrated gift books on animal burial, there is Edward C. Martin's *Dr. Johnson's Apple Orchard: The Story of America's First Pet Cemetery*, available directly from the Hartsdale Pet Cemetery (www.petcem.com/books.htm).

Gladstone, Michigan: Pet Casket Capital of the World

No fun-filled family vacation involving death-related destinations can be considered complete without a trip to the Hoegh Pet Casket Company in Gladstone, Michigan, where visitors can take a guided tour of the factory, the world's largest of its kind.

Founded in 1966, Hoegh (pronounced "Hoig") produces caskets made of high-impact styrene. Eight different sizes are available for creatures ranging from parakeets to St. Bernards (they are also ideal for human arms and legs and are occasionally purchased by amputees who wish to give their severed limbs a decent burial). During the tour, visitors learn how the caskets are molded, trimmed, and finished. Other highlights include a simulated pet funeral and a detailed scale-model pet cemetery.

All in all, a highly educational experience and easily the number one tourist attraction in all of Gladstone (though the local walleye fishing runs a close second).

The Hoegh Pet Casket Company is located at 337 Delta Avenue, just east of Fourth Avenue, east of downtown Gladstone. Call 906-428-2151 to arrange a tour, available year-round, weekdays 8 A.M.–4 P.M.

In Memoriam: Fluffy

Pet obituaries, which began to appear in small-town newspapers a number of years ago under such titles as "Pet Passings" and "Pause to Remember" (Get it?), have become increasingly popular in recent years. Weirdly, they are often more heart-wrenching than the ones composed for humans. It would take a pretty callous person not to choke up at tributes such as this one, to a faithful pooch named Hoops: "My

May the memories you've made and the moments you've shared with your beloved cat bring you comfort in the time of your loss.

Pet-loss condolence card. Courtesy of Dr. Wallace Sife and the Association for Pet Loss and Bereavement.

beloved Hoops passed away today. Watching him suffer was one of the most difficult things I've ever had to deal with. He was helpless—and I couldn't do anything. There is a stillness in my home that is indescribable. In the time I had him, he provided me with a love that I never experienced. I thank God for bringing him to me. He loved me unconditionally, and I hope that in his final hours he knew just how much I loved him."

Not every pet obituary, of course, is this moving. Some have a charmingly childlike quality ("Bubbles was a loving hamster full of life and he never even bit anyone"); others are sweetly amusing ("To my beloved chicken, Milo—may you R.I.P. in chicken heaven"). And a few are just, well, strange: "Thoughts flicker in my mind like faint stars. I glint like a drop of dew in the morning sun and vanish. This space into which I now dissolve and disappear is the eternal color of your eyes." This actually seems rather poetic until you realize it was written for a deceased rat named Dale.

Besides newspapers, various websites now offer a handy way to post obituaries for beloved pets. Three of the most popular are www.thefuneraldirectory.com, www.ilovedmypet.com, and www.heavenlypawsonline.com.

ASK DR. DEATH

Dear Dr. Death:
I've owned dogs my whole life and like to think I know just about everything regarding the canine species. One thing puzzles me, though. What exactly is the difference between a dog cadaver and a cadaver dog?

A Puzzled Pet Lover

Dear Puzzled:
Simply put, a dog cadaver is the dead body of a dog. Preserved dog cadavers are commonly used to teach basic canine anatomy in veterinary schools, which obtain specimens in various ways—from biological supply companies, breeders, animal shelters, and, increasingly, from ordinary pet owners who donate their deceased pets to educational institutions.

Cadaver dogs are a whole other kettle of fish (or bowl of kibble, ha ha). These remarkable police canines are similar to their bomb- and narcotics-sniffing cousins, only instead of the telltale scents of explosives or drugs, they have been taught to detect the odor of human remains.

Endowed with amazing olfactory organs—thousands of times more sensitive than a human's—these dogs undergo an extensive training period during which they are exposed either to chemicals that simulate the smells of human cadavers at different stages of decomposition or to actual body parts. Once this phase of their conditioning is complete, they are taught how to track the source of the odor and to signal the location either by barking or lying down.

A well-trained cadaver dog can perform feats that seem positively supernatural, distinguishing the faintest whiff of human decomposition in places suffused with other powerful smells. In one demonstration, a cadaver dog was able to locate a small piece of human pinky finger that had been sealed inside a plastic bag and stuck in a garbage-filled Dumpster. This ability makes them invaluable tools in the area of HRD (human remains detection). They have proven highly effective not only in locating the corpses of long-buried murder victims but also in recovering remains from disaster sites such as the rubble of the World Trade Center.

Corpse-Napping: Ransoming the Dead

Since the business of kidnapping relies on a simple, straightforward threat—"Pay up or you'll never see this person alive again"—you wouldn't think that abducting someone who's already dead makes sound financial sense. Still, that hasn't stopped certain criminals from digging up corpses and holding them for ransom. Few of these crimes have panned out for the perpetrators. In 1876, for example, an Illinois gang hatched a plot to steal Abraham Lincoln's corpse and ransom it for $200,000 in gold. Breaking into the martyred president's vault at the Oak Ridge Cemetery in Springfield, they pried off the lid of his marble sarcophagus and were in the process of removing the remains when Secret Service agents—who had gotten wind of the nefarious plot—swarmed inside and arrested the culprits.

Five years later, British body snatchers attempted to extort £6,000 by stealing the body of Alexander William Crawford Lindsay, 25th Earl of Crawford and 8th Earl of Balcarres. Relatives refused to fork over the ransom, however, and the body was eventually recovered. Equally unsuccessful were the pair of enterprising corpse-nappers who in 1976 snuck into the Swiss cemetery where the great silent-film comedian Charlie Chaplin was buried, dug up the heavy oak casket containing his remains, and carted it away. Announcing that "my husband lives on in my heart and mind, and it really doesn't matter where his remains are," his widow, Lady Oona O'Neill Chaplin, steadfastly refused to pay any ransom, even as the thieves kept lowering their demands from $600,000 to $250,000. Eventually, the two culprits were arrested and the Little Tramp's unopened casket—after being recovered in a farmer's cornfield—was reinterred. This time, however, it was sealed in concrete for good measure.

One of the few cases of successful corpse-napping occured in post–Civil War New York City when the body of Alexander T. Stewart (1803–1876) was abducted from what was supposed to be its final resting place. An Irish immigrant who settled in America at the age of eighteen, Stewart—dubbed the "Merchant Prince" of Manhattan—built a dry goods empire that eventually included two of the most imposing retail stores in New York. At the time of his death at the age of seventy-three, his personal fortune was estimated to be between $40 million and $50 million—equivalent to about $50 *billion* in today's currency.

In November 1878, two and a half years after his death, Stewart's unembalmed remains were stolen from his tomb in the cemetery of St. Mark's Church in lower Manhattan. The stench issuing from the ransacked tomb was so intense that police were confident that the crime would be solved within days. After all, they reasoned, the thieves couldn't possibly conceal such reeking plunder for long. In the event, Stewart's corpse—or what remained of it—was not recovered until 1882, when his widow reportedly paid $20,000 for a bag of bones that were supposedly her husband's. This time, his remains were interred beneath a Long Island cathedral in a crypt that—according to legend—is rigged with a security device that will cause the church bells to ring in the event of another break-in.

The "Baker" Patent Burglar-Proof Grave Vault.

THE BAKER VAULT sheds the water into the earth, instead of draining into the bottom of Vault and Casket. THE BAKER has eight large handsome Bar Drop Handles.

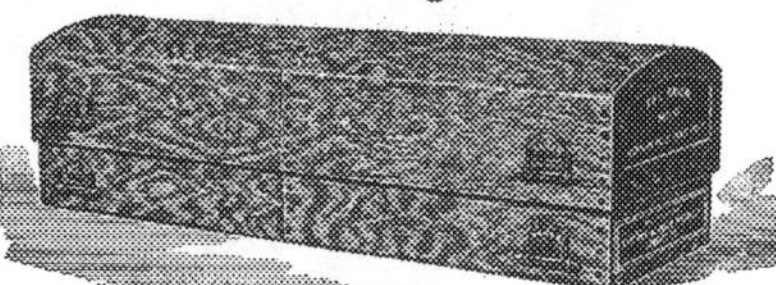

THE BAKER has heavy malleable iron ends, beautifully paneled with raised letters, finished in bronze. The most desirable Vault in every particulars made.

SPRINGFIELD METALLIC CASKET CO. SPRINGFIELD, OHIO.

RECOMMENDED READING

The definitive account of the Stewart affair is Wayne Fanebust's *The Missing Corpse: Grave Robbing a Gilded Age Tycoon* (Praeger, 2005), which supplements the story with lots of information on the Lincoln corpse-napping plot as well as the business of nineteenth-century body snatching in general.

Burke and Hare: Making a Killing from Corpses

Prior to the 1830s, British laws placed severe restrictions on human dissections, making it exceptionally difficult for doctors and medical students to obtain cadavers for anatomical study. As a result, aspiring surgeons and their teachers were often forced to turn to grave robbers—or "resurrection men," as they were called—to supply them with raw material.

Though the names of William Burke and William Hare would become synonymous with this ghoulish breed of entrepreneur—the loathsome body snatcher who would sneak into a graveyard at night, dig up a freshly buried corpse, and sell it for a few pounds to an anatomy school—they were not, in fact, grave robbers but financially motivated serial killers. In 1827, Hare and his common-law wife were running a squalid boardinghouse in the Edinburgh slums when an elderly lodger died, owing them £4. To cover the debt, Hare hit upon the idea of selling the old man's corpse to an anatomist. With the help of his friend Burke, he conveyed the cadaver to a medical school run by a celebrated surgeon, Dr. Robert Knox, who paid them £7 10s—an enormous sum to two poor Irish immigrants who normally made a pittance as laborers.

Impressed with the monetary potential of dead bodies but disinclined to engage in the difficult, dirty, and dangerous business of grave robbing, Burke and Hare opted for an easier method of obtaining marketable corpses: they decided to produce their own. Not long afterward, when another of Hare's lodgers fell ill, the two men eased him into a coma by feeding him whiskey, then suffocated him by pinching his nose and sealing his mouth. This time, they got £10 from Dr. Knox. Another ailing inmate of Hare's hostelry soon met the same end.

Having exhausted the supply of sick lodgers at Hare's boardinghouse, the two men began preying on neighborhood beggars, local prostitutes, and other street people. Luring them to Hare's place with the promise of liquor and food, the two men would suddenly pounce upon the unwary victims and suffocate them. Fifteen people—twelve women, two handicapped boys, and

The body snatchers, William Burke (left) *and William Hare.*

an old man—were murdered this way before the two killers were caught.

To save his own skin, Hare turned king's evidence. In January 1829, Burke was hanged before a cheering crowd of twenty-five thousand spectators and his body publicly dissected. His name would enter the English language, the verb *burke* meaning to murder someone for the purpose of dissection.

Two excellent books on the subject of body snatching are Ruth Richardson, *Death, Dissection, and the Destitute* (Penguin, 1988) and Michael Sappol, *A Traffic of Dead Bodies: Anatomy and Embodied Social Identity in Nineteenth-Century America* (Princeton University Press, 2002).

Digging Up the Goods

In the 1961 fright film, *Mr. Sardonicus*, the title character learns that a lottery ticket—purchased by his father prior to the old man's death—has won the jackpot. But where's the ticket? After a frantic search, he realizes to his horror that it is in the breast pocket of his father's burial suit! Goaded by his shrewish wife, he sneaks into the cemetery at night, digs up the grave, and pries open the coffin—with highly traumatic results (when he sees his father's hideous death-contorted features, his own face becomes frozen in a grotesque, skull-like rictus).

Mr. Sardonicus is, of course, pure Gothic fantasy. But something similar happened in real life to the Pre-Raphaelite painter-poet Dante Gabriel Rossetti. In 1860, Rossetti wed the beautiful Elizabeth Siddal, his primary muse and model and a talented artist in her own right. Just two years later, Siddal died, apparently of a self-administered overdose of laudanum. At her funeral, the grief-stricken Rossetti placed a small notebook containing his latest, handwritten love poems into her coffin, slipping it under her flowing copper-red hair.

Seven years after her burial, Rossetti decided that it was time to publish the poems. Unfortunately, he had failed to keep copies. At the urging of his publisher, Rossetti agreed to have his wife's coffin exhumed. The job was done at midnight. The box was opened and the book slipped from beneath the body, a few strands of corpse hair still clinging to it. Rossetti, who refused to attend and spent the night in an agony of horror, was told by those present that the years in the ground had not altered his wife's appearance at all, except for her flowing red hair, which had grown so luxuriantly that it filled up the coffin.

Though perfectly intact (apart from a worm hole or two), the little volume carried an "evil smell" and had to be disinfected page by page. Eventually, the poems were published—to generally unfavorable reviews. Though Rossetti had not witnessed the unearthing of his wife's remains, he was haunted by thoughts of the exhumation for the rest of his life.

The moral? When burying a loved one, take care not to place anything in the coffin that you might want to retrieve at a later date.

Necrophilia

In his classic study of aberrant behavior, *Psychopathia Sexualis*, the German psychiatrist Richard von Krafft-Ebing describes necrophilia as the most "repugnant" of all perversions. Considering that his case histories include a man who paid prostitutes to "tear out the eyes and entrails" of live bunnies while he masturbated and another who could only become aroused by having women "spit, urinate, and defecate in his mouth," that's saying quite a lot.

In an oft-cited essay on the subject, "Sexual Attraction to Corpses: A Psychiatric Review of Necrophilia," Drs. Jonathan P. Rosman and Phillip J. Resnick distinguish between "necrophiliac homicide," in which a psychopath deliberately murders someone to have sex with the corpse, and what the good doctors somewhat oxymoronically label "regular necrophilia," by which they apparently mean people who have sex with corpses in a more socially acceptable way. (The example they give is a female embalmer who "had sexual intercourse with 20–40 male corpses." Exactly how she achieved this feat, Rosman and Resnick do not say.) They also identify two other categories: "necrophiliac fantasy," in which a person regularly indulges in masturbatory daydreams about sex with the dead, and something the authors call "pseudonecrophilia." The example they cite for the latter is a "37-year-old single white man [who] went out drinking with his 49-year-old girlfriend" and "on the way home shot her in the head by accident." He then "became sexually excited and had anal intercourse with the corpse" (which, to a layman, sounds a lot like actual necrophilia but apparently doesn't count because it wasn't premeditated and therefore qualifies as pseudonecrophilia).

In *Psychopathia Sexualis*, Krafft-Ebing describes a number of particularly appalling cases, including a French soldier named Bertrand, who would sneak into cemeteries, exhume female corpses, and violate them "with a madman's frenzy"; a feebleminded gravedigger named Viktor Ardisson, who would sneak cadavers back to his rooms and have sex with them until they were too rotten even for his own depraved tastes; and a pervert named Henri Blot, who achieved a certain immortality in the annals of psychopathology when, at his trial, he blithely declared: "Everyone to his own taste. Mine is for corpses."

While degenerates such as these arouse only revulsion, there have been a number of other well-known cases in which necrophiliac acts have been motivated by what can only be described as desperate romantic love. A notorious case is that of Carl Tanzler, aka Carl von Cosel, a middle-aged radiologist who worked at a sanitarium in Key West, Florida, where in the early 1930s he became obsessed with a beautiful twenty-two-year-old patient named Maria Elena de Hoyos. When she died of tuberculosis, he smuggled her body back home and slept with it for seven years, jury-rigging it with piano wire, plaster of Paris, rags, glass eyes, and a wig as it gradually decomposed. (He also reportedly inserted a tube of some sort between her legs so that he could continue to enjoy sex with his ghastly bride.)

In analyzing the causes of this perversion, Rosman and Resnick identify a number of "psychodynamic events that could lead to necrophilia," including "poor self-esteem," a "desire for a sexual object who is incapable of rejecting" the lover, and a tendency to indulge in "exciting fantasies of sex with a corpse." Frankly, none of these explanations is very persuasive (lots of people who don't sleep with corpses have low self-esteem and a fear of rejection, and anyone who fantasizes about sex with a cadaver is already in the grip of necrophiliac tendencies). More intriguing is their notion that at the root of necrophila is an inordinate terror of death, which—through the defense mechanism Freudians call a "reaction formation"—is transformed into its opposite, a pathological desire for the dead.

RECOMMENDED READING

Rosman and Resnick's essay can be found in the *Bulletin of the American Academy of Psychiatry and Law*, vol. 17, no. 2, 1989, pp. 153–63. Krafft-Ebing's 1886 classic has appeared in many editions, including a relatively recent paperback published by Bloat Books (1999). For a thorough retelling of the ghoulish tale of Carl Tanzler, see Ben Harrison, *Undying Love: The True Story of a Passion That Defied Death* (New Horizon Press, 1996).

A very comprehensive discussion of necrophila by crime writer Katherine Ramsland can be found online at www.crimelibrary.com/serial_killers/notorious/necrophiles/necro_4.html.

"The Unquiet Grave"

Though Carl Tanzler was clearly in a class by himself, the loss of a true love can be so overpowering that it drives even less obsessed men to necrophiliac extremes. No less a figure than Ralph Waldo Emerson—one of America's greatest writers—is a case in point. Still devastated by grief a year after the death of his beloved first wife, Ellen, Emerson—as we know from his journal—snuck off to the cemetery one night and violated her grave ("I visited Ellen's tomb and opened the coffin").

The same impulse is recorded in one of the most famous of all English ballads, "The Unquiet Grave":

"The wind doth blow today, my love,
And a few small drops of rain;
I never had but one true-love,
In cold grave she was lain.

"I'll do as much for my true-love
As any young man may;
I'll sit and mourn all at her grave
For twelvemonth and a day."

The twelvemonth and a day being up,
The dead began to speak:
"Oh who sits weeping on my grave,
And will not let me sleep?"

" 'Tis I, my love, sits on your grave,
And will not let you sleep;
For I crave one kiss of your clay-cold lips,
And that is all I seek."

"You crave one kiss of my clay-cold lips,
But my breath smells earthy strong;
If you have one kiss of my clay-cold lips,
Your time will not be long.

" 'Tis down in yonder garden green,
Love, where we used to walk,
The finest flower that e'er was seen
Is withered to a stalk.

"The stalk is withered dry, my love,
So will our hearts decay;
So make yourself content, my love,
Till God calls you away."

5

CREMATION, CRYONICS, and OTHER POSTMORTEM POSSIBILITIES

To Burn or Not to Burn?

Archaeological evidence makes it clear that cremation has been around since the Stone Age, though—viewing humanity as a whole—there has always been a certain amount of ambivalence about the practice. In some cultures, it was regarded as the only way to go. As Stephen Prothero writes in his highly informative book *Purified by Fire* (University of California Press, 2001):

> We know cremation was widely practiced in ancient India. The Vedas, Hinduism's earliest scriptures, contain cremation hymns from the late second millennium BCE. The priests who sang those hymns expected the soul to survive its fiery ordeal, then to fly birdlike to the world of the ancestors or the world of the gods. Later Hindu scriptures, principally the Upanishads (texts from the middle of the first millennium BCE that popularized concepts such as reincarnation and karma), describe cremation as a purification process in which burning the body cleans the soul, preparing it for rebirth.
>
> In ancient Greece, cremation was the preferred method of corpse disposal. Homer provides a vivid picture of an elaborate cremation ceremony in Book 23 of the *Iliad*, when the grief-stricken Achilles stages a spectacular funeral for his fallen friend Patroclus. After gathering immense quantities of timber, the Achaeans construct an enormous pyre, each side a hundred feet long, and place the corpse atop the highest point. The body is covered with fat from sacrificed sheep and cattle and surrounded by two-handled jars of oil and honey. The flayed carcasses of the animals are added to the pyre, along with several butchered stallions, a pair of freshly killed dogs, and a dozen captive Trojans. When the fire won't light, Achilles appeals to the gods, who send a roaring wind that sets the pyre ablaze. The next

morning, Achilles and his comrades douse the flames with wine, then collect the bones and place them in a golden urn, protected by a double layer of animal fat.

The ancient Romans also embraced cremation, at least for wealthier citizens. Julius Caesar, Brutus, Nero, and Caligula were among the luminaries whose corpses were cremated. Uncoffined bodies were placed atop pyres with vessels of aromatic gum and other sweet-smelling substances (according to Dr. Kenneth Iserson, the ever-excessive Nero "reportedly used more myrrh, incense, and fragrant oils to cremate one of his wives than was produced in all of Arabia that year"). After the corpse had been reduced to ashes, the bone fragments would be collected, bathed in milk, and placed in perfumed urns.

Victorian cremation urn.

In contrast, the ancient Israelites forbade cremation, which—like embalming—was viewed as a desecration of the body. Early Christians likewise repudiated the practice, which they associated with the paganism of the Greco-Roman world. By the fifth century, cremation had virtually vanished from Europe and was officially criminalized by the emperor Charlemagne in 789. For the next thousand-plus years, earth burial was essentially the only acceptable form of body disposal in the Christian West.

It was not until the late nineteenth century that the situation began to change. A turning point occurred in 1869, when a group of medical experts at an international conference in Florence attacked earth burial as a threat to public health and endorsed cremation as a more sanitary alternative. In 1873, an Italian professor named Brunetti displayed a prototype cremation furnace, along with a glass box holding four pounds of incinerated human remains, at the Vienna Exposition. Accompanied by a sign that read "*Vermibus erepti, puro consumimur igni*" ("Saved from the worms, we are consumed by the flames"), Brunetti's exhibit created a sensation. Before long, societies to promote cremation had sprung up in a number of major European cities, including London, where in 1874 Queen Victoria's personal surgeon, Sir Henry Thompson, published what Stephen Prothero calls "the most influential pro-cremation book of the century," *The Treatment of the Body After Death*.

Two years later, in December 1876, a landmark event in the history of modern cremation took place in the United States. Amid increasing concerns that graveyards were a source of disease-bearing "miasmas," the corpse of a gentleman named Charles De Palm was incinerated with much fanfare by a pro-cremation activist, Francis Julius LeMoyne, who constructed America's first crematory on his estate in rural Pennsylvania. Newspapers all over the country covered the event. Other highly publicized cremations soon followed, including that of Mrs. Benjamin Pitman of Cincinnati, the second person to be consigned to LeMoyne's flames and the first female to be cremated in the United States.

In the following years, a debate raged between burial traditionalists and reform-minded "cremationists." Resistance to the practice among religious leaders—who argued that the eventual resurrection of the body required an intact corpse—was forcefully answered by various freethinking clerics. In a sermon delivered to a standing-room-only crowd at New York City's Lyric Hall, for example, the Reverend O. B. Frothingham insisted that an omnipotent God could just as easily "recover a shape from a heap of ashes" as "from a mound of dust."

Despite the arguments of Frothingham and other advocates who touted the sanitary, financial, and even spiritual benefits of cremation, the American public failed to embrace the practice. For nearly a decade, LeMoyne's crematory remained the only one in operation in this country. In 1884, the cremation movement received a much-needed boost from Samuel D. Gross, one of the nation's leading surgeons (and the subject of Thomas Eakins's masterpiece "The Gross Clinic"). After decades of dissecting corpses, Gross knew exactly what happens to human bodies when they decay, and he recoiled from the thought of earth burial. When he died in 1884, his cremation was big news and legitimized the practice in the eyes of many people.

By the turn of the century, the controversy that had raged over cremation had largely gone away. In 1913, the Cremation Association of America was created by Hugo Erichsen, author of *The Cremation of the Dead Considered from an Aesthetic, Sanitary, Religious, Historical, Medico-legal, and Economical Standpoint*, "the first great pro-cremation work written by an American," according to Stephen Prothero. Six years after its founding, its membership totaled seventy U.S. crematories. Over the next half century, public acceptance of cremation continued to grow at a slow but steady pace. By the outbreak of World War II, there were two hundred crematories in the United States.

In the immediate aftermath of the war, however, interest in cremation declined, partly because it evoked associations with the horrors of the Nazi death camps, partly because of the country's plunge into postwar conspicuous consumption, reflected as much in its taste for gaudy funerals as for the tail-finned automotive behemoths coming out of Detroit. That trend began to be reversed with the publication of Jessica Mitford's anti-funeral-industry diatribe, *The American Way of Death*, in 1963. The sixties counterculture, which was in full swing by 1967, also saw cremation as a hip alternative to the stodgy funeral customs of the "establishment." By the dawn of the new millennium, fully one-quarter of all corpses in the United States were disposed of by cremation, and the future looks even brighter. With a range of new and exciting postincineration options available to aging baby boomers—having their cremains shot into space, turned into synthetic diamond jewelry, incorporated into a coral reef, or stored in a one-of-a-kind objet d'art—cremation is hotter than ever!

RECOMMENDED READING

Stephen Prothero's book is a highly readable chronicle of U.S. cremation history from its Gilded Age beginnings to the customized, consumer-conscious send-offs of today. Its bibliography lists most of the key works on the subject, dating back to the post–Civil War era.

Death Fun Fact

Did you know that when you see a bunch of carefree college students disporting themselves around a beach bonfire while on spring break, you are actually watching the unwitting performance of an archaic mortuary ritual? Etymologically, the word *bonfire* derives from *bone fire*, referring to a blaze on which the bones of corpses were consumed. In later centuries, bonfires continued to retain their association with human incineration since they were commonly employed to immolate heretics, martyrs, and those accused of witchcraft. Thankfully, we now live in an age where the only thing likely to get roasted on a bonfire is a hot dog.

Cremation: Then and Now

Cremation has come a long way since 1876, when Francis LeMoyne built America's first crematory on his estate in rural Pennsylvania. LeMoyne's facility was a plain, one-story red-brick affair that (according to one scandalized contemporary) had all the architectural appeal of a "large cigar box." Its public space consisted of two bare chambers: a haphazardly furnished "reception room" with a few mismatched pieces of furniture and a "makeshift columbarium which looked no more sacred than an ordinary bookcase" (in the words of historian Stephen Prothero). The furnace room was equally unsightly, striking one observer as "loathsomely cheap and plain for its purpose"—"as unaesthetic as a bake-oven."

The inaugural cremation to be held at LeMoyne's facility took place on December 6, 1876, when an émigré Austrian nobleman named Charles De Palm earned his place in American mortuary history by becoming the first person in the country to undergo what one newspaper called "scientific roasting"—"the careful and inodorous baking of a human being in an oven." Preparatory to this landmark incineration, De Palm's corpse was sprinkled with aromatic herbs and spices and covered with flowers and evergreen branches. From the initial firing of the fur-

Early postcards of the LeMoyne Crematory. Courtesy of the Washington County Historical Society.

nace to the final collection of the ashes, the entire process took nearly two days to complete. De Palm's cremains were then sprinkled with perfume, placed in a Hindu-style urn, and transported to New York City—all, that is, except for a few bone fragments that were kept as a memento by LeMoyne or given away to curiosity seekers as souvenirs of the occasion.

Things happen much more expeditiously nowadays—and (for the most part) in far more attractive settings. Modern crematories often resemble chapels and feature comfortably appointed viewing rooms where family members can observe—and even participate in—the process. The body, enclosed in anything from a linen shroud to a cardboard container to a wood casket, is conveyed by motorized trolley from the viewing room to the cremator, a high-tech, computer-controlled furnace fired by one of several fuels, generally natural gas, propane, or oil.

The actual chamber in which the incineration takes place is known as a retort and is capable of reaching temperatures high enough—between 1,400° and 2,100° F—to vaporize the internal organs, muscle tissue, and flesh, amounting to about 95 percent of the body. After an hour or two, all that's left is about five to seven pounds of bone fragments, which are swept out of the retort by the operator and pulverized in a rotating drum known as a cremulator.

Death Fun Fact

The highly publicized incineration of Charles De Palm on December 6, 1876, was a milestone event in U.S. mortuary history—"the first cremation in modern America," as it was widely billed. De Palm, however, was *not* the first Caucasian to be cremated in this country. That distinction belongs to Colonel Henry Laurens, described by Stephen Prothero as "a prominent merchant-planter from South Carolina and president of the Continental Congress" who had learned about cremation from his studies of Greek and Roman culture. In his will, Laurens directed his survivors to cremate his corpse in the open air, a wish that was carried out on his Charleston estate following his death in 1792.

Laurens's motivation in seeking cremation, however, was very different from De Palm's. The latter was part of a burgeoning late-nineteenth-century reform movement promoting cremation as a scientifically superior alternative to earth burial. Laurens, on the other hand, was prompted by something far more primal: fear of being buried alive. As Prothero explains, "His daughter had been pronounced dead after being stricken with smallpox and was close to being interred when she suddenly sprang back to life." Traumatized by the event, Laurens insisted that his own corpse be incinerated as a surefire way (so to speak) of avoiding premature burial.

The powdered cremains can then be disposed of in any of a growing number of ways: placed in an urn and ceremonially installed in a columbarium, buried in a grave, or displayed on the living room mantel; scattered at sea; turned into a synthetic diamond; launched into deep space; incorporated into a "memorial reef"; or (for the cost-conscious) stored in a cardboard box and kept on a closet shelf.

CANA

Founded in 1913 as the cremationist counterpart of the National Funeral Directors Association, CANA—the Cremation Association of North America—was the brainchild of Hugo Erichsen (1860–1942), a tireless worker for the cause of human corpse incineration. Known for the first six decades of its existence as the Cremation Association of America, the organization—which originally consisted of fifty-two crematory owners—now numbers fifteen hundred members. In Erichsen's day, cremation was touted by its supporters as a superior means of corpse disposal—cheap, scientific, and supposedly more sanitary than earth burial. Nowadays, CANA chooses to stress the more ceremonial aspects of the practice, requiring members to sign the following declaration:

> In the practice of cremation, we believe:
>
> In dignity and respect in the care of Human Remains, in compassion for the living who survive them, and in the Memorialization of the dead.
>
> That a Cremation Authority should be responsible for creating and maintaining an atmosphere of respect at all times;
>
> That the greatest care should be taken in the appointment of crematory staff members, any of whom must not, by conduct or demeanor, bring the ceremony or cremation into disrepute;
>
> That cremation should be considered as preparation for Memorialization;
>
> That the dead of our human society should be memorialized through a commemorative means suitable to the survivors.

Like the NFDA, CANA operates a website (www.cremationassociation.org) that includes a crematory directory, career advice center, and consumer information, along with links to such informative articles as "The History of Cremation," "Getting Creative with Cremains," "Ten Steps to Ensure Safe Cremation of Obese Individuals," and "Why Cremated Remains Cannot Be Sent by Express Mail." Membership in the association—which is open to anyone in the death care industry who "recognizes that cremation is impacting their professional future and wants to be proactive in turning this into a positive rather than a negative force"—includes a subscription to the quarterly magazine the *Cremationist.*

Every cremationist must be a missionary for the cause, and embrace every suitable occasion to spread its gospel, the glad tidings of a more sanitary and more aesthetic method of disposing of our beloved dead.

—HUGO ERICHSEN

Ashes to Art

Thanks to the growing trend in cool customized burial containers, your corpse can now spend eternity in anything from a handcrafted folk-art coffin from Ghana in the shape of a crocodile to a fancy bronze casket adorned with the logo of your favorite sports team. But why should slowly decomposing cadavers have all the fun? What about people who choose cremation instead of burial? Shouldn't their ashes have a stylish place to reside, not just some boring old urn or a shoebox shoved away on a closet shelf?

Title: *Anubis* Artist: *Jack Thompson* Medium: *Painted ceramic* Copyright © 2003 Jack Thompson

Maureen Lomasney clearly thinks so. An artist and photographer dedicated to the proposition that beauty "can help to heal a troubled heart," Lomasney is the founder of Art Honors Life, a unique gallery in Sonoma County, California, specializing in original handcrafted cremation vessels. Priced from $800 to $1,900, these one-of-a-kind funerary *objets* range from the elegant to the playful: a ceramic prayer wheel etched with autumn leaves, an earthenware jar made to resemble a lichen-covered rock, a Flash Gordon–style rocket ship of glistening aluminum, a delicate angel-adorned box of glazed porcelain clay, an exquisite "cinerary vessel" of black walnut and gold leaf, even a vintage vacuum cleaner (the "Urn-a-matic") that can play "Seasons in the Sun" at the push of a button. Each is so sheerly beautiful that you may want to buy one for yourself and display it on a shelf even if you aren't quite ready yet to store your ashes inside it.

Title: *Koa* Artists: *Carol Green and Lynn Hayes* Medium: *Cast bronze* Copyright © Carol Green and Lynn Hayes

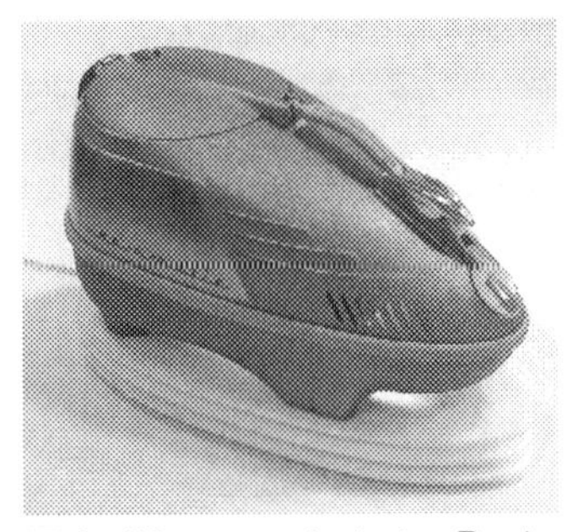

Title: *Urn-a-matic* Artist: *Darin Montgomery* Media: *Vintage vacuum cleaner, Plexiglas, home video and audio featuring the song "Seasons in the Sun"* Copyright © Darin Montgomery

Besides her gallery, Lomasney sponsors an international "Ashes to Art" exhibition showcasing the work of her clients and runs a website called Funeria (www.funeria.com), where you can view examples of their work.

The Perfect Final Resting Place for Snack Lovers

Fancy-shmancy art urns are all well and good for the chardonnay-sipping, sushi-eating, NPR-listening crowd. But if you're more of a beer, pizza, and NASCAR type, you'll want something a little more down-to-earth. Thanks to Fredric Baur, the perfect solution is no farther away than your nearest supermarket.

A Cincinnati organic chemist and food storage technician, Baur was the inventor of the iconic Pringles potato chip package—the tall, tube-shaped canister with resealable plastic lid and tinfoil lining. According to a widely published report from the Associated Press, Baur was so proud of his creation that when he died on May 4, 2008, his ashes—as per his request—were buried inside a Pringles can.

Conveniently preprinted with such touching sentiments as "Ingredients: dried potatoes, maltodextrin, mono- and diglycerides, and dextrose," the Pringles can makes a perfect final resting place for your loved one's cremains, particularly if your loved one happened to resemble a hard-boiled egg decked out with walrus mustache, parted bangs, and bow tie. Plus, each of these handy-dandy burial containers comes packed with a supply of yummy "potato" chips in case you get hit with a bad case of the munchies during the memorial service!

Fly Me to the Moon

Whether you're a die-hard Trekkie who has always yearned to explore the "final frontier" or just a normal person who thinks it would be really cool to take part in a space mission, a company called Celestis can make your dream come true. Sort of. You won't exactly be whizzing around the solar system on a sightseeing trip. But for prices ranging from a mere $500 all the way up to $67,500, a small portion of your cremated ashes can hitch a ride on a rocket ship into outer space.

Based, appropriately enough, in Houston—home of NASA—Celestis offers four different types of "memorial spaceflight." In the least expensive—the so-called Earth-Return Service—a few grams of your cremains are packed into a small capsule resembling a lipstick holder, which is then launched into space. After experiencing the thrill of the "zero-gravity environment" (in the words of the online advertising brochure), your ashes then return to earth, where they are handed over as a keepsake to your loved ones.

If you'd like to enjoy something a bit more adventurous when you're dead, you can sign up for the Earth Orbit Service, which allows your cremains to "ride alongside a commercial or scientific satellite" as "part of a real space mission." After orbiting the earth for anywhere from 10 to 240 years, the spacecraft will reenter the atmosphere, "harmlessly vaporizing like a blazing shooting star in final tribute."

For those who have always dreamed of replicating the exploits of the Apollo astronauts, Celestis will place a thimbleful of your ashes on a rocket that will either put you into permanent lunar orbit or actually land you on the surface of the moon. Finally—for the true aerospace enthusiast or any boomer who watched *2001: A Space Odyssey* one too many times while under the influence of mind-altering drugs—the company offers the ultimate trip, a spot on a Voyager mission that will propel you on "a permanent celestial journey" into "deepest space," where you will have the "opportunity to be at one with the cosmos." Groovy!

Whatever option you choose, your "memorial spaceflight" includes such amenities as an invitation to the launch for your loved ones, a professional-quality DVD of the event, an inscription on a special name plaque included on the spacecraft, a "personalized online memorial" placed on the company website, and a handsome, suitable-for-framing postlaunch certificate.

For more detailed information, go to the Celestis website, www.memorialspace flights.com.

Sleeping with the Fishes

Have you ever gone snorkeling during a tropical vacation and then, when it was time to head back to the boat, thought: "Boy, this is nice. Wish I could stay out here longer"? Well, thanks to a company called Eternal Reefs, you *can* stay there longer. A lot longer. Like, forever.

Eternal Reefs (www.eternalreefs.com) is an offshoot of the Reef Ball Development Group, the brainchild of Atlanta businessman Don Brawley. During spring-break diving trips to the Florida Keys in the mid-1980s with his college roommate, Todd Barber, Brawley was struck by how quickly the coral reefs were deteriorating, largely as a result of the usual manmade causes: pollution, discarded debris, the destructive effects of dropped anchors, motorboat propellers, et cetera.

Determined to do something about the problem, the pair went on to found a company that produces environmentally sound artificial reefs. The literal building blocks of the enterprise are uniquely designed "reef balls"—hollow domelike modules resembling perforated concrete igloos. Deposited on the ocean floor, these structures provide a suitable habitat for the various forms of marine life—sponges, anemone, sea fans, and so on—that thrive in natural reef formations. To date, the oceans have been seeded with nearly a half million reef balls worldwide, helping to restore teeming life and diversity to once-moribund underwater environments.

It was a comment by Brawley's father-in-law, Carleton Palmer, that put the company in the body disposal business. After being diagnosed with liver cancer in the late 1990s, Carleton, a devoted deep-sea fisherman, asked his son-in-law to take his cremated ashes, mix them into a reef ball, and sink him underwater. "I'd rather spend eternity down there with all that life than in a field full of dead people." As to location, Carleton wasn't fussy—as long as the spot "had lots of red snapper and grouper."

Not long after his death, Carleton got his wish when his cremains were added to a load of concrete that yielded the raw material for thirty reef balls, which were then ferried six miles off the Florida coast and dropped into the blue waters of the Gulf. When word of Carleton's unique sea burial spread, others began contacting the company to ask if their own departed loved ones could be "reefed." A new memorial enterprise, Eternal Reefs, was born.

For prices ranging from $2,500 to $6,500, depending on which model you choose, the company will incorporate your ashes into a small, medium, or large "memorial reef" at its casting facility in Sarasota, Florida. You can also choose a lower-cost option, a "community reef," in which your ashes are mixed together with a bunch of other cremains. And if you want Fido to join you in Davy Jones's locker, a mini-reef designed specifically for house pets is available for just $695.

Survivors can participate in the process by adding their loved one's ashes to the fresh concrete as it's poured into the mold and leaving a handprint on the module while it's drying. Once the reef has hardened, it is transported by boat, with family members on board, to its final resting place, where it is dropped into the waters to form a permanent habitat for the local sea life. Prices include a bronze memorial plaque affixed to the module and a handsome certificate that gives the precise longitude and latitude of the reef's location. Sites are generally close to resort areas, so survivors can combine a yearly visit to their loved one's final resting place with a fun beach vacation!

A more recent entry in the rapidly growing, highly competitive area of subaquatic cremains disposal is Great Burial Reef, a company founded by former Wall Street trader Jason Rew. As befitting an ex-investment banker, Rew offers a slightly more upscale version of the experience. For $7,500, customers receive a maple urn made by artists in New Mexico. After being filled with ashes, this handcrafted receptacle—which, given its ultimate purpose, is almost gratuitously beautiful—is placed by scuba divers into an artificial concrete reef two miles west of Sarasota, Florida, in the Gulf of Mexico. For more information, go to www.greatburialreef.com.

If you're looking for something even more splashy (so to speak) in the way of a memorial reef—a permanent resting place that resembles an underwater theme park or the submerged lobby of a Las Vegas hotel—you might want to explore the glories of Atlantis Memorial Reef (www.atlantisreefproject.com). Located off the coast of Miami, in the emerald waters just east of Key Biscayne, this sprawling aquatic site is a fanciful reconstruction of the lost city of Atlantis as it might be imagined by a Disney designer. There are various options for perpetual residency in Atlantis, all of which involve placing your cremains in a special container and installing them in one of the architectural features of the enchanted underwater city: the foundation of an ancient palace, say, or the horizontal lintel spanning two columns in the ruined temple of the sea god Poseidon. Judging from the publicity material, it actually looks like a fun place to spend eternity. The only real drawback is that you'll be dead the whole time.

Ashes Aweigh

Sea burial is a venerable corpse disposal method, dating back to ancient times and practiced by sailors throughout the centuries. Nowadays, having your body consigned to Davy Jones's Locker is rare for civilians, though a few companies offer the service as an environmentally friendly alternative to earth burial.

Nature's Passage, a company headquartered in Amityville, Long Island, markets a range of watery interments, including "full body/casket submersion," in which the embalmed, encoffined cadaver is submerged in the open ocean at depths exceeding 100 fathoms, and "sail-cloth wrapped submersion," in which an unembalmed body is wrapped in weighted sail cloth and similarly disposed of. Veterans are qualified for a "full military honors" ceremony (complete with commemorative American flag provided to the family at no additional cost as a handsome souvenir of the occasion). Civilians who opt for full-body sea burial can choose from various options, from elaborate on-board funerals with full religious services to more secular affairs designed for die-hard unbelievers (the company's website declares that "we are proud to offer burials that are sanctioned by the American Atheists, Inc."). For further information, go to www.naturespassage.com.

Far more common than full-body nautical burial is having your ashes scattered at sea. A growing number of companies (including Nature's Passage) offer this service. The best-known is the Neptune Society, founded in 1973 by California chiropractor Charles Denning. A dapper, goateed gent whose resemblance to KFC's Colonel Sanders earned him the nickname "Colonel Cinders," Denning enjoyed heaping scorn on funeral directors, deriding them as purveyors of "tin boxes that rust in the ground, pink gowns and booties, and scenic plots overlooking freeways." Specializing in low-cost, no-frills cremations, Neptune will pick up a body at the place of death, handle all the necessary paperwork, transport the corpse to a refrigerated holding facility, incinerate it in a simple container, place the cremains in an urn, and either return them to the family or (for an extra fee) scatter them at sea. Though some of Neptune's business practices have recently come in for criticism by activists such as Lisa Carlon of the Funeral Consumers Alliance, it continues to provide simple, affordable cremations in various states around the country. For more information go to www.neptunesociety.com. Other companies that have sprung up in Neptune's wake (as it were) include Pacific Coast Ashes at Sea (www.cremainsatsea.com), Maritime Funeral Services (www.maritimefuneralservices.com), Sea Services (www.seaservices.com), and Sea Burial (www.seaburial.com). Besides the standard cremains-scattering option, some of these outfits offer other types of nautical disposal. Sea Burial, for example, will have a diver carry an ash-filled urn to the

DEATH QUIZ

All but one of the following dead celebrities had their ashes scattered at sea. Who is the sole exception?

A. Steve McQueen

B. Humphrey Bogart

C. Vincent Price

D. Jerry Garcia

E. Robert Mitchum

F. Rock Hudson

ANSWER: B. Somewhat ironically—since three of his signature roles were Harry Morgan, the world-weary fishing boat captain in *To Have and Have Not*; Charlie Allnut, the hard-drinking captain of a ramshackle tramp steamer in *The African Queen*; and the seriously nutty Captain Queeg in *The Caine Mutiny*—Bogie is the only one of these celebs whose cremains were not scattered over the water. They are interred in the Glendale branch of Forest Lawn Memorial Park.

seabed floor and bury it in the sand, while Sea Services offers a trademarked "seashell urn" that begins to biodegrade as it descends through the water until it "respectfully deposits the remains in their final resting spot at the ocean's depths."

The Eternal Alumni Club

Are you the kind of person who looks back on your undergraduate years as the best time of your life and wishes you could have stayed in college forever? Well, thanks to a new development in the realm of American higher education, your dream can now come true, in a manner of speaking.

You won't exactly be enjoying toga parties or other fun-filled nights of frathouse binge drinking. As a matter of fact, you won't be enjoying anything at all since you'll be sealed up inside a stone wall. Still, you'll never have to leave college again!

According to an article in the May 18, 2007, *New York Times*, a growing number of U.S. colleges and universities—including the University of Richmond, Notre Dame, the Citadel, and Hendrix College in Conway, Arkansas—are constructing on-campus columbaria: memorial walls designed to hold cremation urns. For a few thousand dollars, faculty or alumni can purchase a niche and "have their ashes maintained on campus in perpetuity."

The practice seems to have originated at the University of Virginia. In 1991, a Charlottesville lawyer named Leigh B. Middleditch Jr.—a product of both Virginia's undergraduate and law schools who wished to be buried on the grounds of his beloved alma mater—discovered that the university's venerable graveyard was already full. After some lobbying and fund-raising, he managed to get a columbarium built in place of a cemetery wall. The 180 niches, priced at $1,800 apiece, quickly sold out.

Since then, at least a half dozen other institutions of higher learning have followed suit. Though the notion of going into the mortuary business strikes some educators as bizarre, others see it as a natural product of our modern age. "Many people don't identify with their churches, or their churches don't have cemeteries like they used to," says one former college chaplain. "But people feel very connected to their colleges, and there are some beautiful places on campuses."

The practice has benefits for the universities as well, which are always looking for new ways to raise money. The hope, as the article points out, is that "by building stronger bonds with alumni and their families," a nice on-campus columbarium for postgraduate cremains "might lead to substantial donations."

Hair Today, Memorial Gemstone Tomorrow

Remember that old *Superman* TV show where the Man of Steel took a lump of coal and squeezed it until it became a diamond? Well, thanks to a company called

LifeGem, something similar can now be done to your departed loved one.

Imagine turning your late hubby into a beautiful one-half-carat princess diamond and mounting him on a lovely pendant necklace that you can wear to your next dinner party! Or converting Grandpa into a handsome pair of diamond-studded cufflinks! You can even have the remains of your beloved pet tabby made into a "God Bless America" lapel pin!

For prices ranging from a mere $2,699 all the way up to $24,999 (depending on weight, color, and shape), LifeGem will take a lock of your loved one's hair or a portion of his/her/its cremated ashes and convert this precious material into a high-grade synthetic "memorial diamond." (Clearly, CorpseGem would be a more accurate name for the company, though we can certainly understand why they opted for LifeGem.) This miracle is accomplished through a unique four-step process that involves extracting carbon from the organic remains, subjecting it to intense heat, then placing the resulting graphite inside a special machine that "replicates the awesome forces deep within the earth." Eventually, a rough diamond crystal is produced, which is then finished by expert diamond cutters to the customer's specifications.

The diamonds are offered in a variety of cuts and colors. Of course, like natural diamonds, they are not absolutely flawless. But then again—in the words of one satisfied customer who gave her spouse the patented postmortem LifeGem treatment—neither was her late husband.

You'll find lots more about LifeGem, including a handsome brochure, at www.lifegem.com.

Going Out in Viking Style

Leave it to the Vikings—the same folks who reputedly enjoyed drinking mead from human skulls—to come up with the manliest way of cremating someone. When one of their warriors died, he was loaded onto a dragon-prowed ship with his weapons, enough food and drink for the trip to Valhalla, and a sacrificed slave to keep him company. Then the boat was set afire.

Usually, the ship was burned on land, then buried under a mound of earth. Sometimes, however, it was towed out to sea before being torched—at least according to legend. Since blazing, waterborne wooden boats don't leave any archaeological evidence, there is no actual proof of such a practice. Still, it is described in a number of Norse sagas. It is also memorably portrayed at the climax of the 1958 movie *The Vikings*, in which the ship bearing the slain chieftain, Einar, is set afloat, then ignited by a shower of flaming arrows fired from shore by his fellow warriors. No ax-wielding, seafaring marauder could ask for a more touching send-off.

Keith, Coke, and Funerary Cannibalism

In her best-selling 1963 exposé, *The American Way of Death*, Jessica Mitford attacks our national funeral habits—particularly our insistence on embalming and open-casket viewing—as nothing less than "barbaric." This judgment seems a tad harsh, particularly when American mortuary customs are compared to those of certain other groups—the Fore tribe of New Guinea, for example. This aboriginal people practiced what anthropologists call "funerary cannibalism": the ritual eating of dead family members as part of the grieving process.

Archaeological evidence suggests that funerary cannibalism dates all the way back to the Paleolithic era and persisted well into the modern age, not only among the Fore (who frequently came down with a mad-cow-like disease called kuru from eating human brains) but among other primitive people as well, such as another New Guinea tribe called the Gimi. According to Kenneth Iserson, author of the encyclopedic *Death to Dust: What Happens to Dead Bodies?* (Galen Press, 1994), "In the Gimi ritual, relatives placed a dead man's body on a platform, so that he could decompose. . . . His female relatives then dragged him off the scaffold, dismembered the corpse, and carried the pieces into the normally forbidden men's hut. There they ate their portions over several days." The Yanomamo tribe of the Amazon also reputedly practiced funerary cannibalism. When one of their children died, the parents held a funeral feast during which they consumed the little one's entire body, including the bones, which were ground up, cooked, and mixed with plantain.

Shocking as it seems to modern sensibilities, the practice of funerary cannibalism springs from a deep and very human impulse: the desire to incorporate the essence of a loved one into your own body—to make the vanished family member a very literal part of yourself.

Maybe that's what Keith Richards had in mind when he performed his own unique act of funerary cannibalism. Richards didn't exactly eat the flesh of a dead relative. The hard-living guitarist for the Rolling Stones did something more in keeping with his wild-man reputation: he ingested his father's remains as a drug.

In an interview with the British music magazine *NME*, Richards claimed that following the death and cremation of his father, Bert, in 2002, he mixed some of the old man's ashes with cocaine and snorted them. The blend of cremains and coke "went down pretty well," Richards observed. The tabloid press had a field day with the story ("Father Nose Best" was a typical headline).

Richards's PR people issued immediate retractions, claiming that it was all just an April Fool's joke. If Richards was, in fact, telling the truth (and it says something about his wild-man reputation that his claim seems perfectly credible), it's possible that he was simply experimenting with one of the few substances he had never tried before. But maybe—without even consciously knowing it—he was performing a rock-and-roll version of a primordial ritual: consuming ("with a little bit of blow") the body of his departed ancestor.

Cryonic Preservation: Cooling Your Heels (Along with the Rest of Your Anatomy) for a Few Millennia

Once upon a time, young women of royal birth were occasionally killed by poisoned apples, preserved in glass coffins, and eventually brought back to life by handsome princes who happened to be wandering by. Nowadays things are different. Thanks to enormous strides in the science of human refrigeration, we no longer have to depend on things like dwarf-constructed caskets and magical kisses. Instead we can turn to a sophisticated technique known as *cryonic preservation*, aka *cryopreservation* or simply *cryonics* (not to be confused with *cryogenics*, the branch of physics that studies very low temperatures).

In the simplest terms, cryonics consists of putting a dead person into an indefinite deep freeze in the hope that science will eventually come up with a way to thaw him out and revivify him. Though the concept can be traced back to science fiction stories of the 1930s, the person universally regarded as the driving force behind the contemporary cryonics movement is former physics professor Robert C. W. Ettinger.

In his influential book *The Prospect of Immortality* (self-published in 1962 and subsequently reissued by Doubleday), Ettinger argues that "most of us now breathing have a good chance of physical life after death—a sober, scientific probability of revival and rejuvenation of our frozen bodies." While acknowledging that a few wrinkles remain to be ironed out—like, how exactly do you bring a long-frozen dead person back to life?—he expresses the utmost confidence that scientists of the future will possess not only the technological know-how but the active desire to resurrect us. "No matter what kills us, whether old age or disease, and even if freezing techniques are still crude when we die, sooner or later our friends of the future should be equal to the task of reviving and curing us."

Indeed, Ettinger is so optimistic about the future that he describes a "tired old man" of today placing himself in cryonic suspension and awakening centuries hence "with the physique of a Charles Atlas," having been "rejuvenated while unconscious" by our benevolent "friends of the future," who evidently will have nothing better to do than spend their time sprucing up and reanimating frozen corpses. Today's cryopreserved dead, Ettinger

Body preservation, Grimm-style.

insists, will wake up "young and virile" in "a wonderful world, a vista to excite the mind and thrill the heart." They will "not merely be revived and cured, but enlarged and improved, made fit to work and play on a grand scale and in a grand style." That the future might not turn out to be quite so rosy—that we might reawaken to find ourselves, say, caged in a futuristic petting zoo or trapped in some *Matrix*-like inferno where we serve as human battery packs for a race of malevolent machines—is a possibility that he fails to consider.

The process of cryonic suspension is exceptionally complicated—not just a matter of packing a corpse in ice and periodically refilling the cooler. In her book *Modern Mummies: The Preservation of the Human Body in the Twentieth Century* (McFarland, 1996), Christine Quigley describes at some length the procedure performed on James H. Bedford, the world's first human being to undergo voluntary cryopreservation.

At 6:30 P.M. on January 12, 1967, Bedford—a seventy-three-year-old retired psychology professor—died of lung cancer in a convalescent home in Glendale, California. At his bedside were members of the Los Angeles Cryonics Society (LACS), along with Bedford's physician, Dr. B. Renault Able, who shared his patient's interest in cryonics. After making the determination of death, Able connected Bedford's body to a heart-lung machine and flooded it with nutrients and oxygen to keep the brain from degenerating. He injected Bedford's body with heparin to prevent the blood from clotting. With LACS member Dr. Dante Bruno, Able intravenously injected dimethyl sulfoxide to prevent ice crystals from forming in the body tissues. The men packed Bedford's body in dry ice and turned off the heart-lung machine when the body temperature had reached near freezing.

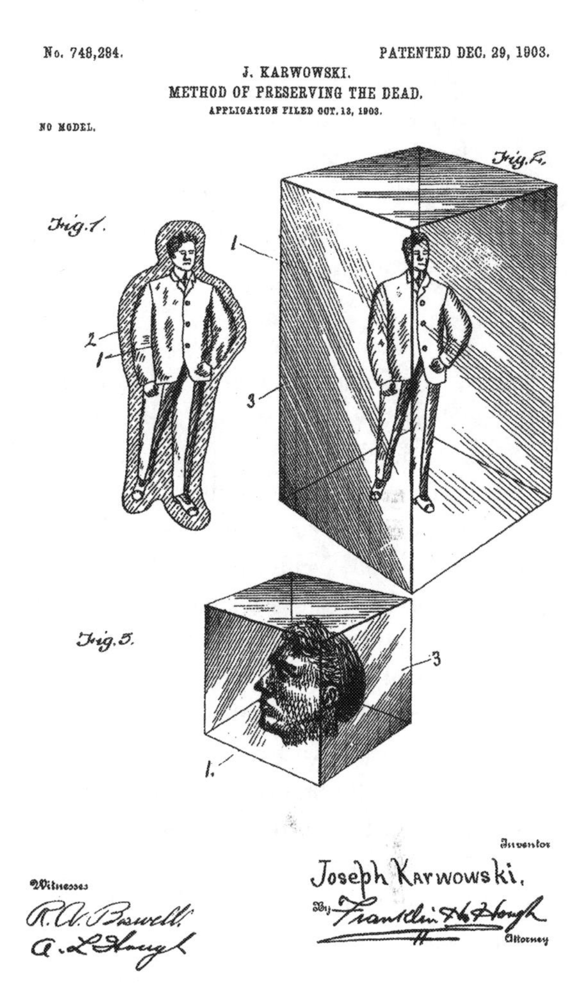

1903 patent applications for a precryonics method of corpse preservation.

By 2 A.M., the temperature of Bedford's body had been lowered to –100°F, equal to that of dry ice. A horizontal cryogenic storage capsule manufactured by Cryocare Equipment Corporation was brought into the room. The stainless steel cylinder was seven feet long and had been constructed with double walls to insulate the body. Bedford's frozen body was wrapped in alu-

> minum foil, enclosed in a sleeping bag, and placed inside the capsule. The inner container was welded shut. The chamber was filled with liquid nitrogen, a liquefied gas with a temperature of about 320 degrees below zero, and within seconds Bedford's tissues had become as brittle as glass.

As you may imagine, turning a dead person into a human Popsicle—or a "corpsicle," as Kenneth V. Iserson so aptly puts it—isn't cheap, particularly when you add in the expense of extended (if not eternal) maintenance and storage. Prices run from roughly $30,000 up to $120,000 for full-body cryopreservation, though you can save a bundle by opting for the head-only option, also known as "neurosuspension"—a procedure that received a great deal of publicity a few years back when it was revealed that the decapitated head of baseball immortal Ted Williams had been preserved apart from his body.

Needless to say, a great deal of controversy has surrounded cryonics from the start. Many scientists deride it as a form of high-tech quackery. "Believing cryonics could reanimate somebody who has been frozen," says one eminent physician, "is like believing you can turn hamburger back into a cow." Other equally prominent scientists, however, are not so quick to dismiss it, particularly in light of the rapid advances in fields such as nanotechnology that might—at least theoretically—make the resurrection of cryopreserved corpses possible in the far future.

Besides the issue of its feasibility, other objections to the procedure have been raised. These range from the psychological ("How will I survive emotionally in the future without the people I love?") to the ethical ("Won't cryonics lead to the overpopulation of the earth?") and the religious ("Doesn't God intend for humans to die?"). Proponents, however, have carefully reasoned and persuasive answers to most of these questions. For example, your loved ones can also be cryonically preserved and join you in the future. (Alternatively, you can always make new friends.) As for concerns about overcrowding, the percentage of present-day people who can afford the procedure is so small that their future resurrection will have no impact on the world population. And while God might want us to die, who can say when? After all, according to the Bible, Noah lived 950 years and Methuselah even longer—969 years.

RECOMMENDED RESOURCES

The world's foremost cryopreservation company is the Alcor Life Extension Foundation of Scottsdale, Arizona. Its website (www.alcor.org) not only describes the process in detail but also debunks the major "myths" surrounding cryonics and addresses, in a frank and sensible way, some of the problems that still attend the procedure. Another leading organization in the field is the Cryonics Institute of Clinton Township, Michigan, which maintains an equally informative website (www.crynonics.org) and publishes a bimonthly magazine for cryonics enthusiasts, the *Immortalist*. The American Cryonics Society of Cupertino, California (www.americancryonics.org) has been in existence since 1969. While offering a full cryonic suspension program, it does not have long-term storage facilities and contracts with other organizations, primarily the Cryonics Institute, for this service.

The single most comprehensive online source for information about cryonics is the website of self-declared "life-extensionist and inveterate scribbler" Ben Best (www.benbest.com/cryonics/cryonics.html). Deeply informed, exceptionally thorough, and highly readable, Best's encyclopedic site not only tells you everything you've ever wanted to know about cryonics (how it works, what it costs, etc.), but also addresses questions that would never occur to most people: Where does the soul go when a person is cryopreserved? Is it immoral to spend thousands of dollars to have your body frozen when people in poor countries are starving? How will reanimated people live in the future without marketable skills?

Ted Williams: Dead Head

If you've always wondered what a decapitated cryopreserved head looks like—at least as portrayed by one of America's leading sculptors—now's your chance to find out. In 2005, Daniel Edwards—controversial creator of such outlandishly amusing pieces as *Monument to Pro-life: The Birth of Sean Preston* (a naked Britney Spears down on all fours giving birth to a newborn), *Presidential Bust of Hillary Rodham Clinton* (a topless and surprisingly well-endowed Hillary), and *Suri Cruise's First Poop* (pretty much what it sounds like)—whipped up a storm of publicity with a work called *The Ted Williams Memorial Display with Death Mask, from the Ben Affleck 2004 World Series Collection.*

Presented as the ultimate sports collectible, this prankishly gruesome work consists of three lifelike sculptures that purport to be genuine plastic casts of the clinically severed head of the great Boston Red Sox slugger, made while Williams was "in cryonic slumber" (in reality, they were modeled on photographs of the living Williams). Each head is posed with a different piece of memorabilia: a 1941 *Life* magazine with Williams on the cover, a pair of 1950s cleats, and an autographed baseball.

You can see the work at various sites on the Web. For best results, type "Daniel Edwards" and "Ted Williams" at Google Image Search.

Death Fun Fact

Ever since his death in 1966, stories have circulated that Walt Disney's corpse was cryogenically preserved and stored below the Pirates of the Caribbean ride at Disneyland for future resuscitation. This, however, is an urban legend. In reality, Disney was cremated and interred in the Court of Freedom section of Forest Lawn Memorial Park.

Green Burials

If you are a concerned, ecologically aware citizen who cares deeply about environmental issues (in other words, a tree-hugging hippie), you'll want to look into the increasingly popular form of interment known as "green burial."

A relatively recent outgrowth of the back-to-nature movement that first sprang up in the late 1960s, green burials dispense with all the costly and elaborate accoutrements of traditional interments: fancy coffins, heavy-duty burial vaults, ostentatious memorials, "perpetual care" cemeteries as neatly manicured as suburban lawns. Instead, they offer a simple, back-to-the-earth form of burial in bucolic settings: lush meadows, grassy fields, and shady forests.

The practice originated in Great Brit-

DEATH DEFINITION: *Excarnation*

THE DEFINITION OF *EXCARNATE* IS "TO DEPRIVE OF FLESH"—FOR EXAMPLE, TO REMOVE THE MEAT FROM bones. (The word is the opposite of *incarnate*, which means "to invest with flesh," "to give something bodily form.") Stripping flesh from skeletons is, of course, exactly what carnivorous beasts do to their prey. Hence, the term *excarnation* is sometimes used to describe the funerary practice of disposing of dead bodies by feeding them to wild animals.

As Kenneth Iserson documents in his exhaustive volume *Death to Dust: What Happens to Dead Bodies?* (Galen Press, 1994), this method has been used by people throughout the world from prehistoric times to the present. In ancient Egypt, dead slaves were tossed into the Nile as croc chow. Elsewhere in Africa, corpses were carted off to the desert for the jackals and hyenas. The ancient Bactrians who resided in what is present-day Afghanistan kept dogs for the precise purpose of body disposal (the elderly and infirm were also occasionally fed to the hounds). And tribal people from Australia to North America have placed their dead in trees or elevated platforms to be devoured by vultures and other scavengers.

Nowadays, the practice is still carried out by the Parsees of India, who—to avoid polluting the sacred elements of earth, fire, and water—refrain from burial, cremation, or casting corpses into rivers. Instead, they erect stone parapets known as Towers of Silence and place dead bodies within to be consumed by vultures. Some modern-day serial killers have also favored excarnation as a means of eliminating incriminating evidence. In the 1930s, a sociopath named Joe Ball disposed of his female victims by tossing their bodies into an alligator-stocked pond behind his seedy Texas roadhouse. More recently, a Canadian pig farmer named Robert Pickton, accused of murdering more than two dozen women, allegedly got rid of the remains by feeding them to his porkers.

ain, which currently boasts more than 150 "green cemeteries." In our own country, the acknowledged pioneers of the eco-friendly funeral movement are Billy Campbell—a small-town physician in the farming community of Westminster, South Carolina—and his wife, Kimberly. In 1996, the Campbells turned a thirty-eight-acre stretch of Westminster woodlands known as the Ramsey Creek Preserve into our nation's first back-to-nature burial ground (or, in the somewhat more pretentious phrase preferred by its founders, "memorial ecosystem"). The strict environmental rules enforced at Ramsey Creek have become the model for other natural cemeteries that have begun to appear across the United States:

1. Bodies may not be embalmed (to prevent any toxic fluids from leaking into the groundwater).
2. Coffins must be made of biodegradable materials (simple wood, wicker, cardboard, papier-mâché). Shrouds made of natural fiber are also permitted.
3. Tombstones are not allowed. A flat rock from the preserve can be placed on the grave and, if the family wishes, engraved with the name of the deceased. (A person can also choose to leave his or her grave unmarked, in which case the site is entered into a database to provide a permanent record of its location.)
4. Flowers or shrubs can be planted at the gravesite but only if they are native to the area. (A checklist is provided by the preserve and runs the gamut from heart-leaved aster to hairy yucca. You won't be pushing up anything as mundane as daisies at Ramsey Creek Preserve.)

Besides protecting the planet from embalming-fluid leakage and nonbiodegradable caskets, green burials are easy on the pocketbook. Nowadays, an average funeral costs in the neighborhood of $6,500, not including the price of the cemetery plot. By contrast, being planted in a beautiful woodsy area such as Ramsey Creek Preserve will set you back less than half that amount. Plus, it serves the purpose of land conservation since no one is going to turn a cemetery into a condo development.

As Billy Campbell says, "By setting aside a woods for natural burials, we preserve it from development. At the same time, I think we put death in its rightful place, as part of the cycle of life. Our burials honor the idea of dust to dust."

Or dust to mulch, as the case may be.

RECOMMENDED READING

Mark Harris, a former environmental columnist with the *Los Angeles Times* syndicate, has written a highly readable book on alternative, ecofriendly burials, *Grave Matters: A Journey Through the Modern Funeral Industry* (Scribner's, 2007). For someone whose sympathies are clearly on the side of the green burial movement, he's also pretty fair and balanced, noting, for example, the dubious environmental advantages of "air-freighting a body to a distant woodland ground for shrouded interment, as has happened."

An excellent online source of information about green burials is the Forest of Memories Natural Burial website at www.forestofmemories.org.

On no subject are our ideas more warped and pitiable than on death. Instead of the friendly union of life and death so apparent in Nature, we are taught that death is an accident, a deplorable punishment for the oldest sin, the archenemy of life. But let children walk with Nature, let them see the beautiful blendings and communions of death and life, their joyous insuperable unity as taught in woods and meadows, plains and mountains and streams of our blessed star, and they will learn that death is stingless indeed, and as beautiful as life, and that the grave has no victory, for it never fights. All is divine harmony.

—John Muir (used as an epigraph for the Ramsey Creek Preserve website)

Isn't It Ironic? (Part II)

According to the London *Daily Mail* of July 4, 1997, a woman named Rolande Genève planted an oak tree in her garden in Isère, France, when she was six years old. Sixty years later, following a severe thunderstorm, the tree fell over and killed her.

Ecopods: Designer Coffins for the Save-the-Earth Crowd

If you decide to take the green burial route, the simplest (and cheapest) way to go is inside a plain pine coffin. But if you're looking for something more stylish than an unvarnished box, the Ecopod may be the right choice for you.

The brainchild of British designer Hazel Selina, the Ecopod came into being when Selina was called upon to arrange the funeral of an old friend. A passionate environmentalist who ran a natural childbirth center in Devon, England, she was horrified to discover that traditional coffins not only relied on endangered species such as mahogany but allowed precious natural resources to go to waste by preventing dead bodies from turning into compost. On a train ride to Wales, she came up with the concept of a coffin made of papier-mâché

Ecopod. Courtesy of ARKA Ltd.

and shaped like a seedpod. The result was the Ecopod.

A sleek, slightly curved container made of 100 percent recycled paper and toxin-free resin, the Ecopod comes in two different sizes and a variety of colors, with simple decorative devices made of natural silk-screened paper. Compared to ordinary coffins, they are such strikingly elegant objects that it almost seems a shame to hide them underground.

For more information on the Ecopod, go to www.ecopod.co.uk.

How to Make a Mummy

You've probably always wondered how the ancient Egyptians turned corpses into mummies. Perhaps you've even thought about having your own body preserved in this traditional manner when you die. Well, here's the authentic recipe as handed down from the time of the pharaohs!

INGREDIENTS

Natron (a mineral salt, also used to make Bavarian pretzels; you will need 400 pounds, give or take a few teaspoons)
Juniper oil
Palm wine
Sawdust
Tree resin
Wax
1 human corpse

SPECIAL EQUIPMENT

Stone slab
Hooked embalming rod (a crochet hook may be substituted in a pinch)
Obsidian knife
Jars (preferably of the beautifully sculpted canopic variety)
Linen (approximately 1,000 yards)
Priceless gold jewelry such as rings, bangles, amulets (optional)

PREP TIME

About 60 days

DIRECTIONS

1. Place body on slab.
2. Poke hooked rod through nasal cavity and extract brain in clumps until it is completely removed. Dispose of brain tissue. Rinse interior of cranium with palm wine, then pack with tree resin and sawdust.
3. With obsidian knife, open a small incision in the abdomen. Remove liver, lungs, intestines, and stomach and store in jars. Leave heart in place to be weighed by Osiris in the afterlife.
4. Cover body with natron and let dehydrate for 40 days. Rinse. Dry. Anoint with juniper oil.
5. Stuff body cavity with tree resin, sawdust, and leftover natron. Seal incision with wax.
6. Add jewelry, amulets, etc.
7. Tear linen into strips, 16 yards long and 2–8 inches wide. Decorate with hieroglyphic prayers. Spend next 15 days wrapping body in intricate geometrical patterns.
8. Voilà! Your mummy may now be outfitted with a gold mask, placed in a human-shaped sarcophagus, and transported to the burial chamber

of your choice, where (barring the depredations of treasure-seeking tomb raiders) it will reside for all eternity.

You are young again. You live again. You are young again. You live again. Forever.

—Ancient Egyptian prayer for the dead

You, Too, Can Be a Mummy (and So Can Fido)

Have you always envied King Tut? Harbored a secret yen to be eviscerated, anointed in oil, and entirely swaddled in gauze? Dreamed of having your body discovered in a perfect state of preservation by archaeologists of the future? Thanks to the miracle of modern "mummification" pioneered by an organization called Summum, that dream can now come true!

Summum was founded by a former aerobics instructor named Claude "Corky" Nowell, who subsequently became a licensed funeral director and legally changed his name to Summum Bonum Amon Ra, supposedly ancient Egyptian for "Worker of Creation." (His friends still call him "Corky.") Along with Salt Lake City mortician Ron Zefferer (who also adopted a moniker from Egyptian mythology and is now known as Ron Temu), Ra spent years developing a state-of-the-art "mummification" process. The two men began by experimenting on lower life forms before working their way up to Corky's pet cat (which had died of feline leukemia). Having finally perfected their technique, they patented their formula, set themselves up as professional "thanatogeneticists," and established their company, the world's first (and only) commercial mummification service.

Headquartered in a shining golden pyramid just five blocks from the Mormon Temple in Salt Lake City, Summum offers what its advertising brochure describes as a

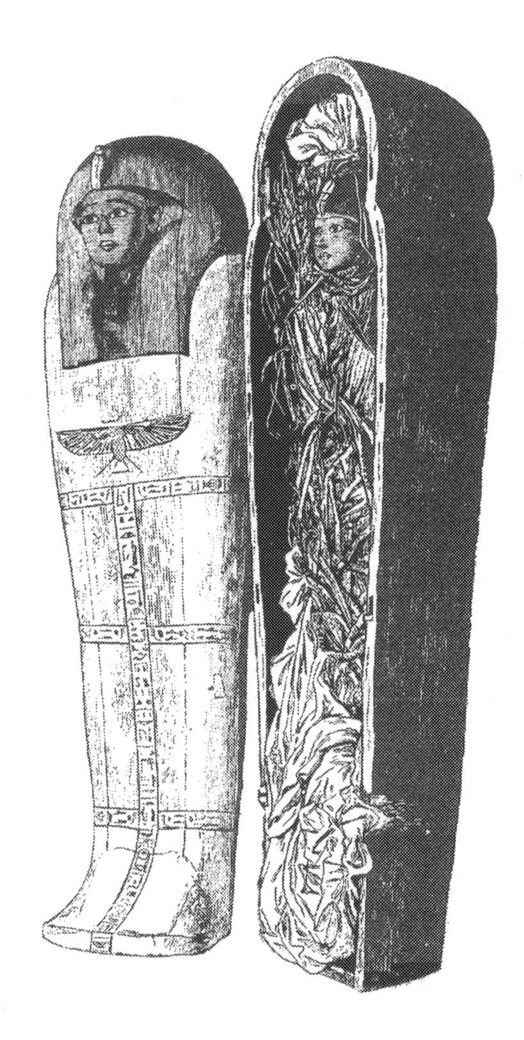

"very thorough and gentle process that allows you to leave this life in as beautiful a manner as possible"—a process tagged with the trademarked phrase "eternal memorialization." A page on its very handsome website, (www.summum.org/mummification) supplies further details.

Once the deceased has been transported to Summum's mortuary-cum-temple in Salt Lake City, "the rites of Transference begin and are officiated as the body is bathed and cleansed. An incision is made to remove the internal organs. The organs are thoroughly cleansed and placed back in the body." The body is then "immersed in a baptismal font filled with a special preservation solution." After a period ranging from a week to a month—"long enough to achieve maximum penetration as the rites of Transference continue"—the body is "removed, cleansed again, then covered with a lotion." Next comes the wrapping in "several layers of cotton gauze," followed by the application of successive layers of polyurethane, fiberglass, and resin. Finally the mummy is encased within a custom-made casket called a Mummiform, which is then filled with "an amber resin, completely surrounding the

Herotodus on Mummy Making

The most famous firsthand description of the Egyptian mummification process was written by the great Greek historian Herodotus (aka the "father of history"). It appears in his book *The Persian Wars*, composed in the fifth century B.C.

"The mode of embalming, according to the most perfect process, is the following: They take first a crooked piece of iron, and with it draw out the brain through the nostrils, thus getting rid of a portion, while the skull is cleared of the rest by rinsing with drugs; next they make a cut along the flank with a sharp Ethiopian stone, and take out the whole contents of the abdomen, which they then cleanse, washing it thoroughly with palm wine, and again frequently with an infusion of pounded aromatics. After this they fill the cavity with the purest powdered myrrh, with cassia, and every other sort of spicery except frankincense, and sew up the opening. Then the body is placed in nitre for seventy days, and covered entirely over. At the end of this period, which must not be exceeded, the body is washed, and wrapped round, from head to foot, with bandages of fine linen cloth, smeared over with gum, which is used generally by the Egyptians in the place of glue, and in this state it is given back to the relations, who enclose it in a wooden case, made to resemble a human figure. Then fastening the case, they place it in a sepulchral chamber, upright against the wall."

mummy and protecting the perfection that has been created." The entire process requires a minimum of 120 days.

Needless to say, such elaborate postmortem ministrations don't come cheap. After noting that "the rites of mummification are something we would offer free of charge if we could," the folks at Summum point out that they "incur extensive costs" in preparing each mummy and therefore "suggest a donation" for anyone who wishes to undergo their procedure. The minimal cost is currently $67,000, though total expenses can amount to "well over a hundred thousand dollars," depending on the exact style of Mummiform one chooses to be encased within. (The simplest is a sleek, shiny capsule, though other, far more elaborate handcrafted models are available, including ones "inlaid with gold, ceramics, or jewels.") Little wonder that the customers who have so far signed up for "eternal memorialization" tend to be the rich and famous.

For those with a little extra cash to toss around, mummification is also available for pets. Costs range from $6,000 to over $128,000, depending on species, weight of animal, and "type of Mummiform chosen."

Mummy Bear: The Cutest Darn Mummy *Ever!*

If you're the parent of a preschooler, you've undoubtedly found yourself faced with an all-too-common dilemma: just how do you introduce your child to the wonderful world of mummification? Well, thanks to the folks at Summum, the world's leading provider of "modern mummification" services, that worry is a thing of the past. Just proceed to the company's kids' website at http://kids.summum.us.

There, you and your offspring will be introduced to Mummy Bear, an absolutely adorable, bandage-swathed teddy who has undergone the mummification process and is bursting with eagerness to share its joys with all the little visitors to his interactive home page. ("Hi everyone! My name is Mummy Bear. Do you like mummification? I sure do. I think it's cool.") Mummy Bear will not only lead your children on a guided tour of mummification through the ages but teach them jokes, riddles, games, poems, and even the "Mummy Bear Prayer" ("Now I lay me down to rest / I leave this life, I've done my best / Please clean my body, head to toe / Wrap me up and make me whole").

There's also a slide show of Mummy Bear undergoing the mummification process, from evisceration (you'll get to see his furry little tummy opened up and his cute little innards exposed) to wrapping. All we can say is . . . awwwww.

The price might seem a tad steep, but after all, as Summum's website proclaims "Through this singular form of Permanent Body Preservation, your pet, at his natural earthly passing, will enter eternity in all of his splendor and beauty."

100 Percent All-Natural Mummies

Besides the kind of mummy that everyone is familiar with—the bandage-wrapped ancient Egyptian type that resides in a fancy sarcophagus and can be brought back to life with the proper ritual incantation—there is an entirely different variety found in many parts of the world. This sort of mummy is not the product of a sophisticated method of embalming but rather the result of natural processes.

Human corpses can be naturally mummified under different environmental conditions. After as little as two weeks in a hot, arid climate, for example, an exposed human body weighing 150 pounds may be converted into a completely dessicated, parchment-colored, 45-pound mummy. One of the more startling discoveries of recent times occurred in the remote Chinese wasteland known as the Taklamakan desert, where perfectly preserved three-thousand-year-old mummies with long blond hair and blue eyes were discovered in the late 1980s. Certain areas of South America have also been fertile grounds for modern mummy hunters. In a major find that took place in 2002, several thousand Inca mummies—many with their hair, eyes, and skin intact—were uncovered from an ancient graveyard on the outskirts of Lima, Peru, a region that receives virtually no rainfall and whose exceptionally dry soil provides ideal conditions for natural mummification.

By the same token, dry, *frigid* conditions can also preserve a corpse indefinitely. In 1991, a pair of German climbers discovered the body of a 5,300-year-old man garbed in a woven-grass vest, leather loincloth, bearskin cap, and primitive snowshoes. Nicknamed Ötzi (for the region in which he was found), this remarkable Copper Age mummy was so well preserved that scientists were able to determine the contents of his last meal (red deer meat) and the cause of his death (apparent homicide from an arrow to the left shoulder). Other famous "ice mummies" include the so-called Siberian Ice Princess—a 2,500-year-old female shaman whose corpse was adorned with vivid tattoos of mythical creatures—and Juanita, an Inca sacrificial victim found high atop a Peruvian mountain in 1995.

The particular chemical constituents of a burial site can also be conducive to long-term corpse preservation. More than one thousand Ice Age corpses have been found in the sphagnum bogs of northern Europe. The most famous of these—Denmark's 2,400-year-old Tollund Man—has kept so extraordinarily well that when two brothers discovered him in 1950, they assumed he was a recent murder victim.

Unique soil conditions in the Mexican city of Guanajuato are also thought to be responsible for the numerous mummies exhumed from the local cemetery. These singularly ghastly corpses—victims of a cholera epidemic in 1833—include a tiny infant trumpeted as *la momia más pequeño del mundo* (the smallest mummy in the world) and a woman accused of witchcraft. Some wear agonized expressions, suggesting that they may have been buried alive. They can be viewed at the Museo de las Momias next time you're down Guanajato way. (Alternatively, you can see them online at www.mummytombs.com/mummylocator/group/guanajuato.closeup.htm.

RECOMMENDED READING

For a detailed, scientific look at the various forms of mummification, you can't beat Christine Quigley's *Modern Mummies: The Preservation of the Human Body in the Twentieth Century* (McFarland, 1998). There's also much to be learned from her earlier book, *The Corpse: A History* (McFarland, 1996). Johan Reinhard, discoverer of the ice mummy nicknamed Juanita, recounts his adventures in *The Ice Maiden: Inca Mummies, Mountain Gods, and Sacred Sites in the Andes* (National Geographic, 2005). A particularly fun and fascinating read is Heather Pringle's *The Mummy Congress: Science, Obsession, and the Everlasting Dead* (Theia, 2001).

6

LOSS and HOPE

The Hour of Lead

For various cultural reasons—our belief in personal freedom, our pride in not being enslaved to the past—Americans have never had much use for the kinds of rigid social customs that define life in so many other parts of the world. Here in the good old U.S.A., we are free (within strict legal limits) to act as we please. We're not obliged to do things a certain way just because that's how they've always been done. Even immigrants who try to cling to their long-established traditions generally find themselves adapting to our American way of life, where the only communal rituals everyone is more or less compelled to obey are attending a pizza party on Super Bowl Sunday and undergoing the nightmare of Thanksgiving travel so you can spend time with relatives you don't particularly get along with.

Clearly, there are distinct advantages to living in a country where every aspect of existence—how you're supposed to dress, what you're allowed to eat, whom you're permitted to marry, when you're required to pray—isn't dictated by centuries-old tradition. Still, as is so often the case, the benefits come with a downside. Social rituals, after all, evolved for a reason. Among other things, they come in very handy at moments of crisis, when they provide us with a clear set of behavioral rules that help us cope with the calamity at hand. This is particularly true when people are faced with the greatest calamity of all, the death of a loved one.

Throughout human history, societies all over the world have established specific rituals for mourning. These practices amount to a time-tested communal support system, devised to help the newly bereaved get through the immediate shock and trauma of their loss and begin the process of healing. Some groups in America still adhere to such ancient customs. For example, following the death of a first-degree relative (father, mother, son, daughter, brother, sister, or spouse), practicing Jews observe the week-long ritual known as sitting *shiva*, during which the mourner forgoes personal grooming, wears a torn outer garment (such as a shirt or blouse ripped at the heart), sits on a low chair when visitors come to offer condolences, and obeys other rules and prohibitions. Generally speaking, however, there are no fixed mourning rituals for most Americans, who are often left to their own emotional devices when confronted with the death of a loved one.

In the absence of such sustaining rituals, an entire grief industry has sprung up in modern America. Publishing constitutes one major area of this business. As of December 2007, for example, more than three thousand books were included under Amazon.com's "Grief and Bereavement" subject listing, the bulk of them self-help manuals with titles such as *How to Survive the Loss of a Love*, *Healing After Loss*, *How to Go on Living When Someone You Love Dies*, *Getting to the Other Side of Grief*, and *The Grief Recovery Handbook*. There are also scores of more narrowly focused books addressed to specific forms of bereavement: *Finding Your Way After Your Spouse Dies*, *Grieving the Death of a Mother*, *Surviving the Death of Your Baby*, *35 Ways to Help a Grieving Child*, and so on.

Besides this ever-growing mountain of self-help books, there is also the burgeoning field of grief counseling. Practiced primarily by licensed psychologists and social workers (the kinds of trained human-service professionals who, in our secular society, provide the guidance traditionally offered by priests and other spiritual advisors), grief counseling is designed to help bereaved people work their way through the normal process of mourning. A more radical approach—aimed at those whose reaction to a death is so extreme than it can fairly be called pathological—is known as grief therapy.

Though many of the myriad books on the subject insist that there is no "correct" way to mourn, certain general rules apply. To begin with, virtually all experts agree that a bereaved person must allow himself to fully vent his grief. This can be difficult, especially in a society such as ours that doesn't encourage its members (especially men) to openly express their feelings. Even more than other pent-up emotions, however, suppressed grief can lead to all kinds of physical symptoms, from insomnia and ulcers to migraine and heart disease—a truth recognized at least as far back as the sixteenth century, when Shakespeare put this insight into the mouth of a character in *Macbeth*:

> Give sorrow words; the grief that does not speak,
> Whispers the o'er-fraught heart and bids it break.

According to a standard text, J. William Worden's *Grief Counseling and Grief Therapy* (Springer, 1982), mourners must accomplish four "tasks"—collectively known as "grief work"—before they can transcend their loss and return to normal functioning. These tasks are (1) to accept the reality of the loss, (2) to experience the pain of grief, (3) to adjust to an environment in which the deceased is missing, and (4) to withdraw emotional energy and reinvest it in another relationship.

Though Worden's book derives from a pioneering investigation of spousal loss conducted in the late 1960s—a project known as the Harvard Bereavement Study—the basic ideas it sets out were recognized much earlier. In his landmark 1917 paper, "Mourning and Melancholia," for example, Sigmund Freud describes the "work of mourning" that individuals must undergo in order to restore their psychological equilibrium after a devastating loss. Freud's findings are concisely summed up by Katherine Ashenburg in her fine book, *The Mourner's Dance: What We Do When People Die* (North Point, 2002):

> The task, as Freud saw it, involves an acceptance that the beloved person is no more, and a slow, piecemeal, and above all effortful withdrawal of the mourner's attachment to that living person. This bit-by-bit labor—which entails a mental if not literal poring over keepsakes of the dead, each memory, each dashed expectation—is carried out, as Freud says, at "great expense" of time and emotional energy. While it takes place, the "existence of the lost object is continued in the mind." Although Freud could not explain why this process, which we take for granted, is "so extraordinarily painful," he did not doubt its effectiveness: "When the work of mourning is completed, the ego becomes free and uninhibited again."

That "grief work" consists of distinct stages culminating in the withdrawal of one's deepest emotional attachment to the lost loved object is a truth understood by America's greatest poet of death and mourning, Emily Dickinson. Her famous poem "After great pain, a formal feeling comes" concludes with a stanza that precisely conveys this wisdom:

> This is the Hour of Lead—
> Remembered, if outlived,
> As Freezing persons recollect the Snow—
> First—Chill—then Stupor—then the letting go—

RECOMMENDED RESOURCES

Among the hundreds of books dealing with grief and bereavement, the following are particularly useful:

Harold Bloomfield, *How to Survive the Loss of a Love* (Bantam, 1976).

Helen Fitzgerald, *The Mourning Handbook* (Fireside, 1994).

Sandra M. Gilbert, *Death's Door: Modern Dying and the Ways We Grieve* (Norton, 2006).

Earl A. Grollman, *Living When a Loved One Has Died* (Beacon Press, 1977).

John W. James, *The Grief Recovery Handbook* (Perennial, 1989).

Patricia Kelley, *Companion to Grief* (Simon & Schuster, 1997).

Bernadine Kreis, *Up from Grief* (Seabury Press, 1969).

Harold Kushner, *When Bad Things Happen to Good People* (Schocken, 1981).

Eda LeShan, *Learning to Say Good-bye* (Avon, 1988).

Elizabeth Mehren, *After the Darkest Hour the Sun Will Shine Again* (Fireside, 1997).

Elizabeth Harper Neeld, *Seven Choices: Taking the Steps to New Life After Losing Someone You Love* (Delacorte, 1992).

Therese Rando, *How to Go On Living When Someone You Love Dies* (Bantam, 1988).

Harriet Schiff, *Living Through Mourning* (Viking, 1984).

Carol Staudacher, *Beyond Grief* (New Harbinger, 1987).

Judith Viorst, *Necessary Losses* (Fawcett Gold Medal, 1986).

Alan Wolfelt, *Understanding Grief* (Accelerated Development, 1992).

Of particular note is Joan Didion's devastating memoir, *The Year of Magical Thinking* (Alfred A. Knopf, 2006), one of the most powerful portraits of bereavement ever written.

The Internet, of course, abounds with information on loss, grief, and mourning. Among the most useful websites are:

The Grief Recovery Institute (www.griefrecovery.com)

Center for Loss and Renewal (www.lossandrenewal.com)

GriefNet.org (www.griefnet.org)

Good Grief Resources (www.goodgriefresources.com).

Particularly good online articles and pamphlets include:

"Coping with Grief and Loss: A Guide to Grieving and Bereavement" (www.helpguide.org/mental/grief_loss.htm)

"Coping with Bereavement" (www.nmha.org/index.cfm?objectid=C7DF9618-1372-4D20-C807F41CB3E97654)

"Life After Loss: Dealing with Grief" (cmhc.utexas.edu/booklets/Grief/grief.html)

"Grief, Bereavement, and Mourning" (www.healthsystem.virginia.edu/internet/chaplaincy/bereavement/grief.cfm)

Grief and Mourning

Though the words are often used interchangeably, there is a crucial difference between grief and mourning. *Grief* is the profound pain we suffer when we lose someone or something precious; it is a wound to our souls. *Mourning*, on the other hand, refers to the ways we cope with grief, the process we undergo to help us deal with our bereavement.

As opposed to grief, which is a completely internal phenomenon, something we feel deep inside us, there is an external dimension to mourning. When Victorian women lost a husband, for example, they signified their grief by wearing black mourning clothes for several years. For this reason, psychologist David E. Balk defines mourning as "the social expression of grief as shaped by cultural prescription, expectations, and norms." Far more eloquently, Shakespeare nails down the distinction in these doleful words spoken by the fallen monarch Richard II:

> My grief lies all within,
> And these external manners of lament
> Are merely shadows to the unseen grief
> That swells with silence in the tortured soul.

Dr. Lindemann and the Inferno

After Sigmund Freud's pioneering 1917 paper, "Mourning and Melancholia"—the first work to explore the importance of mourning for the mental health of the bereaved—the most significant essay on the subject is "Symptomatology and Management of Acute Grief" by psychologist Erich Lindemann. This groundbreaking essay, published in the September 1944 issue of the *American Journal of Psychiatry*, grew directly out of one of the worst disasters in modern American history, the inferno that destroyed Boston's Cocoanut Grove nightclub on November 29, 1942.

A former speakeasy located at 17 Piedmont Street, the Cocoanut Grove was one of the city's swankiest nightspots. Its tropical décor, complete with artificial palm trees, gave it a romantic atmosphere straight out of that year's Hollywood hit, *Casablanca*. Though its legal capacity was limited to 460 occupants, approximately one thousand people were packed into the club on that frigid fall evening.

At around 10:15 P.M., one of the patrons—a young soldier looking for some privacy while he and his date nuzzled in the downstairs lounge—unscrewed a low-wattage bulb glowing amid the decorative palm leaves above their table. Instructed by a bartender to restore the light, a sixteen-year-old busboy climbed onto a seat and, unable to see the socket, struck a match and held it close to the fake—and, as it turned out, highly flammable—fronds. Almost immediately, the ceiling was in flames.

Waiters quickly tried—and failed—to douse the blaze by squirting it with water from seltzer bottles. Within minutes the flames had swept across the ceiling, raced up a stairwell, burst onto the dance floor, and engulfed the main dining room. Frantic patrons scrambled for the front entrance. Only a few made it through the revolving door before it jammed up with bodies and became a death trap. Others raced to the rear, only to find the back door padlocked—a precaution to keep deadbeats from sneaking out without settling their tabs. Several other doors were unlocked but impassable since they only swung inward and could not be opened against the crush of panic-stricken people struggling to escape. A plate-glass window that might have served as an emergency exit was boarded up.

Nearly two hundred firefighters sped to the scene—twenty-six engine companies, five ladder companies, and three rescue companies. The conflagration was extinguished in fifteen minutes. By then, however, nearly five hundred people had perished inside the building, making it the deadliest nightclub fire in U.S. history.

At the time of the tragedy, Lindemann was chief of psychiatry at Massachusetts General Hospital, where many of the survivors received treatment. His observation of their long-term reactions led to the publication of his now-classic essay.

In it, Lindemann describes five consistent symptoms that characterize acute grief: intense bodily distress, preoccupation with the image of the deceased, guilt, anger, and changes in patterns of conduct. A sixth feature—adopting behavioral traits of the deceased—also appeared in a large number of the bereaved. Lindemann goes on to describe a three-stage therapeutic process necessary to restore the sufferer to normal functioning: (1) emancipation from emotional bondage to the deceased; (2) readjustment to the environment in which the deceased is missing; and (3) the formation of new relationships. For this process, Lindemann coined the now standard term *grief work.*

ASK DR. DEATH

Dear Dr. Death:
When I think about dying, I don't particularly look forward to the prospect of having my gussied-up corpse laid out for all the world to see. At the same time, I've often heard that viewing a loved one's body at a funeral home is an important part of the grieving process. Is this true or false?

Worried About How I'll Look When I'm Dead

Dear Worried:
This is absolutely true. Or completely false. Depends on whom you ask. Some experts argue that an open-casket viewing serves a vital psychological function for survivors by forcing them to accept the finality of death. According to the late Erich Lindemann, professor of psychiatry at Harvard Medical School, the single "most useful" part of a funeral service occurs "when living persons confront the fact of death by looking at the body. People tend to deny painful reality. But when they experience that moment of truth that comes when they stand before the dead body, their denials collapse. They are facing reality, and that is the first important step toward managing their grief." Perhaps unsurprisingly (given the profits they reap from preparing corpses for viewing), undertakers tend to heartily endorse this opinion.

Other mental health experts, however, see things very differently, arguing that open-casket viewings have the exact opposite effect. According to these professionals, viewing a cosmetically made-up corpse makes it easier for family members to *deny* reality by creating the illusion that their loved one is sleeping or resting peacefully. Far from serving a therapeutic purpose, it can also be an actively unpleasant, if not traumatic, experience for some survivors.

As for encouraging children to view a dead body, expert opinion is equally divided. Some psychologists insist that since children are prone to frightening misconceptions about death, it is healthy for them to confront the "reality of the open coffin." Clifton D. Bryant, editor of the authoritative *Handbook of Death and Dying* (Sage, 2003), however, states unequivocally that "small children should not be present during viewing" and that "no child, regardless of age, should be forced to view a body." (If you've ever seen the 1957 movie *The Three Faces of Eve*—in which a little girl develops multiple personality disorder after being forced to kiss her dead grandma on the cheek—you'll undoubtedly agree with the latter view.)

Condolence Letters

There was a time when literate people prided themselves on their ability to compose articulate letters to friends. That, of course, was before the advent of e-mail and instant messaging. Nowadays, letter writing has joined the ranks of other increasingly obsolete skills, such as performing long division by hand and driving a standard-shift car.

Even today, however, there are occasions when no other form of communication will do. Preeminent among these is when a bereaved friend is in need of consolation. Somehow, a heartfelt "Sry 4 ur loss" transmitted via cell phone just won't cut it.

Given how hard some people find it to express themselves in writing—plus the inherent difficulty of conveying one's sympathy in a way that doesn't seem phony or trite—composing a meaningful condolence letter can seem like a daunting task. Experts in the field of grief counseling offer a number of suggestions.

Ideally, you should handwrite a condolence letter on tasteful stationery within two weeks of learning about the death. You should strive for a natural, conversational style that avoids both flowery sentiment and stilted, overly "proper" language. The letter can be as short as a few sentences, though longer letters, running as much as a few pages, are perfectly acceptable.

Since the purpose of a condolence letter is twofold—to pay final respects to the dead and offer comfort to the living—it should consist of the following components, according to grief experts Leonard Zunin and Hilary Stanton Zunin:

1. *Acknowledge the loss.* Assuming that you didn't hear the news from the person you're writing to, you should begin by explaining how you learned about the death and expressing your dismay. ("I was heartbroken when I heard from Bill last night about your father's death.")
2. *Convey your sympathy.* In sincere, straightforward language, offer your sympathy and emotional support. ("No words can adequately express my sadness, but I want you to know that my thoughts and prayers are with you at this difficult time.")
3. *Mention the special qualities of the deceased.* If you knew the deceased well, describe the traits you most admired in him or her. ("Your father was not only an exceptionally generous and warmhearted man but one of the happiest I've ever known. He never seemed to lose his capacity to enjoy the small, simple pleasures of life.")
4. *Recall a specific memory of the deceased.* If possible, relate an anecdote that evokes the special qualities of the person. ("I remember walking through the town park just a few months ago and seeing him in the playground with his granddaughter Suzie. They were together on the seesaw and, from the look on their faces, it was hard to tell who was having more fun, the seven-year-old girl or her seventy-year-old grandpa.")
5. *Remind the bereaved of his or her own personal strengths.* The death of a loved one can render a person so emotionally fragile, so profoundly insecure, that a few reassuring words, bolstering the bereaved's sense of self-worth, can be very important. ("From personal experience, I know how hard it is to lose a father. But I also know that, like your father, you are a person of great inner strength and resilience and that these qualities will help see you through this difficult time.")
6. *Offer assistance.* People in the early stages of grief can always use a little help dealing with the daily demands of life—cooking,

cleaning, errand running, and so on. If you are ready and willing to assist in specific ways, say so. Generalized offers—"If I can help out in any way, let me know"—are much less effective and tend to ring a little hollow. ("As someone who cares deeply about you and your family, I hope you'll allow me to help out in the coming weeks. I'll call in a few days to see if there's anything I can do.")

7. *End with a thoughtful phrase*. Instead of a conventional sign-off—"sincerely," "best wishes," "yours truly," "warmly," or the like—conclude with a final, heartfelt phrase. (Among the suggestions offered by the Zunins: "Our hearts are with you always," "We share in your grief and send you our love," or "You know you have my deepest sympathy and my friendship always.")

If, for whatever reason, you feel absolutely incapable of writing a condolence letter, a store-bought sympathy card will do. Even in this case, however, you should add a brief message of your own—even if it's just a line or two expressing your love and support.

RECOMMENDED READING

For a lucid, comprehensive guide that will tell you how to write condolence letters to everyone from the parents of teenage suicides to military wives whose husbands have been killed in action to children who have suffered the loss of a pet, see Leonard M. Zunin and Hilary Stanton Zunin's *The Art of Condolence: What to Write, What to Say, What to Do at a Time of Loss* (Harper-Perennial, 1991). Also recommended: Helen Fitzgerald's *The Mourning Handbook: The Most Comprehensive Resource Offering Practical and Compassionate Advice on Coping with All Aspects of Death and Dying* (Fireside, 1995). You can also find a useful tip sheet at http://dying.about.com/od/thegrievingprocess/a/condolence.htm.

The cradle rocks above an abyss, and common sense tells us that our existence is but a brief crack of light between two eternities of darkness.

—Vladimir Nabokov

Grief Dreams

Back in 1895, Sigmund Freud became convinced that he had solved one of the great mysteries of the ages: the hidden meaning of dreams. It seemed entirely possible, he wrote to a friend from his home in Vienna, that "some day on this house, one will read on a marble tablet: 'Here revealed itself, on July 24, 1895, the secret of the dream to Dr. Sigm. Freud.' "

Despite his absolute assurance that he had finally decoded this age-old riddle, Freud's theory has not aged well. Nowadays his psychoanalytical interpretation of dreams as fulfillments of repressed erotic wishes has been largely discredited. Indeed, certain scientists insist that dreams are just random neuronal events with no hidden meaning at all. Other researchers, however, continue to believe that dreams do play a significant role in the emotional and psychological life of the dreamer, even if it's not the erotic one insisted on by Freud.

One variety of dream that has drawn particular attention from researchers in recent years has been the dream about a dead loved one. In a pioneering 1992 essay, "Through a Glass Darkly: Images of the Dead in Dreams," Harvard psychology professor Deirdre Barrett analyzed seventy-seven such dreams and found that they fell into four major categories, roughly corresponding to the stages of grief as famously outlined by Elisabeth Kübler-Ross.

The first and most common is the "back-to-life dream," which tends to occur shortly after a death. Though these dreams are sometimes accompanied by intense feelings of joy at the longed-for return of the loved one, they are often intensely disturbing, like this recurrent nightmare by a young woman who had been the primary caretaker of her terminally ill grandmother until the latter's death three months earlier:

> A recurring dream I have is that my grandmother visits me in a hotel. I say, "Oh, you've come back to me," and she says, "Yes, we are going to try it again and see if I live this time." Suddenly, she collapses on the bathroom floor. I try to revive her, but I can't. I am panic-stricken and scream, "You can't die, I have to do it right this time!"

Next in frequency are what Barrett calls "advice dreams," in which the dead person returns to offer words of wisdom to the dreamer. In contrast to the previous category, these dreams generally occur long after the loved one's death and are almost always pleasant, as in this example:

> My father died nine years ago but I often dream that he returns, especially at times of stress in my life. I tell him problems I am having and sometimes he just listens and I feel better. But usually he gives me advice, sometimes very clear, sometimes garbled. In the instances where it is clear, it is always good advice but things I already know I should do. But just seeing him and hearing it from him makes me feel better.

The third category of death dream, which Barrett calls the "leave-taking" type, also tends to make bereaved people feel better, helping them to "resolve their grief in waking life." Barrett cites the example of a young woman whose grandmother died suddenly in a hospice before they had a chance to say goodbye. For months afterward, the young woman was "tormented by guilt." One night, however, she dreamed that she was awakened by the ringing of the hallway phone:

> As I picked up the phone, the dark hallway became fully illuminated. I said "hello" and my grandmother's voice said, "Hello, Sally, this is grandma." I said, "Hi, how are you?" We spoke for about ten minutes. Finally, my grandmother said she had to go. I said, "OK Gram, take care, I love you." She said, "I love you, too, goodbye." As I hung up the phone, the illuminated hallway became dark again. I walked back to bed and fell asleep. When I woke up for real the next morning, and ever since then, I have been at peace with my grandmother's death.

Telephone calls also figure prominently in the final category, which Barrett labels "state-of-death." These are dreams in which the sleeper is contacted by a dead person who reports on conditions in the afterlife. In the majority of examples collected by Barrett, the deceased gets in touch with the dreamer by phone, though other means of communication are sometimes employed, as in the case of "one young man who dreamed his dead grandmother appeared on a television talk show to be interviewed about what it was like to be dead."

While some researchers question Barrett's direct correlation between death dreams and the phases of waking grief, all agree that they serve an important psychological function, keeping alive our connections to departed loved ones and helping us to come to terms with their loss. Psychologist Patricia Garfield has written an entire book on the subject, *The Dream Messenger: How Dreams of the Departed Bring Healing Gifts* (Simon & Schuster, 1997). Based on her analysis of roughly one thousand examples, Garfield concludes that most dreams about dead loved ones contain nine standard elements: something that signals the imminent arrival of the "dream messenger" (Garfield's term for the image of the deceased); the arrival itself; details relating to the physical appearance of the dead person (who may or may not look as he or she did in life); other departed family members or friends who may appear as "attendants"; a message delivered by the deceased; a gift conferred by same; a farewell embrace; the departure of the "dream messenger"; and the feelings that the reawakened person experiences in the aftermath of the dream.

Garfield is exceptionally open-minded about the ultimate source of such dreams, refusing to dismiss the possibility that they might be "actual encounters with the spirits of the deceased." Few scientists would entertain such a supernatural explanation. Most would agree, however, that—wherever they spring from—these nocturnal visions tend to be "exceptionally vivid, emotionally packed, and may dramatically alter the life and belief system of the dreamer."

The Victorians: Fetishists of Death

The Victorians might have been inordinately squeamish about sex—covering bare piano legs with crinolines, for example, and insisting that no well-bred young lady would ever feel anything as debased as erotic desire. But they made up for their sexual prudery with an unbridled indulgence in matters relating to death—an almost orgiastic wallow in bereavement rituals.

Queen Victoria herself epitomized—and helped promote—this phenomenon. After the sudden death of her husband, Prince Albert, in December 1861, she plunged into a state of deep mourning from which she never fully emerged. Until her own death forty years later, she dressed exclusively in widow's weeds and maintained a domestic routine that bordered on the necrophilic. "Each morning," as D. Lyn Hunter writes, "servants set out Albert's clothes, brought hot water for his shaving cup, scoured his chamber pot, and changed his bed linens. The glass from which he took his last dose of medicine stayed by his bedside for nearly four decades."

Taking their cue from the beloved

monarch, Victorians on both sides of the Atlantic made a fetish of mourning, giving themselves over to elaborate, highly formalized death rituals. Middle- and upper-class funerals reached new heights of ostentation, with opulent hearses, luxurious coffins, extravagant processions, and professional pallbearers decked out in elaborate costumes. Etiquette manuals such as *The Mourner's Book*, *The Mourner's Friend*, and *The Mourner's Gift* spelled out the often dizzyingly complex dress codes for widows, who were required to remain in mourning attire for more than two years. Memorial "hairwork jewelry," fashioned from locks of the deceased, became a hot-selling item, along with other varieties of mortuary merchandise, from black-edged mourning stationery to embossed "memorial cards" handed out as souvenirs following the obsequies.

Inside the home, parlor walls were adorned with somber lithographs of grief-stricken survivors weeping over tombstones, cupboard shelves displayed little glass domes enclosing the desiccated remains of old funeral wreaths, and fireplace mantels sported framed photographic portraits of dead babies laid out in their cribs. Beautifully landscaped "garden cemeteries" became a favorite site for Sunday outings. Tear-jerking ballads such as "Little Sister Has Gone to Sleep" became sheet-music best sellers, while poetasters grew famous composing doggerel about the tragic demise of innocent victims. Even kiddies got in on the act, gobbling up picture books such as *Who Killed Cock Robin?* that featured lavishly illustrated funeral scenes.

It's for good reason that one British scholar, James Stevens Curl, calls his indispensable study of late-nineteenth-century mortuary practices *The Victorian Celebration of Death*.

RECOMMENDED READING

James Stevens Curl's book (issued in 2000 by Sutton) deals exclusively with British mortuary customs, as does Trevor May's slender but information-packed *The Victorian Undertaker* (Sire, 2000). For the American side of Victorian mourning rituals, see *A Time to Mourn: Expressions of Grief in Nineteenth-Century America* (Museums of Stony Brook, 1980), edited by Martha V. Pike and Janice Gray Armstrong, and Karen Halttunen's *Confidence Men and Painted Women: A Study of Middle-Class Culture in America, 1830–1870* (Yale University Press, 1982).

Widow's Wear

Though it would still be regarded as a breach of decorum to show up at a funeral wearing, say, a Hawaiian shirt and cargo shorts, the rules governing the proper attire for such solemn occasions have relaxed considerably over time. Indeed, even in the not-so-distant past, people here and abroad were required to follow stringent dress codes not only at funerals but during the ensuing (often quite extended) mourning period.

This was particularly true for women. The practice of wearing "widow's weeds" (from the Old English *wæd*, meaning "garment") extends back to the Middle Ages, when wealthy women—who were expected

Renaissance lady in widow's weeds.

to forsake their social and sexual lives following the death of their husbands—often retired to convents and dressed in the austere, somber manner of nuns.

In succeeding centuries, mourning garments became increasingly stylish, at least among the aristocracy. As early as the fifteenth century (according to costume historian Lou Taylor), "the temptations of fashionable dress became too much for aristocratic widows, and from that date onward, very slowly at first and then with increasing speed, widows' dresses became more and more fashionable." In Elizabethan England, some shameless aristocratic widows went so far as to deck themselves out in wheeled farthingales, long stomachers, and neck ruffs. At this point, black was not yet the exclusive color of mourning. On the contrary, the French style known as *deuil blanc*, or "white mourning," was common among European royalty.

By the Victorian era, mourning dress had turned into something of a fashion fetish on both sides of the Atlantic. To a great extent, the craze was inspired by Queen Victoria herself, who—following the sudden death of her beloved husband, Albert, in 1861—shrouded herself in crape-covered black garments and continued to wear mourning clothes for the remaining forty years of her life.

Victorian women's magazines such as *Godey's Lady's Book*, *Gentlewoman*, and *Sylvia's Home Journal* devoted endless articles to the subject of widow's wardrobes, complete with engraved illustrations of the latest in stylish mourning wear. A typical picture might show a Victorian beauty arrayed in "tasteful mourning toilette consisting of a dress in soft black silk, with dull surface, which is veiled with a tunic of transparent spotted net ornamented with a fine design in narrow braiding, while the collar is in black silk guipure lace."

At the same time manuals, with titles such as *Notes on Fashionable Mourning*, set forth the complex, if not utterly bewildering, rules of mourning etiquette. Readers were instructed, for example, that "mothers should wear black without crape for six weeks after the death of the mothers- or fathers-in-law of their married children," while "a second wife, on the death of her husband's first wife's parents, was expected to wear black silk, without crape, for six weeks."

The dress code was especially onerous for widows, who were required to be in "full mourning" for no less than two years. This protracted period of public bereavement consisted of three distinct stages: "deep mourning," a year-and-a-day-long stretch during which the widow wore dull black garments shrouded from shoulder to floor in heavy black crape, along with a long black "weeping veil" when venturing outside; "second mourning," a nine-month period when she was allowed to ease up a bit on the crape and add a few black silk trimmings to her toilette; and "third (or ordinary) mourning," when she could dispense with the crape altogether and adorn her somber apparel with a certain amount of funereal frippery—"black ribbon, embroidery or lace."

Even after enduring the two-year sartorial restrictions of full mourning, widows were required to enter into a period of "half mourning," which, as Lou Taylor explains, "lasted anywhere from six months to a lifetime. Many widows never came out of half mourning. . . . Half mourning consisted of the fashions of the day but made up in special half mourning colors. These included a range of soft mauves, variously called violet, pansy, lilac, scabious, and heliotrope."

Along with all the other hallmarks of Victorian society—from bustles and whalebone corsets to the view of women as docile "domestic angels" devoid of sexual feelings—these elaborate rituals were killed off by the enormous social upheavals of the post–World War I era. Mourning dress became increasingly rare in both the United States and Great Britain as the century progressed. By now, things have reached such a pass that, as Lou Taylor somewhat wistfully notes, "It has become difficult to identify widows."

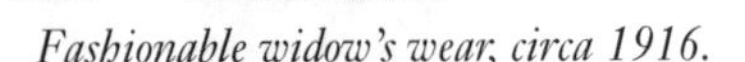

Fashionable widow's wear, circa 1916.

RECOMMENDED READING

Lou Taylor's *Mourning Dress: A Costume and Social History* (Allen & Unwin, 1983) is a comprehensive, richly illustrated survey of this subject that will be of particular interest to readers who thrill to such passages as: "The portrait shows her wearing a black dress over a white yoke, which replaces the bib-type barbe. She wears a deep ruff and cuffs in white lawn edged with reticella lace and a white lawn Paris head, without the hanging back panel. Edged with lace, it is covered on the crown of the head with a transparent white veil or 'head-rail.' Veils of this type replaced the tippeted mourning hoods by the end of the sixteenth century and were known as arched hoods."

An excellent essay by costume historian Barbara Dodd Hillerman, "Chrysalis of Gloom: Nineteenth-Century American Mourning Costume," appears in Martha V. Pike and Janice Gray Armstrong's *A Time to Mourn: Expressions of Grief in Nineteenth-Century America* (Museums of Stony Brook, 1980), published as the catalogue for the exhibition of that name.

Mourning for father or mother should last one year. During half a year should be worn Henrietta cloth or serge trimmed with crape, at first with black tulle at the wrists and neck. A deep veil is worn at the back of the bonnet, but not over the head or face like the widow's veil, which covers the entire person when down. Mourning for brother or sister may be the same; for step-father or step-mother the same; for grandparents the same; but the duration may be shorter. Mourning for children should last nine months. The first three the dress should be crape-trimmed, the mourning less deep than that for a husband. Wives wear mourning for the relatives of their husband precisely as they would their own, as would husbands for relatives of their wives.

—*Harper's Bazaar*, April 17, 1886

Death Quiz

Black might seem like the appropriate shade to wear when you're grieving the loss of a loved one, but mourning colors actually vary quite a bit around the world. Match the culture below with the color associated with mourning:

1. Egypt	A. Red
2. Abyssinia	B. Yellow
3. Iran	C. Brown
4. China	D. Blue
5. Thailand	E. White
6. South Africa	F. Purple

Answers: 1-B; 2-C; 3-D; 4-E; 5-F; 6-A

Hairwork Jewelry

The superstitious belief that possessing a lock of someone's hair gives you power over that person is ancient and widespread. In many cultures, a haircut can be a dangerous proposition. If the clippings aren't properly disposed of, a sorcerer might get hold of them and gain control of your soul. Conversely, to voluntarily bestow a lock of your hair on another person is a mark of absolute trust.

Even in our modern, scientific society, there's a sense that a person's spirit inheres in his hair—which is why, in the not-so-distant past, young women routinely kept strands of their sweetheart's hair in heart-shaped gold lockets (or, in a somewhat creepier vein, why serial killer aficionados will pay good money for some of, say, Charles Manson's barbershop trimmings).

The Victorian era witnessed a vogue for so-called hairwork jewelry—everything from bracelets and brooches to necklaces, rings, and stickpins fashioned from intricately woven hair. Some of these items were love tokens, others were made to commemorate important events, while still others were purely decorative (nothing like a nice set of human-hair earrings to complement a ball gown). Many of these pieces, however, were made for memorial purposes—to accessorize the elaborate bereavement costumes that were de rigueur for Victorian widows. Wearing them was a way for mourners to keep a piece of their loved ones close to their hearts.

Victorian memorial hair jewelry (which has become an increasingly pricey collectible) came in various shapes and styles. One of the most popular was an oval pendant or pin with

Victorian hairwork brooch.

a glazed compartment containing a lock of the loved one's hair and surrounded by the words "In Memory" inlaid in Gothic gold letters. Even more common was the rectangular brooch or medallion depicting a gravestone inscribed with a memorial motto: "Not lost, but gone before," "I weep, heaven rejoices," "Sacred to the memory," and so on. Rising beside the tombstone was a weeping willow tree whose dripping branches were composed of actual wisps of the deceased's hair.

(Nowadays, the tradition of turning little bits of dead people into memorial jewelry is being carried on by a company called LifeGem, which converts hair clippings or cremains into synthetic diamonds. See "Hair Today, Memorial Gemstone Tomorrow" in the "Cremation" section.)

If you'd like to read more about this subject (or begin a collection of your own), you won't do better than C. Jeanenne Bell's lavishly illustrated *Collector's Encyclopedia of Hairwork Jewelry* (Collectors Books, 1998). You'll also find lots of useful information at www.hairwork.com.

Hold That Pose

In the 2001 fright film *The Others*, an Englishwoman (played by Nicole Kidman) and her two young children inhabit a big spooky house that appears to be haunted by a family of ghosts. (*Spoiler alert:* It turns out that Nicole and the kids are the ghosts!) At one point in the movie, Kidman's character comes upon a dusty old album filled with photographs of dead people.

It's natural for viewers to assume that these pictures are fakes—creepily convincing images cooked up by the folks in the special-effects department. In point of fact, however, most of them are the real deal—actual specimens of what are known as postmortem portraits, morbid photographic keepsakes that were particularly popular during the death-besotted days of the Victorian era.

The practice of making artistic likenesses of corpses did not, of course, begin (or end) with the Victorians. The ancient Egyptians outfitted their royal mummies with sumptuous gilded death masks. In fifteenth-century Europe, wax death masks were routinely created for newly deceased kings. As cultural critic Alan Riding explains, "When a king died, it was considered important that his body lie in state long enough for people to travel from distant towns to pay it homage. Since the corpse could not be exposed for as long as three weeks, it was discreetly replaced by a mannequin with only molded copies of the head and hands on public view."

By the late eighteenth century, the sale of celebrity death masks had become a lucrative business. The doctor who molded a death mask from Napoleon's entire head made a bundle selling bronze and plaster reproductions. Madame Tussaud got her start making a wax death mask from Robespierre's decapitated head, hot off the guillotine. In the following century, reproduction death masks of great composers—Beethoven, Liszt, Chopin—were especially big sellers.

Death masks haven't been the only form of postmortem portraiture. In the past, wealthy families frequently commissioned paintings of their newly deceased loved ones, a practice that apparently began in seventeenth-century Holland. Artworks of this kind fall into two major categories:

commemorative portraits showing the corpse on its deathbed, and so-called posthumous mourning pictures depicting the dead subject (generally a child) as if he or she were still alive.

This latter type of memorial painting was especially popular in mid-nineteenth-century America. Typically, the grieving parents, wishing to possess a visual record of their lost little one, would call in an artist to make a life-size portrait within days of the child's passing. Though modeled on the corpse, the picture would show the child as he or she was in life: playing with a favorite toy, for example, or cuddling with the family cat.

At the same time, the artist would include a conspicuous allegorical emblem to indicate that the child was actually deceased. A bright-eyed little girl might be shown holding a rose with a broken stem, signifying that her blossoming life had been cut short. Or a somber young boy might be posed beside a lake with a receding boat in the background—a symbol of the passage of life to the distant shores of death. So popular were these paintings in the middle decades of the nineteenth century that many struggling American artists were able to keep body and soul together by specializing in the genre. As one painter wrote to a friend, "It sometimes appears as if my only patron is Death."

With the invention of the daguerreotype in 1840, photography began to replace painting as the preferred medium for mortuary portraiture. Framed photographs of corpses—especially babies and young children—became a common feature of the American household. Professional photographers advertised their ability to "take pictures of dead persons on one hour's notice" at either their studios or the residence of the deceased. The practice was so common that, as scholar Jay Ruby notes, photographic supply houses manufactured special accessories for "sepulchral daguerreotypes," such as black mats decorated with floral patterns on which a dead baby could be artfully posed. In keeping with the intensely sentimental nature of the Victorian "cult of mourning," the subjects were made to appear peacefully asleep, often in their cribs, baby carriages, or cradles.

Though postmortem photographs are generally regarded as a unique hallmark (if not a pathological symptom) of the Victorian era, the practice of taking pictures of the dead has persisted into modern times, albeit in a somewhat altered form. Throughout the twentieth century and up to the present (as Jay Ruby demonstrates), American families have continued to take snapshots of their departed family members. In contrast to the typical nineteenth-century postmortem picture, however, these images tend not to be close-ups of corpses but photos of the open coffin on display at the funeral home.

Morbid as this practice might seem, there is really nothing surprising about it. We live, after all, in an age when people feel compelled to capture every instant of their lives on camera. In a society where fathers feel free to bring camcorders into the delivery room to record their children's birth, it's natural that the opposite pole of existence would end up as a picture in the family album.

RECOMMENDED READING

A seminal essay on American memorial paintings is Phoebe Lloyd's "Posthumous Mourning Portraiture," included in Pike and Armstrong's *A Time to Mourn: Expressions of Grief in Nineteenth-Century America* (Museums of Stony Brook, 1980). Jay Ruby's *Secure the Shadow: Death and Photography in America* (MIT Press, 1995) is a fascinating, richly illustrated survey of the subject. Stunning examples of American postmortem photographs can be found in Stanley Burns's *Sleeping Beauty* (Twelve Trees Press, 1992)—the source of many of the dead-people pictures shown in the film *The Others*—and its sequel, *Sleeping Beauty II* (Burns Archive Press, 2002).

Victorian Postmortem Photography: A How-to Guide

The process of taking postmortem pictures is detailed in this excerpt from an article by a gent named Charles E. Orr that appeared in an 1877 issue of the trade journal the *Philadelpha Photographer*:

> My mode of procedure is as follows: where the corpse is at some distance and cannot be conveyed to the [studio], my first step is to secure proper conveyance, select and carefully prepare a sufficient quantity of plates, pack necessary instruments, implements, chemicals, etc., being careful not to forget any little thing necessary. Proceed at once to the cellar or basement of the house, that being more spacious, and generally affording better opportunity of shutting out the light than any other room, set up the bath, have your collodian and developer in readiness, your fixer, etc., handy, secure sufficient help to do the lifting and handling, for it is

no easy task to bend a corpse that has been dead more than twenty-four hours. Place the body on a lounge or sofa, have the friends dress the head and shoulders as near as in life as possible, then politely request them to leave the room to you and your aides.

If the room be in the northeast or northwest corner of the house, you can almost always find a window at the right and left of a corner. Roll the lounge or sofa containing the body as near into the corner as possible, raise it to a sitting position, and bolster firmly, using for a background a drab shawl or some material suitable to the circumstance. By turning the face slightly into the light, you can produce a fine shadow effect, if so desired.

Place your camera in front of the body at the foot of the lounge, get your plate ready, and then comes the most important part of the operation—opening the eyes. This you can effect handily by using the handle of a teaspoon. Put the upper lids up; they will stay. Turn the eyeball around to its proper place, and you have the face as nearly as natural as life. Proper retouching will remove the blank expression and the stare of the eyes. Such with me has proved a successful experience.

Little girl with a red necklace and curled hair. Daguerreotype, circa 1850. Courtesy of Stanley B. Burns, MD, and the Burns Archive.

We die only once, and for such a long time!

—Molière

Widow Sacrifice

Being forced to wear mourning clothes for two and a half years after the death of your husband might seem like a heavy burden to bear. But compared to the ordeals inflicted on women in other parts of the world, Victorian widows had it easy.

In many traditional societies, women have had only one function: to serve their spouses with a slavish devotion, even in death. When a husband expired, his wife, having lost her raison d'être, was expected to follow suit, so that she could continue to perform her matrimonial duties in the afterlife.

In some societies, the newly bereaved widow was ritually strangled, poisoned, or clubbed to death. In others, such as the Bena Kanioka tribe of the Congo, she might be buried alive (women who were not overly enthusiastic about this procedure had their arms and legs broken so they could not escape from the grave). Or more exotic sacrificial methods might be used. "In the Melanesian New Hebrides," writes social historian Lou Taylor, "a special conical cap made of spiders' webs was used for smothering widows—the task being performed by the widow's son."

The best-known form of this practice is the Hindu ritual known as sati, or widow burning. The term derives from one of the names applied to the goddess of marital felicity and also denotes a faithful wife or chaste woman. Its more common meaning refers to the once-widespread custom in which an Indian woman would immolate herself on her husband's funeral pyre either by lying beside his corpse before the fire was lit or by throwing herself onto the flames.

Though formally prohibited by British colonial law in 1829, sati persisted well into the twentieth century (a highly publicized case took place in September 1987, when a childless eighteen-year-old widow named Roop Kanwar committed sati in the village of Deorala). Even today—and despite the passage of the Sati Prevention Act in the wake of the so-called Deorala affair—it reportedly still occurs on rare occasions in certain remote, rural areas of India.

For a general survey of this subject, see Joerg Fisch, *Burning Women: A Global History of Widow-Sacrifice from Ancient Times to the Present* (Seagull Books, 2006). For more on the specifically Hindu version of this custom, see Sakuntala Narasimhan, *Sati: Widow Burning in India* (Viking, 1990); John Stratton Hawley, *Sati, the Blessing and the Curse: The Burning of Wives in India* (Oxford University Press, 1994); and Catherine Weinberger-Thomas, *Ashes of Immortality: Widow-Burning in India* (University of Chicago Press, 1999).

When Grief Is a Relief

In an essay published in the January 29, 2007, issue of *Newsweek*, Jennifer Elison, a professional grief counselor from Montana, makes a startling admission. Two decades earlier, in October 1985, her physician husband was killed when his subcompact car was struck by a semi as he drove home from work. When informed of his death, Elison experienced a "bewildering mix" of emotions: shock, sadness, anger. Mostly, however, what she felt was "overwhelming relief."

As Elison goes on to explain, her seemingly storybook marriage was really a sham. Dominated and demeaned by her rigid, belittling mate, she was desperately unhappy. Little wonder that she secretly exulted in the news of his death.

Elison eventually discovered that her experience was far from unique. For many people—and not just the wives of abusive spouses—the death of a close relative can be liberating. Think of the middle-aged daughter who has spent years acting as nursemaid to an invalid parent. Or the young couple faced with the prospect of sacrificing their lives to the round-the-clock care of a severely disabled child. Or the grown woman who has watched her once-adored kid brother descend into a nightmarish existence of incurable mental illness.

Of course, it's not very nice "to be glad someone is dead"—particularly when that someone is your nearest kin. In our culture, as Elison points out, Elisabeth Kübler-Ross's now-famous formulation of the five stages of grief has taken on the status of dogma. "Woe to the person who doesn't fit into the mold," Elison writes. To feel relief instead of sorrow at the news of someone's death seems so shameful, if not monstrous, that people can rarely admit to the emotion—even, sometimes, to themselves.

But as Elison argues in her 2004 book, *Liberating Losses: When Death Brings Relief* (co-written with Chris McGonigle), there's no reason for guilt. We need to accept the fact that it's perfectly natural for some people to breathe easier when a relative dies. "It may make us uncomfortable, or even anger us," Elison very sensibly asserts, "but we must realize that it's never our place to force someone to grieve in a way that we find acceptable. When someone dies, the bereaved family members must be forgiven if they are pleased to be getting their lives back, even if they can't say it out loud."

That the phenomenon Elison explores has always existed is made clear in one of the best pieces of "short-short" fiction ever written in this country, "The Story of an Hour" by Kate Chopin, author of the classic novel *The Awakening*. It's a work that remains as relevant—and challenging—today as it was when it was first published in 1894. Here it is in its entirety:

> Knowing that Mrs. Mallard was afflicted with a heart trouble, great care was taken to break to her as gently as possible the news of her husband's death.
>
> It was her sister Josephine who told her, in broken sentences; veiled hints that revealed in half concealing. Her husband's friend Richards was there, too, near her. It was he who had been in the newspaper office when intelligence of the railroad disaster was received, with Brently Mallard's name leading the list of "killed." He had only taken the time to assure himself of its truth by a second telegram, and had hastened to forestall any less careful, less tender friend in bearing the sad message.
>
> She did not hear the story as many women have heard the same, with a paralyzed inability to accept its significance. She wept at once, with sudden, wild abandonment, in her sister's arms. When the storm of grief had spent itself she went away to her room alone. She would have no one follow her.
>
> There stood, facing the open window, a comfortable, roomy armchair. Into this she sank, pressed down by a physical exhaustion that haunted her body and seemed to reach into her soul.
>
> She could see in the open square before her house the tops of trees that were all aquiver with the new spring life. The delicious breath of rain was in the air. In the street below a peddler was crying his wares. The notes of a distant song which some one was singing reached her faintly, and countless sparrows were twittering in the eaves.
>
> There were patches of blue sky showing here and there through the clouds that had met and piled one above the other in the west facing her window.
>
> She sat with her head thrown back upon the cushion of the chair, quite motionless, except when a sob came up into her throat and shook her, as a child who has cried itself to sleep continues to sob in its dreams.
>
> She was young, with a fair, calm face, whose lines bespoke repression and even a certain strength. But now there was a dull stare in her eyes, whose gaze was fixed away off yonder on one of those patches of blue sky. It was not a glance of reflection, but

rather indicated a suspension of intelligent thought.

There was something coming to her and she was waiting for it, fearfully. What was it? She did not know; it was too subtle and elusive to name. But she felt it, creeping out of the sky, reaching toward her through the sounds, the scents, the color that filled the air.

Now her bosom rose and fell tumultuously. She was beginning to recognize this thing that was approaching to possess her, and she was striving to beat it back with her will—as powerless as her two white slender hands would have been.

When she abandoned herself a little whispered word escaped her slightly parted lips. She said it over and over under her breath: "free, free, free!" The vacant stare and the look of terror that had followed it went from her eyes. They stayed keen and bright. Her pulses beat fast, and the coursing blood warmed and relaxed every inch of her body.

She did not stop to ask if it were or were not a monstrous joy that held her. A clear and exalted perception enabled her to dismiss the suggestion as trivial.

She knew that she would weep again when she saw the kind, tender hands folded in death; the face that had never looked save with love upon her, fixed and gray and dead. But she saw beyond that bitter moment a long procession of years to come that would belong to her absolutely. And she opened and spread her arms out to them in welcome.

There would be no one to live for during those coming years; she would live for herself. There would be no powerful will bending hers in that blind persistence with which men and women believe they have a right to impose a private will upon a fellow-creature. A kind intention or a cruel intention made the act seem no less a crime as she looked upon it in that brief moment of illumination.

And yet she had loved him—sometimes. Often she had not. What did it matter! What could love, the unsolved mystery, count for in face of this possession of self-assertion which she suddenly recognized as the strongest impulse of her being!

"Free! Body and soul free!" she kept whispering.

Josephine was kneeling before the closed door with her lips to the keyhole, imploring for admission. "Louise, open the door! I beg, open the door—you will make yourself ill. What are you doing Louise? For heaven's sake open the door."

"Go away. I am not making myself ill." No; she was drinking in a very elixir of life through that open window.

Her fancy was running riot along those days ahead of her. Spring days, and summer days, and all sorts of days that would be her own. She breathed a quick prayer that life might be long. It was only yesterday she had thought with a shudder that life might be long.

She arose at length and opened the door to her sister's importunities. There was a feverish triumph in her eyes, and she carried herself unwittingly like a goddess of Victory. She clasped her sister's waist, and together they descended the stairs. Richards stood waiting for them at the bottom.

Some one was opening the front door with a latchkey. It was Brently Mallard who entered, a little travel-stained, composedly carrying his grip-sack and umbrella. He had been far from the scene of accident, and did not even know there had been one. He stood amazed at Josephine's piercing cry; at

Richards' quick motion to screen him from the view of his wife.

But Richards was too late.

When the doctors came they said she had died of heart disease—of joy that kills.

So death, the most terrifying of ills, is nothing to us, since so long as we exist, death is not with us, but when death comes, then we do not exist.

—EPICURUS

Isn't It Ironic? (Part III)

In the year 1060, Béla of Hungary, after a drawn-out power struggle with his brother, Andràs, finally claimed his country's throne. Two years later, while seated on that selfsame throne, he was killed when its canopy collapsed, crushing him to death.

Grief Goodies

Thanks to Darcie and Tony Sims, founders of the catchily named organization Grief Inc., bereaved consumers can now conveniently shop for all their grief-related merchandise right from the comfort of their own homes. As part of their enterprise, the Simses have established the Grief Store, an online emporium that advertises itself with this lavishly quotation-marked come-on:

> Now you can "shop" at the Grief Store and be assured that the books, tapes, cards, and memorial products you find are the "best of the best" in the death care industry!

Among the many hard-to-find items available at the Grief Store are videos with titles such as *Footprints on Our Hearts*, *Tear Soup*, and *What Color Is Dead?*; memorial items such as tear-shaped silver pendants and "Merry Christmas from Heaven" tree ornaments; and a wide selection of bereavement books, including Darcie's own delightful *Why Are the Casseroles Always Tuna? A Loving Look at the Lighter Side of Grief*. For more information go to www.griefstore.com or call 888-564-6018.

Where Do the Gone Things Go? Children and Death

Considering all the media violence they're bombarded with on a daily basis, it may seem strange to assert that today's children have very little exposure to death. But compared to the way things used to be—when kids watched their loved ones die at home, saw the corpses laid out in the parlor, witnessed (and even participated in) the butchering of farm animals—American life, rife though it may be with make-believe

ASK DR. DEATH

Dear Dr. Death:
I understand that during the seven-day Jewish mourning period known as shiva, *all mirrors in the home of the bereaved must be covered. Can you explain the meaning of this custom?*
Curious About Jewish Death Rituals

Dear Curious:
The usual explanation is that at a time when all thoughts should be on the departed, there is no place for personal vanity. Most anthropologists, however, regard this as a modern rationalization for a practice rooted in primitive superstition.

It is a well-documented fact that fear of the dead is a primal human emotion. This fear, according to experts, springs from the archaic belief that at the moment of death, even the most dearly beloved relative instantly turns into a vengeful demon that seeks to wreak harm on the living. As a result of this belief, humans have always taken extraordinary measures to protect themselves from the malign spirits of the newly departed. Some aboriginal tribes, for example—convinced that souls cannot cross a sheet of water—bury their dead on islands or on the far side of a river. Others make sure to throw open all the doors and windows at the moment of death so that the spirit will make a prompt exit. Still others place heavy slabs of wood on dead bodies before interring them to keep the spirits weighted down.

The Jewish custom of covering up mirrors during the period of mourning stems (so anthropologists believe) from a similar impulse. It is a common superstitious belief throughout the world that mirrors have the power to steal or house human souls. (It is because he has no soul, for example, that Dracula has no reflection when he looks in a mirror. Similarly, breaking a mirror is dangerous because you might damage your soul.) For this reason, covering up all the mirrors when a loved one dies is a way to prevent his or her now-malevolent spirit from taking up permanent residence in the household.

This custom, incidentally, is not the only one still practiced in the modern world that derives from the primitive fear of the dead. Indeed, as Katherine Ashenburg explains in her fascinating book, *The Mourner's Dance: What We Do When People Die* (North Point Press, 2002), "Most of our traditions and rituals are born out of fear and self protectiveness. The dark clothes we wear to funerals hide the living from the malevolent spirit. Crying and speaking well of the dead persuade him that he is regretted. Holding a wake reassures him that he is not forgotten, perhaps even deludes him into thinking he is still living. The tombstone is an attempt to keep the spirit underground, where he can do less harm. So, symbolically, are the small stones Jews leave on tombstones when they visit a cemetery."

mayhem, actively shields children from the harsh realities of death. Seeing a horde of computerized zombies blown away onscreen hardly promotes a realistic understanding of mortality—particularly when the creatures are likely to rise again a few seconds later.

With death so shrouded in taboo in our youth-obsessed, longevity-crazed society, it falls to parents to shed light on the subject. Unfortunately, because of their own deep-seated discomfort, most grown-ups have a harder time talking about the facts of death than about the facts of life. The parent who would never dream of telling his or her kids that they were brought by the stork or found under a cabbage leaf resorts to all kinds of euphemisms and evasions when discussing death. But—as with misinformation about sexual matters—such tactics do more harm than good, exacerbating the child's anxieties and potentially affecting him for life.

When broaching this delicate topic, it helps to know something about the way a child's ideas about death typically evolve. The pioneering study of this subject was conducted in 1948 by Hungarian psychologist Maria Nagy. According to her findings, children pass through three developmental stages in their conception of death. Between the ages of three and five, they tend to see death as a kind of diminished form of life, a state akin to sleep from which the person will eventually awaken. During stage two, which occurs between the ages of five and nine, they understand that death is permanent but tend to believe it happens mostly to others, particularly the elderly. They generally personify death as some sort of monster—a ghost, skeleton, bogeyman, and so on—and believe that it can be evaded through luck and skill. It is not until they reach the third stage, around age nine, that they begin to understand that death is universal.

Mourning teddy from Plush Sentiments/Comfort Gifts.
Courtesy of Beth Sanderson.

Of course, not every child conforms to this model. There are ten-year-olds who still believe that only old people die, while some preschoolers have a precocious understanding of the finality of death. As every parent knows, children mature both physically and emotionally at dramatically different rates. Still, Nagy's findings have largely been confirmed by subsequent studies.

Based on her work, psychologists now offer a standard set of guidelines when advising parents on the best way to talk about death with their young ones. While experts agree that the subject should be dealt with in an honest and straightforward way, they stress that the information must be suitable for the child's age. Clearly, telling your little one about the process of bodily decay that Grandpa's corpse will undergo in the coffin is just as inappropriate as describing the mechanics of sexual intercourse to a preschooler who asks where babies come from.

For parents looking for help, one of the best and most widely admired resources is Earl Grollman's *Talking About Death: A Dialogue Between Parent and Child* (Beacon Press,

1976). This slender volume begins with a twenty-five-page read-along picture book, beautifully tailored to the emotional needs and mental capacities of young children. This is followed by a straightforward and eminently sensible guide addressed to parents.

Grollman recommends that children be told right away about a death in the family since delay only increases the risk that the news will be conveyed "by the wrong person in the wrong way." Though the impulse to soften the blow is understandable, parents should avoid euphemisms like "We lost Grandpa today," "Grandpa was such a good person that God wanted him," or "Grandpa went away on a long trip and will be gone for a very long time." Such explanations are bound to produce confusion and anxiety on the part of the child, who may blame his parents for not going out to look for Grandpa, or feel heartbroken that Grandpa left without saying goodbye, or decide that it makes more sense to behave badly if being good means getting snatched away by God. By the same token, saying that Grandpa is no longer around because he went to sleep or got sick and was taken to the hospital can produce a pathological dread of bedtime in a child or cause him to develop a terror of ever falling ill.

In a gentle and loving but unambiguous way, the parent should let the child know that death is real and irrevocable—that, as Grollman writes, "Dead is dead. Grandfather is gone. He will never come back." Comparisons to nature can be helpful: "You put seeds in the ground. They bud. Beautiful flowers appear. After a time, the flowers fade. They fall off. They die."

Children should be permitted, even encouraged, to express their sorrow openly. Particularly in a culture like ours, which has traditionally frowned on excessive displays of emotion in males, little boys must be told that it's okay to cry. Small children are also apt to feel guilty when a loved one dies—to experience the loss as a punishment for their own misbehavior. Parents must therefore reassure them that they are in no way to blame. ("Grandfather did not die because you may have been bad. You did nothing to make him die.")

One of the trickiest issues for parents to deal with is the inevitable question "Where is he now?" Here, too, it's important to avoid fanciful explanations. In a famous poem, "First Death in Nova Scotia," Elizabeth Bishop poignantly evokes her own childhood confusion when her well-meaning but misguided parents told her that her little cousin Arthur, who had recently died, was going off to live with the royal family. Though intended to make the child feel better, this explanation only left her more deeply troubled. "But how could Arthur go," she wonders, "clutching his tiny lily, / with his eyes shut up so tight / and the roads deep in snow?"

Grollman (himself a rabbi) acknowledges that some parents might wish to offer a religious view involving the hereafter. But he also strongly recommends that children be supplied with a factual answer about the final disposal of the body: for example, "When life stopped and grandfather died, his body was placed in a casket and placed in the earth in a cemetery. A stone or plaque will identify the place of burial. The cemetery will be kept beautiful with flowers and shrubs." (Or, alternatively, "His body was burned in a place called a crematory. The ashes were placed in a small box which was placed in the wall of a building called a columbarium.")

Finally, parents should stress that although the loved one is gone forever, he will continue to live on in the child's memories of him. ("Of course we shall have grandfather in other ways. We can never forget that he died. But we will always remember that he lived.")

Never tell your children what they will need to unlearn later. Avoid fairy tales and half-truths. Imaginative fancy only gets in the way when they are already having enough trouble separating the real from the make-believe. Youngsters need direct, simple, and honest information about death as about everything else. They need continuing reassurance and understanding.

—Earl A. Grollman

RECOMMENDED READING

Grollman's book is the best available choice for parents looking for a sensitive, highly accessible text they can share with their children. But there are plenty of other works on the subject. Hannelore Wass and Charles A. Corr's *Helping Children Cope with Death: Guidelines and Resources* (Hemisphere, 1982) contains two extensive, annotated bibliographies. The first consists of forty-four books for adults that are "related to helping children cope with death." The second lists 160 children's books in which death is treated in a sensitive and meaningful way, ranging from classics such as Marjorie Kinnan Rawlings's *The Yearling* and E. B. White's *Charlotte's Web* to more recent works such as Joan Fassler's *My Grandpa Died Today* and Phyllis Rash Hughes's *Dying Is Different*.

For those interested in a more technical treatment of the subject, Richard Lonetto's *Children's Conceptions of Death* (Springer, 1980) contains much useful information.

"In Childhood"

As Maria Nagy was the first to demonstrate, very young children tend to see death not as a permanent condition but as a transformed state of being. This fanciful conception is beautifully rendered in this moving poem by Kimiko Hahn from her book *The Artist's Daughter* (Norton, 2002).

In Childhood

things don't die or remain damaged
but return: stumps grow back hands,
a head reconnects to a neck,
a whole corpse rises blushing and newly
  elastic.
Later this vision is not True:
the grandmother remains dead
not hibernating in a wolf's belly.
Or the blue parakeet does not return
from the little grave in the fern garden
though one may wake in the morning

thinking mother's call is the bird.
Or maybe the bird is with grandmother
inside light. Or grandmother was the bird
and is now the dog
gnawing on the chair leg.
Where do the gone things go
when the child is old enough
to walk herself to school,
her playmates already
pumping so high the swing hiccups?

Kids and Pet Loss

Losing a beloved dog or cat is painful for anyone, but it can be particularly hard on children since it's likely to be the first time in their young lives that they are faced with the harsh reality of death. In his invaluable book *The Loss of a Pet: A Guide to Coping with the Grieving Process When a Pet Dies* (Wiley, 1998), Wallace Sife advises parents to avoid the following common "explanations" for a pet's demise:

1. *Your pet was loved so much that God took it back to heaven.* According to Sife, "The child may wonder if God will take him or other dear family members back, as well."
2. *The animal doctor made a mistake and the pet died.* "A child may think that this may happen with people and their doctors, too," says Sife.
3. *The pet ran away from home.* Unless this is true, it should—like all prevarications—be avoided. "Such an attempt at deception," writes Sife, "may easily lead to distortions in the child's mind, causing feelings that he or she is undeserving or guilty and cannot be trusted with the truth."
4. *The pet got sick and died.* "The misperceived notion that dying is the result of getting sick may be very upsetting. Children and loved ones also get sick."
5. *The pet went to sleep forever.* A statement such as this can create terrifying associations in a child's mind between dying and sleeping. You might find yourself with a kid too frightened to close his or her eyes at night.

As for positive recommendations, Sife offers the following:

1. Ask the child how he feels about the pet's death. Reassure him that his feelings are natural.
2. Hold a ceremony for the pet.
3. Keep your pet alive in the family memory. Reminisce fondly with the child about the pet.
4. Inform the child's teacher about the pet's death.
5. Discuss the possibility of getting another pet in the future—not as a replacement

Pet-loss condolence card. Courtesy of Dr. Walter Sife and the Association for Pet Loss and Bereavement.

but as a new and different companion for the child.

6. Have the child read a book on the subject. A very good one for young children is Fred Rogers's *When a Pet Dies* (Putnam, 1988), a slender illustrated volume whose plainspoken text perfectly captures the comforting tone of the late Mr. Rogers.

For more information, Sife's book—available online at Amazon.com or directly from the Association for Pet Loss and Bereavement (www.aplb.org/resources/books.html)—is highly recommended.

Death Comes to Mr. Rogers's Neighborhood

The loss of a beloved pet is hard for everyone in a household. But it can be especially devastating for small children who have never experienced death and bereavement before. To help your little ones cope with the trauma, you might want to give them a copy of Fred Rogers's *When a Pet Dies* (Putnam, 1998), part of his excellent "First Experience" series.

Illustrated with color photos and written in the author's inimitably gentle but straightforward style, this slender volume is perfectly calibrated to the emotional needs and comprehension level of its target audience. Capturing the lulling cadence of Mr. Rogers's voice, it offers wisdom and reassurance without evading the painful realities of the situation. ("One thing we know about dying is that it isn't like going to sleep" reads the text on a typical page. "When a pet dies, it can't wake up again. A pet that dies stops breathing and moving. It doesn't see or hear anymore. And it doesn't need to eat anymore.") It's the perfect introduction to a topic that—in our death-phobic society—most parents have trouble handling on their own.

APLB

The Web's finest resource for grieving pet owners can be found at www.aplb.org, the official site of the Association for Pet Loss and Bereavement. Founded by Brooklyn psychologist Walter Sife after the death of his beloved miniature dachshund, the APLB is a nonprofit organization that serves as an online clearinghouse for all subjects related to pet bereavement.

People coping with the loss of a pet will find a wealth of tools to assist them: a comprehensive state-by-state list of pet cemeteries and crematories; a directory of pet bereavement counselors; a complete bibliography of relevant books (including Sife's own award-winning *The Loss of a Pet*, now in its third edition); advice on helping children deal with the death of a pet; and much more (including virtual condolence cards that can be e-mailed to the newly bereaved). There are also hotlines, chat rooms, and a quarterly newsletter featuring memorial tributes, poems, profiles, book reviews, and articles such as "Guilt in Pet Loss," "Pet Loss in the Gay/Lesbian Community," and "Ways to Commemorate the Memory of Your Pet."

The Undiscovered Country: Where Do We Go from Here?

What's it like to be dead? That, of course, is the ultimate mystery—the question that keeps Hamlet from making his quietus with a bare bodkin (or, as we say in English, committing suicide). As the melancholy Dane so poetically puts it:

> To die, to sleep—
> To sleep—perchance to dream: ay, there's the rub,
> For in that sleep of death what dreams may come
> When we have shuffled off this mortal coil,
> Must give us pause.

Of course, even as Hamlet expresses his terrible uncertainty about death, it's clear that he thinks of it as a place: "an undiscovered country, from whose bourn / No traveler returns." What gives him pause is not knowing exactly what he's likely to find there.

Hamlet's view of death as an unexplored realm that might hold some intensely unpleasant surprises is just one of many ways that humans have visualized the postlife experience. To the ancient Sumerians, for example, the hereafter held no surprises. They knew exactly what it was like—a cheerless shadowland where the disembodied dead pass an endless succession of gray, dreary days—a place, as it is described in the epic of Gilgamesh, "where people sit in darkness; dust is their food and clay is their meat."

The early Hebrews took a similarly bleak view of the afterlife. In their conception, everyone who died—righteous and wicked, slave and king—ended up in a pit called Sheol, a grim underground realm analogous to the Greek netherworld, Hades. In later centuries, a different notion, stressing posthumous reward and punishment, evolved. Sheol (or, alternatively, an infernal realm called Gehenna) was reserved as a place of suffering for the wicked, while the righteous could expect to

Isn't It Ironic? (Part IV)

On Friday, June 24, 2005, Paul Winchell died at the age of eighty-two. A legendary ventriloquist and beloved star of the boomer-era kiddie show *Winchell Mahoney Time,* he was also renowned as the voice of Tigger in Disney's animated Winnie-the-Pooh movies.

Just one day later, on Saturday, June 25, the well-known character actor John Fiedler died at the age of eighty. In his long career, Fiedler appeared in many celebrated films, from *12 Angry Men* to *The Odd Couple*. He also provided voices for animated characters. His most famous vocal role? Piglet in Disney's Winnie-the-Pooh cartoons.

enjoy bodily resurrection on the Day of Judgment.

Christianity elaborated on this latter conception in its vision of heaven and hell. Sinners were consigned to eternal damnation in a place commonly visualized as a sea of fire. Trapped in this "ocean of burning liquid brimstone," the souls of the damned were subjected to unending torture, described in vivid detail by revivalist preacher Charles G. Finney:

> Look! Look! . . . see the millions of wretches, biting and gnawing their tongues, as they lift their scalding heads from the burning lake! See! see! how they are tossed, and how they howl. . . . Hear them groan, amidst the fiery billows, as they Lash! and Lash! and Lash! their burning shores.

Hell, as imagined in a 1496 woodcut.

Traditional depictions of hell are pretty consistent in their emphasis on hideous, never-ending torments inflicted by jeering devils in a flaming, pandemoniac environment. Heaven, on the other hand, has been visualized in various ways: a transcendent paradise of lush forests, unfading flowers, and pristine, noncombustible lakes; a celestial realm inhabited by harp-playing angels who spend their days singing the praises of the Lord; or more or less anything that represents your own personal idea of eternal bliss. One common element found in most views of heaven that makes the concept so irresistibly appealing is the promise of being reunited forever with beloved friends and family members.

Floating blissfully on a cloud, bathing miserably in brimstone, or drifting wraithlike in a shadowy twilight zone aren't the only options for postmortem existence. Some societies have pictured the afterworld as a place pretty much like the here and now, only better. Viking warriors who died a glorious death, for example, went straight to Valhalla, where they got to spend their evenings indulging in orgiastic banquets of boar's meat and liquor after long, bracing afternoons of savage, blood-drenched warfare. Similarly, as one scholar notes, "Many traditional Plains Indian societies imagined the deceased as existing on a rolling prairie, successfully hunting buffalo, living in teepees, feasting and dancing."

This type of hereafter—in which the departed moves on to an existence not so very different from the one he enjoyed while alive—is labeled "life as usual" by thanatologist Robert Kastenbaum, who identifies the main varieties of afterlife belief in his book *Death, Society, and Human Experience* (C. V. Mosby, 1977). Another of Kastenbaum's categories is "cycling and recycling," by which he means the perception of death "as a temporary condition that alternates with life or that represents a transition stage between one form of life and another." An example is the Hindu belief in reincarnation, the notion that the soul passes through a succession of lives until it achieves enlightenment.

Other categories of afterlife belief include "cosmic melding" (the idea that "each person is like a drop of water that returns to the ocean to become a continuing but transformed part of the universal flow") and what Kastenbaum calls "symbolic immortality," the notion that a human being can conquer death by creating something that lives on in society: a great work of art, for example, or a self-named college endowment. This form of posthumous survival, however, seems disappointing at best, at least if you share the philosophy of Woody Allen, who has famously remarked: "I don't want to achieve immortality through my work. I want to achieve it through not dying."

Indeed, the only postlife scenario less appealing than symbolic immortality is eternal extinction—the disheartening possibility that we cease to exist forever at death. Despite the supposedly secular outlook of modern Western society, however, the vast majority of Americans continue to believe in an afterlife. According to a recent survey by AARP, nearly three-quarters of the over-fifty population are convinced that there is life beyond the grave. Of that hefty cohort, nearly 90 percent expect to end up in heaven. Opinions differ, however, as to exactly what paradise consists of. One respondent ventured that it is a place where "everybody gets along. It's always a beautifully clear day, and sunny, with great landscaping." Others seem to visualize it as a kind of all-expenses-paid resort, where you get to spend eternity surrounded by family and friends, enjoying all kinds of fun-filled activities, including (this being the boomer generation) great sex.

In his richly illuminating study, *Life After Death: A History of the Afterlife in Western Religion* (Doubleday, 2004), Alan F. Segal lists the following points that define the typical American view of the hereafter:

- The afterlife will be a better life.
- There will be no more problems or troubles.
- There will be no more sickness or pain.
- It will be peaceful.
- The afterlife will be happy and joyful, no sorrow.
- There will be love between people.
- God's love will be the center of life after death.
- Crippled people will be made whole.
- People in heaven will grow spiritually.
- They will see friends, relatives, or spouses.
- They will live forever.
- There will be humor.
- People in heaven will grow intellectually.
- Those in heaven will be recognizable as the same people that they were on earth.
- There will be angels in heaven.

Though a religious outlook would seem to be necessary for a faith in the afterlife—how, after all, can there be such a thing as heaven without phenomena such as the soul and God?—even nonbelievers cling to the hope of immortality. In a *New York Times Magazine* piece, "Eternity for Atheists," writer

Jim Holt surveys a number of current theories of the afterlife, all "based on hard science with a dash of speculation." Relativity specialist Frank J. Tipler of Tulane University, for example, proposes "future beings might, in their drive for total knowledge, 'resurrect' us in the form of computer simulations." In the view of John Leslie, one of the world's leading philosophers of cosmology, "each of us is immortal because our life patterns are but an aspect of an 'existentially unified' cosmos that will persist after our death." For both Tipler and Leslie, "the mind or 'soul,' as they see it, consists of information, not matter. And one of the deepest principles of quantum theory, called 'unitarity,' forbids the disappearance of information."

The notion that we might end up as resurrected computer simulations or traces of information in an "existentially unified cosmos" is clearly good news for quantum physicists and relativity theorists. For the rest of us, however, the Club Med in the sky preferred by graying boomers seems distinctly more appealing.

RECOMMENDED READING

So many books have been written about afterlife beliefs that a bibliography on the subject would constitute a volume of its own. Besides Segal's indispensable study, outstanding works include S.G.F. Brandon, *The Judgment of the Dead: The Idea of Life After Death in the Major Religions* (Scribner, 1967); J. Bremer, *The Rise and Fall of the Afterlife* (Routledge, 2002); Stephen T. Davis, *Death and Afterlife* (St. Martin's, 1989); and Colleen McDannell and Bernhard Lang, *Heaven: A History* (Yale University Press, 1988). Jenny Randles and Peter Hough's *The Afterlife: An Investigation into the Mysteries of Life after Death* (BCA, 1993) is an illustrated pop examination of the subject, covering a wide range of topics, from spiritualism to poltergeist phenomena to past-life regression.

For an entertaining, firsthand account of one person's quest for evidence of an afterlife, don't miss Mary Roach's *Spook: Science Tackles the Afterlife* (W. W. Norton, 2005), a worthy follow-up to *Stiff*, her improbably delightful book about dead bodies and the many bizarre uses to which they have been put.

What happens when we die? Does the light just go out and that's that—the million-year nap? Or will some part of my personality, my me-ness persist? What will that feel like? What will I do all day? Is there a place to plug in my laptop?

—Mary Roach

"The Indian Burying Ground"

Modern scientists like Timothy Taylor operate under the assumption that the positions in which corpses are buried reveal a great deal about a society's attitude toward death. But there is nothing new about this insight. In this poem by the early American author Philip Freneau, first published in 1787, the speaker evokes the Native American view of the afterlife by contrasting Indian and European burial practices.

ENTERING HEAVEN.

In spite of all the learned have said,
I still my old opinion keep;
The posture that we give the dead,
Points out the soul's eternal sleep.

Not so the ancients of these lands—
The Indian, when from life released,
Again is seated with his friends,
And shares again the joyous feast.

His imaged birds, and painted bowl,
And venison, for a journey dressed,
Bespeak the nature of the soul,
Activity, that knows no rest.

His bow, for action ready bent,
And arrows, with a head of stone,
Can only mean that life is spent,
And not the old ideas gone.

Thou, stranger, that shalt come this way,
No fraud upon the dead commit,
Observe the swelling turf, and say,
They do not lie, but here they sit.

Here, still a lofty rock remains,
On which the curious eye may trace
(Now wasted half by wearing rains)
The fancies of a ruder race.

Here, still an aged elm aspires,
Beneath whose far-projecting shade
(And which the shepherd still admires)
The children of the forest played.

There oft a restless Indian queen,
(Pale Shebah, with her braided hair)
And many a barbarous form is seen
To chide the man that lingers there.

By midnight moons, o'er moistening dews,
In habit for the chase arrayed,
The hunter still the deer pursues,
The hunter and the deer—a shade!

And long shall timorous fancy see
The painted chief, and pointed spear,
And Reason's self shall bow the knee
To shadows and delusions here.

Heaven as Home

The Victorian tendency to sugarcoat death—to disguise its bitter realities beneath a cloying glaze of sentimentality—is epitomized by a popular volume, *Golden Thoughts on Mother, Home, and Heaven*. Compiled by the Reverend Theodore L. Culyer and published in New York City in 1882, this handsomely bound collection contains hundreds of poems and prose pieces celebrating the joys of its three titular subjects: motherhood, domestic bliss, and the afterlife.

For a sense of its intensely saccharine flavor, here is a typical selection, a bit of verse by a poetaster named Fanny J. Crosby with the simple title "Heaven":

Oh! Where shall human grief be stilled
  And joy for pain be given,
Where dwells the sunshine of a love
In which the soul may always rove?
  A sweet voice answered—Heaven.

O heart, I said, when death shall come
  And all the cords be riven,
What lies beyond the swelling tide?
That same sweet voice to mine replied
  In loving accents—Heaven.

Where, where shall friendship never die,
  Nor parting hand be given?
My heart was filled with strange delight,
For in that silent hush of night,
  I heard the answer—Heaven.

O, voyager, on life's fitful sea;
  By stormy billows driven;
Say, what can soothe thy aching breast,
Or give thee comfort, joy, and rest,
  Like Mother, Home, and Heaven!

The Corpse Brides

When you vacation at a deluxe resort hotel, all your needs are taken of. There's the minibar, the fruit basket, the nifty little toiletry items. You'd think the same situation would exist in heaven—that the management would supply every amenity to make your stay a happy one. Certain people, however—the ancient Chinese, the Vikings, and various aboriginal tribes, among others—have had a kind of BYO conception of the afterlife, burying their dead with assorted goodies to enjoy on the other side: food, drink, even human companionship.

The same custom continues to this day in certain parts of the world, including rural China, where—as *New York Times* reporter Jim Yardley explains—"families burn offerings of fake money or paper models of luxury cars in case an ancestor might need pocket change or a stylish ride in the netherworld." But the practice doesn't stop there. Villagers who have lost a young unmarried son will go to even greater lengths to ensure their child's contentment in the hereafter. Not infrequently, reports Yardley, they will "search for a dead woman to be his bride and, once a corpse is obtained, bury the pair together as a married couple."

The tradition—known as *minghun* or "afterlife marriage"—extends back many centuries and is rooted in Chinese ancestor worship, "which holds that people continue to exist after death and that the living are obligated to tend to their wants." People in the market for a marriageable female corpse search around for a family that has recently lost a daughter. Though commercial trafficking in cadavers is illegal in China, money always changes hands in these private transactions. The going rate for a corpse bride is the equivalent of $1,200—about four times the yearly income of an average farmer. In a poor region where young people frequently leave home in search of a better life, the steep price reflects the scarcity of the commodity in question. One family was able to sell their drowned teenage daughter as soon as her body washed up.

If parents *do* manage to find a nice dead young woman for their departed son, they hold a ceremony that varies in quality according to the family's wealth. "Poor people just bring the bodies over and put them in the earth," one local woman explains. "People with money will have a reception."

It is impossible that anything so natural, so necessary, and so universal as death should ever have been designed by Providence as an evil to mankind.

—Jonathan Swift

The Light at the End of the Tunnel

For people desperately seeking proof of an afterlife, new hope appeared in 1975 when Raymond Moody—a highly respected figure who held both a Ph.D. in philosophy and a medical degree—published his international best seller, *Life After Life*. Based on eleven years of research, Moody's groundbreaking book offered compelling evidence of a remarkable (and quite heartening) possibility: that our conscious minds might actually survive our bodily deaths.

Having studied the cases of 150 people who had been brought back from the brink of extinction—including many who had been pronounced clinically dead before being resuscitated—Moody found a remarkable consistency in the way they described their experiences. Nearly all reported that they had first been infused with an overwhelming sense of well-being. This was followed by the distinct sensation of floating above their bodies and observing themselves from a height. Next, they found themselves hurtling through a dark tunnel toward an indescribably brilliant light, where they were welcomed by their long-deceased relatives and encountered a glorious being that radiated absolute acceptance and love. After viewing a panoramic replay of their lives, they returned—often reluctantly—to their bodies (often reentering through the top of the head). Taken together, these and other elements constitute the phenomenon that Moody dubbed "near-death experience," or NDE.

Inspired by Moody's book, other researchers began to study the NDE phenomenon, including psychologist Kenneth Ring and cardiologist Michael Sabom, whose own investigations largely confirmed Moody's conclusions, leaving little doubt that the phenomenon is both authentic and widespread.

For the religiously inclined, these findings serve as a triumphant vindication of their beliefs since the common features of the near-death experience conform so closely to traditional conceptions of the newly departed soul's voyage to heaven. Most scientists, however—while accepting that NDEs really happen to a significant percentage of dying people—offer less spiritually comforting explanations, attributing the experience to purely physiological causes, such as a lack of oxygen to the brain. According to a 2007 *Time* magazine article on the latest research in the field, "The brain-based theory of NDEs goes something like this":

> Survival is our most powerful instinct. When the heart stops and oxygen is cut, the brain goes into all-out defense. Torrents of neurotransmitters are randomly generated, releasing countless fragmentary images and feelings from the memory-storing temporal lobes. Perhaps the life review is the brain frantically scanning its memory banks for a way out of this crisis. The images of a bright light and tunnel could be due to impairment at the rear and sides of the brain respectively, while the euphoria may be a neurochemical anti-panic mechanism triggered by extreme danger. As for perhaps the strangest element of NDEs, the out-of-body experience, studies led by Swiss neuroscientist Olaf Blanke have shed light on what might be going on there. In 2002, Blanke and others reported how they were able to induce OBEs in an epilepsy patient by stimulating the brain's temporoparietal junction (TPJ), thought to play a role in self-perception. . . . It's probable that stress in the TPJ causes the dissociation of NDEs—a dissociation that's entirely illusory.

Though neuroscientists differ as to the precise cause of the phenomenon, they generally agree that, as the *Time* piece puts it, "NDEs occur in the theater of one's mind, and that in the absence of resuscitation, it's the brain's final sound and light show, followed by oblivion." Still, those looking forward to a life after death will find nothing in even the most up-to-date studies to definitively disprove their belief.

Are NDEs a genuine glimpse of the afterlife or a mere trick of the expiring mind? In the immortal words of Mark Twain: "You pays your money and you takes your choice."

RECOMMENDED RESOURCES

Besides Moody's seminal book, classic works on the subject include Kenneth Ring's *Life at Death: An Investigation of the Near-Death Experience* (Coward, McCann & Geohegan, 1980) and Michael Sabom's *Recollections of Death: A Medical Investigation* (Harper and Row, 1982). Mary Roach devotes a chapter of her book *Spook: Science Tackles the Afterlife* (Norton, 2005) to current NDE research. The *Time* magazine article cited previously, written by Daniel Williams, appeared in the August 31, 2007, issue of the magazine. For the latest developments in the field, check out the extensive website maintained by the International Association for Near-Death Studies at www.iands.org.

The Near-Death Scenario

Extrapolating from the accounts of 150 people who had undergone extremely close calls with death, Raymond Moody put together a list of traits that constitute the prototypical near-death experience. Here, in the most common order of their occurrence, are the outstanding ones:

1. *Hearing the news.* At the moment of crisis, the dying person hears himself pronounced dead by his physician.
2. *Feelings of peace and quiet.* Despite his physical distress, he is suffused with an overwhelming sense of calm and relaxation.
3. *The noise.* A peculiar sound—either extremely annoying (buzzing, banging, roaring) or intensely pleasant (orchestral music, wind chimes, etc.)—fills the dying person's ears.
4. *Out of the body.* Detached from his physical self, the dying person floats above his own body, gazing down on it from a height.
5. *The dark tunnel.* The person has the sensation of being drawn, sucked, or hurled through a long tunnel-shaped space.
6. *Meeting others.* Otherworldly spirits—often those of deceased loved ones—appear to offer comfort and guidance to the dying person as he proceeds on his journey.
7. *The being of light.* An indescribably brilliant light appears in the distance. As the dying person draws nearer, it takes the form of a mysterious being that radiates warmth and love.
8. *The review.* In the presence of the radiant being, the dying person experiences an extraordinarily vivid playback of the high points of his life.
9. *The border or limit.* The dying person has the sensation of arriving at a fence or threshold or some other type of border—the final boundary between life and death.
10. *Coming back.* Though the person may earnestly wish to cross over to the other side, his soul is inexorably drawn back into life, sometimes reentering his body through the top of the head.

The aftermath of this experience also tends to be the same for every individual who experiences it. "Later," says Moody, "he tries to tell others, but he has trouble doing so. In the first place, he has no human words adequate to describe these unearthly experiences. He also finds that others scoff, so he stops telling other people. Still, the experience affects his life profoundly, especially his view about death and its relationship to life."

7

DEATH CAN BE FUN!

Death in the Movies

As even a cursory glance at the American Film Institute's list of the all-time greatest movies makes clear, death has always been a major theme in motion pictures. Of the hundred films selected by the AFI, only about a dozen are devoid of death scenes. The rest (beginning with *Citizen Kane*, which opens with its dying hero breathing his famous last word, "Rosebud") portray death in a staggering variety of forms: by revolver (*High Noon*), submachine gun (*The Godfather*), arrow (*Stagecoach*), dynamite (*The Bridge on the River Kwai*), switchblade knife (*West Side Story*), light saber (*Star Wars*), quicksand (*Lawrence of Arabia*), Roman chariot (*Ben-Hur*), hot rod (*Rebel Without a Cause*), mop water (*The Wizard of Oz*), knife-wielding transvestite (*Psycho*), machete-wielding bandito (*The Treasure of the Sierra Madre*), shotgun-wielding redneck (*Easy Rider*), great white shark (*Jaws*), biblical artifact (*Raiders of the Lost Ark*), homicidal computer (*2001: A Space Odyssey*), nuclear Armageddon (*Dr. Strangelove*), Russian roulette (*The Deer Hunter*), plunge from convent bell tower (*Vertigo*), betrayal by double-crossing femme fatale (*The Maltese Falcon*), and many, many more.

Even heartwarming family films such as *It's a Wonderful Life*, *Snow White and the Seven Dwarfs*, and *E.T.* bring their heroes perilously close to death. It's hard to avoid the conclusion that, for filmgoers everywhere, watching other people die on-screen is rich in entertainment value.

Clearly, there is no way of compiling a comprehensive list of death in the cinema without producing a thousand-page doorstop like Leonard Maltin's annual movie guide. Here is a purely subjective list of a dozen personal favorites, arranged into helpful catgories.

MOST HEART-WRENCHING FUNERAL

Imitation of Life (1959). The single most agonizing scene in this ten-hankie tear-jerker occurs during the funeral procession of the saintly African American maid Annie (Juanita Moore). As the hearse makes its way along the streets, Annie's light-skinned adult daughter Sarah Jane (Susan Kohner)—who, in her efforts to pass as white, has cruelly rejected her mother—suddenly appears and throws herself on the coffin, begging her mommy's forgiveness. If this moment doesn't reduce you to a state of helpless blubbering, you might want to visit your cardiologist to see if your heart is still functioning.

MOST AMBIGUOUS DEATH

Shane (1953). The final shot of this classic Western shows the heroic gunslinger (Alan Ladd)—who has been badly wounded during the climactic shootout—riding through a cemetery, holding himself in a very unnatural position, as though he is barely alive. Are we supposed to think that he is literally dying? Or is the scene merely allegorical, symbolizing the end of the frontier way of life that Shane personifies? This burning question will continue to be debated for as long as there are guys with nothing better to do than sit around with their buddies and engage in pointless arguments about old cowboy movies.

NOBLEST DEATH

Angels with Dirty Faces (1938). At the end of this classic gangster film, tough guy Rocky Sullivan (James Cagney)—who is ready to spit in the eye of any copper who lays a finger on him—is being led to the electric chair after plugging the double-crossing rat played by Humphrey Bogart. As Rocky swaggers down the corridor to the death chamber, his childhood-friend-turned-neighborhood-priest (Pat O'Brien) begs a final favor. Rocky is worshipped by a gang of young punks who still have a chance to go straight. If they see that their idol has feet of clay, maybe they'll stop regarding him as a role model and think twice about following in his criminal footsteps. At first Rocky refuses, but at the last minute—in a redemptive self-sacrificial act that brings tears to the good father's eyes—he pretends to break down and goes screaming and crying to his death.

MOST EMOTIONALLY SATISFYING DEATH

Dirty Harry (1971). Few, if any, other moments in cinematic history are as profoundly gratifying as the climax of this two-fisted classic, when Clint Eastwood's heroic police officer puts a well-deserved .44 Magnum slug into the worthless carcass of the sniveling long-haired psycho killer after asking, "Are you feeling lucky, punk?"

BEST 3-D DEATH

Dial M for Murder (1954). Originally meant to be shown in 3-D (which enjoyed a brief vogue in the 1950s), this Alfred Hitchcock thriller concerns evil hubby Tony Wendice (Ray Milland), who sets up his rich wife, Margot (Grace Kelly), to be killed by an intruder. During the attempted murder, Margot fights back and manages to bury a pair of scissors between the shoulder blades of her attacker. In a tight close-up, we see the scissors sink into his body as he falls onto his back—a shocking image in any format but especially powerful when viewed, as intended, in 3-D.

☠ MOST DIABOLICALLY INGENIOUS DEATHS

Final Destination (2000), *Final Destination 2* (2003), *Final Destination 3* (2006). In the original entry in this series, Death—feeling cheated after a few intended teenage victims escape destruction by refusing to board a doomed airplane—sets out to reclaim them by devising ingenious Rube Goldberg–like accidents. The most thrilling is the elaborate accident that starts off the second installment with a colossal bang.

☠ MOST SHOCKING DEATH IN A CLASSIC FILM NOIR

Kiss of Death (1947). In a scene that still shocks with its brutality (even in our age of *Saw*, *Hostel*, and other works of cinematic "torture porn"), a cackling psychopath named Tommy Udo (Richard Widmark) ties a crippled old lady to her wheelchair and hurls her down a flight of steps—basically just for the fun of it.

☠ MOST SURPRISING DEATH OF A CHARACTER YOU EXPECT TO MAKE IT TO THE END OF THE MOVIE

Million Dollar Baby (2004). For the first three-quarters of this Oscar winner, everything leads the audience to expect that they are watching a *Rocky*-like Cinderella story about a scrappy underdog who ends up as champ. So it comes as a tremendous shock when Hilary Swank's character is paralyzed by a sucker punch delivered by a vicious female opponent and has to be euthanized by her mentor, Clint Eastwood.

☠ MOST SHATTERING CARTOON DEATH

Bambi (1942). There's no contest in this category. Even though it happens off-screen, the killing of Bambi's mother is far and away the single most devastating death ever to occur in a feature-length animated movie.

☠ MOST TRAUMATIC PET DEATH

Old Yeller (1957). No baby boomer who saw this Disney film upon its initial release has ever recovered from the climactic scene, in which the towheaded young hero has to shoot his beloved pooch (who has contracted rabies following a heroic battle with an infected wolf). *Runner-up:* the cold-blooded murder of Gertrude the Duck by the evil (and hungry) Count Saknussem in the 1959 film version of Jules Verne's *Journey to the Center of the Earth*.

☠ FUNNIEST EMBALMING SCENES

The Loved One (1965). A highlight of this uneven but intermittently hilarious adaptation of Evelyn Waugh's satirical look at the American way of death is Rod Steiger's portrayal of the priggish chief embalmer, Mr. Joyboy, who communicates with his embalmer girlfriend by arranging the faces of cadavers so that their expressions mirror his own feelings.

Liberace as the jolly mortician, Mr. Starker, in The Loved One *(1965).* The Loved One *© Turner Entertainment Co. A Warner Bros. Entertainment Company. All Rights Reserved.*

☠ MOST ENCHANTING MOVIE ABOUT SOMEONE DYING TRAGICALLY IN THE PRIME OF LIFE

Here Comes Mr. Jordan (1941). In this thoroughly delightful fantasy, a lovable young palooka named Joe Pendleton (Robert Montgomery) is killed in a plane crash fifty years before his designated time, owing to a screw-up by a blundering angel. When the mistake is discovered, the angel's dapper, dulcet-voiced boss (Claude Rains) reincarnates Joe in the body of a playboy millionaire named Farnsworth, who has just been murdered by his two-timing wife. Various amusing and romantic complications ensue. In the end, Joe gets his chance at the title by transmigrating into the body of a prizefighter named Murdoch, who has just been bumped off by gamblers for refusing to throw the fight. Untimely death, marital betrayal, cold-blooded murder, and gangland corruption have never seemed so charming. (Remade in 1978 as the Warren Beatty vehicle *Heaven Can Wait.*)

Of course, though movies are rife with death, both natural and violent, few films portray it in an accurate way. In Hollywood movies, beautiful people die picturesquely of wasting diseases (as in the 1970 tear-jerker *Love Story*), while graphic, ostensibly hyper-realistic mayhem (such as the climactic bloodbath in the 1969 classic *The Wild Bunch*) tends to be "as stylized as the sword-play in Japanese Noh theater" (in the words of critic Jib Fowler).

One searing cinematic exception is the 2003 documentary *Dying at Grace*. Directed by Canadian filmmaker Allan King, this critically acclaimed feature records the final days, hours, and minutes of five terminally ill patients in the palliative care unit of the Salvation Army Toronto Grace Health Centre who agreed to share their experience on film. Regarded by its many admirers as the most brutally honest movie ever made on the subject, King's documentary not only forces the viewer to confront the often harrowing physical and emotional realities of dying but also (as *Toronto Star* critic Geoff Pevere puts it) "offers an oblique critique of our ritualized, pop-culture denial of this primal human event."

Death Lit 101

Since virtually all great works of literature (along with countless crummy ones) deal with the same two subjects—love and death—it's impossible to create a manageable list of every major work that deals with mortality. But if you were going to teach a college course called, say, "The Death Theme in

Fiction and Poetry," here are some short stories and poems you'd want to include in your syllabus.

- Leo Tolstoy, "The Death of Ivan Ilyich." This harrowing masterpiece is arguably the single greatest literary evocation of the experience of dying. If you want to know exactly what it must feel like to be enjoying a vital and active middle age one day and then suddenly fall sick and die in protracted agony, this is the story for you.
- Katherine Anne Porter, "The Jilting of Granny Weatherall." A tour de force of stream-of-consciousness writing, this famous story takes us inside the mind of the eighty-year-old title character as she lies on her deathbed, reliving the high (though mostly low) points of her long and generally depressing life.
- Edgar Allan Poe, "The Masque of the Red Death." Poe's version of the *danse macabre*, this classically creepy story about the world's least welcome party crasher conveys an age-old message: the futility of trying to escape from death's clutches.
- Ambrose Bierce, "An Occurrence at Owl Creek Bridge." This famous Civil War story about a Confederate sympathizer who is about to be hanged from a railroad bridge features a nifty twist ending that would not be out of place on *The Twilight Zone* (which is probably why a cinematic version of it was aired as an episode on *The Twilight Zone*). But the ending is not just a clever gimmick; it gives the story—which is ultimately about the tricks of perception that go on inside a dying brain—a terrible poignancy.
- Sarah Orne Jewett, "Miss Tempy's Watchers." This small gem of nineteenth-century American "local color" writing portrays two New England farm women as they pass a long night watching over the body of their newly deceased neighbor. A quietly moving story that evokes a bygone funerary custom while dealing with the ways that the spirits of our departed friends and relatives continue to touch our lives.
- W. W. Jacobs, "The Monkey's Paw." Playing on a proverbial theme—be careful what you wish for!—this classic tale of terror (arguably the scariest ever written) serves as an effective reminder that the very human impulse to pray for the return of a deceased loved one might not be such a hot idea.
- William Faulkner, "A Rose for Emily." This story deals with such typically Faulknerian themes as the decay of traditional southern culture and its usurpation by the crass forces of industrialized modernity. But mostly it's a really cool story about necrophilia.
- Ernest Hemingway, "Snows of Kilimanjaro." A typically Hemingwayesque writer who has failed to treat a thorn scratch with iodine reviews the moral and artistic failings of his life as he lies dying of gangrene within sight of the titular mountain. The powerful and sweeping tale conveys a vitally important message: never neglect to put antiseptic on a cut while on an African safari.
- Robert Penn Warren, "Blackberry Winter." In the form of first-person reminiscence about a single day in the life of a nine-year-old farm boy, this story by Pulitzer Prize–winning novelist and American poet laureate Robert Penn Warren embodies a profound and universal theme: the fall from the paradise of childhood

innocence into the adult world of time, change, aging, and death.

- Vladimir Nabokov, "Christmas." In this ravishing tale, rich in traditional symbols of death and resurrection, a man named Slepstov, grieving for the loss of his recently deceased teenage son, is vouchsafed a vision of life renewed in the form of a metamorphosing insect. Read it and weep.
- Emily Dickinson, "After great pain, a formal feeling comes—." Given the range and depth of her morbid preoccupations, there are any number of amazing Emily Dickinson death poems to choose from. This one, however, is arguably the greatest poem about bereavement ever written, compressing the essence of the experience into thirteen shattering lines.
- Thomas Hardy, "Are You Digging on My Grave?" A darkly sardonic poem, told from the point of view of a dead and buried young woman who hears the earth being disturbed over her head and assumes that someone who misses her terribly is digging on her grave. We won't spoil the punch line, but let's just say that the theme of the poem can be summed up in a familiar phrase: how quickly they forget!
- A. E. Housman, "To an Athlete Dying Young." If you saw the Academy Award–winning movie *Out of Africa*, you know that this is the poem Meryl Streep recites at the funeral of her dashing great-white-hunter lover, Robert Redford. A timeless classic (the poem, not the movie), it conveys a pretty world-weary message about life (particularly from an author who was still a young man himself when he wrote it): get out while the getting's good.
- Philip Larkin, "The Old Fools." One of the greatest of recent English poets, Larkin had (depending on your point of view) either an unhealthy preoccupation with death or an unblinkingly realistic sense of its ultimate horror. In any case, this savage poem about aging and mortality will in no way make you feel better about the prospect of aging.
- Dylan Thomas, "Do Not Go Gentle into That Good Night." Addressed to the poet's dying father, this stirring plea to "rage against the dying of the light" has the essential characteristic of all great poetry: no matter how many times you hear it, it still has the power to send shivers down your spine.
- Edgar Allan Poe, "The Conqueror Worm." Playing on the same metaphor used by Shakespeare—"all the world's a stage"—Poe presents human life as a theatrical spectacle. Only in his case (as you'd expect), the play turns out to be a mad, tormented horror show that climaxes when all the actors end up as worm chow.
- Conrad Aiken, "Blind Date." With jazzy diction and imagery drawn from the world of tawdry amusement parks and blaring juke joints, Aiken paints a vivid picture of the fleetingness of existence and the inevitability of death. "Baby, it is the last of all blind dates / And this we keep with the keeper of the golden gates."
- Sylvia Plath, "Death & Co." This bone-chilling portrait of personified death—represented as two equally creepy figures, one a vulture-headed connoisseur of dead babies, the other a long-haired would-be lover with a seductive smile and a dangling cigarette—is typical of the death-obsessed poet. That Plath ended up with her head in an oven will come as no surprise to any reader of this poem.

- Elizabeth Bishop, "First Death in Nova Scotia." A deeply moving poem about a young girl's first experience of death as she views the body of her little cousin Arthur, laid out in his white coffin. Told from the child's point of view, the poem beautifully captures her confusion as she struggles to make sense of the fanciful explanation that her parents offer (Arthur, they tell her, is going off to be a page in Buckingham Palace) in a misguided effort to protect her from the truth.
- Sharon Olds, "The Exact Moment of His Death." In her 1992 collection *The Father*, Olds confronts the physical facts of dying with an unsparing directness. Like the other poems in the volume, this one packs such visceral power that we seem to be standing at her father's deathbed at the instant his cancer-ravaged body is transformed into a corpse.

Death's Poet Laureate

Back in the 1870s, America witnessed a craze for so-called obituary verse—sappy, sentimental poems about tragic deaths, preferably of innocent young children. The best-known exponent of this wildly morbid genre was Julia A. Moore, aka the "Sweet Singer of Michigan."

The daughter of a farmer, Julia began churning out tear-jerking doggerel in her late teens, usually in response to newspaper stories about lethal accidents, fatal diseases, and various manmade and natural disasters. Her first volume, *The Sentimental Song Book*, appeared in 1876, when she was twenty-nine years old, and became an immediate best seller, despite its somewhat cool reception by critics ("Shakespeare, could he read it, would be glad that he was dead," wrote one reviewer). Still, she had her literary admirers, most notably Mark Twain, who got such a kick out of the sheer jaw-dropping awfulness of her death-besotted work that he modeled one of his characters after her: Emmeline Grangerford, author of a particularly atrocious funeral ode in *The Adventures of Huckleberry Finn*.

Here's a sample of the work that has earned the Sweet Singer a special place in the hearts of lovers of truly bad poetry:

"Little Andrew"

Andrew was a little infant,
And his life was two years old;
He was his parents' eldest boy,
And he was drowned, I was told.
His parents never more can see him
In this world of grief and pain,
And Oh! they will not forget him
While on earth they do remain.

On one bright and pleasant morning
His uncle thought it would be nice
To take his dear little nephew
Down to play upon a raft,
Where he was to work upon it,
And this little child would company be—
The raft the water rushed around it,
Yet he the danger did not see.

This little child knew no danger—
Its little soul was free from sin—
He was looking in the water,
When, alas, this child fell in.
Beneath the raft the water took him,
For the current was so strong,
And before they could rescue him
He was drowned and was gone.

Oh! how sad were his kind parents
When they saw their drowned child,
As they brought him from the water,
It almost made their hearts grow wild.
Oh! how mournful was the parting
From that little infant son.
Friends, I pray you, all take warning,
Be careful of your little ones.

Death's Playlist

Okay, full disclosure: we don't really know what the Grim Reaper listens to on his iPod. But here's an educated guess.

- Jim Carroll, "People Who Died." This wildly morbid catalogue of catastrophe stands as one of the catchiest punk recordings ever.
- Rolling Stones, "Paint It Black." A driving, sitar-laced elegy to a dead girlfriend, ranked number 174 on *Rolling Stone* magazine's list of the all-time greatest rock songs.
- Bob Dylan, "Knockin' on Heaven's Door." The moving last words of a dying frontier sheriff, this Dylan classic sounds even better when heard on the sound track of Sam Peckinpah's *Pat Garrett and Billy the Kid*, for which it was originally composed.
- George Jones, "He Stopped Loving Her Today." If you don't bawl like a baby when listening to this tear-jerking country classic, make an immediate appointment with your cardiologist to see if your heart's still functioning.
- Eric Clapton, "Tears in Heaven." This heartrending tribute to the singer's four-year-old son, Conor, who died in a tragic fall in 1991, is a little mawkish for some tastes. But writing it was clearly cathartic for the grieving father.
- Kansas, "Dust in the Wind." A catchy pop acknowledgment of our cosmic insignificance. Hokey but strangely profound.
- Blue Öyster Cult, "(Don't Fear) The Reaper." Ranked by *Rolling Stone* magazine as one of the "500 Greatest Singles of All Time" (number 397 to be precise), this rockin' tune about the inevitability of death has only one flaw: it needs more cowbell.
- Warren Zevon, "Life'll Kill Ya." The title track of Zevon's 2000 album, this characteristically unsentimental song about mortality proved sadly prescient: two years after its release, Zevon was diagnosed with terminal cancer.
- Hank Williams, "I'll Never Get Out of the World Alive." Another weirdly prophetic song that was the last ever recorded by the "hillbilly Shakespeare."
- Lucinda Williams, "Fancy Funeral." This heartfelt plea for simple, inexpensive burial might make the Grim Reaper's playlist, but it certainly isn't going to be on the iPod of any member of the National Funeral Directors Association.
- Loudon Wainwright III, "Doin' the Math." Though Wainwright is known for his sardonic humor, there's nothing funny—at least to a fellow baby boomer—about this cool-eyed contemplation of encroaching old age and all-too-imminent death.
- Johnny Cash, "God's Gonna Cut You Down." There are many versions of this traditional folk song, but few are as memorable as the one recorded by the "Man in Black" not long before his own death in 2003.
- Jan and Dean, "Surfin' Hearse." With

lyrics worthy of Cole Porter ("My dad thinks there's nothing worse / Than my big black Cadillac surfin' hearse") and a melody that blends the Beach Boys' "Little Deuce Coupe" with Chopin's funeral march, this toe-tapping paean to a "big black Cadillac" funeral car converted into a bitchin' beach buggy easily rivals "The Little Old Lady from Pasadena" as one of Jan and Dean's finest musical achievements.

A Death Song That Could Make Even John Wayne Cry

Arguably the most two-fisted tear-jerker ever composed, "The Cowboy's Lament"—aka "Streets of Laredo"—is guaranteed to make even the manliest buckaroo choke up. There have been many variants, but here are the complete lyrics to the traditional version:

As I walked out on the streets of Laredo,
As I walked out in Laredo one day,
I spied a young cowboy all wrapped in white linen,
Wrapped in white linen as cold as the clay.

"I can see by your outfit that you are a cowboy,"
These words he did say as I boldly walked by.
"Come sit down beside me and hear my sad story,
I'm shot in the breast and I know I must die.

"It was once in the saddle, I used to go dashing,
Once in the saddle, I used to go gay.
First to the cardhouse, and then down to Rosie's,
But I'm shot in the breast and I'm dyin' today.

"Get six jolly fellows to carry my coffin,
And six pretty maidens to bear up my pall.
Throw bunches of roses all over my coffin,
That they might not smell me as they bear me along.

"Then beat the drum slowly, play the fife lowly,
Play the dead march as you carry me along.
Take me to the green valley, lay the sod o'er me,
I'm a young cowboy, and I know I've done wrong.

"Then go write a letter to my gray-haired mother,
And tell her the cowboy that she loved is gone.
But please not one word of the man who had killed me,
Don't mention his name, and his name will pass on."

When thus he had spoken, the hot sun was setting.
The streets of Laredo grew cold as the clay.
We took the young cowboy down to the green valley,
And there stands his marker we made to this day.

"We beat the drum slowly, played the fife lowly,

Played the dead march as we carried him along.
Down in the green valley, laid the sod o'er him.
He was a young cowboy, and he said he'd done wrong.

Lullabies: Ditties of Death

Anyone who has paid attention to the words of "Rock-a-bye Baby" knows that this ostensibly soothing, slumber-inducing lyric is scary as hell: "When the bough breaks / The cradle will fall / And down will come baby / Cradle and all." Exactly how is a song about plunging to your death while trapped in a cradle supposed to lull you to sleep?

As it happens, "Rock-a-bye Baby" isn't the only terrifying lullaby. In certain parts of the world, parents commonly croon their infants to sleep with lyrics that either describe the imminent death of the child or threaten him with extreme bodily injury if he doesn't quit crying and go to sleep.

According to Finnish scholar Kalle Achté, who has made an extensive survey of the subject, his own countrymen—for whatever unexplained cultural reasons—are particularly fond of such unnerving ditties. Popular Finnish lullabies include "Rock the Child into the Grave" and "Come, Death, in Little Socks," in which "the singer promises to reward death with a pair of socks or shoes for taking the child away."

But Finnish babies aren't the only ones who grow up hearing such dismal tunes. Newborn Estonians are expected to fall asleep while listening to their grandmas sing:

Rock the child, swing the child,
Rock the child into death.
Swing the child into the coffin,
Cross the arms upon the breast.

And then there's this deeply reassuring Russian lullaby:

Sleep, sleep,
If you die today
I shall make a little coffin
Of pine boards.
I shall carry you to the churchyard,
I shall cry and I shall mourn
When I bury you in a little grave.

What exactly is going on here? Achté speculates that in a preindustrial world where infant mortality rates were shockingly high, such funereal songs offered mothers a way of confronting their worst fears. And given the hard lot of peasant women in those bygone days, mothers might actually have seen death as preferable to earthly existence and "wished that on their children."

Whatever the case, all we can say is, it's a good thing the target audience for these bedtime dirges are too little to understand the words.

Six Feet Under: Must-See TV for Morticians

Sure, everyone is aware that death figures prominently in the daily experience of funeral directors. But who knew that their lives are so full of sex, drugs, and extreme family dysfunction? That long-kept secret was finally made public in the hit HBO series *Six Feet Under*, which came to the end of its five-season run in 2005 but continues to enjoy a healthy afterlife in DVD format.

Created by Alan Ball (Academy Award–winning screenwriter of the film *American Beauty*), this critically acclaimed show revolves around the Fisher clan, proprietors of a family-owned funeral parlor. Their lives take an unexpected turn when their patriarch, Nathaniel Senior (Richard Jenkins), is killed in a traffic accident in the opening moments of the first episode. The sudden death of the elder Nathaniel (who, though deceased, puts in regular appearances throughout the series) introduced one of the signature features of the show, each episode of which begins with the shocking (though often darkly humorous) death of a character who is then brought to the Fisher funeral home for disposal.

The complicated (and occasionally soap-opera-ish) story lines focus on the dynamics among the surviving family members—mother Ruth (Frances Conroy), teenage daughter Claire (Lauren Ambrose), gay younger brother David (Michael C. Hall), and older black-sheep sibling Nate junior (Peter Krause)—along with their assorted lovers and friends. For the more morbidly inclined members of the audience, however, the real distinction of the program has to do with its exceptionally realistic depiction of the day-to-day operations of an old-fashioned funeral home, from the arrangement conference and the embalming (performed for the Fishers by their ace employee Federico Diaz, played by Freddy Rodriguez) to the viewing and service.

Die-hard fans of the show will want to visit the official website, www.hbo.com/sixfeetunder, which offers a host of nifty features, including obituaries of all the leading characters, trivia games, and an online gift shop where you can order your own "Fisher & Diaz" T-shirts!

Death is here and death is there,
Death is busy everywhere,
All around, within, beneath,
Above is death—and we are death.

—Percy Bysshe Shelley

Magazines You Are Unlikely to Find in Your Doctor's Waiting Room

Since every profession from aerospace engineering to zymurgy (the branch of chemistry dealing with the fermentation of beer) has its own trade publication, you won't be surprised to learn that embalmers have one, too. It's called—surprise!—the *Embalmer*. The official journal of the British Institute of Embalmers, this handsomely produced quarterly is "devoted to furthering the interest, acceptance, and practice of embalming throughout the world" (as its masthead announces). To that end, it publishes a wide range of entertaining and informative pieces, including "The Great Salisbury Train Disaster: A Landmark for English Embalmers," "Advanced Embalming and Reconstruction Workshops," and "Funeral Service Training in Australia."

The occasional issue even features a removable centerfold that—like the kind invented by Hugh Hefner—offers graphic glimpses of exposed human flesh, albeit of a somewhat less erotic nature (unless you happen to be a necrophile). Typical is the pullout in the October 2006 issue, which demonstrates, though a series of explicit full-color close-ups, the advantages of injecting embalming fluid through the superior axillary artery as opposed to the more traditional femoral. It's quite eye-catching—though if your adolescent son prefers it to the *Playboy* variety, it might be time for that talk with the school psychologist. For more information, check out the British Institute of Embalmers website, www.bioe.co.uk.

Other mortuary mags that deal with topics not normally covered in *People*, *Entertainment Weekly*, and the children's magazine *Highlights* are:

- *American Cemetery* ("The Independent Magazine of Mortuary Management"), which offers helpful features such as "Winterizing Your Cemetery" and "Top Ten Marketing Ideas for Cemeteries" (www.katesboylston.com).
- *Mortuary Management*, a venerable trade publication that has been serving the needs of funeral directors and others in the death biz since 1914 (www.mortuarymanagement.com).
- *The Director*, the official magazine of the National Funeral Directors Association, offering articles such as "The Seven Habits of Highly Effective Grievers" and "Why You Should Bring Those Oversize Caskets Out of the Backroom" (www.nfda.com).
- *American Funeral Director*, the country's leading independent trade magazine for funeral directors and other funeral service professionals, now in its 130th year of publication. Recent must-read articles include "Pet Loss Services: Mentally Positioned to Succeed" and "Are You Prepared for the Next Pandemic?" (www.katesboylston.com).

Sick Jokes

Question: What's funnier than a dead baby?

A. Anything. Dead babies aren't funny.

B. Two dead babies?

C. A priest, a rabbi, and a lawyer.

D. None of the above.

Answer: None of the above. What's funnier than a dead baby is . . . a dead baby in a clown costume!

This, of course, is an example of a particularly tasteless brand of humor, the dead baby joke, of which there are scores of examples (If you don't believe me, check out www.dead-baby-joke.com). Though this genre didn't arise until the 1960s, it was preceded by other forms of gross-out humor, some dating back to the turn of the last century. Between 1899 and 1930, morbid little poems known as "Little Willies" enjoyed a vogue in America. Some of these were as sadistic as any sixties-era dead baby joke:

Willie, with a thirst for gore,
Nailed the baby to the door.

Mother said, with humor quaint:
"Willie dear, don't spoil the paint."

While ghoulish humor like this might seem to reflect nothing more than the debased sensibilities of the audience, psychologists and others tell us that sick jokes actually serve an important function. As eminent folklorist Alan Dundes argues in his fascinating study, *Cracking Jokes: Studies of Sick Humor Cycles and Stereotypes* (Ten Speed Press, 1987), they provide "a socially sanctioned outlet for the discussion of the forbidden and taboo" and thus offer us a way to ventilate and relieve our anxieties. Viewed from this perspective, dead baby jokes can be seen not just as a form of crude adolescent humor told for nothing more than raw shock value, but also as a means of dealing with the most taboo and anxiety-provoking subject of all: death.

"The Hearse Song"

Jokes aren't the only way children have of coping with death anxieties. Another is the creepily comical song "The Worms Crawl In," aka "The Hearse Song," a macabre favorite for generations of children. It exists in dozens of variant forms. Here's one of the best known:

Did you ever think when a hearse goes by,
That you may be the next to die?
They take you to the family plot,
And there you wither, decay, and rot.
They wrap you in a bloody sheet,
And then they bury you six feet deep.
All goes well for a week or two,
And then things start to happen to you.
The worms crawl in, the worms crawl out
They eat your guts and they spit them out.
One of the worms that's not so shy
Crawls in one ear and out one eye.
And then your blood turns yellow-green
And oozes out like sour cream.
Your eyes fall in, your teeth fall out,
Your liver turns to sauerkraut.
So never laugh when a hearse goes by,
For you might be the next to die.

Memento Mori

Not so very long ago, the only people who sported death's-head jewelry were members of outlaw biker gangs and the kind of teens who paint their fingernails black, cultivate corpse-pale complexions, and decorate their rooms with posters of Marilyn Manson. All that has changed. According to a front-page article by David Colman in the July 27, 2006, Styles section of the *New York Times*, we

Memento mori: Renaissance death's-head timepiece.

have entered the era of "graveyard chic," when the human skull has become a trendy design logo on everything from necklaces, wristwatches, and bracelets to boxer shorts, umbrellas, and even toilet brushes. "With the full force of the American consumer marketing establishment behind it," writes Colman, "the skull has lost virtually all of its fearsome outsider meaning. It has become the Happy Face of the 2000s."

As with so many other phenomena that seem uniquely symptomatic of the modern era, however, there is nothing particularly new about skull-based jewelry and household decor. To be sure, people in past ages didn't flaunt skulls as a fashion statement or (like an unnamed Manhattan hostess in Colman's article) blow four thousand bucks on a set of skull-shaped sterling placecard holders with hinged jaws to clasp the cards. But they *did*, at times, wear death's-head jewelry and even decorate their homes with human skulls.

Among the New England Puritans, for example, it was not uncommon for the devout to wear silver skull rings. And seventeenth-century portraits of Puritan dignitaries frequently depict their subjects seated at desks that hold paperweights made of actual human skulls. Mary, Queen of Scots, owned a skull-shaped silver watch, while Martin Luther had a gold ring with a death's-head in enamel.

Items such as these are technically known as memento mori, a Latin phrase generally translated as "remember you will die." For pious Christians of earlier centuries, these grim emblems of mortality had a deeply spiritual function, reminding them of the urgency of attending to their souls in a world where death can come at any instant.

In other times and places, memento mori served a more worldly, if not hedonistic, purpose—"as an intensifier for enjoying the good life in the here and now," in the words of thanatologist Robert Kastenbaum. In ancient Rome, for example, miniature coffins were sometimes passed out as party favors to remind the guests to eat, drink, and be merry—"to dance footloose upon the earth,"

Danse macabre: *fifteenth-century woodcut.*

as Horace writes in his *Odes* since there will be no such pleasure in the afterlife.

By the Middle Ages, the memento mori tradition had not only taken on a far more somber emphasis but also assumed a variety of new and often grotesque guises. Largely in response to the devastation wrought by the Black Plague, gruesome depictions of death—focusing on the horrors of physical decay and conveying a visceral sense of the precariousness of existence—became a dominant motif of medieval art. In woodcut illustrations such as Hans Holbein's famous *danse macabre* series (showing a ghastly grim reaper carrying off the rich and poor alike) and paintings such as Pieter Breughel the Elder's *The Triumph of Death* (in which a horde of armed skeletons descends upon a field of victims engaged in a variety of worldly pursuits), viewers were reminded in the most graphically unnerving way of their inescapable fate.

Though the memento mori craze of the medieval period eventually petered out, the tradition has never entirely disappeared. During the seventeenth century, for example, a genre of still-life painting known as *vanitas* (Latin for "vanity") flourished in the Netherlands. Works of this type depict a variety of objects—most commonly skulls, hourglasses, and wilting flowers—meant to symbolize the transience of life and the vanity of all earthly achievements and pleasures. Some people have even gone to the extreme of furnishing their homes with the receptacles in which they plan to be interred. Sarah Bernhardt, for example, liked to relax in a coffin, which she kept in her bedroom. A famous photograph of the legendary actress shows her reposing in the open casket as though rehearsing for her burial.

Perhaps the most striking and widely publicized memento mori of the present day—one that says as much about our glamour-obsessed, consumerist age as Holbein's *danse macabre* woodcuts reveal about the medieval mentality—is British bad-boy artist Damien Hirst's *For the Love of God*: a life-size platinum cast of a human skull encrusted with 8,601 high-quality diamonds, including a fifty-two-carat gem in the center of the brow. The single most expensive piece of contemporary art ever created, it can be yours for a mere $100 million and change.

Memento Mori Calendars

Not so very long ago, wall calendars came in two basic varieties: (1) the advertising calendar handed out free by local businesses—insurance agencies, dry cleaners, hardware stores, and the like—and illustrated with cheesy photographs of butterflies, tropical sunsets, and Alpine landscapes, and (2) the "cheesecake" calendar that featured full-color photos of scantily clad cuties or demurely posed nudes and that could invariably be found on the walls of auto repair shops everywhere.

Things are very different today. Glossy,

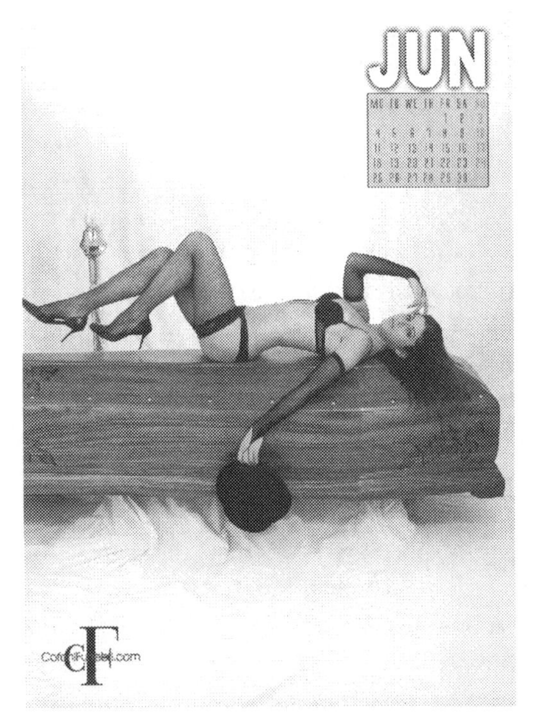

Sexytime coffins. From the 2007 CofaniFunebri.com "The Last 2 Let You Down" calendar. Courtesy of CofaniFunebri.com.

lavishly produced wall calendars have become a big part of the publishing business and are available for every conceivable interest and taste. Whether you're a Beatles fan, an aficionado of French Impressionist art, a cat fancier, a *Star Wars* geek, or a lover of any of a thousand other things—comic strips, pets, vintage cars, rock musicians, Renaissance artists, hit TV shows, franchise films, best-selling fantasy books, et cetera, et cetera, you'll find a calendar perfectly suited for you. So it's no surprise that there are calendars for the memento mori crowd. After all, what better way to keep track of the passage of every fleeting day, week, month, and year of your life than with a death-themed wall calendar?

Take the "Last 2 Let You Down" calendar produced by the Italian coffin-making concern, Cofani Funebri. Featuring a pair of hot babes dressed like porn stars and striking salacious poses atop a selection of handsomely carved caskets, this slick, oversize item is guaranteed to be a major turn-on to anyone who has ever fantasized about having sex in a funeral home. To order, go to www.cofanifune bri.com.

For those who prefer beefcake to cheesecake, there is the "Men of Mortuaries" calendar, depicting a bunch of hunky young all-American morticians, some posed formally in graveyards and funeral homes, others assuming playfully suggestive attitudes while engaged in various mortuary-related activities (check out the shot of the tank-topped "Mr. June" hosing down his hearse). "The Men of Mortuaries" calendar is issued by KAMM Cares, a nonprofit organization benefiting women suffering from breast cancer. It can be ordered at www.menofmortuaries.com.

If vehicles are more to your taste than flesh-and-blood human beings, you'll undoubtedly prefer the Society of Funeral Coaches calendar, featuring artsy, sepia-toned photographs of classic hearses juxtaposed with blow-ups of beautiful Victorian-era memorial statuary. You'll find it at www .societyoffuneralcoaches.com.

If you prefer a desk calendar to the hanging kind, you might consider the *Where Are They Buried? How Did They Die?* calendar, based on Tod Benoit's book of the same name. Each of the 365 detachable pages is devoted to a famous person who died on that day and includes a capsule obituary, along with the location of his or her grave. You can also download a calendar of "famous demises" at www.whataslacker.com/calendar. Organized, like Benoit's, around celebrity death anniversaries, it lists a number of famous names for each day of the month and provides additional information about them with a click of the mouse.

Days of the Dead

Halloween may be rooted in pagan religion, but it has become so thoroughly commercialized that it sometimes seems like a corporate creation, invented for the sole purpose of peddling bite-size candy bars and spookhouse novelty items to the American public. Happily, that spirit of rampant consumerism has not yet trivialized the Mexican counterpart of Halloween, the holiday known as Día de los Muertos—the Day of the Dead. A multiday festival that traces its origins to pre-Columbian times, Día de los Muertos is equal parts commemoration and carnival: both a loving remembrance of departed family and friends and a mocking defiance of death itself. Its seemingly paradoxical mix of reverence and revelry allows participants to commune with their deceased loved ones while mitigating their own mortal terrors by making the Grim Reaper himself into a kind of laughingstock—by treating death with what the essayist F. Gonzalez-Crussi calls a "joking familiarity."

In the days leading up to the holiday, which culminates on November 2, celebrants devote themselves to a variety of activities. To honor their deceased loved

ones—whose souls will come home for a few brief hours to enjoy the pleasures they once knew in life—families set up household shrines laden with offerings: the food and drink most prized by the departed, along with a few of his or her favorite possessions. Burial plots are weeded, tombstones scrubbed and decorated. Town marketplaces overflow with colorful goods: huge arrays of marigolds to lay on the graves; ghoulish treats like *pan de muerto* (bread of the dead) and sugar skulls; leering masks of devils, vampires, and witches; and, of course, the delightfully macabre folk-art figurines known as *calacas*, hand-carved little skeletons engaged in every imaginable form of human behavior. Costumed mummers and singing minstrels parade through the village squares, performing burlesque skits and reciting comical verses.

On the evening of November 1—when the adult dead return—families converge on the village cemetery for an all-night vigil, vividly evoked by cultural historian Rosalind Rosoff Beimler:

> Candles are lit on the gravestones, one for each lost soul. Women kneel or sit all night to pray; the men keep watch, talking and drinking. In some places food is placed on the graves. By midnight the cemetery is filled with candles flickering in the windy autumn night. Both city folk and villagers spend the following day in the company of their dead, but also enjoying the sociability of the living. Gossip and drink are shared at gravestones. Strolling musicians play the ghosts' favorite tunes.

"By the evening of November 2," writes Beimler, "the party is over." The ghosts return to their world, while families settle back to their normal routines. "Thus," concludes Beimler, "are the living and the dead left at peace with each other for another year."

RECOMMENDED READING

An excellent, lavishly illustrated book on the history, meaning, and practice of the Day of the Dead is Elizabeth Carmichael and Chloë Sayer's *The Skeleton at the Feast: The Day of the Dead in Mexico* (University of Texas Press, 1991). Photographer John Greenleigh, who traveled to various small villages throughout Mexico in four different years to document the holiday, provides a vivid evocation in *The Days of the Dead: Mexico's Festival of Communion with the Departed* (Collins, 1991), with informative commentary by Rosalind Beimler. Also highly recommended: "The Grin of the *Calavera*," a typically elegant meditation on the Mexican attitude toward death by the physician-essayist F. Gonzalez-Crussi. It can be found in his collection, *The Day of the Dead and Other Mortal Reflections* (Harcourt Brace, 1993).

Strange but True

The history of death has produced some amazing coincidences. For example:

- John Adams and Thomas Jefferson died in separate states on the same day, July 4, 1826—the fiftieth anniversary of the signing of the Declaration of Independence.
- Babe Ruth, the home run king, and Elvis Presley, the king of rock and roll, died on the same date, August 16, twenty-nine years apart (Ruth in 1948, Presley in 1977).
- Thomas Edison was buried on October 21, 1931, exactly fifty-two years to the day after he invented the electric lightbulb.
- Sir Winston Churchill and his father, Lord Randolph Churchill, died on the same date, January 24, seventy years apart.

Most amazing of all are the weird connections between Abraham Lincoln and John F. Kennedy, to wit:

- Lincoln's secretary was named Kennedy, and Kennedy's secretary was named Lincoln.
- The two men were elected exactly one hundred years apart, in 1860 and 1960.
- Both were shot on a Friday.
- Both of their successors were named Johnson.
- John Wilkes Booth ran from the theater and was caught in a warehouse; Lee Harvey Oswald ran from a warehouse and was caught in a theater.
- Both assassins had three names composed of a total of fifteen letters.

Eerie!

Death: King of Terrors or Really Fun Hobby?

Since (as the daily offerings on eBay verify) there are people in the world willing to spend good money on things such as antique ink blotters, vintage cough syrup bottles, and Depression-era gum-ball charms, it should come as no surprise that there are also hobbyists devoted to the acquisition of death-related artifacts. Occupying the more outré end of this pursuit are collectors who traffic in objects such as actual shrunken heads made by Jivaro tribesmen and similar bizarre human

Postmortem postcards.

relics. It is more common, however—and far less illegal—for mortuary enthusiasts to invest in such fascinating items as old embalming merchandise, mortuary school memorabilia, and other funereal ephemera.

Topping the list of death-related desirables are Victorian postmortem photographs. As with any collectibles, prices for these macabre treasures vary widely, depending on factors such as rarity, condition, and subject matter. A cracked and faded carte de visite of somebody's grandmother laid out in a flower-strewn casket can be had for forty or fifty bucks. By contrast, a mint-condition daguerreotype of a beautifully dressed and carefully posed dead baby can command upward of a thousand. Other vintage photographs, such as pictures of turn-of-the-century medical students posed with dissected cadavers, are also much coveted by collectors. The most affordable pictorial items are old cemetery postcards, which rarely cost more than a few dollars.

Day of the Dead figures, available from bluelips.com. Courtesy of Bluelips.

Like other hobbyists—for example, the numismatist who limits himself to Colonial American currency, or the comic book collector who sticks to the "funny animal" genre—many mortuary enthusiasts prefer to focus on a single, highly specialized area. Some, for example, collect only specimens of antique embalming equipment, everything from early injection pumps to vintage bottles of arterial fluid to tins of restorative putty. Others prefer the promotional items handed out by neighborhood funeral parlors—wall calendars, matchbooks, ashtrays, and the like. Still others focus on Victorian mourning paraphernalia, including embossed memorial cards, black-bordered condolence stationery, and hairwork jewelry. Certain fashion-conscious individuals seek out material from the makers of traditional burial wear: trade magazine advertisements or manufacturer's catalogues showing the latest styles for the well-dressed corpse. There are even collectors of actual antique coffins—though this particular pursuit clearly requires the kind of storage space unavailable to the average apartment dweller.

Indeed, given the commercial scope of the American death industry—the sheer variety of merchandise it has generated since the Civil

War—the possibilities for death-related collecting are nearly boundless. For an excellent introduction to this delightful and edifying hobby, you won't do better than C. L. Miller's handsomely illustrated trade paperback, *Postmortem Collectibles* (2001). (If, by some bizarre oversight, your local bookstore doesn't stock it, you can order it directly from Schiffer Publishing, 4880 Lower Valley Road, Atglen, PA 19310. Or go to www.schifferbooks.com.)

Bluelips: Your One-Stop Online Shopping Site for Those Hard-to-Find Mortuary Novelty Items

Founded in 1999 as an online store specializing in videos and books about death, Bluelips has evolved into the Web's leading source for funeral-related novelties and gift items, perfect for every occasion.

Throwing a birthday party for your preschooler? Just imagine the joy of his little guests when they open their goody bags and discover their very own foil-wrapped chocolate caskets. Tired of giving your girlfriend the same old jewelry on Valentine's Day? Nothing shouts "I love you" louder than a sterling silver pendant in the shape of an embalmer's trocar. Want to impress your boss at the law firm with your sartorial sophistication? How about a tie clasp in the shape of Anubis, the jackal-headed Egyptian god of the dead? Starting high school in a new neighborhood and want to impress the other kids with how cool you are? They'll be shaking their heads in amazement when you show up for the first day of class in that nifty T-shirt emblazoned with a silk-screened image of King Tut's skull!

These are just a fraction of the treasures available at Bluelips. Whether you're looking for Death Row Bubblegum Cigarettes, DVDs of actual autopsies, femur-shaped ballpoint pens, or one-pound anatomically correct chocolate hearts, you'll find them all at www.bluelips.com.

Coffin key ring, one of the many fun funereal novelty items available at Pushin' Daisies.

If you're looking for a particular item not available at Bluelips—say, a cookie cutter in the shape of a hearse or a skull-head toilet-brush holder—you should check out Pushin' Daisies, another excellent online mortuary novelty shop started by a female New Jersey funeral director who goes by the moniker of Cadaver Cat. You'll find it at www.pushindaisies.com.

Build-a-Corpse: Fun for the Whole Family!

Are you one of the many ardent fans of Alfred Hitchcock's *Psycho* who think it would be neat to be just like Norman Bates and keep a mummified corpse around the house but don't want to deal with the fuss and bother of looting your mother's grave? Well, an outfit called Di Stefano Productions has come up with the perfect solution, one that not only eliminates all the moral, legal, and

Build your own corpse! Courtesy of Jaime Di Stefano.

hygienic drawbacks of grave robbing but also provides a really fun hobby you can share with the kids!

For a mere $19.95, the company will send you a handsome, spiral-bound publication, *How to Build a Corpse: Easy Step by Step Instruction Manual* that will permit you (as the online advertisement puts it) to "build a lifesize, realistic decaying corpse in the privacy of your own home." By following the simple, illustrated instructions, anyone, no matter how devoid of artistic talent or basic human judgment, will be able to assemble an amazingly deathlike replica of a hideously decomposed human corpse using materials readily available at most hardware stores and hobby shops. (One caveat: "If your favorite hobby store doesn't supply some of the needed materials," cautions the ad, "you may have to visit a theatrical supply shop or even your local dentist.")

Once completed, your uncannily realistic corpse can be decked out in any style you choose—for instance, in a grizzled female wig and an old calico frock. Just imagine the amazed and delighted reactions of your friends and family members when they visit your home and discover what appears to be the exhumed body of your long-dead mother occupying a rocking chair in the center of your dimly lit fruit cellar!

For more information on *How to Build a Corpse*, visit the company's website, www.corpsesforsale.com. Or contact Di Stefano Productions, 2629 Stephenson Drive, Wilmington, DE 19808, 302-993-0494.

Mortuary Museums

While snooty European types like to brag about cultural attractions such as the Louvre, the Prado, and the Uffizi, we Americans can certainly hold our own when it comes to world-class museums. After all, where else can you find such magnificent and edifying institutions as the Burlingame Museum of Pez Memorabilia, the World

Kite Museum and Hall of Fame, the Kansas Barbed Wire Museum, Frederick of Hollywood's Lingerie Museum, and the New York Museum of Water? ("Discover the secrets of water! Enjoy fun, inspiring exhibits and learn why water is the most important part of your future on planet earth!")

Along with these meccas, our country boasts a number of outstanding museums dedicated to the wonderful world of death, burial, and bereavement. Among the most rewarding:

1. NATIONAL MUSEUM OF FUNERAL HISTORY

While the external appearance of this Houston, Texas, landmark may not match the architectural splendor of, say, the Louvre—or even, for that matter, the architectural splendor of the average Home Depot—don't let its unprepossessing exterior fool you. Within its prefabricated walls resides America's premier collection of mortuary-related artifacts. Here, you will marvel at an astonishing assemblage of rare and exotic coffins (including a one-of-a-kind casket built for three, intended for a married couple and their deceased child); a spectacular lineup of international hearses (among them the world's only funeral bus, designed to transport a coffin, six pallbearers, and twenty mourners to the

Scale-model 1966 Cadillac S&S limousine-style hearse. Courtesy of the Abbott & Hast Death Care Web Store.

Mini-Hearses: Save 'Em! Swap 'Em! Collect the Whole Set!

If you're looking for a hobby you can share with the kids but aren't into stamps, coins, or baseball cards, you might think about collecting exquisitely detailed scale-model hearses.

Each of these beauties measures approximately fourteen inches in length, comes in various colors, and features a number of cool accessories, including removable wood-grain caskets and church trucks. They cover the whole historical range of automotive hearses, from a 1921 Model T and a 1938 Cadillac with carved window panels to an elegant 1966 Cadillac landau complete with extending rear loading table. The gem of the bunch, however, is the maroon 1959 Cadillac limo-style hearse, featuring rocket-ship fins, bullet taillights, fully opening doors, flocked drapes, and more. Sweet!

Compared to your average Matchbox car, these babies aren't cheap. Most of them will run you a hundred bucks apiece. (Plus another $41.99 per acrylic display case.) But we're talking heirloom items here. You can find them online at Die Cast Auto (www.diecastauto.com) or the Abbott & Hast Death Care Store, your one-stop shopping source for mortuary merchandise (www.abbottandhast.com).

cemetery); a full-scale replica of a 1920s embalming room; a diorama of a 1900s casket factory; and much much more. You can take a peek at its offerings by checking out the online exhibition at www.nmfh.org, but any serious student of death will want to visit this in person.

ADDRESS: 415 Barren Springs Drive
Houston, TX 77090
HOURS: Mon.–Fri., 10 A.M.–4 P.M; Sat.–Sun. 12 P.M.–4 P.M.
TEL.: 281-876-3063

2. MUSEUM OF FUNERAL CUSTOMS

"Death is only the beginning" is the rather inscrutable motto of this outstanding collection of mid-nineteenth-century funerary artifacts. Trumpeting itself as America's "second-largest funeral museum" (after the NMFH in Houston), it exists (in the words of its mission statement) to "provide the public with a deeper understanding of the history of American funeral and mourning customs, funerary art, and funerary practice; foster an appreciation of history within the funeral profession; and encourage further study on the subject." Its 3,500 square feet of exhibition space is devoted to such attractions as:

- Re-created 1920s embalming room
- Re-created middle-class American home funeral setting, circa 1870
- Horse-drawn and motorized hearses that show city and rural funeral services
- Embalming equipment and instruments
- Caskets and coffins that represent changing tastes and designs
- Portable funeral equipment
- Chapel equipment and furnishings
- Examples of postmortem photography
- Full-size reproduction of Abraham Lincoln's coffin
- Scale model of Lincoln's tomb
- Articles of mourning clothing, jewelry, and adornment
- Fraternal mourning badges
- Rare books on embalming, dating back to as early as the sixteenth century
- Funeral trade catalogues and publications
- Gift shop featuring such items as Christmas tree ornaments adorned with silhouettes of hearses and miniature milk chocolate coffins (the perfect treat for the kiddies!)

ADDRESS: 1440 Monument Avenue
Springfield, IL 62702
HOURS: Tues.–Sat., 10 A.M.–4 P.M., Sun., 1 P.M.–4 P.M. (closed on Mondays and holidays)
TEL.: 217-544-3480
If you can't make it to Springfield, you can take a virtual tour at www.funeralmuseum.org/museumonline6.html.

3. THE MUSEUM OF DEATH

In 1995, artists J. D. Healy and Cathee Schultz opened their original Museum of Death in the basement of a former mortuary in San Diego's Gaslamp District. Displaying a variety of ghoulish relics—everything from vintage embalming tables to the badly stained T-shirt of a prisoner put to death in the electric chair—along with grisly accident photos and original serial killer artwork, the museum generated the sort of publicity that, in the view of the building's owners, did little to enhance its market value. Evicted after their four-year lease expired, Healy and Schultz moved their operation to the heart of Hollywood, where its ever-growing collection of bizarre memorabilia—a baseball signed by Charles Manson, John Wayne Gacy's "Pogo the Clown" paintings, a working guillotine, hand-carved Tibetan funerary skulls, among its many macabre curiosities—was housed in a defunct Mexican restaurant. The current museum is the third incarnation of this worthy establishment and, with its expanded collection and enlarged exhibition space, is bigger and better than ever. Definitely a must-see experience, especially if you've always dreamed of watching actual video footage of people getting run over by trains, jumping from burning buildings, or having their arms ripped off by jeeps.

Address: 6031 Hollywood Boulevard
Hollywood, CA 90028
Hours: 12 P.M.–8 P.M. daily, except
Christmas and New Year's Day
Tel. 323-466-8011

4. THE MUSEUM OF MOURNING ART AT ARLINGTON

Situated in Arlington Cemetery in Drexel Hill, Pennsylvania (not to be confused with the national cemetery in Washington, D.C.), this fascinating assemblage of mortuary memorabilia is housed in an exact replica of Mount Vernon, the beloved Virginia home of the father of our country. Devoted to early America's "culture of grief," it includes a wide variety of memorial objects—books, clocks, bells, iron gates, ceramics, and more—adorned with traditional death emblems (skulls, skeletons, crossed bones, angels, lambs, wreaths, urns, etc.). It also features a magnificent horse-drawn hearse, seventy pieces of mourning jewelry made between 1610 and 1810, and—the single weirdest object in the collection—a booby-trapped "cemetery gun," designed to discourage body snatchers by going off when someone tripped over it in a graveyard.

Address: 2900 State Road, Drexel Hill, PA
Hours: Mon.–Fri., 8 A.M.–4:30 P.M. by appointment only (prospective visitors should call at least a week in advance to make arrangements for a guided tour)
Tel.: 215-259-5800

5. THE MÜTTER MUSEUM

Though not a death museum per se, this venerable Philadelphia institution contains a veritable treasure trove of ghoulish goodies for the morbidly inclined. Housed in the College of Physicians, it dates back to 1858, when one Thomas Dent Mütter, a retired professor of surgery, donated his impressive collection of anatomical specimens, including seventeen hundred human bones and preserved body parts, to the medical school. Since then, the original holdings have been supplemented by a dizzying array of grotesque acquisitions, including the world's largest distended colon, the cancerous tumor secretly removed from the jaw of President Grover Cleveland, the thorax of Lincoln assassin John Wilkes Booth, the actual liver shared by conjoined twins Chang and Eng, and scores of hideously deformed fetuses neatly shelved in preservative-filled jars. Death devotees will particularly appreciate the museum's one-of-a-kind "Soap Woman," an exhumed nineteenth-century female corpse that—owing to the peculiar chemical properties of the soil in which it was interred—underwent the highly revolting process known as saponification, which transformed her fatty tissue into the waxy substance adipocere.

ADDRESS: 19 S. 22nd Street
Philadelphia, PA 19103
HOURS: 10 A.M.–5 P.M., daily except Thanksgiving, Christmas, and New Year's Day
TEL.: 215-563-3737

6. THE MUSEUM OF MOURNING PHOTOGRAPHY AND MEMORIAL PRACTICE

Though the name is perhaps a tad grandiose (the "museum" is basically an alcove in the proprietors' living room), this outstanding collection of memorial photographs and related mortuary ephemera is one of the best in the country, perhaps second only to that of the estimable Stanley Burns. Assembled by Chicago architect and photographer Anthony Vizzari and his wife, Andrea, it consists of about fifteen hundred pieces, circa 1840 to the present. At present, the collection, housed in the Vizzaris' apartment in Chicago's historic Logan Square neighborhood, can be viewed only by appointment. To arrange a visit, contact the museum director at viewing@mourningphoto.com. Some of the Vizzaris' holdings can also be seen online by going to the museum's home page at mourningphotography.com and clicking on "Gallery."

THE VIRTUAL AUTOPSY

Always had a hankering to dissect a cadaver but didn't want to take the time and trouble to attend med school? Thanks to the folks at the Australian Museum website, anyone can now find out exactly what goes on during an autopsy. Just go to www.deathonline.net/movies/index.cfm and follow the menu to "Interactive Autopsy." Have fun!

Death Ed

For many years now, classes in human sexual behavior have been a regular (if often controversial) feature of the U.S. educational system. As Sigmund Freud pointed out long ago, however, sex isn't the only primal force that shapes human existence. The other is death. The recognition of this fact has begun to filter into the academic world. To be sure, courses in death and dying aren't exactly a standard part of the liberal arts curriculum. But at least death education has become a recognized area of teaching and study.

Scholars and researchers involved in this field acknowledge Herman Feifel as one of its great pioneers. Chief psychologist at the Los Angeles Veterans Administration Mental Hygiene Clinic and a professor of psychology at the University of Southern California, Feifel was the editor of the groundbreaking book *The Meaning of Death* (McGraw-Hill, 1959), a collection of essays by twenty-one theologians and scientists that is universally credited with jump-starting the modern "death awareness" movement. By the mid-1960s, death-related courses were beginning to pop up in universities across the country. Before long, the field of death education had legitimized itself with all the requisite academic trappings: its very own journal (*Omega: The Journal of Death and Dying*), think tank (the Center for Death Education and Bioethics at the University of Wisconsin, La Crosse), professional organization (the Association for Death Education and Counseling), and regular national and regional conferences.

Nowadays, most colleges and universities offer courses on death and dying, many of which take an interdisciplinary approach, drawing on faculty from various departments: psychology, sociology, anthropology, religious studies, literature, and the arts. A few educational institutions even offer special programs allowing students to earn degrees with a concentration in thanatology.

A typical survey course—Death and Dying 101—might cover such areas as cross-cultural perspectives on death, the dying process, worldwide funeral practices and rituals, grief and bereavement, medical ethics and euthanasia, near-death experiences, and the afterlife. Readings might range from such seminal works as Geoffrey Gorer's 1955 essay "The Pornography of Death" and Jessica Mitford's *The American Way of Death* to pop best sellers such as Mitch Albom's *Tuesdays with Morrie* and literary classics including Tolstoy's "The Death of Ivan Ilyich."

While this type of elective offers a nice change of pace from the monotony of the usual humanities seminar, there is also a more practical, vocational side to death education: programs for people who wish to pursue a hands-on career in the death industry as a funeral director and licensed embalmer. This branch of learning is the specialty of the country's many accredited schools of mortuary science. While requirements differ by state, college degrees in this field usually take two to four years and consist of both general education classes in such core areas as writing, math, and science and specialized courses in all the areas necessary to operate a successful funeral home: embalming techniques, restorative art, mortuary administration, grief counseling, and so on. The American Board of Funeral Service Education (ABFSE), whose roots go back to the 1940s, is recognized by the U.S. Department of Education as the sole accrediting agency for academic programs that prepare funeral service directors. A state-by-state directory of these programs can be found at the organization's website, www.abfse.org.

RECOMMENDED READING

For a very thorough survey of this subject, see the entry on "Death Education" by Charles A. Corr and Donna M. Corr in vol. 1 of *The Handbook of Death and Dying* (Sage, 2003), edited by Clifton D. Bryant. Another illuminating essay is J. E. Knott's "Death Education for All" in the collection *Dying: Facing the Facts* (McGraw-Hill, 1979), edited by Hannelore Wass.

And Following Our Midafternoon Séance, There'll Be Lanyard Braiding at the Arts and Crafts Center

As each school year draws to a close, millions of American parents confront a dilemma. Should they send their kids to summer camp? And if so, what kind—art camp, science camp, baseball camp, drama camp, weight-loss camp? Obviously, the final decision will depend on the child's particular desires, skills, and needs. If you happen to have a child like the one in the hit 1999 movie *The Sixth Sense*—that is, the kind who sees dead people—the choice is pretty obvious. You'll want to send him to the Wonewoc Spiritualist Camp in Wonewoc, Wisconsin.

Actually, you don't have to be a child to enjoy the delights of Wonewoc—just a believer in spiritualism, the movement that started in upstate New York in the mid-1800s when a trio of sisters, Margaret, Kate, and Leah Fox, began communicating with the dead via mediumistic trances. Before long, a séance craze had swept the country and spread to England, where it peaked in the aftermath of World War I, when millions of bereaved parents tried desperately to make contact with the spirits of their slaughtered sons.

Nowadays, spiritualism isn't quite the sensation it used to be when people flocked to darkened auditoriums to see self-professed mediums speak to departed souls and conjure up ectoplasmic phantoms. But it's still a vital movement that, among other activities, operates thirteen camps throughout the United States.

Wonewoc, established in 1893, occupies thirty-seven rustic acres in western Wisconsin. Consisting of three dozen cabins, a dining hall, and a derelict chapel, it is attended by mediums, clairvoyants, and psychics from around the Midwest and offers a variety of fun-filled activities, including classes on past-life regression and workshops on how to see auras, along with ice cream socials and campfires. For prices ranging from $20 to $40, visitors to the camp can receive messages from the Great Beyond as transmitted through resident mediums such as Judy Ulrich, who claims to be able to see dead people "so close, I see the stubble on their face." (Evidently, razors are in short supply in the afterlife.)

For more information about spiritualist camps around the United States, go to www.nsac.org/camps.htm.

Cemetery Fun

Sure, a cemetery is a death-haunted place full of moldering human remains. But that doesn't mean it isn't the perfect spot for a fun-filled weekend visit, offering all kinds of entertaining and educational activities suitable for kids of all ages.

That, at any rate, is the message of Sharon DeBartolo Carmack's oversize trade paperback book, *Your Guide to Cemetery Research* (Betterway Books, 2002). A certified genealogist and self-confessed cemetery enthusiast who developed a lifelong fascination with old graveyards in childhood, Carmack shows readers how to fill in the gaps in their family history by locating their ancestors' burial places, analyzing the information on headstones, tracking down death records, and so on.

Her book, however, is aimed not only at amateur genealogists trying to chart the family tree but also at anyone who is looking to spend a carefree day among the long-buried dead. To that end, Carmack offers lively how-to advice on all kinds of delightful activities, from cemetery picnics and family reunions to assorted arts-and-crafts projects such as cemetery scrapbooks, quilts, and samplers. She also teaches aspiring hobbyists how to make gravestone rubbings and plaster-cast replicas of old tombstones—perfect projects that Junior can bring to school for his next show-and-tell.

In short, Carmack's book is a delightful addition to the library of any taphophile from eight to eighty.

Love and Death

In the age of AIDS, we've become all too familiar with the fact that sex can have fatal consequences. But the connection between sex and death actually extends back many centuries.

In France, the phrase *la petit mort*—"the little death"—has long been used to describe an orgasm. Similarly, in Elizabethan England, "to die" meant to have a sexual climax—the equivalent of our slang expression "to come." When one of Shakespeare's characters tells his girlfriend that he wants to "die in [her] lap," or when another remarks that he will "die bravely, like a smug bridegroom," they're talking about sex.

And the Bard isn't just being metaphorical. Back then, it was a common folk belief that every man was born with a limited supply of "vital fluid" and that every orgasm deprived him of a day of life.

Still, it was a trade-off Shakespeare seemed willing to make. As he puns in one of his sonnets: "Happy to have thy love, happy to die!"

The Bride Wore Black

Every starry-eyed young bride- and groom-to-be wants to consecrate their love with a perfect wedding ceremony. If you're looking to tie the knot in a very special way—one that's sure to make a deep and lasting (not to say potentially traumatic) impression on your family and friends—you might want to consider one of America's fastest-growing trends: the cemetery wedding.

Well, okay, it's not exactly one of America's fastest-growing trends. Actually, as far as we can tell, only one young couple has actually gone ahead and gotten married in a graveyard—though the story received so much attention in the national press that you'd think cemetery weddings really *are* sweeping the country.

The lovebirds in question are named Scott Amsler and Miranda Patterson, both residents of Troy, Illinois, a St. Louis suburb. Amsler works with computers by day and devotes his evenings to his true passion: restoring old hearses. After meeting and falling for his future fiancée, he proposed in a way guaranteed to win any young woman's heart: by affixing an engraved metal sign to the side of his prized 1965 funeral coach. The message read: "Will You Marry Me?" How could a girl refuse?

Driving home to share the happy news with her family, Patterson spotted a perfect location for an outdoor ceremony: a beautiful gazebo perched atop a grassy hill. That the gazebo was part of the city cemetery and surrounded by hundreds of tombstones, some dating back to the Civil War, only made the site more appealing to this real-life Morticia and Gomez.

After contacting the city clerk's office, the couple learned that they would need the permission of the town cemetery committee. At least one alderman, seventy-one-year-old William Hohman, had his doubts, fearing that the graveyard nuptials would set a dangerous precedent. "Once you let that horse out of the barn, people could ask to do anything out there," Hohman told reporters. "You've got various cults running around, and we don't want to get into that nonsense."

There was also some concern that a burial might take place on the same day, casting a literal pall on the festivities. In the end, however, everything apparently worked out well. Permission was granted, no one was inconsiderate enough to require interment while the wedding was taking place, and the bride and groom were able to exchange vows on their charming hilltop setting while surrounded by family, friends, and a few hundred spectral witnesses—what the Bible calls "the congregation of the dead."

The Last Word

Since I've spent the whole book urging readers to take responsibility and not leave final matters to either chance or the questionable judgment of their survivors, it seems only appropriate that I specify my own wishes for an epitaph. Here is how I devoutly wish my tombstone to read:

Courtesy of Kaz Prapuolenis.

Acknowledgments

My gratitude to the following for their kindness and generosity:

Cynthia Beal
Kurt Brown
Elizabeth Burns
Dr. Stanley Burns
Elizabeth Clementson
Joe Coleman
Jaime Di Stefano
Jim Eaton
Rick Geary
Ned Grathwohl
Joseph Grattan
J. D. Gill
Tom Gilson
Emily Guthrie
Jan Heller-Levi
Mary Jones
Christoph Keller
Clay Kilgore
Maureen Lomasney
Maurizio Matteucci
Walter M. P. McCall
Erika Navarette
Ulrike Neurath-Sippel
Minda Powers-Douglas
Kaz Prapuolenis
Michelle Sanders
Beth Sanderson
Laura Schechter
Hazel Selina
Dr. Walter Sife
Al Skinner
Terry Starwalt
Suzy Stjohn
Julie Wiskind

Index

About the Author

HAROLD SCHECHTER is a professor of American literature and culture at Queens College, the City University of New York. He is widely celebrated for both fiction and true-crime writing, including *The Serial Killer Files*. He lives in Brooklyn and Mattituck, Long Island, with his wife, the poet Kimiko Hahn.